Imperium Press was founded in 2018 to supply students and laymen with works in the history of rightist thought. If these works are available at all in modern editions, they are rarely ever available in editions that place them where they belong: outside the liberal weltanschauung. Imperium Press' mission is to provide right thinkers with authoritative editions of the works that make up their own canon. These editions include introductions and commentary which place these canonical works squarely within the context of tradition, reaction, and counter-Enlightenment thought—the only context in which they can be properly understood.

JOSEPH DE MAISTRE was one of the strongest voices in 18th and 19th century reaction. Born into minor Savoyard nobility in 1753, he enjoyed a distinguished law career until he fled the French Republic's annexation, whereupon he acted as chief magistrate to Charles-Emmanuel's Sardinian court, later attaining a number of high offices. Maistre distinguished himself as a political commentator in *Considerations on France*, publishing many works over his life to great acclaim, particularly the posthumous *St. Petersburg Dialogues.*

MAJOR WORKS

VOLUME I

JOSEPH
DE MAISTRE

PERTH
IMPERIUM PRESS
2021

Published by Imperium Press
www.imperiumpress.org

Essai sur le Principe Générateur des Constitutions Politiques,
published by la Société typographique, 1814
Considérations sur la France, published by J. B. Pélagaud, 1796
Étude sur la souveraineté, published s.n., 1794

First Edition

A catalogue record for this
book is available from the
National Library of Australia

ISBN 978-1-922602-22-0 Paperback
ISBN 978-1-922602-23-7 EPUB
ISBN 978-1-922602-24-4 Kindle

Contents

The Cosmic Cachinnations of Joseph de Maistre: Founder of Reaction

In his essay on "Historical Fact" (1932), the refined but somewhat dour Paul Valéry makes passing reference to the Chambéry-born aristocrat, Savoyard jurist, Sardinian diplomatic envoy to the Czar, and arch-critic of the Revolution in France, Joseph de Maistre (1753–1821), who figures as the subject of these paragraphs. Valéry describes Maistre's style as partaking of a "noble, pure, and gentle severity" (124), while bracketing him with such other and later Francophone writer-thinkers as Jules Michelet, Hippolyte Taine, and Alexis de Tocqueville. Valéry himself, in his writerly genealogy, stood, somewhat at an angle perhaps, in the line of Maistre, whose tutelary influence over the young Charles Baudelaire gave rise to the High Symbolist phase of French poetry—Valéry being a third generation Symbolist in his tantalizingly ambiguous verse. Valéry's dictional choice of "severity" nominates itself as appropriate to its object and so, too, the adjectival "noble" and its companion, "pure." In Valéry's "gentle," however, a question arises, and this despite the fact that in French *gentille* (as in, *une gentille sévérité*) need not denote the quiet, forgiving character that its English cognate suggests, but rather a quality of high-born reserve. Is Maistre reserved? Hardly: Maistre discovers his *forte* in the counterattack. Where Monsieur Voltaire launches his barrage of contempt against religion, Maistre fires off his mighty counter-battery, so as to leave the obnoxious contemnor, as though he still lived, in a state of shell-shocked indignity. Where John Locke makes insipid claims about human understanding, Maistre demonstrates that insipidity, point by point relentlessly, until of Locke's case nothing remains except a few ignoble tatters. Where Jean-Jacques Rousseau gushes and foments against the established order Maistre like Zeus thunders back, pointing out the topsy-turvy character of Rousseau's bad logic, to leave standing only the man's egotism and sentimentality. In a cavalry-metaphor, Maistre qualifies himself as a veritable Blücher of polemic.

Compare Maistre, for example, with his contemporary and peer René de Chateaubriand. In his masterly *Genius of Christianity* (1802), Chateaubriand on the one hand insistently, but in a manner authentically *gentle*, presses his case for the centrality of the Catholic religion to European civilization. The presentation never strays from politeness and advances itself in a carefully reasoned way. Maistre's great posthumous publication *The St. Petersburg Dialogues or Conversations on the Temporal Government of Providence* (1821), on the other hand, while complementing Chateaubriand's *Genius* in its content, employs a style, typical of its author, quite different from Chateaubriand's. Maistre, who acknowledges every nuance of courtesy, nevertheless readies himself at every moment to set loose his Olympian indignation; couching himself always, however, in a mood of ebullient and godlike humor he meanwhile articulates his thesis in the rhetoric of ironically self-aware hyperbole. In his ironical self-awareness Maistre indeed ranks with the author of the *Quixote*, Part II, or with Gustave Flaubert. In his exposition, Maistre shows himself a great role-player. He pretends to be flabbergasted that bad arguments have so great a currency and he delights in revealing their sources as so many *faux monnayeurs*. For Maistre, the game is always afoot, and the hunter is always ready to spring. He is the hunter, sure of his shot. Maistre, conceiver of the subtle, not the gross, counter-revolution and sublime founder of the reactionary right, wielded his pen as a cosmic satirist of the most exalted office and as he might have wielded a sword.

Isaiah Berlin remarks in an introduction to an American edition of *Considerations on France* (1797) that Maistre belonged to Romanticism, especially in his view of history. "Maistre," Berlin writes, "like other romantic writers, took the panoramic rather than the particular view of history, seeking, not to describe and relate the unique event, but to find behind the sweep of history some logic, some divine pattern, that would satisfy the selfsame urge for design and order so strongly felt by Enlightenment thinkers" (39). Berlin's description would make of Maistre a precursor to Twentieth Century figures such as Oswald Spengler and José Ortega, whose *oeuvres* combine the search for principles of order that manifest themselves only in sequences of centuries with the analysis of recent events. Spengler, however, never gives evidence of possessing a sense of humor; he is hardly to be described even as possessing a sense of irony. Ortega resembles Spengler in his elevated detachment from that about which he writes; like his contemporary Valéry, Ortega's defense of tradition, as well as his disdain for the contemporary situation, issues from an ice-cold intellectual realm. Not so with Maistre. Passion, faith, and a qualified optimism animate Maistre. That he invested the time and effort late in life to translate from the Greek Plutarch's essay on the question of why the gods seem to delay in the implementation of divine justice testifies to his confidence in a Christian version of the Karmic Law or of *Nemesis*. As Maistre sees it, justice always prevails, even though it might observe an interval, because the universe manifests not only an intelligible physical order but also an intelligible moral order, quite as Plutarch had suspected. Maistre, anticipating, in addition to Spengler and Ortega, certain Traditionalist thinkers of the first half of the last century—René Guénon and Julius Evola come to mind—speaks to the Twenty-First Century as cogently as he did to his own era. The time is ripe for a Maistrian revival.

I. On the St. Petersburg Dialogues.

Because Maistre's masterpiece *The St. Petersburg Dialogues* resumes and amplifies the major themes and theses of his numerous previous works, a selective tour through several of its eleven *soirées* will set the stage for an understanding of *Considerations on France,* the *Essay on the Generative Principle of Political Constitutions* (1809), and the *Study on Sovereignty* (1794). To a reader approaching it for the first time *The St. Petersburg Dialogues* must seem a daunting challenge. Richard Lebrun's English translation (1993) runs to some three hundred and fifty pages. It is not the work's length alone that intimidates, but its immense erudition, and its compositional principle. *The St. Petersburg Dialogues* purports to be the record of conversations late into the night among "the Count," no doubt an autobiographical projection of Maistre himself, "the Senator," and "the Chevalier." The Count hails presumably from a French-speaking country, but not necessarily from France; the Chevalier, the youngest of the three, is French, an expatriate now living in Russia. The Senator is Russian. The Senator and the Chevalier obviously revere the Count—for his wisdom and his experience, but likewise for his witticisms, jokes, and his extraordinary oratorical ability. Once the reader begins reading, Maistre's quasi-Socratic dialogues throw off their intimidating quality and prove themselves to be a rare delight. The experience resembles that of immersing oneself in the epic speeches of George Bernard Shaw's book-length dramas. One has the sense of being present at these extraordinary occasions, with their baroque exchanges and subtle disagreements, the latter being invariably resolved. Maistre knows that he will achieve this effect. He plays with the suspension of readerly disbelief. In the First Dialogue, the Count, responding to the Chevalier's request to end a detour into the realm of Latin apothegmatic and to return to the declared topic of Providence, says: "Whatever subject we treat, my dear friend, we are still talking about Providence. Moreover, a conversation is not a book; perhaps it is even better than a book precisely because it permits us to ramble a bit" (12).

As many a commentator remarks, Maistre judges the self-denominating Enlightenment to have been a civilizational disaster. For Maistre the rhetoric of *progress* furnishes only so much mendacious cant. The century of Enlightenment ushered in an age of unprecedented mendacity, sacrilege, and criminality, which immiserated the European nations. Maistre, believing in the Fall of Man, invokes a species of anti-progress in order to characterize the events and trends of recent history. Beginning with Protestantism, what Maistre calls derisively *the sect* proliferated, not only in Northern Europe, but also in the French-speaking countries, fomenting civil war and dragging the kingdoms and principalities into a phase of prolonged and destructive violence. At one point in the Second Dialogue, the Count rehearses his anthropological theory of how civilization relates to savagery and barbarism. Maistre clearly intends this fascinating "ramble" to apply to the continuity of Protestantism—which he labels the Mohammedanism of Europe—with Jacobinism. The Count defers to the Greeks and other ancient peoples who, in their myths, set the Golden Age, when men observed a natural morality, deeply in the past. "Listen to what wise antiquity has to say about the first men," the Count advises his interlocutors: "It will tell you that they were marvellous men and that beings of a superior order deigned to favor them with the most precious communications" (40). The Count—who speaks for Maistre—suspects the existence in the past of a lost, sacred science superior to modern science. Yet everywhere and always the tendency of *degradation* takes hold. This law holds true both for knowledge of the natural domain and for moral acuity. "Some leader," the Count continues, "having altered a people's moral principle by some transgressions... transmitted the anathema to his posterity; and since every constant force accelerates by its very nature since it is always acting on itself, this degradation bearing on his descendants... has finally made them into... savages" (44-45).

The Count adduces the indigenes of the New World, as they revealed themselves to the early explorers and to the *conquistadors,* as a specimen instance of his claim. In a disquisition that would with certainty cause him to be banished from Twenty-First Century social media, and that forthrightly rebukes the clerical defense of the aborigines of Mexico and South America, the Count denounces the putative *"state of nature"* in which the New-World "savages" (45) dwelt. It was, he says, cruel, bloody, and animalistic. Maistre anticipated the prevailing multiculturalism of the contemporary West, which his prospective critique demolishes in advance. Maistre writes: "There was only too much truth in the first reaction of Europeans, in the time of Columbus, to refuse to recognize as equals the degraded men who peopled the new world" (45). This attitude would change in the direction of sentimentality. Maistre omits to name Bartolomé de Las Casas, but it must be to that author's *Short Account of the Destruction of the Indies* that the Count refers. Maistre gives to the Count to say that, "The merciful priest exalted [the tribes] to make them precious"; and "he played down the evil, he exaggerated the good, he promised what he hoped would be," that is to say, something contrary to the self-evident reality of the situation. Observers like Bartolomé took a stance, in the Count's opinion, *"too favorable to the natives"* (45). Such men thereby contributed to the Rousseauvian cult of the Noble Savage which itself represents a resurgence of savagery. Exercising his powerful intuition, which reflects that of his author, the Count avers that, "One cannot glance at the savage without reading the curse that is written not only on his soul but even on the exterior form of his body" (46). The savage "has known us for three centuries," the Count adds, "without having wanted anything from us, except gunpowder to kill his fellows and brandy to kill himself" (46).

Maistre's chastisement of priestly mushiness *vis-à-vis* the Tainos and Caribes points to an important element of his hybrid Catholic-Gallicanism. He adhered to Greek and Latin Pagan tradition—of the refined and philosophical variety—as much as he did to the Gospel. He also admired the Hindus, of whose primordial lawgiver Manu he writes favorably in the *Dialogues.* He saw Christianity as attaching itself to a moral continuum that descended from an original *"supernatural enlightenment"* (44), which the parables of Christ in no way contradict. In the Eleventh Dialogue, the Senator, in amplifying a remark of the Count, opines how, "it will be shown that all the ancient traditions are true, that all of paganism is nothing but a system of corrupted and displaced truths, which only need *cleaning,* so to speak, and restoring to their place, to shine forth all their light" (326). In the same section of the book, readers will encounter again Maistre's belief in an ancient science and related technique that surpass what passes for science and technique in the present, spiritually depleted moment. Science and religion thrive together, so that a decline in scientific competence will naturally accompany a decline in healthy religiosity. The Senator cites the religious piety and scientific acuity of Sir Isaac Newton. The great Englishman's accomplishment consists, not so much in bringing knowledge of the cosmos *forward,* but rather in "bringing us back to Pythagoras," so that "it will soon be demonstrated that the heavenly bodies are moved precisely like the human body, by intelligences that are united to them" (325). Men might recover elements of the ancient lore. In that case, says the Senator, people of the future "will talk of our present *stupidity* as we talk of the superstition of the Middle Ages" (325). Maistre might well be referring to the advocates of *climate change*, as they now ambiguously denominate their claim, when he arranges for the Senator to affirm that "European scientists are presently a species of conjurers or initiates… who absolutely will not have anyone know *more* or *other* than they" (326).

Maistre devotes large swathes of the *Dialogues* to his dissection of Voltaire and Locke; and scattered remarks to the refutation of Rousseau, whom he had treated at length in previous works. Voltaire, building his argument, as it might be put, on the rubble and the corpse-count in the aftermath of the Lisbon earthquake of 1755, attacked the Christian dogma of Providence and through it the related concept of the Justice of God. He articulated his case in the *Poème sur le désastre de Lisbonne*, which he published in 1756. Maistre devotes the Fourth Dialogue to his refutation of Voltaire, who, in his verses, had cited the *suffering of the innocent*, not so much as the logical, but as the emotional weapon to wield against the supposed Loving God who yet (as he claims) permits the crippling and killing of children through his own acts. Maistre knows that the diatribe against Voltaire's follies, the opening salvo of which has already occurred, will strike a certain overly polite conscience as exaggerated. He cares not. He gives it to the Chevalier to ask: "How can you keep so much rancour towards the dead" (108). The Count replies, "However his works are not dead," but rather "they are alive, and they are killing us" (109). In his poem, Voltaire asks, *why do we suffer under a just master?* The Count replies: "BECAUSE WE DESERVE IT" (118). Original sin contaminates humanity universally, depriving everyone of the claim to pristine moral status. Voltaire asks pleadingly, *why infants, who could not yet merit punishments or rewards, are… subject to the same evils that can afflict grown men?* The Count responds with a proto-Darwinian formulation: "If it is agreed that a certain number of infants must perish, I do not see how it matters to them whether they die in one way or another" (120). If, moreover, a child fall victim to a collapsing wall, might its swift death not be preferable to a lingering one, say, by smallpox? Maistre's is not a Twenty-First Century way of thinking, or rather of "thinking," but that is because it is not a substitution of *maudlin emotion* for *actual thought*.

Maistre argues that punishments are never *necessary* but only *contingent*. Any punishment must be understood as the response of Providence to sin, which Providence wishes to correct. In respect of any sin, moreover, as the Count says, "Innocence could have prevented it" and "prayer could have held it off" (125). The Count identifies what he labels "a sophism of impiety" (125). He posits that "the all powerful goodness knows how to use one evil to exterminate another" (126) and it often does so. Yet observing this perfectly visible principle, obtuse people conclude that "evil is an integral part of the whole" (126). Evil corresponds, rather, to an aberration, a lapse, from the whole. Evil commenced when Adam and Eve flouted the prohibition. Evil intensified when Cain slew Abel; and it intensified, later again, when Sodom and Gomorrah violated the sexual order. The world will restore its wholeness only at the end of time when the divine power redeems it, but that redemption will entail the world's translation under eternity, as the transcendent City of God. Rebels who trespass *against nature,* who selfishly believe that they can ignore the visible principles of reality, believe also that they can establish perfect justice in the temporal realm. The effort to establish perfect justice is, in itself, however, a prideful *injustice* under whose perpetration decent people must invariably suffer, as *actual victims* of a criminal program. The perpetrators bring *Nemesis* on themselves, too, as the Terror well demonstrated. On the tribulations of conscientious and virtuous people, Maistre holds the position that ordeals test conscience and virtue and can strengthen them. Conscience and virtue express themselves, precisely, in prayer. In a mythological allusion to the Hesiodic chaos-monster and emblem of evil, *Typhon,* the Count concludes the Fourth Dialogue as follows: "Our prayers being only the effort of an intelligent being against the action of *Typhon,* their utility, and even their necessity, has been philosophically demonstrated" (126).

In the Sixth Dialogue, Maistre grapples with Locke. Maistre defends a fixed and knowable human nature against Locke's nihilistic assertion of the *blank slate*—the *tabula rasa*. Of Locke's *Essay on Human Understanding,* the Count tells the Chevalier that, "One must traverse this book, like the sands of Libya, without ever encountering the least oasis, the least green point where one can catch one's breath" (165). In the pages that follow, Maistre heaps up examples of Locke's simplistic, literal-minded observations, his absurdities, his risible metaphors, and his tedious prose. "Sometimes he will speak to you of the memory as a box in which one holds ideas until they are needed"; while "elsewhere he makes memory a secretary that keeps registers"; or "he presents the human intelligence to us as a dark room pierced by some windows through which the light comes" (166). Voltaire wrote of Locke that he was the first philosopher who taught the necessity of precise definition. Maistre takes issue: "Locke is precisely the first philosopher who told us *not to define,*" but who "never ceased to define, and in a way surpassing all the boundaries of ridicule" (168). Locke, in Maistre's view, reduced the ancient refinements of moral philosophy to a crude question of "taste or caprice" (168). Maistre obviously savors the opportunity rhetorically to draw and quarter Locke's *Essay.* The prosecutorial rodomontade continues for many amusing pages. Ultimately, Maistre objects to Locke's assertion of the malleability of the subject.

The *tabula rasa* being characterless, it cannot acquire character nor can it generate character. As the *tabula rasa*'s malleability makes of it a thing *acted upon* rather than a subject that *acts*, the concept permits no such thing as freedom. If there were no such thing as freedom—or *free will*—there would be no such thing as morality; and then there would be no such thing as justice. Locke's Man is a thing that cannot be and therefore cannot function as the basis of law.

Rousseau's turn in the docket comes at the climax of the Eighth Dialogue and in the Ninth Dialogue. Maistre applies to Rousseau the categorical label of *savant*. The *savant* is a recent nasty phenomenon symptomatic of the degeneration of society. The *savant* propagates "insolent doctrines" (259) which serve no positive agenda but merely confuse and dismay the easily cajoled—who are the very people most in need of the dogmatic certitude and good guidance inherent in Christian doctrine. The *savant*, usually a professor of this or that faculty, arrogates to himself the title of philosopher without, however, understanding it; he puts his verbal cleverness on public display and he invites adulation. He more resembles an anti-philosopher than he does an Aristotle or an Aquinas. The *savant* belongs to the class of "learned men," whom "we in this century have not known how to keep in their place, which is a secondary one" (259). Maistre uses the adjective "learned" with scathing irony. Whereas in the past *savants* numbered but a few, "today we see nothing but *savants*" (259). In Rousseau's claim that society originates in a convention of primitive deliberators, who produce a social contract, Maistre identifies a prime specimen of *savantism;* so too again in Rousseau's endowment, on the wholly appetitive prehistoric man, of the title of *noble*, and in his notion of property as usurpation. Maistre makes the Count say that, "As for the one who speaks or writes to deprive people of a national dogma, he must be hung like a housebreaker" (260). The Count poses the question rhetorically, "Why have we been so imprudent as to grant freedom of speech to everyone" (260). In the Eighth Dialogue, Rousseau becomes "that *all-purpose fool*... who had so much influence on a century quite worthy of listening to him" (280).

II. On the Generative Principle of Political Constitutions – Considerations on France – Study on Sovereignty.

In *The Generative Principle of Political Constitutions*, Maistre asserts that all legitimate political authority originates with God; and that only God deserves the title of Supreme Sovereign. Polities constitute themselves, not in the way that an architect draws up blue-prints for a large edifice, which the builders then efficiently construct, but by long-term adaptation and improvisation with constant back-reference to an originary and divinely inspired vision. Maistre compares the gradual articulation of a polity to the burgeoning of a great oak, with the acorn symbolizing the divine seed. That the ancients understood these matters with clarity becomes evident in their myths of foundation, in which divinity invariably participates. In the beginning, God created nature, from the clay of which man arose. Institutions thrive to the degree that they nourish themselves on divine inspiration, and they wither to the degree that they alienate themselves from such nourishment. "The origin of sovereignty," Maistre writes, "must always be outside the sphere of human power, so that the very men who appear to be directly involved are nevertheless only circumstances" (p. 24). Maistre has previously quoted himself, but only as "the author of the *Considerations on France,*" to the effect that *"the people will always accept their masters, and never choose them"* (p. 24). How so? Divinity awes men and men defer to those of their co-mortals who seem to embody the divine. "Kings above all, chiefs of fledgling empires, are constantly designated and almost *marked* by Heaven in some extraordinary manner" (p. 25). Longevity strengthens the numinosity of institutions because hoary age appears a defiance of mortality hence also an approximation of immortality. Maistre writes, "As for legitimacy, if it should seem ambiguous in its origin, God is explained by His prime minister to the province of this world: *time*" (p. 24). Maistre remarks that in the foundation stories of the Greek *poleis,* "It is always an oracle which founds cities" (p. 25). One might add with a nod to the *Dialogues* that the oracle often springs into being where a god or hero has slain a monster, shedding its blood, and thereby sacralizing the spot.

In a recurrent thesis of *The Generative Principle,* Maistre insists that, at their origin, not only are all lasting political dispensations divine, but they are *oral,* belonging not to the written but to the spoken word. In Maistre's opening salvo: "One of the grand errors of an age that professed them all was to believe that a political constitution could be written and created *a priori*, while reason and experience meet in establishing that a constitution is a divine work, and that precisely what is most fundamental and most essentially constitutional in the laws of a nation cannot be written" (p. 9). That which speaks, and in so doing participates in the capitalized *Word,* addresses men more directly than that which scribbles. What has sustained itself through pure speech may, of course, later commit itself in writing, but in this case the writer originates nothing, only making a record of what previously existed in another, better form. Maistre goes even further. The impulse to write down and codify the laws signals the degeneration of the laws. It is tantamount to forgetfulness. In addition, an oral commandment codified in script falls subject to so-called improvement. The improver of the law might well think that he has reasoned his way to a just modification, but Maistre has little trust in reason, as the *savants* use that word. Indeed the penchant for reform spurs competition such that the sequence of amendments and re-codifications stretches potentially without end, turning the notion of law on its head. Maistre writes: "Hence primordial good sense, fortunately anterior to sophisms, has sought on all sides the sanction of laws in a power above man, either in recognizing that sovereignty comes from God, or by worshiping certain unwritten laws as emanating from Him" (p. 10). Effective law is also *vague;* it never stipulates *too much,* but reserves itself in generalities and leaves much unsaid. No document, Maistre observes by way of example, delineated the powers of the Roman Senate, a situation that he regards as practical and good.

Maistre's theory of vagueness as an advantageous characteristic of the unwritten law links itself to his belief in free will. In *The Generative Principle,* Maistre discusses Christianity, which he qualifies as "the greatest of all imaginable institutions" (p. 16). While it is true that Christianity has a set of Scriptures, the Author of Christianity was not the author of them. Christ, like Socrates, confined himself to the spoken word. The Gospel in which Christ figures post-dates Him, undoubtedly basing itself on an oral tradition worked up by the Apostles. Whereas, Maistre argues, "The Evangelists, in recounting this Last *Supper*… had a fine opportunity to command our belief in writing"; nevertheless, "they carefully refrained from declaring or ordaining anything" (p. 16). Maistre points to a feature of Gospel rhetoric: "we read in their admirable history: *Go, teach*; but by no means: *teach this or that*" (p. 16). In that same rhetoric, the profession "*We believe*" appears, but never the commandment, "*you shall believe*" (p. 16). The New Testament moreover never pretends to constitute an encyclopedia of Christian doctrine: a parable never mandates but it invites the addressee to meditate and to think. Maistre writes, "there is not a line in these writings which declares, which even allows us to glimpse, a plan to make it a code or a dogmatic statement of all articles of faith" (p. 17). What he calls "*codes of belief*" (p. 17) arouse Maistre's suspicion. Maistre certainly has in mind Calvinism and Lutheranism, but also in all likelihood *Islam*. Totalizing doctrinaire declarations signify for Maistre that whatever religion they advance "is false"; that the authors "have written [their] religious code in a bout of fever"; and that "the code will soon be mocked in this very nation" (p. 17). Islam fits the paradigm in that the Koran's weird verses convey an exemplary delirium. The Protestant sects having largely devolved into mere departments of reigning Western nihilism, Maistre announces himself as something of a prophet. The *ethos* of any people, as

Maistre sees it, is more to be spoken than to be written and more to be felt, and thereby observed, than to be spoken. One remarks that contemporaneity cannot shut its mouth.

The Generative Principle introduces a theory of language under a theory of names. Language is an institution. With religion, in fact, language is one of two *primordial institutions* that constitute man *qua* himself. Plato's *Cratylus* strongly informs Maistre, who adopts that dialogue's hypothesis that the names of the gods stem not from arbitrary coinage but from positive motivation and are thus aboriginally apt and meaningful; and that this fact implicates nomenclature in general. (It is worthy of note that in *The Generative Principle* Maistre classifies Plato as one of the "Greek Fathers" and pairs him with Origen.) He who creates owns title to the naming of what he has created. God being the creator of all and everything—He alone possesses the license to name. Maistre observes how "God is called: *I am*; and every creature is called, *I am that*" (p. 37). The creature must accept its subordination: it names itself first through imitation of the Godhead and then through a witting subaltern qualification. God grants men only a limited *privilege to name*, but not the *right* to do so. Such naming as men propose should function under a rule of modesty. Like the oak from the acorn, the name must properly *"germinate"* (p. 41). Any name must acquire its intertwined branches of meaning through long usage, as the oak gradually and beautifully ramifies. Maistre objects to *prideful* or *extravagant naming*—a noticeable disease of the vile century against which he wages war. In its baroque sophistries, the Eighteenth Century's "rebellious pride," as Maistre puts it, "which cannot deceive itself, seeks at least to deceive others by inventing an honourable name which pretends to exactly the opposite merit" (p. 39). Abuses of language invariably burst forth when men exalt themselves above God. The same crimes arise when those men believe that with quill and black tincture, on laid-cream *feuilles,* they might reorganize reality, including the human reality, according to their whim or pleasure. In Nominalism, Maistre scents the demonic principle.

Considerations on France, Maistre's assessment of the Revolution, and his *Study on Sovereignty,* a critique of Rousseau and Condorcet, are of a piece with *The Generative Principle.* All of Maistre's works, including his formidable correspondence and voluble *memoirs,* constitute elements of an organic whole which their author sums up in the *Dialogues,* of which they are the tributaries. Other commentators on Maistre emphasize his fascination with violence and bloodletting as functions of a providential scheme, a facet of their author's work that these present paragraphs have hitherto skirted, if only so as to differentiate themselves from typical commentary. This theme, however, pushes itself to the fore in *Considerations of France.*

In the *Dialogues,* Maistre elaborates his theory that punishment—in the manner of *Karma* or *Nemesis*—operates as part of the cosmic constitution, whose legislator is God. At the same time, punishment never corresponds to necessity, but only to contingency. Always, punishment might have been prevented, but for the perversity of the human ego. Sin actually affirms that gift of God, free will. In *Considerations,* Chapter I, Maistre writes of men that they are "Freely slaves," who "act both voluntarily and necessarily" and who "do what they will, but without being able to disturb [God's] general plans" (p. 53). The Eighteenth Century has amounted to an acute phase of doing what one wills, and so egregiously has this wicked liberty indulged itself that in response to its transgressions, "we see actions suspended, causes paralysed, and new effects" (p. 53). The Revolution, that fruit of God-hating resentment, has metamorphosed into "a *miracle,*" as Maistre writes, "an effect produced by a divine or superhuman cause which suspends or contradicts an ordinary cause" (p. 53).

The Revolution appears in its full anomaly to its opponents, whom it astonishes. Regicide, that most heinous of crimes, occurs seemingly without consequence; great schemes of mischief, which in stable times would have faced obstacles, enact themselves with absurd ease; and "the good party is unfortunate and ridiculous in all that it undertakes" (p. 54). In the meantime mediocrities attain political prominence and wield the prerogatives that accompany station. Anticipating Gustave Le Bon, Maistre opines how "the French Revolution leads men more than men lead it" (p. 55). Being the rejection of all order, the Revolution unfolds in obedience to no plan, but it is as improvisatory as it is bloodthirsty. Immediately after its initial gains, the Revolution began to feed on itself, a fact that demonstrates the instrumental character of those who believe themselves the Revolution's agents. The Revolution is therefore indeed improvisatory, but it is other than spontaneous. Providence employs the Revolution against itself. What of the innocent parties, however? Maistre points out that sixty thousand people gathered to witness the beheading of Louis XVI and that no one, on that occasion, endangered himself by calling *halt!* The innocents of the Revolution number fewer than the broad complaint would suggest; and if they perished innocently, they perished as martyrs. In enormities like that of 1789, the guilty ones inevitably expiate their guilt by their own blood. In *Considerations,* Chapter II, Maistre pens this excellent maxim: "when a philosopher consoles himself of these misfortunes in view of the results; when he says in his heart, *let a hundred thousand be murdered, provided we are free*; if Providence answers him: *I accept your recommendation, but you shall be counted among that number,* where is the injustice?" (p. 58). And so it is that, "Every drop of Louis XVI's blood will cost France torrents"

(p. 61).

An earlier paragraph accredited Maistre with the innovation, not of the gross, but of the subtle counter-revolution. Maistre opposed the scheme whereby a nucleus of French contra-revolutionaries would enlist the assistance of external powers to invade France and suppress the rebellion. Maistre desired the preservation of French sovereignty, which invasion by foreign powers would sabotage. Foreign armies would occupy French territory. Foreign princes would likely exploit the situation to annex French territory. A restored monarch, in addition to owing a debt to those who re-installed him, would be constrained by his adherence to Christian doctrines from inflicting on rebels the condign penalties that their crimes demand. The sovereign would need to exercise clemency, for example, and extend mercy. Or, if determined magistrates gained sway, "justice… would have had an air of vengeance" (p. 61). Punishments would in that case lend themselves to misrepresentation. Providentially, the Revolution must, by the mechanics of its progress, grind itself to stoppage. It will do so with appropriate inward-turning ferocity. Maistre asserts in *Considerations,* Chapter IV, that "a large republic is impossible" (p. 79). The Revolution presuming the form of a large republic, its endurance comes with the opposite of a guarantee. Once the Revolution reaches its inevitable end, the renewed monarchy will content itself with the Christian task of rebuilding the nation. While it is true that Maistre praised the hangman as absolutely necessary for the stability of the state, he never advocated violence, but merely remarked its persistence and ubiquity. Maistre stands out as a theoretician of violence, a phenomenon that he studied closely and scientifically.

Readers will encounter the heart of *Considerations* in Chapter III, which its author entitles "Of the Violent Destruction of the Human Species." Any number of commentators have quoted Maistre's line. It must nevertheless be quoted again: "History unfortunately proves that war is the usual state of the human race in a certain sense, that is to say that human blood must flow without interruption somewhere or other on the globe; and that peace, for every nation, is but a respite" (p. 70). Maistre crowds a sequence of paragraphs with details of war since the Roman Republic. He then launches into one of his proto-Darwinian discussions, arguing that war *re-tempers* the human spirit when a civilization has become lazy and decadent, and that it stimulates the arts and sciences. Maistre points out as evidence for his assertion that the great age of Greece, the Fifth Century, corresponded to a series of destructive wars that left the *poleis* bankrupt and exhausted. War need not be inevitable. Like all punishments, war falls subject to preemption, even if such preemption were rare. Nevertheless, as Maistre sees things, war, once it breaks out, boasts a *sacred* quality. War is sacrificial. War makes manifest the principle that *"the innocent suffer for the benefit of the guilty"* (p. 75). Maistre believes that "It was from this dogma… that the ancients derived the usage of sacrifice that they practiced throughout the world, and judged useful not only for the living, but also for the dead" (p. 75). Self-sacrifice for the sake of others follows the same intuition as the hecatomb or human sacrifice, but it accords itself better with Christian principles. Maistre reminds his readers that men live in a fallen world, where evil taints everything and disorder obtains. Yet in Maistre's words: "there is no disorder that ETERNAL LOVE does not turn against the principle of evil" (p. 76). The Revolution cannot exempt itself from this implacable law.

The *Study on Sovereignty* represents an earlier stage in the same line of Maistre's thinking as the later *Generative Principle.* The *Study* names Rousseau many times, but even where Maistre omits to put Rousseau under direct inquisition, his chapters tend to confront the earlier writer's *Social Contract* and *Discourse on Inequality.* In the *Study,* Maistre first comes to the fore as an anthropologist. He does so by conducting a thorough critique of Rousseau's assumption that "there was a human era before society": this assumption, however, is "the only thing that had to be proven" (p. 170). The *Study* rejects the hypothesis of *scattered* or *isolated men*—Rousseau's self-absorbed and anti-social savage. Even supposing Rousseau's non-binding sexual encounters between primitive men and women, with the men free from any obligation to stay for the night or call in the morning, the mothers and their children would have constituted social units. Man's nature, Maistre argues, emerges only in society. Maistre writes that history, which constitutes a plausible account of man's sojourn on earth, and which therefore better recommends itself than Rousseau's speculation, "constantly shows us men united into more or less numerous societies, ruled by different sovereignties" (p. 169). The conclusion follows that no pre-social phase of human nature existed: "because before the formation of political societies, man is not altogether man" (p. 169). Maistre deals with Rousseau as he had dealt with Locke. Rousseau deploys a vocabulary of *nature, right,* and *order,* but in context, or due to the lack of a context, these terms elude definition. Rousseau juggles with words. According to Maistre nations exhibit an organic quality. Nations experience birth, have fathers and teachers; nations have a *soul,* such that, "When we speak of the *spirit* of a nation, the expression is not as metaphorical as we think" (p. 176). Finally, nations *die.* History is littered with their corpses.

Sovereignty flows from Providence, that is, from the Will of God. Just as men are instruments of Providence, they are equally instruments of the sovereignty that moulds them. Each nation has its sovereign founder who "divines those hidden forces and qualities which form his nation's character" and finds, as Maistre writes, "the means of fertilizing them, of putting them into action" (p. 186). The sovereign founder never reveals himself in the act of writing or deliberating. If the time came when the descendants of the sovereign founder felt the need to write down the laws that he had bequeathed them, they would merely remind themselves with ink on paper of the *ethos* that previously obtained, but they would invent nothing. Nations grow from instinct, not from deliberation, Maistre insists. The maturation of the policy must furthermore at every stage acknowledge the order of being. It is faith that apperceives divinity, but it is also faith that apperceives the order of being. The aboriginal task to instill that faith befalls the sovereign founder as a supreme obligation. The student of history will gather many examples of the sovereign founder from the early medieval period. Charlemagne famously, according to his biographers, acquired literacy only late in life and never really got the hang of reading and writing. He *rode* at the head of his cavalry. Joan of Arc, arguably the genetrix of the French nation, had as much to do with letters as did Charlemagne. The King of the Franks and the Maid of Orleans acted, in Maistre's precise sense, as instruments of Providence. The Barons in submitting the *Magna Carta* to Prince John constituted no convention. Like Homer the Barons committed to writing *a living oral tradition* that their document never originated but only belatedly reaffirmed. Maistre writes of "*prejudices*, fathers of the laws and stronger than the laws" (p. 206). *What—civilization is founded on prejudice? Yes, emphatically,* Maistre answers: *Civilization is the prejudice for the natural order of things.* Modernity, taking offense from anything not itself, eschews the apocalypse of God and along with it the necessary connotative lexicon of theology. Modernity consists, in striking contrast with its utopianism, in a long procession of extraordinary national and global catastrophes, with colossal bloodletting, culminating in the atomic attacks on the two most Christian cities of Japan. Maistre's apocalyptic language offers a vocabulary and perspective vastly different from those of modernity but supremely meet to the discussion thereof. Modernity because of its literal-mindedness can never carry out an adequate critique of itself.

The language-theoretician Eric L. Gans qualifies Maistre, in his *Scenic Imagination* (2007), as the *first anthropologist.* Gans finds it possible to extract from Maistre's writings the thesis that the first organizing principle of humanity, of nations, and indeed of sovereignty took the form of sacrifice. In *The St. Petersburg Dialogues* and *The Generative Principle,* Maistre insists that language and law descend on humanity from a transcendental origin, which men usually call Zeus or Jupiter or God. Language and law *dawned on men* in an event. This is why Maistre argues that no one ever invented language or the code of law, but that the individual only ever *learns* language or the code of law. Gans writes that, "De Maistre's religiously tinged rhetoric should not blind us to the fact that the discussion of pagan sacrifice that opens the [*Elucidation on Sacrifices*] is essentially functionalist; the pagan gods are less supernatural beings than manifestations of an 'idea of God' that [Maistre] considers coeval with humanity" (108). As Gans remarks, Maistre understands sacrifice as redemptive on the model of the Passion. Maistre's description of Louis XVI's execution in the *Elucidations* particularly impresses Gans for its *scenic* quality. In the *Considerations,* perhaps even more than in the *Elucidations,* the regicide constitutes a vast public spectacle that exercises albeit in a wicked way a socially unifying effect. For Maistre, in Gans' view, sacrifice and language have an intimate connection in that Christ is not only the redeemer, but also in John's theology, the Word. Gans concludes that Maistre "is the first thinker to find in Christianity the basis for a science of anthropology" (110). Maistre becomes under Gans' description something of a precursor to René Girard whose study of *Things Hidden since the Foundation of the World* (1978) picks up where the *Elucidation* leaves off.

III. A Brief Life of Maistre.

Maistre's life is bound up inextricably with the fortunes of the Kingdom of Sardinia or Piedmont-Sardinia, to which the Duchy of Savoy belonged—with an interregnum—in the late Eighteenth and Early Nineteenth Centuries. Joseph-Marie, Comte de Maistre, entered this mortal life at Chambéry, in the Duchy of Savoy, on 1 April 1753, the eldest of two sons of François-Xavier, a magistrate and senator of Piedmont-Sardinia whom the king had elevated to the rank of count. According to Charles Augustin Sainte-Beuve's *Portraits Littéraires, Tome II* (1862), Maistre responded in a lively way to public events even in childhood. Sainte-Beuve tells the story of how, at the age of eleven, on hearing that the French government had suppressed the Jesuits, the young Maistre joyously and volubly repeated the story. Sainte-Beuve continues: "His mother heard him and stopped him. 'Never speak thus,' she said; 'you will understand one day that it is one of the greatest misfortunes for religion.'" So solemn was the mother's rebuke that it "remained ever present to him." Maistre passed under the tutelage, at home, of the Savoyard Jesuits in Chambéry. He also took courses at the college there, proving himself adept in languages. Sainte-Beuve reports that in early adolescence Maistre had memorized an entire book of Vergil's *Aeneid* and liked to recite it. Many years later when a friend reminded him of this feat, he found his memory intact. Maistre attended the University of Turin, where, in 1773, he took his law degree. In Sainte-Beuve's telling: "The following year… he entered as substitute-lawyer [and] fiscal-general supernumerary… to the Senate of Savoy, and he followed the various degrees of this career of the public prosecutor until in April, 1788, he was promoted to the seat of senator, as a councilor to parliament." Sainte-Beuve comments on Maistre's deportment as a judge: "His emotion, whenever it was a capital condemnation, was lively; he did not hesitate in the sentence when he thought it dictated by conscience and by truth; but his scruples, his anxiety on this subject, quite deny those who… would have liked to make [of him] an inhuman soul."

The French Republic invaded Savoy in 1792, annexed its territory, and imposed its violent and confiscatory regime. The occupation would remain in force until 1815. No doubt fearing for his life, Maistre fled to Lausanne, which served him as his base for three years. While residing in Switzerland Maistre became a familiar of Madame de Staël and participated in her *salon*. The product of that association was the *Considerations*. Although Maistre had been an inveterate writer since adolescence, the *Considerations*, appearing when he had reached the age of forty, marked the beginning of his public career as a *littérateur*. Early in 1797 Maistre responded to a plea from King Charles-Emmanuel IV to rejoin the court, but he arrived in the midst of Napoleon's Italian campaign. Sainte-Beuve writes how Maistre "returned only to witness the vicissitudes of his country and the ruin of his sovereign, whom Napoleon had deprived of his Piedmontese estates. Maistre, traveling with his family, fled to Venice where, according to Sainte-Beuve, they domiciled "in a single room on the ground floor of the Austrian residents' Hotel." Maistre rejoined Charles-Emmanuel, who had reorganized his court at Cagliari in Sardinia, in January of 1800, serving as a member of the senate and chief magistrate of the much-reduced state. According to Georg Brandes, writing in *Main Currents in the Literature of the Nineteenth Century*, Volume III, "he labored hard to improve the slovenly administration of justice which he found prevailing there." He spent his spare time in study. As Sainte-Beuve reports, Maistre "renewed and strengthened his already extensive philological knowledge, anxious to go back to the hidden roots, and never separating the spirit from the letter."

The epochal event in Maistre's life came in 1803, when Charles-Emmanuel appointed him envoy extraordinary and minister plenipotentiary to the Imperial Court in St. Petersburg. By a circuitous route that took him through Rome, Maistre arrived in St. Petersburg in May of that year.

Brandes writes: "His acceptance of this appointment obliged him to part from his wife, Françoise-Marguerite (née de Morand), and children, to whom he was tenderly attached. The pay was so miserable that it barely sufficed to cover his own necessary expenses—he could not afford to provide himself with a fur-lined coat." (Maistre had two daughters, Adele and Constance, and a son, Rodolphe.) Maistre's duties, however, were light so that he could devote himself to study and writing. Sainte-Beuve describes his routine. He sat at a desk, from early morning, attending to correspondence. The task done, he took up his books and his quill. He had his meals served at the same desk, invariably resuming his researches after he had replenished himself—often until late in the night. "Most of M. de Maistre's works," writes Sainte-Beuve, "have been composed in solitude, without audience, as by an ardent, animated thinker who speaks with himself." Maistre was nevertheless not a hermit. The Czar warmed to him and introduced him to aristocratic and intellectual circles. Brandes relates how Alexander, "as proof of his favor and esteem for de Maistre… gave commissions in the Russian Army to his brother and son"; and he adds that "the brother was wounded during the campaign in the Caucasus." Maistre kept a pet dog named *Biribi* whose affection partly compensated the absence of his family. He particularly missed being apart from his daughters and wrote them numerous letters over the years of their mutual separation.

In 1808 Maistre undertook a surprising project. He attempted to gain an audience with Napoleon in order to plead the cause of his straightened Sardinia. As Brandes writes, "he took this step not in his capacity as minister, but privately and on his own responsibility." Maistre composed a letter and sent it to the Emperor, who, while he omitted to respond directly, requested the French ambassador in St. Petersburg to favor its writer discreetly. According to Brandes, Napoleon admired Maistre and thus "did not take his audacity at all amiss." When the Sardinian government learned of Maistre's attempt at communication with Bonaparte, it rebuked him, but it made no move to recall the plenipotentiary from his mission. One can only imagine what would have transpired in a dialogue between Maistre and Napoleon. It would have been an exchange for the ages. But it was not to be. Napoleon's Russian campaign of 1812 reinforced Maistre's notion of war as a supernatural occurrence—and he naturally took the Russian victory at the Battle of Borodino as evidence for his providential view of history. Isaiah Berlin mentions that Maistre's letters concerning the reaction of Russian society to Napoleon's violent incursion provided Leo Tolstoy with useful research material while writing *War and Peace*. In addition to his copious personal and diplomatic correspondence, Maistre wrote six of his books during his Russian sojourn: *Of the Pope, Of the Gallican Church, Examination of the Philosophy of Bacon*, and the *St.-Petersburg Dialogues*. The last remained incomplete (though vast) at Maistre's death and saw publication posthumously; *Of the Gallican Church* also saw publication posthumously. As the commentaries of Sainte-Beuve and Brandes tell, these works maintained their currency in the mid- and even unto the late-Nineteenth Century, but in later decades, Maistre spoke to fewer and fewer readers. When authors addressed him, as the leftwing Harold Laski did in the 1940s, it was mainly to denounce him.

Maistre left Russia in May of 1817. For part of his journey he traveled as an honored guest on one of the warships of Alexander's Imperial Flotilla. Before returning at long last to Turin to be reunited with his family, Maistre, for the first time in his life, visited Paris, where he stayed from late June until late August. Then it was on to Turin. Sainte-Beuve writes that "all the dignities and highest functions awaited him there." Victor-Emmanuel bestowed on the man the titles of Minister of State and Regent of the Grand Chancellery. Despite the titles, Maistre went basically into retirement. He had entered a period, moreover, of physical decline. He became distinctly aware of his mortality and foresaw his death. No doubt but his Spartan existence in Russia had cost him a measure of his life-energy. Even so, as Brandes writes, he kept his sense of ironic humor. Sainte-Beuve relates a story told to him by a painter acquaintance of Maistre, who, in 1820, proposed that he sit for a portrait in his chancellor's uniform. On the day when he made his formal visit to the king, he presented himself to the painter. "He came indeed," as Sainte-Beuve quotes his source; "and as I told him that he should not have come that day, for he seemed very tired on having climbed our stairs, he answered me [that he] wanted to come today, because [he would] not be able to come back." The old man was making a joke at his own expense. Maistre's condition worsened, including a loss of appetite. Even so, he continued his correspondence by dictation and listened intently while his family and friends read to him. After six weeks in bed, Maistre died on 26 February 1821 at the age of sixty-seven. "To the end," writes Brandes, "de Maistre was true to his character; he would not yield a foot of the ground that had been lost centuries before."

Maistre's best-known disciple, the Symbolist poet Baudelaire, links him somewhat paradoxically to Twentieth Century modernity and to contemporary Western Civilization in the third decade of the Twenty-First Century. Cultivated people—those who have acquired their education outside the institutions—still read and appreciate Baudelaire, whose poems and essays remain in print. Those who read Baudelaire enter the aura of Maistre, even if unbeknownst. Yet the name of Maistre nowadays relegates itself mainly to encyclopedia articles. Another poet, the American Ezra Pound, also valued Maistre, as did the right-wing French philosopher Charles Maurras. Those two still have a few readers. Gustave Le Bon suggests himself as related genealogically to Maistre although Le Bon, while a critic of mass movements such as Jacobinism, observed a purely secular orientation rather than a religious one. Le Bon's *World Unbalanced* (1923) nevertheless looks at the social disorder and psychological schisms of the then-contemporary political and cultural scene through Maistrian lenses. The English-language translators of Maistre, Richard Lebrun and Jack Lively, labored like Hercules to make his works available to contemporary readers. Lebrun translated *The St. Petersburg Dialogues* and the *Examination of the Philosophy of Bacon,* two immense books. *Alas!*—these saw publication in limited, expensive editions intended for university libraries. In the present moment of resurgent political sectarianism in the West—a descent into something like a Maoist Cultural Revolution increasingly prone to confrontation and violence—Maistre's pertinence to the situation renews itself urgently. Our crisis of Puritan conformism and its attendant restriction of consciousness solicit Maistre's thundering voice more than ever.

Thomas F. Bertonneau

March, 2019

Works Cited

Brandes: *Main Currents in Nineteenth Century Literature,* Vol. III – *Joseph de Maistre.*

Gans: *The Scenic Imagination: Originary Thinking from Hobbes to the Present Day.* Stanford University Press, 2008.

Maistre: *Considerations on France.* Translated and edited by Richard A. Lebrun, with an introduction by Isaiah Berlin. Cambridge University Press, 1994.

Maistre: *Essay on the Generative Principle.* Edited by Elisha Greifer and translated with the assistance of Laurence M. Porter. Gateway Edition, Henry Regnery Company, Chicago, 1959.

Maistre: *St. Petersburg Dialogues.* Translated and edited by Richard A. Lebrun. McGill University Press, 1993.

Maistre: *Study on Sovereignty.* In *Studies on Sovereignty, Religion, and Enlightenment,* translated and edited by Jack Lively. Transaction Publishers, 1965.

Sainte-Beuve: *Portraits Littéraires, Tome II* (1862).

Valéry: *The Outlook for Intelligence.* Translated by Denise Folliot and Jackson Matthews. Princeton University Press, 1962.

Note on the Text

Maistre's punctuation, paragraph structure, and typographical emphasis have been closely preserved in this edition. Some longer direct quotations are now quoted verbatim—Maistre's use of the reporting verb "he says" has been removed in those cases where it is redundant, i.e. where he adds no further comment on the quotation in the same paragraph. In some cases where Maistre has inserted fragmentary quotations, the entire quotation has been included for context.

Source editions are as follows:

Essai sur le Principe Générateur des Constitutions Politiques (Lyon and Paris: H. Pelagaud et fils Roblot, 1873)

Considérations sur la France (Lyon and Paris: La Librairie Ecclésiastique de Rusand, 1829)

Étude sur la souveraineté (*Sine nomine*, 1829)

Plato's Greek has been sourced from *Platonis Opera*, ed. John Burnet (Oxford University Press, 1903).

Notes by the editor of this edition are in [square brackets]. Notes by the editors of the source editions are in <angled brackets>. All Latin and Greek passages the translator of which is not specified have been translated by the present editor.

MAJOR WORKS

VOLUME I

Essay on the Generative Principle of Political Constitutions and Other Human Institutions

O ye sons of men, how long will ye turn my glory into shame? how long will ye love vanity, and seek after leasing?

Psalms 4:3

Editor's Notice.

Whoever has wished to find the cause of this uneasy spirit which has agitated the universe for more than thirty years has recognized that the systems spawned by modern philosophy have displaced or destroyed the true foundations of society.

By fostering man in his pretended rights, and by letting him ignore part of his first duties, bold innovators have flattered his passions, inspired him with unheard-of pretensions, and soon led him to question those precious truths which the experience of all ages had confirmed. Since then, everything has been problematic, the most inviolable laws have vanished, the government of states has ceased to be conducted according to rule, political harmony has collapsed, and we have nearly reaped in the field of the revolution the too numerous fruits of new doctrines.

The most ancient legislators had placed their laws under the protection of the gods, they had established religious ceremonies, they had recognized the constitutive principles of states; and if, in those remote times, so many peoples have successively risen and fallen, it is because, relying on religions false and of little duration, they could not have a solid foundation.

The establishment of Christianity has made revolutions less frequent, and it is to this that we owe the happiness which France has enjoyed for fourteen centuries. If Providence has allowed our country to suffer such disastrous catastrophes, it is because we had strayed from the holy maxims of our ancestors, and because it wished to remind us, by this terrible lesson, that without religion all is error and calamity.

This first truth, from which all the others flow, was developed by M. de Maistre, with as much force as logic, in his book entitled: *Essay on the Generative Principle of Political Constitutions*. Already he had established it in his *Considerations on France*; but he thought it ought to be the subject of a separate treatise to make it yet clearer by freeing it from all the particular circumstances which seemed to apply only to the French Revolution.

This second work being in a way the complement of the first, a new edition of which we have just produced, we cannot refuse to reprint it on the same paper, with the same typeface, and in the same format as the other works of M. de Maistre, to meet the demands of those who wish to collect them.

Preface.

Politics—which is perhaps the thorniest of the sciences due to the perennial difficulty of discerning what is stable or changeable in its elements—presents a very strange phenomenon, well suited to make every wise man called to the administration of states tremble. It is this: all in this science that good sense first regards as an evident truth is almost always found, when experience has spoken, not only false, but disastrous.

To begin at the foundation, if we had never heard of governments, and men were called to deliberate, for example, on hereditary or elective monarchy, we would justly regard one who should decide for the former as a fool. The arguments against it appear so naturally to reason that it is pointless to recount them.

History, however, which is experimental politics, demonstrates that hereditary monarchy is the government most stable, most happy, and most natural to man, and elective monarchy, on the contrary, the worst kind of government known.

In fact, concerning population, commerce, prohibitive laws, and a thousand other important subjects, one almost always finds the most plausible theory contradicted and annulled by experience. Let us cite a few examples.

How does one go about making a state powerful? — "Above all, it is necessary to favour population by all possible means." On the contrary, any law tending directly to favour population, without regard to other considerations, is bad. We must even try to establish in the state a certain moral force which tends to diminish the number of marriages, and to render them less hasty. The excess of births over deaths as determined by tables usually only proves the number of the destitute, etc. The French economists had sketched out the demonstration of these truths; the fine work of Mr. *Malthus* has come to finish it.

How to prevent scarcities and famines? — "Nothing is easier. We must forbid the export of grain." — On the contrary, a premium must be granted to those who export them. The example and authority of England have forced us to *swallow* this paradox.

How to maintain the exchange rate in favour of a country? — "It must, no doubt, prevent the export of currency; and consequently, it must ensure, by strong prohibitive laws, that the state buy no more than it sells." On the contrary, these means have never been employed without bringing down the exchange rate, or, what amounts to the same thing, without increasing the nation's debt; and one can never take the opposite route without raising it, that is to say, without proving that the credit of the nation over its neighbours has increased, etc.

But it is in what is most substantial and fundamental in politics, I mean in the very constitution of empires, that the observation in question recurs. I hear that the German philosophers have invented the word *metapolitics* to be to *politics* what the word *metaphysics* is to *physics*; this new expression seems very well-formed to express the *metaphysics of politics*; for there is such a thing, and this science deserves the profound attention of observers.

Nearly twenty years ago, an anonymous writer, who was much occupied with these kinds of speculations and who sought to plumb the hidden foundations of the social edifice, thought himself entitled to advance, like so many incontestable axioms, the following propositions diametrically opposed to the theories of time.

1. No constitution results from deliberation: the rights of the people are never written, or only as simple declarations of pre-existing unwritten rights.

2. Human action is circumscribed in these sorts of cases,[1] to the point that the men who act are only circumstances.

3. The rights of the people, properly so-called, almost always arise from the concession of sovereigns, and then they can be traced histor-

1 [i.e., in forming constitutions.]

ically: but the rights of the sovereign and the aristocracy have neither date nor known authors.

4. These concessions themselves have always been preceded by a state of affairs which necessitated them, and which did not depend on the sovereign.

5. Although written laws are nothing but declarations of pre-existing rights, it is nowhere near possible for all these rights to be written.

6. The more one writes, the weaker the constitution.

7. No nation can give itself liberty if it does not have it;[2] human influence does not extend beyond the development of existing rights.

8. Lawgivers, properly so-called, are extraordinary men who perhaps belong only to the ancient world and the youth of nations.

9. These legislators, even with their marvellous power, have only ever gathered together pre-existing elements, and have always acted in the name of the Deity.

10. Liberty is, in a sense, the gift of kings; for almost all free nations were constituted by kings.[3]

11. There has never existed a free nation which did not have, in its natural constitution, seeds of liberty as old as itself; and no nation has ever successfully attempted to develop, by its fundamental written laws, rights other than those which existed in its natural constitution.

12. No assembly of men whatever can constitute a nation. An enterprise of this kind must even be ranked among the most memorable acts of folly.[4]

2 Machiavelli is called here to testify: *Un populo uso a vivere solto un principe, se per qualohe accidente diventa libero, con difficoltà mantiene la libertà.* ["A people accustomed to live under a prince, should they by some eventuality become free, will with difficulty maintain their freedom."] *Discourses on Livy*, I, XVI.

3 This must be taken under serious consideration in modern monarchies. As all legitimate and holy immunities of this kind must start from the sovereign, all that is wrested from him by force is cursed. *To write a law*, said Demosthenes very well, is nothing: *to MAKE IT WANTED is everything.* (*Olynthiacs*, III) But if this is true of the sovereign vis-à-vis the people, what shall we say of a nation; that is to say—to use a euphemism—of a handful of overheated theorists who would propose a constitution to the legitimate sovereign, as one would propose a capitulation to a besieged general? All this would be indecent, absurd, and especially, futile.

4 Machiavelli is again cited here: *E necessario che uno sia quello che dia il modo e delta oui mente dipenda qualunque simile ordinazione.* ["It is essential that there should be but one person upon whose mind and method depends any similar

It does not seem that, since the year 1796, the date of the first edition of the book that we quote,[5] anything has happened in the world that could have led the author to repent of his theory. On the contrary, we believe that at this moment it may be useful to develop it fully and to follow it in all its implications, one of the most important of which, no doubt, is that stated in these words in chapter X, from the same book:

> Man cannot create a sovereign. At most, he can serve as an instrument to dethrone a sovereign and deliver his kingdom to another sovereign already royal ... "*Moreover, there has never been a sovereign family which can be assigned a plebeian origin. If such a phenomenon should appear, it would mark a new epoch in the world.*"[6]

One can reflect on this thesis, which *divine judgement* has just approved in a rather solemn way. But who knows if the ignorant levity of our age will not say earnestly: *If he had willed it, he would still be in his place!* as she repeats again after two centuries: *If Richard Cromwell had possessed his father's genius, he would have fixed the protectorate in his family;* which is exactly like saying: *If this family had not ceased to reign, it would still reign.*

It is written: BY ME PRINCES RULE.[7] This is not a church phrase, a preacher's metaphor; it is the literal truth, simple and palpable. It is a law of the political world. God *makes* kings, literally. He prepares the royal races; He matures them under a cloud that hides their origin. Thereafter they appear *crowned with glory and honour*; they take their places; and here is the greatest sign of their legitimacy.

This is because they arise of themselves, without violence on the one hand, and without marked deliberation on the other: it is a kind of magnificent tranquillity which it is not easy to express. *Legitimate usurpation* would seem to me the proper expression (if it were not too bold) to characterize such origins, which time hastens to consecrate.

Let no one allow himself to be dazzled, then, by the most splendid human appearances. Who has ever assembled in himself more than the extraordinary personage whose fall still echoes throughout Europe? Have we ever seen sovereignty so outwardly firm, a greater consolidation of means, a man more powerful, more active, more formidable? For a long time, we

process of organization."] *Discourses on Livy*, I, IV.

5 *Considerations on France*, ch. IV. p. 93 [the chapter in this edition is actually VI].

6 *Considerations on France*, ch. X, §3, p. 141

7 *Per me Reget regnant. Proverbs* VIII, 15.

saw him trample under foot twenty nations, speechless and frozen with dread; and his power finally threw out roots which could make *hope itself despair.* — Yet he is so far fallen that Pity, who contemplates him, recoils for fear of being *touched.* Moreover, one may observe here that, for a *somewhat* different reason, it has become equally difficult to speak of this man, and of the august rival who has rid the world of him. The one escapes from insult, and the other from praise. — But I digress.

In a work known only to a few people in St. Petersburg, the author wrote in the year 1810:

> When two parties clash in a revolution, if we see precious victims fall on one side, we can bet that this side will win at last, despite all appearances to the contrary.

This is yet another assertion whose truth has just been borne out in a manner most striking, and least expected. The moral order has its laws just as the physical, and their study is altogether worthy of occupying the meditations of the true philosopher. After a whole age of criminal trifling, it is high time to recall what we are, and to trace all knowledge back to its source. It is this which has induced the author of this little work to let it escape the portfolio that held it for five years. He lets its date stand,[8] and it is given word for word as it was written at that time. Friendship has brought about this publication, and perhaps it is so much the worse for the author; for this good lady is, on certain occasions, as blind as her brother. Be that as it may, the spirit which has dictated the work enjoys a well-known privilege: he may, no doubt, sometimes be mistaken on trivial points, he may exaggerate or speak too confidently; he may, in fine, offend against language or taste, and in this case, so much the better for the wicked, *if by chance there be any*; but there will always be left to him the well-founded hope of not offending anyone, since he loves all the world, and, moreover, the perfect assurance of interesting a class of men very numerous and estimable, without the possibility of harming a single one: this belief is indeed soothing.

8 [May, 1809.]

Essay on the Generative Principle of Political Constitutions and Other Human Institutions.

I. One of the grand errors of an age that professed them all was to believe that a political constitution could be written and created *a priori,* while reason and experience meet in establishing that a constitution is a divine work, and that precisely what is most fundamental and most essentially constitutional in the laws of a nation cannot be written.

II. It has often been thought that it would make an excellent joke at the expense of the French to ask them *in what book was the Salic law written?* but Jérôme Bignon answered very aptly, and probably without knowing how right he was, *that it was written* IN *the hearts of the French.* In fact, suppose that a law of such importance exists only because it is written—it is certain that whatever authority wrote it should have the right to annul it; the law, then, will not have that character of sanctity and immutability which distinguishes truly constitutional laws. The essence of a fundamental law is that no one has the right to abolish it: but how can it be above *all* if some *one* has made it? The agreement of the people is impossible; and even if it were not, an agreement is not a law, and binds no one unless there is a superior authority which guarantees it. *Locke* sought the character of the law in the expression of united wills; we must be happy thus to meet precisely that trait which excludes the idea of *law.* In fact, united wills form the *regulation* and not the *law,* which necessarily and manifestly presupposes a superior will which makes itself obeyed.[9] "In Hobbes' system" (the same one which was so ubiquitous in our century under the pen of Locke), "the force of civil laws rests only on convention; but if there is no natural law that orders the execution of the laws which have been made, what are they for? Promises, covenants, oaths are only words: it is as easy to break this frivolous bond as to form it. Without the doctrine of a Divine Lawgiver, every moral obligation is chimerical. Force on the one hand, impotence on the other: here is the whole bond of human society."[10]

What a wise and profound theologian has said here of moral obligation applies with equal truth to political or civil obligation. Law is not proper-

9 "Man in the state of nature had only rights ... On entering society, I relinquish my particular will to comply with the law, *which is the general will.*" *Le Spectateur Français* (I, p.194) has rightly mocked this definition; but it could have observed, moreover, that it belongs to the age, and especially to Locke, who opened this century in such a disastrous manner.

10 Bergier, *Traite Historique et Dogmatique de la Religion*, III, ch. IV, §19, pp. 330, 331. (After Tertullian, *Apologeticus*, 45)

ly *law*, nor is it truly sanctioned, except in supposing it emanates from a superior will; so that its essential character is *that it is not the will of all.* Otherwise the laws will be, as we have just said, *only regulations*; and as the author just quoted observes, "those who have had the liberty of making these conventions have not given up the power of revoking them; and their descendants, who have had no part in it, are still less bound to observe them."[11] Hence primordial good sense, fortunately anterior to sophisms, has sought on all sides the sanction of laws in a power above man, either in recognizing that sovereignty comes from God, or by worshiping certain unwritten laws as emanating from Him.

III. The codifiers of Roman law have unpretentiously placed in the first chapter of their collection a fragment of Greek jurisprudence quite remarkable. *Among the laws which govern us*, says this passage, *some are written and others are not*. Nothing more simple; nothing more profound. Do we know any Turkish law which expressly allows the sovereign to condemn a man to death immediately, without the intervening decision of a tribunal? Do we know any *written* law, even religious, which forbids this to the sovereigns of Christian Europe?[12] Yet the Turk is no more surprised to see his master promptly order a man's death than to see him go to the mosque. He believes, with all Asia, and even with all antiquity, that the right to promptly inflict capital punishment is a legitimate prerogative of sovereignty. But our princes would shudder at the mere idea of condemning a man to death; for as we see it, this condemnation would be an abominable murder; and yet I doubt whether it would be possible to defend it by a fundamental written law without bringing on greater evils than those we might wish to prevent.

IV. Ask of Roman history what precisely was the power of the senate; she will remain silent, at least as to the precise limits of this power. It is generally seen that the power of the people and that of the Senate mutually *balanced* one another, and ceased not to fight each other; it is clear that patriotism or weariness, weakness or violence ended these dangerous strug-

11 Bergier, *Traite Historique*, III, ch. IV, §12.

12 "The Church forbids her children, even more strongly than the civil laws, to judge themselves; and it is in this spirit that Christian kings do not judge themselves in the first place, even in cases of *lèse-majesté*, and that they place criminals in the hands of judges to punish them according to the laws and the procedures of justice." (Pascal, *Lettres Provinciales* XIV.) This passage is very important and should be published more widely.

gles, but we do not know any more.[13] In viewing these great scenes of history, one sometimes feels tempted to believe that things would have gone much better if there had been definite laws circumscribing these powers; but this would have been a great mistake: such laws, always compromised by unforeseen cases and compelling exceptions, would not have lasted six months, or they would have overthrown the republic.

V. The English Constitution is an example closer to us, and therefore more striking. Let it be examined with attention: we will see that *it proceeds only insofar as it is inert*[14] (if this pun is allowed). It is sustained only by exceptions. *Habeas corpus*, for example, has been so often and so long suspended that it is doubtful whether the exception has not become the rule. Suppose for a moment that the authors of this famous act had undertaken to fix the cases where it could be suspended; in so doing, they would have annihilated it.

VI. At the sitting of the House of Commons on June 26, 1807, a lord cited the authority of a great statesman to establish *that the King has no right to dissolve Parliament during the session*; but this opinion was contradicted. Where is the law? Try to do it, try to fix exclusively *in writing* the case where the King has this right; you will bring about a revolution. *The King*, said one of the members, *has this right when the occasion is important*; but what is an *important* occasion? Try once again to decide in writing.

VII. But here is an event yet more singular. Everyone remembers the great question agitated with such fervour in England in the year 1806: it was a question of *whether the holding of a judicial appointment together with a place on the Privy Council was or was not in accordance with the principles of the English Constitution*; at the meeting of the same House of Commons on the 3rd of March, a member observed *that England is governed by a body* (the Privy Council) *not known by Legislature*.[15] *Only*, he added, *it is*

13 I have often reflected on this passage from Cicero: *Leges Liviae praesertim uno versiculo senatus puncto temporis sublatae sunt* ["in particular, the laws of Livius were annulled in a moment by a single utterance of the senate"] (*De Legibus*, II, 6). By what right did the senate take this liberty? and how could the people let it? Surely, it is not easy to say: but why should this surprise us, since after all that has been written on history and Roman antiquities, it was necessary in our times to write discourses to learn how the Senate was recruited?

14 [French *qu'elle ne va qu'en n'allant pas*, lit. "it goes, in that it does not go", i.e. it works when it does not change.]

15 *Thy country is governed by a body not known by Legislature.*

connived at.[16]

So here, in this wise and justly famous England, there is a body that governs and in truth does everything, but *that the constitution does not recognize.* Delolme has overlooked this feature, which I could corroborate with many others.

After this, tell us of written constitutions and constitutional laws made *a priori.* One cannot conceive how a sensible man could imagine the possibility of such a chimera. If one were to make a law in England to give a constitutional existence to the Privy Council, and then to regulate and circumscribe rigorously its privileges and powers, with the precautions necessary to limit its influence and to prevent its abuse, one would overthrow the state.

The true *English Constitution* is that admirable, unique, and infallible public spirit, beyond all praise, which directs everything, which protects everything. — What is written is nothing.[17]

VIII. Toward the end of the last century a loud cry was raised up against a minister who had formed the idea of introducing the same English Constitution (or what was called by that name) into a realm in turmoil, and which demanded a constitution of any kind with a sort of fury. He was wrong, if you will, as much as one can be wrong when acting in good faith; it is right to suppose he was, and I believe this with all my heart. But who, then, was entitled to condemn him? *Vel duo, vel nemo* ["either two, or none"]. He did not declare that he wished to destroy anything of his own accord; he only wished, he said, to substitute one thing which seemed reasonable to him for another which was no longer wanted; and which *ipso facto* no longer existed. Moreover, if the principle is granted (and indeed it was), *that man can create a constitution,* this minister (who was certainly a man) had the right to make his own just as well as, and more than, any other. Were doctrines on this point doubtful? Did we not believe, on all sides, that a constitution is a work of the intellect like an ode or a tragedy? Had not *Thomas Paine* declared with a profundity that ravished the universities *that a constitution does not exist until it can be put in his pocket?* The eighteenth century, which doubted itself in nothing, balked at noth-

16 *Connived at,* see the *London Chronicle* of March 4, 1806. Observe that this word *Legislature* comprises the three powers; it follows from this assertion that the King himself *does not know of the Privy Council.* — But I think he might.

17 *The turbulent government of England,* says Hume, *ever fluctuating between privilege and prerogative, would afford a variety of precedents, which might be pleaded on both sides.* (*History of England,* 1621, James I, ch. XLVII) Hume, speaking the truth thus, does not lack respect for his country; he says what it is and must be.

ing: this is the rule; and I do not think it has produced a single fledgling of any talent who did not make three things straight out of college: an *educational system*, a constitution, and a world. If, then, a man, in the maturity of age and talent, deeply versed in economics and in the philosophy of the time, had undertaken only the second of these things, I should have found him already exceedingly moderate; but I confess that he seems to me a real prodigy of wisdom and modesty when I see him, putting (at least, as he thinks) experience in place of foolish theories, respectfully asking a constitution of the English instead of making one himself. One says: *even this was not possible*. I know it, but he did not, and how would he know? Name the one who told him.

IX. The more one examines the play of human agency in forming political constitutions, the more one will be convinced that human agency enters into it only in an infinitely subordinate manner, or as a simple instrument; and I do not think the least doubt remains as to the incontestable truth of the following propositions:

1. That the roots of political constitutions exist before any written law;
2. That a constitutional law is, and can only be, the development or sanction of a pre-existing and unwritten right;
3. That what is most essential, most intrinsically constitutional, and truly fundamental, is never written, nor even can be, without endangering the state;
4. That the weakness and fragility of a constitution are precisely in direct proportion to the multiplicity of written constitutional articles.[18]

X. We are deceived on this point by a sophism so natural that it entirely escapes our attention. Because man acts, he believes he acts alone, and because he has the consciousness of his freedom, he forgets his dependence. In the physical order he perceives reason; and though he may, for example, plant an acorn, water it, etc., yet he can agree that he does not make oaks, because he sees the tree grow and perfect itself without an intervening human power, and besides, he has not made the acorn; but in the social order, where he is present and acts, he comes to believe that he is really the direct author of all that is done by himself: it is, in a sense, as though the trowel believes itself to be the architect. Man is intelligent, he is free, he is sublime, no doubt; but he is no less a *tool of God*, according to the happy

18 Which can serve as commentary on the famous motto of Tacitus: *pessimae reipublicae plurimae leges* ["the more numerous the laws, the more corrupt the state"].

expression of Plutarch in a beautiful passage which has, of its own accord, just placed itself here.

> We must not marvel if the greatest and most beautiful things in the world are done by the will and providence of God, since in all the greatest and most principal parts of the world there is a soul; for the organ and tool of the soul is the body, and the soul is THE INSTRUMENT OF GOD. And since the body has of itself many movements, and the greater and more noble derive from the soul, so it is with the soul, with some of its operations being self-moved; in others, it lets itself be wielded, directed, and led by God, as He pleases, being the most beautiful and most adroit organ that could be. For it would be a strange thing for the wind, the clouds, and the rains to be instruments of God, with which He nourishes and preserves many creatures, and destroys many others, and that He should not use living creatures to do any of His works. For it is far more reasonable that they, depending totally on the God's power, should obey all His direction, and carry out all His will, than that the bow should obey the Scythians, the lyre and flutes the Greeks.[19]

One could not say it better; and I do not think that these beautiful reflections find any more just application anywhere than in the formation of political constitutions, where one can say with equal truth that man does everything and does nothing.

XI. If there is anything familiar, it is Cicero's analogy of the Epicurean system, which wished to build a world with atoms falling at random in a void. "One would rather believe," said the great orator, "that letters thrown into the air could, on falling, have arranged themselves such as to form a poem." Thousands of voices have repeated and celebrated this thought; I do not see, however, that anyone has thought of giving it the finishing touch that it lacks. Suppose that printed characters thrown from the top of a tower should happen to form Racine's *Athalie* on the ground—what would this prove? *That an intelligence had presided over the fall and the arrangement of characters.* Common sense would never conclude otherwise.

XII. Now, consider any political constitution; that of England, for example. Certainly, it was not made *a priori*. Never did her statesmen come together and say: *Let us create three powers, balance them in such a way,* etc.; no one ever thought of such a thing. The Constitution is the work of

19 Plutarch, *Banquet of the Seven Sages*, French translation by Amyot.

circumstances, and the number of these circumstances is infinite. Roman laws, ecclesiastical laws, feudal laws; Saxon, Norman, and Danish customs; the privileges, prejudices, and claims of all classes; wars, revolts, revolutions, the Conquest, the Crusades; all the virtues, vices, knowledge, errors, passions—in fine, all these elements acting together and forming, by their admixture and reciprocal action, combinations multiplied by myriads of millions, have finally, after several centuries, produced the most complex unity and the most beautiful balance of political forces ever seen in the world.[20]

XIII. Now, since these elements, thus thrown into the air, have arranged themselves in such beautiful order, without any man of the innumerable host acting in this vast field ever having known what he was doing with respect to the whole, nor having foreseen what was to happen, it follows that these elements were guided in their fall by an infallible hand superior to man. The greatest folly, perhaps, of an age of follies, was to believe that the fundamental laws could be written *a priori*; while they are evidently the work of a force superior to man; and that their very writing, long after, is the surest sign of their nullity.

XIV. It is quite remarkable that God, having deigned to speak to men, has Himself manifested these truths in the two revelations which we have from His goodness. A very skilful man who, in my opinion, has made a sort of epoch in our age—because of the desperate struggle that his writings show between the worst prejudices of an age, of sect, of habits, etc., and the purest intentions, the movements of the most upright heart, the most precious knowledge—this skilful man, I say, has decided *that instruction coming immediately from God, or given only by His orders,* OUGHT *firstly to certify to men the existence of this* BEING. It is precisely the opposite; for the principal character of this instruction is not to reveal directly the existence of God or His attributes; but to suppose the whole known beforehand, without understanding either why or how. So, it does not say: *there is,* or *you shall believe in only one eternal, all-powerful God,* etc., it says (and this

20 Tacitus believed that this form of government would never be more than an ideal theory or a brief experiment. "The best of all governments," he says (echoing Cicero, as we know), "would be what should result from the mixture of the three powers balanced by one another; *but this government will never exist; or, if it should manifest, it will not last.*" (*Annals*, IV, 33) English good sense can, however, make it last much longer than one might imagine by constantly subordinating, to a greater or lesser extent, the theory, or what we call *the principles,* to the lessons of experience and moderation: which would be impossible if the *principles* were written.

is its first word), in a purely narrative form: *In the beginning God created*, etc.; which supposes that the dogma is known before the Scripture.

XV. Let us turn to Christianity, which is the greatest of all imaginable institutions since it is altogether divine and is made for all men and for all ages. We will find it subject to the general law. Certainly, its divine author was indeed able to write Himself or to cause His doctrines to be written; yet He did neither, at least not in legislative form. The New Testament, after the death of the Lawgiver, and even the establishment of His religion, presents a narrative, warnings, moral precepts, exhortations, orders, threats, etc., but by no means a collection of dogmas expressed in imperative form. The Evangelists, in recounting this Last *Supper* where God loved us EVEN UNTO THE END, had a fine opportunity to command our belief in writing; however, they refrain from declaring or ordering anything. In fact, we read in their admirable history: *Go, teach*; but by no means: *teach this or that*. If doctrine presents itself under the pen of the sacred historian, it is simply stated as something previously known.[21] The symbols that have appeared since then are professions of faith in order to recognize itself, or to contradict the errors of the moment. It reads: *We believe*; never *you shall believe*. We recite them alone: we chant them in the temples, *on the lyre, and on the organ*,[22] as true prayers, because they are formulas of submission, confidence, and faith, addressed to God, and not ordinances addressed to man. I would like to see the *Confession of Ausburgh* or the *Thirty-Nine Articles* set to music; that would be pleasant![23]

The first symbols are far from containing the enunciation of *all* our doctrines, the Christians of the time would, on the contrary, have regarded the enunciation of them *all* as a great sin. The same is true of the Holy Scriptures: never was there a shallower idea than that of seeking in them the totality of Christian doctrines: there is not a line in these writings which

21 It is quite remarkable that the same Evangelists did not take up the pen until late, and mainly to contradict the false histories published in their time. Canonical epistles also arose from accidental causes: Scripture never entered into the primitive plan of the founders. *Mill*, though a Protestant, has expressly acknowledged this. (*Proleg. in Nov. Test. Graec.* p. 1, No. 65) And Hobbes had already made the same observation in England (Hobbes' *Tripos in Three Discourses*, Disc. III, p. 265)

22 *In chordis et organo*. Ps. CL, 4.

23 Reason can only *speak*, it is love that *chants*; and this is why we sing our symbols; for *faith* is only a *belief through love*; it does not reside only in the understanding: it penetrates further and is rooted in the will. A philosopher-theologian said with great truth and elegance: "There is a difference between believing and judging what one must believe." *Aliud est credere, aliud judicare esse credendum.* (*Leon. Lessii Opuscula.* Lugd. 1651, in fol. p. 556, col. 2, *De Praedestinatione*)

declares, which even allows us to glimpse, a plan to make it a code or a dogmatic statement of all articles of faith.

XVI. But there is more: if a people has one of these *codes of belief*, we may be sure of three things:

1. That the religion of this people is false;
2. That it has written its religious code in a bout of fever;
3. That the code will soon be mocked in this very nation, and that it can have neither strength nor durability. Such, for example, are those famous ARTICLES, *which one signs more than one reads, and which one reads more than one believes.*[24] Not only does this catalogue of dogmas count for nothing, or nearly so, in the country where it was born; but, moreover, it is obvious, even to the foreign eye, that the illustrious owners of this sheet of paper are very much embarrassed by it. They would like very much to make it disappear, because national good sense, enlightened by the time, is impatient with it, and because it reminds them of an unhappy origin; but the *constitution is written.*

XVII. Never, doubtless, would these Englishmen have demanded the *Magna Carta* if the privileges of the nation had not been violated; nor would they have asked for it unless these privileges had existed before the Charter. It is the same for the Church as for the State: if Christianity had never been attacked, it would never have written in order to establish its dogma; but dogma has never been established in writing except where it existed previously in its natural state, which is that of *speech*.

The true authors of the Council of Trent were the two great innovators of the sixteenth century.[25] Their disciples, having grown calmer, have since proposed to erase this fundamental law because it contains some hard words for them; and they tried to tempt us, holding out the possibility, at this price, of a meeting that would make us accomplices instead of friends; but this demand is neither theological nor philosophical. They themselves once brought into the language of religion those words which weary them and let us desire that today they learn to pronounce them. Faith, if a sophistical opposition had never forced her to write, would be a thousand times more angelic: she weeps over those decisions which revolt extorted from her and which were always evils, since they all suppose doubt or attack and could not be born but amid the most dangerous commotions.

24 Gibbon in his *Memoirs*, Milman edition 1840, ch. III.

25 The same observation can be made as far back as Arius: never has the Church sought to write her dogmas; she was always forced.

The state of war raised these venerable ramparts around the truth; they no doubt defend her, but they hide her; they make her unassailable, but by that very means less accessible. Ah! that is not what she asks, she who would like to hold the whole human race in her arms.

XVIII. I have spoken of Christianity as a belief system; I will now consider it as sovereignty, in its most numerous associations. There she is monarchical, as everyone knows, and this is as it should be, since the monarchy becomes, by the very nature of things, more necessary as the association becomes more numerous. It has not been forgotten that a mouth, however impure, has nonetheless met with approval in our times when it says *that France was geographically monarchical.* It would be difficult, indeed, to better express a more incontestable truth. But if the extent of France alone excludes the idea of any other kind of government, still more this sovereignty, which by the very essence of its constitution will always have subjects in all parts of the globe, could not be other than monarchical; and experience on this point is in agreement with the theory. Given this, who would not believe that such a monarchy is more rigorously defined and circumscribed than all the others in the prerogative of its chief? However, the opposite has happened. Read the innumerable volumes produced by the foreign war, and even by a kind of civil war which has its advantages and its inconveniences—you will see that on all sides only facts are cited; and it is especially remarkable that the supreme tribunal has constantly allowed debate on the question which presents itself to all minds as the most fundamental of the constitution, without having ever wished to decide on it by a formal law; and so should it be, if I am not mistaken, precisely because of the fundamental importance of the question.[26] Some benighted men, reckless only out of weakness, tried to decide on it in 1682, in spite of a great man; and it was one of the most solemn indiscretions ever committed in the world. The monument of it which remains to us is doubtless reprehensible in every respect; but especially so from an aspect which has not been noticed, although it presents itself to enlightened criticism more than any other. The famous declaration dared to decide in writing and without necessity, even apparent necessity (which carries the fault to excess), on a question which must always be left to a certain practical wisdom enlightened by UNIVERSAL conscience.

This is the only point of view in accord with the design of this work; but

26 I do not know whether the English have remarked that the most learned and fervent defender of the sovereignty we are dealing with here has titled one of its chapters: *A mixed monarchy tempered by aristocracy and democracy is better than a pure monarchy*. (Bellarmine, *De Summo Pontiff*, ch. III) Not bad for a fanatic!

it is well worthy of the meditations of every just mind and upright heart.

XIX. These ideas (taken in their general sense) were not foreign to the philosophers of antiquity: they have felt the weakness—I almost said the nothingness—of writing in forming great institutions; but no one has better seen or better expressed this truth than Plato, who one always finds is first on the path to all great truths. First, according to him, "the man who owes all his instruction to writing *will only ever have the appearance of wisdom*."[27] "The word," he adds, "is to writing what a man is to his portrait. The productions of writing present themselves to our eyes as living things; *but if one should question them, they maintain a dignified silence.*[28] It is the same with writing, *which does not know what to say to one man nor what to hide from another*. If one should baselessly attack or insult it, it cannot defend itself; *because its author is never there to support it.*[29] Thus, he who imagines that he can establish a clear and enduring doctrine by writing alone, IS A GREAT FOOL.[30] If he really possessed the true seeds of truth, he would guard well against the thought that *with a little black liquid and a pen*[31] he could make them germinate in the world, defend them against the inclemency of the seasons, and communicate to them the necessary potency. As for one who undertakes to write *laws or civil constitutions*,[32] and who thinks that because he has written them he can give them sufficient self-evidence and stability, whoever he may be, private man or legislator,[33] and whether it be said or left unsaid,[34] he has disgraced himself; for by this he has also proven himself ignorant of the nature of inspiration and delirium, justice and injustice, and good and evil: now, this ignorance is a disgrace, even though the whole mass of the vulgar should applaud."[35]

XX. After hearing *the wisdom of the Gentiles*, it will not be useless, I think,

27 Δοξόσοφοι γεγονότες ἀντὶ σοφῶν (Plato in *Phaedrus*, Opp. book X, Bipont edition, p. 381)

28 Σεμνῶς πάνυ σιγᾷ (Plato, *Phaedrus*, X, p. 382)

29 Τοῦ πατρὸς ἀεὶ δεῖται βοηθοῦ (Plato, *Phaedrus*, X, p. 382)

30 πολλῆς ἂν εὐηθείας γέμοι (Plato, *Phaedrus*, X, 382) Word for word: *He overflows with folly*. Let us be careful, everyone in our country, that this species of *plethora* does not become endemic.

31 Ἐν ὕδατι γράψει μέλανι σπείρων διὰ καλάμου (Plato, *Phaedrus*, X, p. 384)

32 Νόμους τιθείς, σύγγραμμα πολιτικὸν γράφων (Plato, *Phaedrus*, X, p. 386, 126)

33 Ἰδίᾳ ἢ δημοσίᾳ (Plato, *Phaedrus*, X)

34 Εἴτε τίς φησιν εἴτε μή (Plato, *Phaedrus*, X)

35 Οὐκ ἐκφεύγει τῇ ἀληθείᾳ μὴ οὐκ ἐπονείδιστον εἶναι, οὐδὲ ἂν ὁ πᾶς ὄχλος αὐτὸ ἐπαινέσῃ (Plato, *Phaedrus*, X, pp. 380, 387)

to listen again to Christian philosophy.

"Doubtless it would have been desirable," said the most eloquent of the Greek Fathers, "that we had never needed writing, and that the divine precepts were written only in our hearts, by grace, as they are by ink in our books: but since we have lost this grace by our fault, let us seize, as we must, *a plank instead of the vessel*, and without forgetting, however, the superiority of our original condition. God never revealed anything in writing to the elect of the Old Testament; He always spoke to them directly, because He saw the purity of their hearts; but the Hebrew people having fallen into the abyss of sin, books and laws became necessary. The same course was renewed under the reign of the New Revelation; for Christ did not leave a single writing to his Apostles. Instead of a book, he promised them the Holy Spirit. *It is He*, he tells them, *who will inspire you with what you have to say.*[36] But because, in the course of time, sinful men revolted against doctrine and against morality, it was necessary to have recourse to books."

XXI. The whole truth is united in these two authorities. They show the profound imbecility (it is quite permissible to speak like Plato, who never loses his temper), the profound imbecility, I say, of those poor folk who imagine that lawgivers are men,[37] that laws are a piece of paper, and that nations can be comprised *of ink*. On the contrary, they show that writing is invariably a sign of weakness, ignorance, or danger; that so far as an institution is perfect, it writes less; so that what is certainly divine has written nothing at all in establishing itself, making us feel that every written law is only a necessary evil, produced by infirmity or human malice; and that it is of no authority at all unless it has received a previous and unwritten sanction.

XXII. Here one must groan over the fundamental fallacy of a system that has so unfortunately divided Europe. Partisans of this system have said: *We believe only in the word of God* ... What an abuse of words! what a strange and disastrous ignorance of things divine! We alone believe *in the word*, while our *dear enemies* persist in believing only *in Scripture*: as if God could or would change the nature of the things of which He is the author and bestow upon Scripture a life and potency which it lacks! Is not the Holy Scripture *a writing*? Was it not traced out *with a pen and a little black*

36 St. Chrysostom, *Homily on St. Matthew* 1:1.

37 Among a host of admirable verses with which the Psalms of David sparkle, I distinguish the following: *Constitue, Domine, legislatorem super eos, utsciant quoniam homines sunt*; that is to say, "Appoint, O Lord, a lawgiver over them: that the Gentiles may know themselves to be but men." It is a beautiful sentence!

liquid? Does it know what to say to one man and what to hide from another?[38] Did not Leibnitz and his maidservant read the same words? Can it be, this Scripture, anything other than the *portrait of the Word*? And although infinitely estimable in this respect, if one should question it, must it not *keep a divine silence*?[39] In fine, if one attacks or insults it, *can it defend itself in the absence of its Author*? Glory to the truth! If *the Word*, eternally alive, does not give life to the scripture, it will never become *the word*, that is to say, *the life*. Let others, so long as you please, call upon THE SILENT WORD, we will smile in peace at this *false god*; always awaiting, with tender impatience, the moment when its undeceived partisans will throw themselves into our arms, open for nearly three centuries.

XXIII. Any right mind will end in convincing itself on this point if it thinks a little about an axiom equally striking in its importance and universality: that NOTHING GREAT HAS GREAT BEGINNINGS. We will not find in the history of all ages a single exception to this law. *Crescit occulto velut arbor aevo* ["it grows like a tree with the silent lapse of time"]; this is the eternal motto of every great institution; hence the fact that every false institution writes much because it feels its weakness and seeks for support. From the truth just stated follows the unswerving consequence that no great and real institution can be founded on a written law, since the men themselves, the successive instruments of its establishment, do not know what it is to become, and since imperceptible growth is the true sign of durability in all possible orders of things. A remarkable example of this kind is found in the power of the Popes, which I do not intend to consider here in a dogmatic way. Since the sixteenth century, a great number of learned writers have spent a prodigious amount of erudition to determine, as far back as the cradle of Christianity, that the Bishops of Rome were not, in the first centuries, what they have since become; thus supposing, as a point granted, that everything not found in primitive times is an abuse. Now, I say, without the slightest spirit of contention, and without trying to offend anyone, that in so doing they show as much philosophy and real knowledge as if they were looking at an infant in swaddling clothes for the true dimensions of a full-grown man. The sovereignty of which I speak at this moment is born like others, has grown like others. It is a pity to see excellent minds fight to the death to prove by infancy that manhood is an abuse, while an institution full-grown at birth is an absurdity in the first place, a true logical contradiction. If the enlightened and charitable ene-

38 See p. 19 et seq.

39 Σεμνῶς πάνυ σιγᾷ (Plato, *Phaedrus*, X)

mies of this power (and certainly there are many of this kind) examine the question from this point of view, as I pray with love that they do, I have no doubt that all these objections drawn from antiquity will disappear from their eyes like a light mist.

As for abuses, I should not deal with them here. I will only say, since I have already raised it, that there is much to humble the rhetoric which the last century has produced on this great subject. A time will come when the Popes, against whom the greatest cry has been raised, such as Gregory VII, for example, will be regarded in all countries as friends, guardians, and saviours of the human race—as the true founding fathers of Europe.

No one will doubt it once learned Frenchmen become Christians, and once learned Englishmen become Catholics, which must yet come to pass.

XXIV. But by what penetrating word could we, at this moment, make ourselves heard by an age infatuated with Scripture and at odds with the Word, to the point of believing that men can create constitutions, languages, and even sovereignties? By an age for which all realities are falsehoods, and all falsehoods realities; which does not even see what is happening before its eyes; which feasts upon books, and seeks the equivocal lessons from Thucydides or Livy, while closing its eyes to the truth that shines forth in the gazettes of time?

If the wishes of a mere mortal were worthy to obtain from Providence one of those memorable decrees which shape the great epochs of history, I would ask it to inspire some powerful nation which had gravely offended it with the proud thought of constituting itself politically, beginning with the foundations. And if, despite my unworthiness, the ancient familiarity of a Patriarch was permitted to me, I would say: "Grant to the people everything! Give it spirit, knowledge, wealth, esteem, above all a limitless confidence in itself, and that genius at once flexible and enterprising, which nothing embarrasses and nothing intimidates. Extinguish its ancient government; take away its memory; destroy its affections; moreover, spread terror around her; blind or paralyse its enemies; order victory to watch over all its frontiers at once, so that none of its neighbours can interfere in its affairs or disturb it in its operations. May this nation be illustrious in the sciences, rich in philosophy, drunk with human power, free of all prejudices, all ties, all superior influence: give it all it wants, lest it can one day say: *this was lacking or this constrained me*; in fine, let it act freely with this immensity of means, so that it may become, under your inexorable protection, an eternal lesson for the human race."

XXV. Doubtless, one cannot wait for a combination of circumstances that would constitute a literal miracle; but events of the same kind, though less remarkable, manifest themselves here and there in history, even in the history of our days; and although they do not have, for example, that ideal force which I wished for just now, nonetheless they contain great instruction.

Less than twenty-five years ago, we witnessed a solemn effort made to regenerate a great nation mortally ill. It was the first attempt of this great work, and the *preface*, if I may so call it, of the dreadful book that we have since been made to read. Every precaution was taken. The wise men of her country even thought it their duty to consult the modern divinity in its foreign sanctuary. They wrote to *Delphi*, and two famous Pontiffs solemnly replied.[40] The oracles which they pronounced on this occasion were not, as in olden times, light leaves, playthings of the breezes; they were bound:

> … *Quidque haec Sapientia possit,*
> Tunc patuit …
>
> ["then it became clear just what this Wisdom could do"]

Moreover, it is just to admit that in whatever the nation owed only to its own good sense, there were things that can still be admired today. All qualifications, doubtless, united on the wise and august head called to take the reins of government: the chief men interested in maintaining the ancient laws voluntarily made a superb sacrifice to the public, and, to fortify the supreme authority, they lent themselves to changing an epithet of sovereignty. — Alas! all human wisdom was guilty, and all ended in death.

XXVI. It will be said: *But we know the causes which made the enterprise fail.* How then? Do we wish for God to send angels in human form, charged with destroying a constitution? It will always be necessary to employ secondary causes: this one or that, what does it matter? All instruments are good in the hands of the Great Artificer; but such is the blindness of men that if tomorrow some constitution-mongers should come to organize a people, and constitute it *with a little black liquid*, the crowd will hasten again to believe in the miracle announced. It will again be said: *nothing is missing; all is foreseen, all is written;* whereas precisely because all could be foreseen, discussed, and written, it would be shown that the constitution is null, and presents to the eye only an ephemeral appearance.

XXVII. I believe I have read somewhere *that there are very few sovereignties in a position to justify the legitimacy of their origin.* Let us admit the correctness of the assertion—it will not yield the slightest blemish on the

40 Rousseau and Mably.

successors of a chief whose acts could suffer objection: the cloud which could more or less conceal the origin of his authority would only be an inconvenience, a necessary consequence of a law of the moral world. If it were otherwise, it would follow that the sovereign could only reign legitimately by virtue of a deliberation of the whole people, that is, *by the grace of the people*; which will never happen, for there is nothing so true as what has been said by the author of the *Considerations on France*:[41] *that the people will always accept their masters, and never choose them.* The origin of sovereignty must always be outside the sphere of human power, so that the very men who appear to be directly involved are nevertheless only circumstances. As for legitimacy, if it should seem ambiguous in its origin, God is explained by His prime minister to the province of this world: *time.* Nevertheless, it is very true that certain contemporary signs are unmistakable when one is present to observe them; but the details on this point belong to another work.[42]

XXVIII. Thus, everything brings us back to the general rule: *Man cannot make a constitution, and no legitimate constitution can be written.* We have never written—we will never write, *a priori*—a collection of fundamental laws that must constitute a civil or religious society. Only when the society is already constituted, without it being possible to say how, it is possible to declare or to explain in writing certain particular articles; but almost always these declarations are the effect or the cause of great evils, and always cost the people more than they are worth.

XXIX. To this general rule, *that no constitution can be written or made a priori*, only one exception is known; that is, the law of Moses. It alone was *cast*, so to speak, like a statue, and written down, to the smallest detail, by a prodigious man who said FIAT! without his work ever having since needed correction, addition, or modification, by him or by others. It alone could withstand time, because it owed time nothing and expected nothing of it; this alone has lived fifteen hundred years; and even after eighteen new centuries have passed over it, since the great anathema that smote it on that fated day, we see it living, so to speak, a second life, still binding, by some sort of mysterious tie which has no human name, the different families of a people who remain scattered without being disunited; so that, like attraction, and by the same power, it acts at a distance, and makes a whole out of a host of parts widely separated from one another. Thus, for every intelligent conscience, this legislation obviously exceeds the bounds of hu-

41 Ch. IX, p. 116.
42 [p. 121]

man power; and this magnificent exception to a general law, which has yielded only once, and only to its Author, alone demonstrates the divine mission of the great Lawgiver of the Hebrews, far better than the entire work of that English Prelate who, with the strongest mind and an immense erudition, has nevertheless had the misfortune to support a great truth by the sorriest fallacy.

XXX. But since every constitution is divine in its principle, it follows that man can do nothing with one unless he relies on God, of Whom he then becomes the instrument.[43] Now, this is a truth to which the human race as a whole has never ceased to give the most brilliant testimony. Examine history, which is experimental politics—invariably we shall find there the cradle of nations surrounded by priests, and the Divinity always called to the aid of human weakness.[44] Fable, much truer for tutored eyes than ancient history, further strengthens the demonstration. It is always an oracle which founds cities; it is always an oracle which announces divine protection, and the success of the founding hero. Kings above all, chiefs of fledgling empires, are constantly designated and almost *marked* by Heaven in some extraordinary manner.[45] How many unserious men have laughed at the *Holy Ampulla*[46] without thinking that it is a hieroglyph, and that it is

43 One can even generalize the assertion and pronounce without exception: *that no institution whatsoever can last if it is not founded on religion.*

44 Plato, in an admirable and altogether Mosaic passage, speaks of a primitive time *when God had confided the establishment and government of empires not to men, but to genii*; he then adds, speaking of the difficulty of creating lasting constitutions, *the truth is that if God does not preside over the establishment of a city, and if it should have only a human beginning, it could not escape the greatest evils. Therefore, we must endeavour, by every conceivable means, to imitate the primitive regime; and, placing our trust in what is immortal in man, we must found houses as well as states, by consecrating as laws the will of the* (supreme) *intelligence. If a state* (whatever its form) *is founded on vice, and governed by a people who trample on justice, there remains to it no means of safety.* (Plato, *Laws*, book VIII, Bipont edition, p. 180, 181).

45 The controversy of the famous rule of Richard of Saint-Victor has been widely used; *Quod semper, quod ubique, quod omnibus* ["what (is believed) always, everywhere, by all"]. But this rule is general and can, I believe, be expressed as follows: *every belief which is constantly universal is true: and whenever, in separating from one belief any articles particular to different nations, there remains something common to all, this remainder is a truth.*

46 [A glass vial for anointing kings; one of the principal objects in the coronation liturgy of the kings of France at Reims.]

only a question of knowing how to read![47]

XXXI. The coronation of kings springs from the same root. Never was there a ceremony, or to put it better, a profession of faith, more meaningful and respectable. Always the finger of the Pontiff has touched the brow of the nascent sovereignty. The many writers who have seen in these august rites only ambitious views, and even the express agreement of superstition and tyranny, have spoken against the truth, almost all even against their own conscience. This subject deserves to be examined. Sometimes the sovereigns sought the coronation, and sometimes the coronation sought the sovereign. We have seen others denounce the coronation as a sign of dependence. We have sufficient facts to be able to form a healthy enough judgement; but men, times, nations, and forms of worship should be carefully distinguished. Here, it is sufficient to insist on the general and eternal opinion which calls the Divine Power to the establishment of empires.

XXXII. The most famous nations of antiquity, especially the most serious and wise, such as the Egyptians, Etruscans, Lacedaemonians, and Romans, had precisely the most religious constitutions; and the duration of empires has always been proportionate to the degree of influence which the religious principle had acquired in the political constitution: *The cities and nations most devoted to divine worship have always been the most durable and wise, as the most religious ages have always been the most distinguished by genius.*[48]

XXXIII. Never have nations been civilized except by religion. No other known instrument has any hold on the savage man. Without recourse to antiquity, which is very decisive on this point, we see concrete proof of it in America. For three centuries we have been there with our laws, our arts, our sciences, our civilization, our commerce, and our luxury: what have we gained over the savage state? Nothing. We destroy these poor unfortunates with sword and brandy; we push them gradually into the middle of the wastelands, until finally they disappear entirely, victims of our vices and cruel superiority.

XXXIV. Has any philosopher ever imagined leaving his country and its

47 Every religion, by its very nature, *puts forth* a mythology which resembles itself. That of the Christian religion is, for this reason, always chaste, always useful, and often sublime, without ever (by a particular privilege) being possible to confound it with the religion itself. So that no Christian *myth* can do harm, and it often merits the observer's attention.

48 Xenophon, *Memorabilia*, Socr. 1, 4, 16.

pleasures to go to the forests of America to hunt for savages, to inspire in them disgust with all the vices of barbarism, and to give them a moral system?[49] They did much better: they composed beautiful books to prove that the savage was the *natural* man, and that we could wish for nothing better than to resemble him. Condorcet has said *that missionaries have only carried into Asia and America shameful superstitions.*[50] Rousseau has said, with a multiplication of folly truly inconceivable, *that the missionaries did not seem to him wiser than the conquerors.*[51] Finally, their Coryphaeus had the gall (but what had he to lose?) to cast the grossest ridicule upon those pacific conquerors whom antiquity would have deified.[52]

XXXV. However, it is the missionaries who have worked this wonder so far above human forces, and even human will. They alone have traversed the vast continent of America, from one end to the other, to create MEN. They alone did what politics dared not even imagine. But nothing of this kind equals the missions of Paraguay; it is there that the authority and exclusive power of religion for the civilization of men has been most marked. This prodigy has been honoured, but not honoured enough: the spirit of the eighteenth century and another spirit, its accomplice, had the strength to stifle, in part, the voice of justice and even of admiration. One day, perhaps (because one can hope that these great and noble works will be resumed), in an opulent city, sitting on an ancient *savannah*, the father of these missionaries will have a statue. One may read on the pedestal:

> To the CHRISTIAN OSIRIS
>
> *Whose envoys have travelled the earth*
> *to snatch men from misery,*
> *from brutishness and ferocity,*
> *by teaching them agriculture,*
> *by giving them laws,*
> *by teaching them to know and serve God,*
> NOT BY FORCE OF ARMS,

49 Condorcet has promised us, indeed, that the philosophers should be in charge of the civilization and welfare of barbarian nations. (*Sketch for a Historical Picture of the Progress of the Human Mind*, p. 335) We will wait until they are ready to begin.

50 *Sketch*, etc. (*Ibid.* p. 335)

51 Letter to the Archbishop of Paris.

52 "Well! my friends, why do you not remain in your country? You would not have found more devils, but you would have found just as much nonsense." (Voltaire, *Essay on the Manners and Spirit*, etc. Introduction *of Magic.)*

which they never needed,
but by gentle persuasion, moral songs,
AND THE POWER OF HYMNS,
so that one should think them Angels.[53]

XXXVI. Now, when one thinks that this legislative order—which reigned in Paraguay by a unique predominance of virtue and talent, without ever deviating from the humblest submission to legitimate authority, even the most misguided—that this order, I say, was at the same time confronting in our prisons, in our hospitals, and in our quarantine facilities, all the most hideous and repulsive misery, sickness, and despair; that those same men, who hastened, at the first call, to bed down on the straw beside poverty, had no strange air about them in the most polite circles; that they climbed

53 "During his reign in Egypt, Osiris forthwith raised the Egyptians from their indigent, sickly, and savage life, by teaching them to sow and plant; by giving them laws, by teaching them to honour and revere the Gods: and afterward going through all the world, he tamed it too without using any force of arms, but appealing to and winning over the greater part of the peoples by gentle persuasion and remonstrances couched in song and in every kind of music (πειθοῖ καὶ λύγῳ μετ' ᾠδῆς πάσης καὶ μεσικῆς), whom the Greeks thought was Bacchus himself." (Plutarch, *Isis and Osiris*, French translation by Amyot, Vascosan edition, Volume III, p. 287, Henry Stephens edition, book I, p. 634)
"On an island on the Penobscot River, a savage tribe was still found singing a great many pious and instructive Indian songs to the music of the Church, with a precision hardly found in the best constituted choirs; one of the most beautiful airs in the Church of Boston comes from these Indians (who had learned it from their masters more than forty years ago), without these unfortunate Indians having enjoyed any kind of instruction." (*Mercure de France*, July 5, 1806, No. 259, pp. 29 et seq.)
Father *Salvaterra*, (a beautiful name for a missionary!) aptly named the *Apostle of California*, approached the most intractable savages ever known, without any other weapon than a lute which he played superbly. He began to sing: *In voi credo, o Dio mio!* ["I believe in thee, O my God!"] etc. Men and women gathered round him and listened in silence. Muratori says, speaking of this admirable man: *Pare favola quella d'Orfeo; my chi sa che not sia suceeduto in simil caso?* ["This seems like the fable of Orpheus, but who knows whether he should not have succeeded in a similar case?"] Missionaries alone have understood and demonstrated *the truth of that fable*. One even sees that they have discovered the kind of music worthy of being associated with these grand creations. "Send us," they wrote to their friends in Europe, "send us the airs of the great masters of Italy, *per essere armoniosissimi, senza tanti imbrogli di violini obbligati*, ["to be most harmonious without the complicated accompaniment of the violini obbligati"] etc. (Muratori, *Christianesime felice*, etc. Venesia, 752, chapter XII, p. 284)

up the scaffolds *to say the last words* to the victims of human justice, and that from these theatres of horror they dashed into the pulpits to thunder before kings;[54] that they held *the brush* in China, the telescope in our observatories, the lyre of Orpheus in the midst of savages, and that they had ennobled the whole age of Louis XIV; when, in fine, one reflects on the fact that a detestable coalition of perverse ministers, delirious magistrates, and despicable sectarians has today been able to destroy this marvellous institution and to applaud themselves for it, one thinks of the madman who exultingly set his foot upon a watch, saying: *I will stop your noise.* — But what am I saying? a madman is not responsible.

XXXVII. I have had to dwell mainly on the formation of empires as the most important object; but all human institutions are subject to the same rule, and all are null or dangerous if they are not based on the foundation of all existence. This principle being incontestable, what can one think of a generation which has cast everything to the winds, even to the very foundations of the social edifice, by rendering education purely scientific? It was impossible to be mistaken in a more terrible manner; because any system of education that does not rest upon religion will fall in the twinkling of an eye, or will diffuse only poison into the state, *religion being*, as Bacon said excellently, *the aromatic which prevents science from becoming corrupt.*

XXXVIII. It has often been asked: *why a school of theology in all the universities*? The answer is easy: *it is so that the universities may persist, and that instruction not become corrupted.* Originally, they were only theological schools, where the other *faculties* came together as do subjects around a queen. The edifice of public instruction, laid on this foundation, had lasted until our day. Those who have overthrown it at home will long repent it in vain. To burn a city, only a child or a fool is needed; to rebuild it requires architects, materials, workers, wealth, and especially, time.

XXXIX. Those who have contented themselves with corrupting the ancient institutions while retaining the outward forms have perhaps done so much harm to the human race. Already the influence of modern universities on manners and the national spirit, in a considerable part of the continent of Europe, is well-known.[55] The universities of England have,

54 *Loquebar de testimentiis tuis in conspectu regum: et non confundebar* ["I will speak of Thy testimonies also before kings, and will not be ashamed"]. Ps. CXVIII, 46. This is the inscription placed under the portrait of Bourdaloue, and which several of his colleagues have deserved.

55 I will not allow myself to publish notions peculiar to myself, however pre-

in this respect, preserved more reputation than others; perhaps because the English know better how to maintain silence, or to praise themselves in a timely manner; perhaps also because the public spirit, which has an extraordinary strength in that country, knew, better than elsewhere, how to defend these venerable schools from the general anathema. However, they must succumb, and already the wicked heart of Gibbon has yielded strange confessions on this point.[56] In fine, to continue with generalities, if one does not come back to the old maxims, if education is not given over to the priests, and if science is not everywhere placed in the second rank, the evils which await us are incalculable: we will be brutalized by science, and this is the lowest degree of brutality.

XL. Not only does creation not belong to man, but it does not seem that his power, *unaided*, extends to changing established institutions for the better. If there is something obvious to man, it is the existence of two opposing forces struggling relentlessly against one another in the universe. There is nothing good that evil does not defile or alter; there is nothing evil that good does not repress and attack, by constantly impelling all that exists towards a more perfect state.[57] These two forces are present everywhere.

cious they may be; but I believe it is permissible to everyone to reprint what is printed, and to make a German speak on Germany. There is a man, whom no one will accuse of being infatuated with ancient ideals, who expresses himself thus on the universities of his country:
"All our universities in Germany, even the best, need great reforms in terms of morals… Even the best are a gulf in which the innocence, the health, and the future happiness of a host of youth are squandered; and whence emerge beings ruined in body and soul, more burdensome than useful to society, etc. May these pages be a preservative for these young people! May they read on the door of our universities the following inscription: *Young man, it is here that many of your peers lost happiness along with innocence!*" (M. Campe, *Compendium of Travels for the Instruction of Youth*, book II, p. 129)

56 See his memoirs, where, after having made very fine revelations on the universities of his country, he tells us in particular of Oxford: *She will as cheerfully renounce me for a son, as I am willing to disclaim her for a mother*. I have no doubt that this tender mother, sensitive as she ought to be to such a declaration, has bestowed on him a magnificent epitaph: LUBENS MERITO ["gladly, deservedly"]. Sir William Jones, in his letter to Mr. Anquetil, goes to the opposite extreme; but this extreme does him honour.

57 A Greek would have said: Πρὸς ἐπανόρφωσιν. One could say, towards *restitution in full*: an expression that philosophy can very well borrow from jurisprudence, and which will enjoy, under this new meaning, a marvellous accuracy. As for the opposition and the balancing of the two forces, it is enough to open one's eyes. *Good is set against evil, and life against death: so also is the sinner against a just*

They are seen equally in the vegetation of plants, in the generation of animals, in the formation of languages, in that of empires (two inseparable things), etc. Human power perhaps extends only to removing or fighting the evil to liberate the good and to restore to it the power to develop according to its nature. The famous Zanotti has said: *It is difficult to change things for the better.*[58] This thought hides much good sense under the appearance of extreme simplicity. It accords perfectly with another thought of *Origen*, which is alone worth a volume. *Nothing*, he says, *can change for the better among men*, WITHOUT GOD.[59] All men intuit this truth without being able to give an account of it. Hence that automatic aversion of all good minds to innovations. The word *reform*, in itself and prior to all examination, will always be suspect to wisdom, and the experience of all ages justifies this kind of instinct. We know too well what the fruit of the most beautiful speculations of this kind has been.[60]

XLI. To apply these general maxims to a particular case, it is from the sole consideration of the extreme danger of innovations founded on simple human theories, that, without pretending to a decided opinion on the great question of parliamentary reform which has so strongly and endlessly agitated English minds, I am nevertheless led to believe that this idea is disastrous, and that if the English yield themselves up to it too readily they will repent it. *But*, say the partisans of reform (for this is the classic argument), *the abuses are striking, incontestable: now, can a formal abuse, a vice, be constitutional?*—Yes, no doubt, it can be; for every political constitution has essential defects which are due to its nature, and which cannot be separated from it; and what must make all reformers tremble is that these defects may change with circumstances, so that in showing that they

man. And so look upon all the works of the Most High. Two and two, and one against another. Ecclesiasticus [*Sirach*], XXXIII, 15.

We may say in passing: it is thence that is born the rule called *beau idéal* ["perfect model"]. Nothing in nature being what it should be, the true artist, the one who can say: EST DEUS IN NOBIS ["God is in us"], has the mysterious power to discern the least altered traits, and to assemble them to form wholes that exist only in his understanding.

58 *Difficile est mutare in melius*. Zanotti, quoted in the *Transunto della R. Accademia di Torino*. 1788–89, p.6.

59 Αθεεί: or, if one wishes to express this thought in a more laconic way, and free from any grammatical license, WITHOUT GOD, NOTHING BETTER. *Origen Contra Celsum*. 1, 26. de la Rue edition, Paris, 1733, book I. p. 315.

60 *Nihil motum ex antiquo probabile est* ["no departure from ancient usage is admirable"]. Livy, XXXIV, 53.

are new, one has not yet shown that they are not necessary.[61] What sensible man will not therefore shudder when he puts his hand to the work? Social harmony is, like harmony proper, subject to the law of *temperament in the general key*. Rigorously tune the *fifths*, and the octaves will howl, and vice versa. Dissonance being therefore inevitable, instead of driving it out, which is impossible, it must be *tempered* by general distribution. Thus, on both sides, *imperfection is an element of possible perfection*. In this proposition there is only the appearance of paradox. *But*, we will perhaps still say, *what is the rule to discern the accidental defect from that which is due to the nature of things, and which cannot be eliminated?* The men to whom nature has given only ears ask these kinds of questions, and those who have an ear shrug their shoulders.

XLII. When it is a question of abuse, one still must take care to judge political institutions only by their constant effects, and never by causes which signify nothing,[62] still less by certain collateral inconveniences (if it is permissible so to express them) which easily consume men of limited views and prevent them from seeing the whole. In fact, according to our proven hypothesis, the cause having no logical relation to the effect, and the inconveniences of an institution good in itself being, as I said just now, *an inevitable dissonance in the general key*, how could institutions be judged according to causes and inconveniences? Voltaire, who spoke endlessly on everything without ever having pierced the surface,[63] reasoned humor-

61 We have heard that *it is necessary to return to the fundamental and primitive laws of the state which an unjust custom has abolished;* and this is a game sure to lose all. *Nothing weighed on such a scale will be just: however, the people readily lend an ear to these arguments.* (Pascal, *Pensées*, part I, article 6. Paris, Renouard, 1803, pp. 121, 122)
We could not say it better; but such is man! The author of this observation and his hideous sect have never ceased to play *this infallible game in order to lose all*; and indeed, the *game* has succeeded perfectly. Voltaire, moreover, spoke on this point like Pascal: "It is a very vain idea," he says, "a very ungrateful labour, to wish to return everything to ancient usages, etc." (*Essay on the Manners and Spirit*, etc., chapter 85) Hear him then speak of the Popes, and you shall see how he remembers his maxim.

62 At least in relation to the merit of the institution; for, from other points of view, it may be very important to deal with these causes.

63 Dante said to Vergil, in, we must say, doing him too much honour: *Maestro di color che sanno* ["master of those who know"]. — Parini, though he had his head completely turned, has, nevertheless, had the courage to say to Voltaire, parodying Dante: *Sei Maestro... di coloro che credon di sapere* ["master of those who think they know"] (Il Mattino). The quip is apt.

ously on the sale of offices of the magistracy which took place in France; and no example, perhaps, could better illustrate the truth of my proposed theory. *The proof that this sale is an abuse*, he says, *is that it originated only in another abuse.*[64] Voltaire is not deceived here as every man is liable to deceive himself. He deceives himself shamefully. It is a total eclipse of common sense. *All that is born of an abuse is an abuse!* On the contrary, it is one of the most general and most evident laws of this force, at once hidden and striking, and which acts and makes itself felt on all sides, that the remedy of the abuse arises from another abuse, and that the evil, which has reached a certain point, destroys itself, as it should; for the evil, which is only a negation, is measured by the dimension and duration of the being to which it has attached itself, and that it devours. It exists like the ulcer that can only end in self-destruction. But then a new reality rushes in to fill the place of the one that has just disappeared; *for nature abhors a vacuum*, and the good… but I digress too far from Voltaire.

XLIII. This great writer's error originated in the fact that he, *being divided between twenty sciences*, as he himself has somewhere said, and constantly occupied in instructing the world, very rarely had time to think. "A sensuous and dissipated court, reduced to beggary by its expenses, dreams up the sale of offices of the magistracy, and thus creates" (which it would never have done freely and knowingly), "it creates," I say, "a rich, irremovable, and independent magistracy; so that the infinite power *rejoicing in the habitable part of this earth*[65] uses corruption to create incorruptible tribunals" (as far as human weakness permits). There is nothing, indeed, so plausible to the eye of the true philosopher; nothing better conforms to great analogies and to that incontestable law which wills that the most important institutions are never the result of deliberation, but of circumstances. Here is the problem almost solved upon being stated, as happens with all problems: *could a country like France be better judged than by hereditary magistrates?* If, as I suppose, one decides in the affirmative, it will immediately be necessary to propose a second problem, which is this: *the magistrature being hereditary, is there a more advantageous way first to constitute it, and afterward to recruit it, than that which fills the sovereign's coffers with millions at the lowest cost; and which at the same time assures the wealth, the independence, and even the nobility* (of a certain sort) *of the supreme judges?* If we consider only venality as a means of inheritance, every just mind is struck by this point of view, which is a true one. This is

64 *Precis du siecle de Louis XV*, ch. 42.
65 *Ludens in orbe terrarum. Proverbs* VIII, 3.

not the place to go deeper into the question; but it is enough to prove that Voltaire did not so much as see it.

XLIV. Let us now suppose at the head of affairs a man such as himself, bringing together, by a happy agreement, frivolity, incapacity, and rashness: he will not fail to act according to his foolish theories of laws and abuses. He will borrow at seven percent to reimburse account holders and creditors at two percent; he will shape men's minds with a host of paid writings that will insult the magistracy and undermine public confidence in it. Soon patronage, a thousand times more foolish than chance, will start in on its endless list of blunders: the distinguished man, no longer seeing in the right of inheritance a compensation for oppressive labours, will depart without return; the great tribunals will be given over to adventurers without name, without fortune, and without consideration; instead of that venerable magistracy in which virtue and learning had become as hereditary as its dignities of office—a true priesthood in which foreign nations could envy France until the moment when false philosophy, having banished wisdom from everywhere she once dwelt, concluded such fine exploits by driving her out of her own house.

XLV. Such is the natural picture of most reforms; for not only does creation not belong to man, but even reformation belongs to him only in a secondary way, and with a host of terrible restrictions. Starting from these incontestable principles, each man can judge the institutions of his country with perfect certainty; he can especially appreciate all those *creators*, *legislators*, and *restorers* of nations so dear to the eighteenth century, and whom posterity will look upon with pity, perhaps even with horror. We built houses of cards inside and outside Europe. The details would be odious; but we certainly show no lack of respect to anyone by simply asking men to look and judge by events if they persist in refusing any other kind of instruction. Man in relation to his Creator is sublime, and his action is creative: on the contrary, as soon as he separates from God and acts alone, he does not cease to be powerful, for this is a privilege of his nature; but his action is negative, and only destroys.

XLVI. There is not in the history of all ages a single fact which contradicts these maxims. No human institution can last if it is not supported by the Hand that supports all things; that is to say, if it is not specially consecrated to Him at its origin. The more it is penetrated by the divine principle, the more durable it will be. How strange the blindness of men of our age! They boast of their enlightenment, and are ignorant of everything since they are ignorant of themselves. They know not what they are, nor what they are capable of. An indomitable pride incessantly leads them to overthrow everything they have not made; and to create anew they separate themselves from the principle of all existence. Jean-Jacques Rousseau himself, however, has said very well: *Man, small and vain, show me your power, I will show you your weakness.* One could say with as much truth and more profit: *Small, vain man, confess to me your weakness, I will show you your power.* In fact, as soon as man has acknowledged his insignificance, he has taken a great step; for he is very near to seeking a support with which he can do all things. This is precisely the opposite of what has characterized the century just ended (alas! it has ended only in our calendars). Examine all its enterprises, all its institutions whatsoever, and you find it constantly occupied in separating them from the Divinity. Man has thought himself an independent being, and professed a true practical atheism, more dangerous, perhaps, and more culpable than that of theory.

XLVII. Distracted by his vain sciences from the only science that really concerns him, man believed he had the power to *create*, while lacking even the power to *name*. He believed—he who has not even the power to produce an insect or a sprig of moss—that he was the immediate author of sovereignty, the thing most important, most sacred, and most fundamental in the moral and political world;[66] and that such and such a family, for example, reigns because such and such a people had willed it; while he is surrounded by indisputable evidence that every sovereign family reigns because it is chosen by a superior power. If he does not see these proofs, it is because he shuts his eyes, or looks too closely. He has believed that he was the one who invented languages, while it remains to him only to see that every human language is *learned* and never *invented*, and that no imaginable hypothesis within the circle of human power can explain, with the slightest appearance of probability, either the formation or the diversity of languages. He has believed that he could constitute nations, that is, in other words, *that he could create that national unity by virtue of which one nation is not another.* In fine, he has believed that, since he had the power to create institutions, he had a yet stronger reason for borrowing them from other nations and transporting them to his home with the name they bore among these peoples, to enjoy them with like benefits. The French papers furnish me with a singular example on this point.

66 *Having first established a principle, which is noble in itself, and seems specious, but is belied by all history and experience, That the people are the origin of all just power* [...]. Hume, *History of England*, Charles I, ch. LIX, 1649, Bale edition, 1789, p. 120.

XLVIII. Some years ago, the French decided to set up certain races in Paris which were earnestly called, in some writings of the day, *Olympic Games.* The reasoning of those who invented or revived this beautiful name was not complicated. *Men raced,* they said, *on foot and on horseback on the banks of the* Alpheus; *we race on foot and on horseback on the banks of the* Seine: *so it is the same thing.* Nothing could be more *simple*; but without asking them why they had not imagined to call these *Parisian* games instead of calling them *Olympic,* many other observations could be made. To institute *Olympic Games,* Oracles were consulted: the gods and the heroes joined in; they were never commenced without sacrifices and other religious ceremonies; they were regarded as the great *Comitia* of Greece, and nothing was more august. But did the Parisians, before establishing their *revived races of the Greeks,* go to Rome *ad limina Apostolorum* ["to the thresholds of the apostles"] to consult the Pope? Before throwing their daredevils to amuse the shopkeepers, did they sing High Mass? What great political vision did they associate with these races? What was the name of the institutors? — But enough: the most ordinary common sense feels right away the vacuity and even the farce of this imitation.

XLIX. However, in a journal written by men of intelligence whose only fault or misfortune lay in professing modern doctrines, one of these men wrote the following passage about these races a few years ago, with the most amusing enthusiasm:

> I predict it: *the Olympic Games* of the French will one day attract all Europe to the Champ-de-Mars. How cold and emotionless they are, those who see only races here! Me, I see a pageant such as the universe has never given since those of Elis, where Greece was a spectacle to Greece. No, the Roman circuses, the tournaments of our ancient chivalry, did not come near to it.[67]

And as for me, I *believe,* indeed, I *know* that no human institution can last if it does not have a religious basis; *and, moreover* (I beg you to pay attention to this), *if it does not bear a name taken from a national language, and born of itself, without any prior and public deliberation.*

67 *Décade philosophique,* October 1707, No. 1, p. 31, 1809. This passage, in conjunction with its date, has the double merit of being eminently amusing and thought-provoking. It shows with what ideas these children lulled themselves, and how much they knew about what man must know above all. Since then, a new order of things has sufficiently refuted these beautiful conceits; *and if all Europe is now attracted to Paris,* it is certainly not to see the *Olympic Games* (1814).

L. The theory of names is still an object of great importance. Names are by no means arbitrary, as so many men *who have lost their names* have said. God is called: *I am*; and every creature is called, *I am that*. The name of a spiritual being is necessarily relative to its action, which is its distinctive quality; hence, among the ancients, the greatest honour for a divinity was *polyonymy*, that is, the *plurality of names*, which heralded plurality of functions or extent of power. Ancient mythology shows us Diana, still a child, asking this honour of Jupiter; and in the verses attributed to Orpheus, she is paid the honour of being called *démon polyonyme* (genius of many names).[68] Which means, basically, that God alone has the right to give a *name*. Indeed, He *named* all things since He has created all things. He has given names to the stars,[69] He has given them to spirits, and of these last names the Scriptures only pronounce three, but all three are relative to the purpose of these ministers. It is the same with men whom God Himself has chosen to name, and whom the Scripture has made known to us in considerable numbers: always the names are relative to the functions.[70] Did He not say that in His future kingdom He would give the victors a NEW NAME,[71] proportionate to their *exploits*? And have men, *made in the image of God*, found a more solemn way of rewarding conquerors than that of giving them a *new name*, the most honourable of all to the judgment of men, that of the vanquished nation?[72] Whenever a man is supposed to have changed his life and received a new character, he is quite commonly given a *new name*. This can be seen in baptism, in confirmation, in the enlistment of soldiers, on entry into a religion, in the manumission of slaves, etc.; in a word, the name of every being expresses what it is, and in this there is nothing arbitrary. The common expression, he *has a name, he has no name*, is very just and very meaningful; no man can be ranged among

68 See the note by Callimachus on the seventh verse of the hymn to Diana (Spanheim edition); and Lanzi, *Saggio di letteratura etrusca*, etc., book II, p. 241, note. The Homeric hymns are basically collections of epithets; which is in keeping with the same principle of *polyonymy*.

69 Isaiah 40:26.

70 Let us recall the greatest name given divinely and directly to a man. The reason for the name was given, in this case, with the name, and to name expresses precisely the purpose, or, what amounts to the same, the power.

71 Revelations 3:12.

72 This observation was made by the anonymous but well-known author of the German book, *Die Siegsgeschichte der Christlichen Religion, in einer gemeinnützigen Erklarung der Offenbarung*, Johannis, Nuremberg, 1799, p. 89. There is nothing to be said against this page.

those *who are called to assemblies and have a name,*[73] if his family is not marked with a sign that distinguishes it from others.

LI. It is with nations as with individuals; there are some *which have no name*. Herodotus observes that the Thracians would be the most powerful people in the world if they were united: *but,* he adds, *this union is impossible, for they all have a different name.*[74] This is an astute observation. There are also modern peoples *who have no name*, and there are others who have many; but *polyonymy* is as unfortunate for nations as it has been thought honourable for *spirits*.

LII. Names being in no wise arbitrary, and having their origin, like all things, more or less immediately in God, we must not believe that man has the right to name, without restriction, even those things of which he has some right to consider himself the author, nor to impose on them names according to the idea that he forms of them. God has reserved to Himself, in this respect, a sort of immediate jurisdiction which one cannot fail to recognize.[75] "O my dear *Hermogenes*! the imposition of names is a weighty matter, one which can belong neither to the bad man, nor even to the common man ... This right belongs only to a creator of names (*onomaturgos*), that is, as it seems, to the lawgiver alone; but of all your human creatures, the lawgiver is the rarest."[76]

LIII. However, man loves nothing so much as to name. This is what he does, for example, when he applies significant epithets to things; a talent that distinguishes the great writer and especially the great poet. The happy application of an epithet dignifies a substantive, which becomes renowned under this new sign.[77] Examples are found in all languages; but to keep to that of a people who themselves have such a great name—since they have given their name to the *franchise*, or the *franchise* has received it from them—what learned man is ignorant of the *miser Achèron, the attentive steeds, the shameless bed, the timid supplications, the silvered trembling, the*

73 Numbers 16:2.

74 Herodotus, V (Terpsichore), 3.

75 *Origen Against Celsus*, I, 18, 24, p.341, and *Exhortation to Martyrdom*, 46 and in note, de la Rue edition, book I, pp. 305, 341.

76 Plato, *Cratylus*, book III, [390] p. 244.

77 "So that, as Dionysius of Halicarnassus observed, if the epithet is *distinctive* and *natural*, (οἰκεία καὶ προσφυής), in the discourse it carries as much weight as a name." (*On the Poetry of Homer*, chapter 6) One can even say that it is better in a certain sense, since it has the merit of creation without the fault of neologism.

swift destroyer, the pale flatterers, etc.?[78] Man will never forget his primitive rights: it may even be said, in a certain sense, that he will always exercise them, but how much has his degradation restricted them! Here is a law as true as God who made it:

It is forbidden for man to give great names to things of which he is the author, and which he believes to be great; but if he has proceeded legitimately, the vulgar name of the thing will be ennobled by it and will become great.

LIV. Whether for material or political creations, the rule is the same. For example, there is nothing more well-known in Greek history than the word *Ceramicus*: Athens did not know any more august. Long after she had lost her great men and her political existence, Atticus, being in Athens, wrote pretentiously to his illustrious friend: *Finding myself, the other day, in Ceramicus*, etc., and Cicero teased him in his reply.[79] What does this famous word, *Tuileries*,[80] mean in itself?[81] There is nothing more vulgar; but the ashes of heroes, mingled with this earth, had consecrated it, and the earth had consecrated the name. It is rather peculiar that at so great distance of time and place this same word TUILERIES, famous formerly as the name of a burial place, was again dignified under that of a palace. The power which came to inhabit the *Tuileries* did not think of giving them some imposing name which would have a certain proportion to it. If it had committed this fault, there was no reason why the next day this place should not have been inhabited by thieves and prostitutes.

LV. Another reason, which has its value, though it is drawn from a lower altitude, must still impel us to mistrust any pompous name imposed *a priori*. This is because man's conscience almost always warns him of the flaws of the work he has just produced; rebellious pride, which cannot deceive itself, seeks at least to deceive others by inventing an honourable name which pretends to exactly the opposite merit; so that this name, instead of truly testifying to the excellence of the work, is a true expression of the flaws which distinguish it. The eighteenth century, so rich in all that can be imagined false and ridiculous, has furnished on this point several curious examples in the titles of books, in epigraphs, in inscriptions, and in other such things. So, for example, if you read at the head of one of the major

78 I do not remember any famous epithet of Voltaire; this may be a fault of my own memory.

79 In response to your phrase: "*finding myself, the other day, in Ceramicus*," etc. Cicero *ad Atticus* 1, 10.

80 With a certain latitude which still contains the idea of *pottery*.

81 [1847 anonymous translation clarifies with "tile-kiln".]

works of this age:[82]

> *Tantum series juncturaque pollet,*
> *Tantum de medio sumptis accedit honoris.*
>
> ["Such is the power of order and juxtaposition,
> With such beauty does it adorn the commonplace."]

Erase the presumptuous epigraph, and substitute boldly, even before having opened the book, and without the slightest fear of being unjust:

> *Rudis indigestaque moles,*
> *Non bene junotarum discordia semina rerum.*[83]
>
> ["A rough and disordered mass,
> Ill-combined, discordant elements of things."]

Indeed, chaos is the image of this book, and the epigraph exceptionally expresses what is exceptionally absent from the work. If you read at the head of another book, *Philosophical and Political History*,[84] you know, before having read the history announced under this title, that it is neither *philosophical* nor *political*; and you will know, after having read it, that it is the work of a madman. Does any man dare to write below his own portrait: *Vitam impendere vero* ["to devote one's life to truth"]?[85] Wager, with-

82 [*Encyclopédie*, edited by Diderot. The epigraph is taken from Horace's *Ars Poetica*, lines 242–243.]

83 [Ovid's *Metamorphoses*, book I, lines 7 & 9, speaking of the Primal Chaos.]

84 [AKA *Histoire des deux Indes*, collected by Guillaume Thomas Raynal, a large part written by Diderot.]

85 [1847 anonymous translation adds "This was the motto of J. J. Rousseau. It was inscribed on his tomb, as well as under his portrait. On the monument erected to his memory by the Marquis de Girardin, in a grove of poplars, in his beautiful gardens at Ermenonville, about ten leagues from Paris, the traveller reads the following inscription:

> *Ici repose*
> *L'Homme de la Nature*
> Ès de la *Vérité!*
>
> ("Here lies
> The Man of Nature
> And of Truth!")
>
> *Vitam impendere Vero.*
> *Hic jacent Ossa*
>
> ("To devote his life to truth

out knowing any more, that it is the portrait of a liar; and he himself will admit it to you some day when he should fancy to speak the truth. Can we read under another portrait,[86] *Postgenitis hic carus erit, nunc carus amicis* ["this will be dear to posterity, for now it is dear to friends"], without immediately remembering this verse, so happily borrowed from the original, painting him in a slightly different light: *I had worshipers, but not one friend*? And indeed, perhaps there never was any in the class of lettered men less fitted to feel friendship, and less worthy of inspiring it, etc. Works and enterprises of another kind lend themselves to the same observation. Thus, for example, if in a famous nation music suddenly becomes a state affair; if the spirit of the age, blind in every respect, gives to this art a false importance and a false protection very different from that which it would need; if, in fine, a temple is raised to music under the thundering and ancient name of ODEON, it is an infallible proof that art is in decline, and no one should be surprised to hear in this country a famous critic confess, soon after, in vigorous style, that nothing prevents one from writing on the pediment of the temple: ROOM FOR RENT.[87]

LVI. But, as I have said, all this is only a second-order observation; let us go back to the general principle: *That man does not have, or no longer has, the right to name things* (at least in the sense that I explained). One must pay careful attention: the most respectable names have in all languages a vulgar origin. Never is the name proportionate to the thing; the thing always dignifies the name. The name must *germinate*, so to speak, otherwise it is false. What does the word *throne* signify in its origin? *seat*, or even *stool* ["escabelle"]. What does *sceptre* mean? a stick[88] to lean on.[89]

Here lie his bones")]

86 [That of Voltaire.]

87 "It is not the case that the same pieces performed at the *Odeon* produce in me the same sensation that I felt at the old *Théâtre de musique*, where I heard them with rapture. Our artists have lost the tradition of this masterpiece (Pergolesi's *Stabat Mater*); it is written in language foreign to them; they sing the notes without knowing the spirit; their execution is cold, devoid of soul, feeling, and expression. The orchestra itself plays mechanically and with a feebleness that kills the effect. Ancient music (*which*?) is the rival of the highest poetry; ours is only the rival of birds' warbling. Let our modern virtuosos then cease … to dishonour sublime compositions … let them (especially) no longer play Pergolesi; he is too strong for them." (*Journal de l'Empire*, March 28, 1819)

88 [This etymology for *sceptre* is confirmed and elaborated in very interesting fashion in Beneviste's *Dictionary of Indo-European Concepts and Society*, book IV, ch. 3]

89 In the second book of the Iliad, Ulysses wishes to prevent the Greeks from

But the *staff* ["bâton"] of Kings was soon distinguished from all others, and this name, under its *new* meaning, has persisted for three thousand years. What is more noble in literature and more humble in its origin than the word *tragedy*? And the almost foul name of *flag* ["drapeau"], raised and ennobled by the lance of warriors, what fortune has it not had in our language? A host of other names may be mustered more or less in support of the same principle, such as these, for example: *senate, dictator, consul, emperor, church* ["église"], *cardinal, marshal,* etc. Let us end with those of *constable* and *chancellor*, given to two eminent dignitaries of modern times: the first signifies in the beginning only the chief *of the stable*,[90] and the second, *the man who stands behind a railing* (in order not to be overwhelmed by the crowd of supplicants).

LVII. There are, then, two infallible rules for judging all human creations of whatever kind, the *basis* and the *name*; and these two rules, well understood, dispense with any odious application. If the basis is purely human, the edifice cannot stand; and the more men involved in it, the more deliberation, learning, and *especially writing* they will have put into it, in fine, the more human means of all kinds, the more fragile the institution will be. It is principally by this rule that we must judge all that has been undertaken by sovereigns, or by assemblies of men, for the civilization, institution, or regeneration of peoples.

LVIII. On the other hand, the more the institution is divine in its basis, the more durable it is. It is well even to observe, for the sake of clarity, that the religious principle is, in essence, creative and conservative in two ways. In the first place, as it acts more powerfully than any other on the human mind, it stimulates prodigious efforts. Thus, for example, the man persuaded by his religious dogmas that they are of great advantage to him, that after his death his body will be preserved in all possible integrity, without any indiscreet or profane hand being able to approach it; this man, I say, having exhausted the art of embalming, will finish by building the pyramids of Egypt. In the second place, the religious principle, already so strong by what it does, is infinitely more so by what it prevents, because of the respect with which it surrounds all that it takes under its protection.

ignobly abandoning their enterprise. If amid the tumult excited by malcontents he meets a king or a nobleman, he addresses him with sweet words to persuade him; but if he finds under his hand a man of the people δήμον ἄνδρα (a remarkable Gallicism), he beats him *with heavy blows from the sceptre*. (*Iliad*, II, 198, 199)

90 *Constable* is only a Gallic contraction of COMES STABULI, *the companion* or *the minister of the prince for the department of the stables*.

If a simple pebble is consecrated, there is immediately a reason for it to escape from the hands which could misplace or adulterate it. The earth is covered with proofs of this truth. The *Etruscan vases*, for example, *preserved by the religion of the tombs, have reached us, in spite of their fragility, in greater numbers than the marble and bronze monuments of the same epochs.*[91] If you would *preserve* everything, then *dedicate* everything.

LIX. The second rule—that of names—is, I think, neither less clear nor less decisive than the first. If the name is imposed by an assembly; if it is established by prior deliberation, so that it precedes the thing; if the name is pompous,[92] if it has a grammatical proportion to the object which it is to represent; in fine, if it is drawn from a foreign language, and especially from an ancient language, all the characteristics of insignificance are found united, and one can be sure that the name and the thing will disappear in a very short time. Contrary states of affairs herald the legitimacy, and consequently the duration, of the institution. We must be careful not to pass over this subject lightly. A true philosopher must never lose sight of language, a veritable barometer whose variations infallibly announce *good and bad times*. In keeping to the present subject, it is certain that the excessive introduction of foreign words, applied especially to national institutions of all kinds, is one of the most infallible signs of the degradation of a people.

LX. If the formation of all empires, the progress of civilization, and the unanimous accord of all histories and traditions were not yet sufficient to convince us, the death of empires should complete the demonstration begun by their birth. Since it is the religious principle that has created everything, it is the absence of this same principle that has destroyed everything. The sect of Epicurus, which might be called *ancient incredulity*, first degraded and soon destroyed all governments which were so unfortunate as to give it admission. Everywhere *Lucretius* announced *Caesar*.

But all past experience vanished before the dreadful example of the last century. Still intoxicated with its vapours, it is far from the case that men, at least in general, are sufficiently calm to contemplate this example in its true light, and especially to draw the necessary conclusions; it is therefore essential to direct all gazes toward this terrible scene.

91 *Mercure de France*, June 17, 1809, No. 413, p. 679.

92 Thus, for example, if a man other than a sovereign should call himself *legislator*, this is certain proof that he is not one; and if an assembly dares to call itself a *legislative*, not only is this proof that it is not so, but it is proof that it has lost its mind, and that in a short time it will be abandoned to the scorn of the universe.

LXI. There have always been religions in the world, and there have always been wicked men who have opposed them: impiety was also always a crime; for, just as there can be no false religion lacking any admixture of truth, so there can be no impiety which does not oppose some divine truth more or less disfigured; *but there can be no true impiety except in the bosom of the true religion*; and, by a necessary consequence, never has impiety been able in past times to produce the evils that it has produced today; because it is always guilty in proportion to the lights that surround it. It is by this rule that we must judge the eighteenth century; for it is from this point of view that it does not resemble any other. It is commonly said *that all ages are alike, and that all men have always been the same*; but we must be careful not to believe in those general maxims which laziness or triviality invent to dispense with reflection. All ages, on the contrary, and all nations, manifest a peculiar and distinctive character which must be carefully considered. No doubt there have always been vices in the world, but these vices may differ in quantity, in kind, in dominant quality, and in intensity.[93] Now, although there have always been impious ones, never before the eighteenth century had there been, in the midst of Christianity, *an insurrection against God*; never before had we seen a sacrilegious conspiracy of all talents against their author; This is what we have seen today. Vaudeville blasphemed like tragedy; and the novel, like history and physics. The men of this century have prostituted genius to irreligion, and, according to the admirable expression of the dying St. Louis, they have WAGED WAR AGAINST GOD AND HIS GIFTS;[94] Ancient impiety never gets angry; sometimes she reasons; she usually jokes, but always without bitterness. Lucretius himself scarcely ever insults; and though his dark and melancholy temperament drove him to see things in black, and even when he accuses religion of having produced great evils, he is cold-blooded. Ancient religions were not worth the trouble of contemporary disbelief against them.

LXII. When the *good news* was published in the world, the attack became more violent; nevertheless, its enemies always kept a certain moderation. They only show themselves in history at great intervals, and constantly isolated. Never do we see any meeting or formal league: they never give themselves up to the fury to which we have been the witnesses. Bayle him-

93 We must also consider the mixture of virtues whose proportion varies infinitely. When we have shown the same kinds of excesses in different times and places, we think that we have the right to conclude masterfully *that men have always been the same*. There is no sophism more coarse, nor more common.

94 Joinville, in the collection of *Mémoires relatifs à l'histoire de France*.

self, the father of modern incredulity, does not resemble his successors. In his most reprehensible errors, he is not much inclined to persuade, much less does he strike a tone of irritation or party spirit; he denies less than he doubts; he speaks for and against: often, even, he is more eloquent for the good cause than for the bad.[95]

LXIII. It was, therefore, only in the first half of the eighteenth century that impiety really became a power. It is first seen spreading on all sides with an unbelievable activity. From the palace to the cabin, it insinuates itself everywhere, it infests everything; it travels invisible paths, a hidden but infallible action, such that the most attentive observer, seeing the effect, cannot always discover the means. By an unbelievable delusion, it makes itself loved by the very people of whom it is the most mortal enemy; and the authority it is about to sacrifice foolishly embraces it before receiving the blow. Soon a simple system becomes a formal association, which, by a rapid gradation, turns into a plot, and finally into a grand conspiracy which covers Europe.

LXIV. Then, for the first time, is shown this character of impiety which belongs only to the eighteenth century. It is no longer the cold tone of indifference, or at most the malignant irony of scepticism, it is a mortal hatred; it is the tone of anger, and often, of rage. The writers of this period, at least the most prominent, no longer treat Christianity as a human error without consequence, they pursue it as a capital enemy, they fight it to the last extreme; it is a war to the death, and what would seem unbelievable if we did not have the sad proofs before our eyes is that many of those men who called themselves *philosophes* progressed from the hatred of Christianity to the personal hatred of its Divine Author. They hated Him, really as one might hate a living enemy. Two men especially, who will be forever covered by the anathemas of posterity, distinguished themselves by that kind of villainy which seemed far above the power of the most depraved human nature.

LXV. Nevertheless, all Europe having been civilized by Christianity, and the ministers of that religion having obtained in all countries a great political prestige, civil and religious institutions mingled and amalgamated in a surprising way; so that one could say of all the states of Europe, with more or less truth, what *Gibbon* said of France, *that this kingdom had been made by bishops*. It was inevitable, then, that the philosophy of the age would

95 See, for example, with what power of logic he opposed materialism in his dictionary's article on LEUCIPPUS.

soon hate the social institutions from which the religious principle could not be separated. This is what has happened: all the governments, all the institutions of Europe, displeased it *because* they were Christian; and *to the extent* they were Christian, an inquietude of opinion, a universal discontent, seized all minds. In France especially, the philosophical rage knew no bounds; and soon, one formidable voice forming out of so many united voices, we heard it shout in the midst of guilty Europe:

LXVI. "Leave us![96] Shall we, then, eternally tremble before priests, and receive from them the instruction they wish to give us? The truth throughout Europe is hidden by the fumes of the censer; it is time for her to come out of this baneful cloud. We will no longer speak of Thee to our children; it is up to them, when they are men, to know if Thou art, and what Thou art, and what Thou asketh of them. All that exists displeases us because Thy name is written on all that exists. We want to destroy all and remake all without Thee. Depart from our councils; leave our academies; go out of our houses: we would act alone; reason is enough for us. Leave us."

How did God punish this execrable delusion? He punished it as He created the light, by one word, He said: LET IT BE DONE! — And the political world has crumbled.

See, then, how the two kinds of proof come together to impress themselves upon the most benighted of eyes. On the one hand, the religious principle presides over all political creations; and, on the other, all disappears as soon as it is withdrawn.

LXVII. It is for having closed her eyes to these great truths that Europe is guilty, and it is because she is guilty that she suffers. Yet she still rejects the light and fails to recognize the arm that strikes her. Very few men among this material generation are in a position to know the *date*, the *nature*, and the *enormity* of certain crimes committed by individuals, by nations, and by sovereignties; still less to understand the kind of expiation that these crimes require, and the adorable prodigy that forces evil to purify with its own hands the place that the eternal Architect has already measured by eye for His marvellous constructions. The men of this age have taken their side. *They have resolved always to set their eyes upon the earth.*[97] But it would be useless, perhaps even dangerous, to enter into further detail:

96 *Dixerunt Deo:* RECEDE A NOBIS! *Scientiam, viarum tuarum nolumus* ["Therefore they say unto God, DEPART FROM US! for we desire not the knowledge of thy ways."]. Job 21:14.

97 *Oculos suos statuerunt declinare in terram.* Psalms 16:2.

we are enjoined *to profess the truth with love.*[98] On certain occasions it is necessary to profess it only with respect; and, in spite of all imaginable precautions, the step would be slippery even for the calmest and best-intentioned writer. The world, moreover, always contains an innumerable crowd of men so perverse, so deeply corrupted, that, if they should suspect the truth of certain things, they should also redouble their wickedness, and render themselves, so to speak, as guilty as the rebel angels: ah! rather, let their brutishness be further strengthened, if possible, so that they may not become as guilty as even men can be. Blindness is no doubt a terrible punishment; sometimes, however, it still allows us to perceive love; this is all that is useful to say at this moment.

May, 1800

END.

98 Αληθεύοντες ἐν ἀγάπῃ. Ephes, IV. 15. An untranslatable expression. The Vulgate preferring, with good reason, to speak justly than to speak Latin, said: *Facientes veritatem in charitate* ["speaking the truth in love"].

Considerations on France

Dasne igitur hoc nobis, Deorum immortalium nutu, ratione, potestate, mente, numine, sive quod est aliud verbum quo planius significem quod volo, naturam omnem divinitus regi? Nam si hoc non probas, ab eo nobis causa ordienda est potissimum.

["Do you not grant to us, then, that the whole of nature is divinely ruled by the immortal gods' will, reason, power, mind, divinity, or any other word which shall make my meaning clearer? For if you will not grant this, it is imperative that we take up our case from this point."]

Cicero, De Legibus, I, 18.

Editor's Notice.

One of the most remarkable works which appeared during the course of the French Revolution is, without a doubt, that of the Count de Maistre, under the title *Considerations on France.* No one before him had considered the various phases of this terrible epoch with so much fairness and depth, nor had pointed out, with the force of reasoning and clearness of expression that distinguish him, the causes of the disasters we have experienced; no one, especially, had so ably shown the workings of Providence, and foreseen the end of this general upheaval. When we remember that M. de Maistre wrote in 1796, and that we cast our glance across events which have since followed one another, we do not know what to most admire, whether his sagacity in judging the course of human institutions, or that essentially religious spirit which, in relating everything to eternal power, finds in the impiety and corruption of peoples the real principle of the political disturbances they suffer, and in the return to sound doctrines the only cure for their ills. It is not, in fact, with a wholly materialist philosophy that it is possible to explain such great misfortunes, but with this Christian and consoling philosophy which penetrates the consciousness of man, and reveals to him the true origin of decadence, empires, and civil wars.

The first two editions of this work were published in Lausanne in 1796: they were soon out of print. In 1797 there appeared a third at Basel, and the author prepared a new edition at the time of the 18 Fructidor, to circulate it in France according to the King's intentions, which circumstances did not permit. Finally, in 1814 the work was reprinted in Paris; but this edition, made without the participation of M. de Maistre, and very inaccurate besides, contains many additions and deletions which did not reflect his views.

What we offer is such as the author wished, and we obtained from the Countess de Maistre the authorization to include herein a letter addressed to her husband by a Russian gentleman to whom he had sent a copy of *Considerations on France*. Although this letter was written in 1814, it is not, for that fact, of any less interest: it seems that the letter takes on more significance from the events which were then bringing the views of the author to fruition, and which gave his book the character, so to speak, of an accomplished prophecy.

Letter to Maistre.

SIR COUNT,

I have the honour to return to you your work on France. This reading has produced in me such a lively sensation that I cannot hold back from communicating to you the ideas to which it has given birth.

Your work, Monsieur le Comte, is an axiom of the class of those which are not proven because they need no proof; but which are felt because they are rays of natural science. Let me explain; when I am told: "The square of the hypotenuse is equal to the sum of the squares on the two sides of a right triangle," I demand a demonstration—I am convinced, and I allow myself to be convinced. But when one exclaims, "He is a God!" my reason either sees it or is lost in a welter of ideas, but my soul feels it unassailably. It is the same with those grand truths with which your work is filled. These truths are of a high order. This book is not, as I have been told before I read it, *a fine work of circumstance*, but it is the circumstances which have dictated the only fine work I have found on the French Revolution.

Le Moniteur[1] is the most voluminous eventuation of your book. This is where men's efforts in action and words are recorded, as well as the deficiency of these efforts. If there were a philosophical title to give to the *Moniteur*, I would gladly name it "*Compendium of human wisdom and proof of its deficiency*." Your book, the *Moniteur*, history, is the eventuation of this proverb which has become commonplace, but which contains in it the law most fruitful in applications and consequences: "Man proposes and God disposes."

Yes, man can only propose; this is an immense truth. The faculty of combining has been left to man with the power of free will; but events have been withdrawn from his power, and their course obeys only the creative Hand. It is, therefore, in vain that men agitate and *deliberate*, to govern or be governed in this or that way. Nations are like individuals; they may be agitated, but not constituted. When no divine principle presides over their efforts, political convulsions are the result of their free will; but the power of organization is not a human power: order derives from the source of all order.

The epoch of the French Revolution is a great one, it is the age of man and of reason. The end is also noteworthy: it is the hand of God and the age of faith. From the depths of this immense catastrophe, I see a sublime lesson emerge for peoples and kings. This is an example given so as not to be imitated. It belongs in the category of those great scourges with which the human race has been beset and forms the continuation of your eloquent chapter which deals with the violent destruction of the human race. This chapter alone is a work; it is worthy of Bossuet's pen.

The prophetic part of the book equally struck me. This is what it looks like to study God in a speculative manner; what is for reason only an obscure consequence becomes revelation. Everything is understood, everything is explained, when we go back to the great cause. All can be guessed when we rely on it.

You have done me honour in telling me that, as I write, we are busy reprinting this work in Paris. Certainly, it will be very useful as it is; but if you will permit me to give my opinion, I shall make a single observation. I start from this principle: your work is a classic one that cannot be studied too much; it is classic for the host of great and profound ideas it contains. It is circumstantial in one or two chapters, namely that which deals with the *Declaration of the King of France*, in 1795. These chapters were particular to the year 1797 when one believed in the Counter-revolution. Now, how

1 [The main French newspaper during the Revolution, and sometime propaganda outlet.]

many new ideas are there! With what great consequences does history not furnish your principles! This Revolution, concentrated in a single head and fallen with it—the hand of God which sanctified even the faults of the allies; this stupor spread over a nation formerly so active and so terrible; this unknown King in Paris, until the eve of our entry; this great general vanquished in his very art; this new generation, raised in the principles of the new dynasty; this artificial nobility, which sees its first support, and who was the first to abandon it; the Church, tired and panting from the blows that were dealt her; its chief, lowered to the point of sanctifying usurpation, and since raised to the power of martyrdom; the most vigorous genius, armed with the most terrible force, vainly employed in consolidating the edifice of men—this is the picture which I would like to see drawn by your pen, and which would be the obvious demonstration of the principles which you have laid down. I would like to see it in place of those chapters I have indicated to you, and then the work would present to the attentive reader the causes and effects, the actions of men, and the divine response. But it belongs only to you, Monsieur le Comte, to undertake this striking epilogue on your own principles. What I have taken the liberty of sketching here may become, under your hand, a collection of sublime truths; and if I have succeeded by this letter in encouraging you to this great work, I would believe that by that alone I have deserved a place among those who read to educate themselves.

As for me, I limit myself to wishing that you might be willing, by a new *Essay*, to again summon the power to enlighten me, persuaded that your pen shall produce nothing that is not full of grand and powerful lessons.

Please accept assurances that I have the honour of entertaining toward you the highest consideration and respect,

Monsieur le Comte;

OF YOUR EXCELLENCE,

Your most humble and obedient servant,

M. O.,

General in the service of His Majesty
the Emperor of all the Russias.

St. Petersburg, December 24, 1814.

Chapter I:
Revolutions

We are all bound to the throne of the Supreme Being by a flexible chain that restrains us without enslaving us.

What is most admirable in the universal order of things is the action of free beings under the divine hand. Freely slaves, they act both voluntarily and necessarily: they really do what they will, but without being able to disturb the general plans. Each of these beings occupies the centre of a sphere of activity whose diameter varies according to the *Eternal Geometer*, who knows how to extend, restrict, check, or direct the will without altering its nature.

In the works of man, everything is as impoverished as its author; views are restricted, means rigid, springs inflexible, movements painful, and results monotonous. In divine works, the riches of the infinite are revealed down to the very smallest feature; its power works playfully: in its hands all is flexible, nothing resists it; everything is a means for it, even the obstacle: and the irregularities produced by the action of free agents come to be integrated into the general order.

If one imagines a watch whose springs all vary continuously in strength, weight, size, form, and position, and which nevertheless invariably keeps good time, one will form some idea of the action of free beings relative to the plans of the Creator.

In the political and moral world, as in the physical world, there is a normal order, and there are exceptions to that order. Normally we see a series of effects produced by the same causes; but in certain ages we see actions suspended, causes paralysed, and new effects.

The *miracle* is an effect produced by a divine or superhuman cause which suspends or contradicts an ordinary cause. If, in the middle of winter, in front of a thousand witnesses, a man should order a tree to suddenly cover itself with leaves and fruits, and the tree should obey, everyone will cry out at this miracle and bow to the wonder-worker. But the French Revolution, and everything happening in Europe at this moment, is just as marvellous in its own way as the instant fruiting of a tree in the month of January: yet men, instead of admiring, look elsewhere or talk nonsense.

In the physical order, into which man does not enter as a cause, he will readily admire what he does not understand; but in the sphere of his own activity, where he feels that he is a free cause, his pride easily leads him to see *disorder* wherever his action is suspended or disturbed.

Certain measures that are in man's power regularly produce certain effects in the ordinary course of things; if he misses his mark, he knows why, or thinks he knows; he knows the obstacles, he appreciates them, and nothing surprises him.

But in times of revolution, the chain that binds man shortens abruptly, his action diminishes, and his means deceive him. Then, carried along by an unknown force, he hardens himself against it, and instead of kissing the hand that clasps him, he disregards or insults it.

I do not understand anything, is the grand phrase of our day. This phrase is very sensible if it brings us back to the first cause which now presents to men such a great spectacle: it is foolishness if it expresses only a spite or a sterile despondency.

"How, then," the cry is raised on all sides, "can the guiltiest men in the world triumph over all? A hideous regicide has all the success that could have been hoped for by those who committed it! Monarchy is benumbed all over Europe! Its enemies find allies even on the thrones! Everything succeeds for the wicked! The most gigantic projects are executed by them without difficulty, while the good party is unfortunate and ridiculous in all that it undertakes! Opinion persecutes faith throughout Europe! The foremost statesmen are invariably wrong! The greatest generals are humiliated! etc."

No doubt, for the first condition of a consecrated revolution is that all that could prevent it does not exist, and nothing succeeds for those who wish to prevent it. But never is order more visible, never is Providence more palpable, than when superior action substitutes itself for that of man and acts alone. That is what we see at this moment.

What is most striking in the French Revolution is this inexorable force which turns aside all obstacles. Its whirlwind carries away, like light straw, all that human strength has opposed it: no one has thwarted its march with impunity. Purity of motive has been able to make resistance honourable, but no more; and this jealous force, invariably marching to its end, equally rejects Charette, Dumouriez, and Drouet.[1]

1 [Three men characterizing the ideological spectrum during the time of the Revolution. François de Charette was a loyalist, one of the leaders of Counter-rev-

It has been remarked, with good reason, that the French Revolution leads men more than men lead it. This observation is most just; and although it may be applied more or less to all great revolutions, it has never been more striking than in this age.

The very scoundrels who seem to lead the Revolution come into it as mere instruments; and as soon as they pretend to dominate it, they fall ignobly. Those who established the Republic did so without wanting to, and without knowing what they were doing; they were led there by events: a prior design would not have succeeded.

Never did Robespierre, Collot, or Barère think of establishing the revolutionary government and the Reign of Terror; they were led imperceptibly by circumstances, and never shall the like be seen again. These exceedingly mediocre men exercised upon a guilty nation the most frightful despotism in history, and certainly they were the men most astonished in the kingdom at their own power.

But at the very moment when these detestable tyrants had fulfilled the measure of crime necessary for this phase of the revolution, a slight gust overthrew them. This gigantic power, which made France and Europe tremble, did not hold against the first attack; and as there could be nothing great, nothing august in a revolution entirely criminal, Providence willed that the first blow be delivered by the *Septembrists*, so that justice itself might be debased.[2]

We have often been astonished that the most mediocre men have better judged the French Revolution than men of the foremost talent; that they believed in it greatly when accomplished politicians did not yet believe in it. This is because this conviction was one of the components of the Revolution which could only succeed by the extent and energy of the revolu-

olutionary forces in the War in the Vendée. Charles François Dumouriez was a moderate, a military commander who led and then deserted the national army during the Revolutionary War. Jean-Baptiste Drouet was a revolutionary who was instrumental in the arrest of Louis XVI and the royal family in their flight to the frontier.]

2 For the same reason, honour is dishonoured. A journalist (in *le Républicain*) said with much wit and accuracy: "*I understand very well how we can depantheonize Marat, but I will never conceive how we can demaratize the Panthéon.*" [a mausoleum containing French national heroes; Jean-Paul Marat was buried here but disinterred after gaining an association with the radical excesses of the Revolution] Someone complained of seeing the body of Turenne [Henri de La Tour d'Auvergne, Viscount of Turenne, a famous general] forgotten in the corner of a *museum* beside an animal's skeleton: what imprudence! It was enough to give rise to the idea of throwing these venerable remains into the Panthéon.

tionary spirit, or if it is permissible to say, by *faith* in the Revolution. Thus, men without talent and intelligence have very ably driven what they call *the revolutionary chariot*; they have risked all without fear of counter-revolution; they have always walked forward without looking backward; and everything has succeeded for them; this is because they were only the instruments of a force that knew more than them. They made no mistakes in their revolutionary career for the same reason that the *Flute Player* of Vaucanson never hit false notes.[3]

The revolutionary torrent has taken different courses in succession; and the most prominent men in the Revolution have acquired the kind of power and celebrity belonging to them only by following the course of the moment: as soon as they wished to oppose it, or only to withdraw from it into isolation, working too much for themselves, they disappeared from the scene.

Take, for instance, Mirabeau, who was so notable in the Revolution; at bottom he was only the *king of the market hall*.[4] By the crimes he has committed, and by the books he has written, he has seconded the popular movement; he put himself in the train of a mass already set in motion, and pushed it in the direction it was already moving; his power never extended further: he shared with another hero[5] of the Revolution the power to agitate the multitude while lacking the power to dominate it, which forms the true stamp of mediocrity in political troubles. Radicals less brilliant, and fact more skilful and powerful than himself, used his influence for their own profit. He thundered in the tribune, and he was their dupe. He said, in dying, *that if he had lived, he would have collected the scattered parts of the monarchy*; but when he wished, in the moment of his greatest influence, to aim only at a ministry, his subordinates dismissed him like a child.

In fine, the more one looks at the characters most apparently active in the Revolution, the more one finds in them something passive and mechanical. It cannot be too often repeated that it is not men who lead the Revolution; it is the Revolution that uses men. We do not misspeak when

3 [In 1737, Jacques de Vaucanson designed and built a life-size mechanical flute player.]

4 [Maistre's characterization here of Mirabeau is echoed in the *Spectator*: "His voice, often heard, was of little weight, until passion and vanity made him half-scornfully accept the leadership of lesser but more dangerous men in the race towards revolution. He trusted that the first heat of it would spend itself, and that he could direct, if not arrest it, and no doubt he loved to be the king of the market-place not less than to be the chief adviser of the Monarchy; while to be heard at all he had to be in the first instance popular." (*Spectator*, February 20, 1892)]

5 Marquis de Lafayette.

we say that *it proceeds entirely of its own accord*.[6] This phrase indicates that Divinity has never shown itself so clearly in any human event. If it makes use of the vilest instruments, it is because it punishes so as to regenerate.

6 [French *qu'elle va toute seule*, cf. Maistre's pun in §5 of *Essay on the Generative Principle*, p. 14.]

Chapter II: Speculations on the Ways of Providence in the French Revolution

Each nation, like each individual, has received a mission which it must fulfill. France exercises over Europe a true magistracy, which it would be useless to dispute, and which she has abused in the most reprehensible manner. She was, above all, at the head of the religious system, and it is not without reason that her King was called *Most Christian*. Bossuet has not over-emphasized this point. But as she has used her influence to gainsay her vocation and demoralize Europe, it is not surprising that she is being brought back to her mission by terrible means.

It is long since anyone has seen such a frightful punishment inflicted on so many of the guilty. No doubt, there are innocents among the unfortunate, but there are far fewer than is commonly imagined.

All who have worked to divorce the people from their religious beliefs; all who have opposed to the laws of property metaphysical sophistries; all who have said, *strike, so long as we win*; all who have infringed on the fundamental laws of the state; all who have counselled, approved, and favoured the violent measures used against the King, etc.; all these have willed the Revolution, and all those who have willed it have been quite justly its victims, even according to our limited views.

One weeps to see illustrious scholars falling under the axe of Robespierre. One cannot, humanely, bewail them too much; but divine justice has not the slightest respect for mathematicians or scientists. Too many French scholars were the principal authors of the Revolution; too many French scholars loved and favoured it, as long as, like Tarquin's staff, it lopped the tallest heads. Like so many others, they said: *it is impossible for a great revolution to take place without bringing misfortunes*. But when a philosopher consoles himself of these misfortunes in view of the results; when he says in his heart, *let a hundred thousand be murdered, provided we are free*; if Providence answers him: *I accept your recommendation, but you shall be counted among that number*, where is the injustice? Would we judge otherwise in our own courts?

The details would be odious; but there are few French among those they call *innocent victims of the Revolution* to whom their conscience could not say:

> So you see the sad fruits that your faults have produced,
> Now, acknowledge the blows you yourselves have induced.[1]

Our ideas of good and evil, of innocence and guilt, are too often affected by our prejudices. We declare guilty and villainous two men who fight with a three-inch long blade; but if the blade is three feet, the duel becomes honourable. We brand one who steals a *cent* from his friend's pocket; if he steals only his friend's wife, it is as nothing. All brilliant crimes which involve great or likeable qualities—especially those that are rewarded by success—we forgive, even if we do not make virtues of them; while the brilliant qualities which surround the culprit blacken him in the eyes of true justice, whose greatest crime is the abuse of his gifts.

Every man has certain duties to fulfill, and the extent of his duties is relative to his civil position and to the extent of his means. It is far from the case that the same action performed by two given men is equally criminal. So as not to leave our object, an act which was only a mistake or folly on the part of an obscure man, suddenly clothed with unlimited power, could be a crime on the part of a bishop, a duke, or a peer.

Finally, there actions that are excusable, even commendable according to human views, and which are at bottom infinitely criminal. If we are told, for example: *I embraced the French Revolution in good faith, from a pure love of liberty and country; I believed in my soul and conscience that it would bring about the reform of abuses and the public good*; we have nothing to answer. But the eye of Him for Whom all hearts are transparent sees inner guilt; it discovers in a ridiculous misunderstanding, in a little crumpling of pride, in a base or criminal passion, the prime mover of those resolutions which one would like to hold up as exemplary in men's eyes; and for Him the lie of hypocrisy grafted on to treason is a further crime. But let us speak of the nation in general.

One of the greatest crimes that can be committed is undoubtedly the attack on *sovereignty*, no crime bringing more terrible consequences. If sovereignty resides in one head, and that head falls victim to attack, the crime

1 [Racine, *Iphigenia*, 2, lines 1611–12. Maistre's "Alors, de vos erreurs voyant les tristes fruits, / Reconnoissez les coups que vous avez conduits" is a slight misquote; the original has "Alors, de vos respects voyant les tristes fruits, / Reconnaissez les coups, que vous aurez conduits."]

augments the atrocity. But if this sovereign has not deserved his fate by committing no crime, if his very virtues have armed the hand of the guilty against him, the crime is unspeakable. In these features we recognize the death of Louis XVI; but what is important to note—*never did such a great crime have more accomplices.* The death of Charles I had far fewer, and yet one could reproach him, unlike Louis XVI. However, he was given proof of the most tender and courageous concern; the executioner himself, who only obeyed orders, dared not make himself known. In France, Louis XVI marched to his death in the midst of 60,000 armed men, who had not so much as a single shot for *Santerre*:[2] not a voice was raised for the unfortunate monarch, and the provinces were as silent as the capital. *We would have been exposed*, they said. Frenchmen! if you find this a good reason, speak not so highly of your courage, or admit that you use it very badly.

The indifference of the army was no less remarkable. It served Louis XVI's executioners much better than it had served him, for it had betrayed him. One does not see from it the slightest testimony of discontent. In fine, never has a greater crime belonged (in truth, with a multitude of gradations) to a greater number of guilty parties.

An important observation still needs to be made; that every attack committed against sovereignty, *in the name of the nation*, is always more or less a national crime; for it is always more or less the fault of the nation if any number of radicals put themselves in a position to commit the crime in its name. Thus, no doubt not all Frenchmen *willed* the death of Louis XVI; but the immense majority of the people *willed*, for more than two years, all the follies, all the injustices, all the offenses which brought about the disaster of January 21st.

Now, all national crimes against sovereignty are punished without delay and in a manner terrible; this is a law that has never suffered exception. A few days after the execution of Louis XVI, someone wrote in the *Mercure universel*: "Perhaps it did not have to come to this; but since our legislators have taken responsibility for the affair, let us rally around them: extinguish all hatreds, and put the question to rest." Very well: it might have been unnecessary to assassinate the King, but since the deed is done, let us speak of it no more, and let us all be good friends. O madness! Shakespeare knew a little better when he said:

The single and peculiar life is bound,
With all the strength and armour of the mind,
To keep itself from noyance; but much more

2 [The jailer of Louis XVI who escorted him to the guillotine on January 21, 1793.]

That spirit upon whose weal depend and rest
The lives of many. The cease of majesty
Dies not alone; but, like a gulf, doth draw
What's near it with it.[3]

Every drop of Louis XVI's blood will cost France torrents; perhaps four million Frenchmen shall pay, with their heads, for the great national crime of an antireligious and antisocial insurrection, crowned by a regicide.

Where are the first national guards, the first soldiers, the first generals who swore an oath to the nation? Where are the leaders, the idols of this first guilty assembly, for whom the epithet of *constituent* shall be an eternal epigram? where is Mirabeau? where is Bailly with his *beautiful day*? where is Thouret who invented the term *to expropriate*? where is Osselin, proponent of the first law proscribing émigrés? The active instruments of the revolution, who perished by a violent death,[4] could be named by the thousands.

Here again we can admire order in disorder; for it is evident, however little we think about it, that the great culprits of the Revolution could be felled only by the blows of their accomplices. If force alone had produced what is called the *counter-revolution*, and put the King back on the throne, there would have been no means of doing justice. The greatest misfortune that could happen to a sensitive man would be to have to judge the murderer of his father, his relative, his friend, or merely the usurper of his property. Now, this is precisely what would have happened in the case of a counter-revolution, as the term is understood; for the superior judges, by the very nature of things, would have almost all belonged to the injured class; and justice, even if it only punished, would have had an air of vengeance. Moreover, legitimate authority always retains a certain moderation in the punishment of crimes involving a multitude of accomplices. When it sends five or six culprits to their death for the same crime, it is a massacre: if it exceeds certain limits, it becomes odious. In fine, great crimes unfortunately require great torments; and in this way it is easy to exceed the limits when it comes to crimes of *lèse-majesté*, and flattery becomes the executioner. Humanity has not yet forgiven ancient French legislation for the dreadful torment of Damiens.[5] What would the French

3 *Hamlet*, Act 3, Scene 8.

4 [All these radicals, apart from Mirabeau, were executed in the ensuing Reign of Terror.]

5 *Avertere omnes a tanta foeditate spectaculi oculos. Primum ultimumque illud supplicium apud Romanos exempli parum memoris legum humanarum fuit.* ["All averted their eyes from such a terrible spectacle. That was the first and final pun-

magistrates have done with three or four hundred *Damienses*, and all the monsters that covered France? Would the sacred sword of justice have fallen as relentlessly as Robespierre's guillotine? Would all the executioners and artillery horses in the kingdom have been summoned at once to Paris to quarter men? Would lead and pitch have been melted in large boilers to baste limbs torn by red-hot tongs? Moreover, how would different crimes be characterized? how would tortures be proportioned? and especially, how would punishments be levied without laws? *One would have chosen*, it might be said, *some great culprits, and all the rest would have obtained pardon*. This is precisely what Providence did not want. As she can do whatever she wants, she ignores those pardons produced by the inability to punish. It was necessary that the great purification be accomplished, and that eyes should be opened; it was necessary that the metal of France, purged of its sour and impure dross, should devolve cleaner and more malleable upon the hands of a future King. No doubt, Providence does not need to punish contemporaneously to justify its ways; but in our age it comes within our grasp and punishes like a human tribunal.

There have been nations literally sentenced to death as guilty individuals, and we know why.[6] If it entered into God's designs to reveal His plans for the French Revolution, we would read the chastisement of the French like the decree of a parliament. But what more would we know? Is this chastisement not visible? Have not we seen France dishonoured by more than a hundred thousand murders? the whole soil of this beautiful kingdom covered with scaffolds? and this unfortunate land watered with the blood of its children by judicial massacres, while inhuman tyrants squandered it abroad for the support of a cruel war waged for their own interest? Never has the most bloodthirsty despot sported with men's lives with so much insolence, and never has a passive people presented itself at the slaughterhouse with more complacency. Sword and fire, frost and famine, privations, suffering of all kinds, no torment disgusts it: all who are assigned must accomplish their destiny: no disobedience shall be seen until the judgment is accomplished.

And yet in this war, so cruel, so disastrous, what interesting perspectives! and how one passes, by turns, from grief to admiration! Let us transport ourselves to the most terrible epoch of the revolution; let us suppose that,

ishment used among the Romans which was so unmindful of the laws of humanity."] Livy I, 28, *de suppl. Mettii.*

6 *Leviticus* XVIII, 21 *et seq.* XX, 23. *Deuteronomy* XVIII, 9 *et seq. I Kings* XV, 24. *IV Kings* XVII, 7 *et seq.* and XXI, 2. Herodotus book II §46, and Larcher's note on this section.

under the government of the infernal committee,[7] the army, in a sudden metamorphosis, all at once becomes royalist: let us suppose that it rallies to its side the primary assemblies, and that it freely names the most enlightened and esteemed men to trace for it the road to take in this difficult situation: suppose, finally, that one of those representatives of the army rises and says:

"Brave and loyal soldiers, there are circumstances in which all human wisdom is reduced to choosing between different evils. It is hard, no doubt, to fight for the Committee of Public Safety; but there is something more fatal still—to turn our arms against it. The moment the army interferes in politics, the state is dissolved; and the enemies of France, taking advantage of this moment of disorder, will penetrate and divide it. It is not for this moment that we must act, but for future times: above all, it is about maintaining the integrity of France, and this we can only do by fighting for the government, whatever it may be; for in this way France, in spite of her internal schisms, will preserve her military power and external influence. To drive the point home, it is not for the government that we are fighting, but for France and for the future King, who shall be indebted to us for an empire greater, perhaps, than that which the Revolution produced. It is, therefore, a duty for us to overcome the repugnance that makes us sway. Our contemporaries may slander our conduct, but posterity shall do it justice."

This man would have spoken as a great philosopher. Indeed! the army has carried out this fanciful hypothesis without knowing what it was doing; and terror on one side, immorality and extravagance on the other, have done precisely what a consummate and almost prophetic wisdom would have dictated to the army.

On clear reflection, we see that once the revolutionary movement was established, France and the monarchy could only be saved by Jacobinism.

The King has never had an ally; and it is a fact evident enough that there is no imprudence in stating it, that the coalition[8] did not wish France to maintain her integrity. But how to resist the coalition? By what supernatural means could the European conspiracy be broken? The infernal genius of Robespierre alone could work this miracle. The revolutionary government hardened the soul of the French by steeping it in blood; it incensed

7 [The Committee of Public Safety, the de facto executive government during the Reign of Terror, which exercised effective dictatorial control over the military, judiciary, and legislature.]

8 [The War of the First Coalition—European powers allied against France, comprising Spain, Holland, Austria, Prussia, England, and Sardinia—resulted in the formation of the Committee of Public Safety.]

the soldiers' spirit and doubled their power by a ferocious despair and a contempt for life, which drew on rage. The horror of the gallows, pushing the citizen to the frontiers, bolstered military strength in the same measure as it destroyed even the least internal resistance. All lives, all wealth, all power was in the hands of the revolutionary authority; and this monster of power, drunk on blood and success, a frightful phenomenon which had never before been seen, and which no doubt never will be again, was at once a terrible chastisement for the French, and the only means to save France.

What were the royalists asking for when they demanded a counter-revolution such as they imagined it, that is to say, one accomplished abruptly and by force? They were asking for the conquest of France; they therefore demanded its division, the destruction of its influence, and the abasement of its King, that is to say, perhaps three centuries' worth of massacres, the inevitable result of such a rupture of equilibrium. But our descendants, who will trouble themselves very little over our sufferings, and who will dance on our graves, will laugh at our present ignorance; they will easily console themselves for the excesses we have seen, and which will have preserved the integrity *of the most beautiful kingdom after that of Heaven.*[9]

All the monsters the Revolution has hatched have apparently worked only for royalty. Through them, the splendour of victory has won the world's admiration and surrounded the name of France with a glory which the Revolution's crimes have not entirely debased; through them, the King shall return to the throne with all his brilliance and power—perhaps with even greater power. And who knows if, instead of miserably sacrificing some of his provinces to gain the right to reign over others, he may not be restored with the pride of power which gives what it can rightly withhold? We have certainly seen more improbable things happen.

This same idea, that everything is being done for the benefit of the French monarchy, persuades me that any royalist revolution is impossible before peace; for the restoration of royalty would suddenly relax all the machinery of the state. The black magic operating at this moment would vanish like a mist before the sun. Kindness, clemency, justice, all the sweet and peaceful virtues, would suddenly reappear, and would bring with them a certain general mildness in character, a certain cheerfulness entirely opposed to the sombre rigor of revolutionary authority. No more requisitions, no more tolerated theft, no more violence. Would generals, preceded by the white flag, call the inhabitants of the invaded countries *revolutionary* for defending themselves legitimately? and enjoin them not

9 Grotius: *De Jure Belli ac Pacis, Epistle ad Ludovicum* XIII.

to move on pain of being shot as rebels? These horrors, very useful to the future King, could not, however, be used by him; he would have only *humane* means at his disposal. He would be on a par with his enemies; and what would happen in that moment of suspension which necessarily accompanies the transition from one government to another? I do not know. I am well aware that the great conquests of the French seem to protect the integrity of the kingdom (I think I even touch here on the reason for these conquests). However, it seems always more advantageous to France and the monarchy that peace, and a glorious peace for the French, be made by the Republic, and that at the moment when the King should return to his throne, a profound peace should remove him from any sort of danger.

On the other hand, it is evident that an abrupt revolution, far from curing the people, would have confirmed their errors; that it would never have forgiven the power that snatched away their fantasies. As it was the *people*, properly speaking, or the multitude, that the radicals needed to overturn France, it is clear that in general the people had to be spared, and that the great burdens had to fall first on the upper class. It was, therefore, necessary that the usurping power should long weigh upon the people in order to disgust them. The people had only seen the Revolution; it was necessary for them to feel it, that they should, so to speak, savour the bitter consequences. Perhaps, as I write, they have not yet had enough.

The reaction, moreover, must be equal to the action—do not hurry, impatient men, thinking that the very duration of your ills announces to you a *counter-revolution* of which you have no idea. Calm your resentments, and above all, neither complain of kings, nor ask for miracles other than those you see. What! you claim that foreign powers fight for philosophical reasons in order to restore the throne of France, and with no hope of indemnity? But then, you wish men not to be men: you ask for the impossible. You would consent, you may say, to the dismemberment of France *to restore order*; but do you know what *order*? This is what we will see in ten years; perhaps sooner, perhaps later. Moreover, from whom do you gain the right to stipulate for the King, for the French monarchy, and for your posterity? When blind radicals decree the indivisibility of the Republic, see in this only Providence who decrees that of the kingdom.

Let us now take a look at the unheard-of persecution aroused against the national religion and its ministers; it is one of the most interesting *facets* of the revolution.

It cannot be denied that the priesthood in France was in need of regeneration; and although I am very far from adopting the vulgar declamations against the clergy, nonetheless it seems to me incontestable that wealth, luxury, and the general inclination of spirits towards laxity had caused this great body to decline; that one could often find under the surplice a knight instead of an apostle; and that finally, in the time immediately before the Revolution, the clergy had slipped, nearly as much as the army, from the place it had occupied in public opinion.

The first blow to the church was the nationalization of its properties; the second was the constitutional oath;[10] and these two tyrannical measures began the regeneration. The oath sifted the priests, if so it can be said. All who swore it, with a few exceptions which we can ignore, have been led by degrees into the abyss of crime and disgrace: there is not but one view on these apostates.

The faithful priests, recommended to this same opinion by their initial act of firmness, became even more illustrious by the courage with which they managed to confront suffering and even death in defence of their faith. The massacre of the Carmelites is comparable in beauty to anything of this sort in ecclesiastical history.

The tyranny that drove them out of their homeland in the thousands, against all justice and decency, was, without doubt, as revolting as can be imagined; but on this point, as on all others, the crimes of the French tyrants became the instruments of Providence. It was probably necessary that the French priests should be exhibited to foreign nations; they lived among Protestant nations, and this rapprochement has greatly diminished hatreds and prejudices. The considerable emigration to England of the clergy, particularly of the French bishops, seems to me an especially remarkable development. Surely, we will have spoken words of peace! Surely, we will have formed projects for rapprochement during this extraordinary meeting! Even if only common desires were expressed, this would be a great deal. If ever Christians should be reconciled, as everyone invites them to be, it seems that the *initiative* must come from the Church of England. Presbyterianism was a French work, and therefore an exaggerated work. We are too far removed from the followers of this overly insubstantial religion; there is no common language between us. But the Anglican church, which touches us with one hand, touches with the other those whom we cannot approach; and although, from a certain point of view, it is exposed to attack from the two parties, and presents the somewhat ridiculous spectacle of a rebel who preaches obedience, yet it is very valuable under other

10 [On November 27, 1790, the National Assembly voted to require the clergy to swear an oath of loyalty to the Civil Constitution of the Clergy. In this constitution was a clause declaring that the nation of France had ultimate authority over domestic religious matters, a stance later rejected by Pope Pius VI on February 23, 1791. The refusal to take this oath was seen as a challenge to the Civil Constitution of the Clergy, and by extension, the National Assembly which had established it.]

aspects, and may be considered as one of those chemical intermediaries capable of bringing together elements irreconcilable by nature.

The property of the clergy being dissipated, no contemptible motive can provide it with new members for long; so that all circumstances combine to restore this body. There is reason to believe, moreover, that the contemplation of the work with which it seems charged will give it that degree of exaltation which elevates man above himself and enables him to produce great things.

Add to these circumstances the ferment of ideas in certain parts of Europe, the exalted ideas of a few remarkable men, and that kind of anxiety which affects religious natures, especially in Protestant countries, and is pushing them along extraordinary paths.

At the same time, see the storm thundering over Italy; Rome menaced at the same time as Geneva by the power which does not want any worship,[11] and the national supremacy of religion abolished in Holland by a decree of the national convention.[12] If Providence *erases*, no doubt it is *to write*.

I observe, moreover, that when great beliefs have been established in the world, they have been favoured by great conquests, by the formation of great sovereignties: the reason for this is apparent.

Finally, what, in our time, must become of those extraordinary combinations which have deceived all human prudence? In truth, one would be tempted to believe that the political revolution is only a secondary object of the grand plan which unfolds before us with a terrible majesty.

I began by talking about the *magistracy* that France exercises over the rest of Europe. Providence, which always fits means to ends, and which gives to nations, as to individuals, the organs necessary for the accomplishment of their destiny, has given the French nation precisely two instruments, and, so to speak, two *arms*, with which she shakes the world—her language and the spirit of proselytism which forms the essence of her character; so that she always has both the need and the power to influence men.

The power—I almost said the *monarchy*—of the French language is visible: one can, at most, only pretend to doubt it. As for the spirit of proselytism, it is as obvious as the sun; from the fashion designer to the philosopher, it is the salient trait of the national character.

This proselytism commonly comes in for ridicule, and really it often de-

11 [Referring to the 1796–1797 Napoleonic campaign on the Italian peninsula.

12 [On August 5, 1796, an edict was declared by the National Assembly of the Batavian Republic to put an end to the privileged position of the Reformed Church: "A privileged or ruling church will no longer be tolerated in the Netherlands."]

serves it, especially in the forms it takes; at bottom though, it is an *office*.

Now, it is an eternal law of the moral world that every *office* entails a duty. The Gallican church was a cornerstone of the Catholic, or, to put it better, the *Christian* system; for, in truth, there is only one system. Although they perhaps doubt as much, the churches that are enemies of the universal Church exist only by virtue of it, like those parasitic plants, those sterile mistletoes which live only from the substance of the tree which supports them, and which they impoverish.

Because the action and reaction between opposing powers is always equal, the greatest efforts of the *goddess Reason* against Christianity were made in France: the enemy attacked the citadel.

The clergy of France must remain vigilant; it has a thousand reasons to believe that it is called to a great mission; and the same arguments which allow it to see why it has suffered also allow it to believe that it is destined for a crucial task.

In a word, if there is no moral revolution in Europe; if the religious spirit is not reinforced in this part of the world, the social bond will be dissolved. We cannot prophesy anything, and we must expect everything. But if there is to be a change for the better on this point, either there is no more need of analogy, induction, or the art of conjecture—or it is France who is called upon to produce the change.

This is, above all, what makes me think that the French Revolution is a great epoch, and that its consequences shall be felt in a variety of forms far beyond the time of its explosion and the limits of its birthplace.

Considered in its political implications, this opinion is confirmed. How many European powers have deceived themselves over France! How they have *meditated on vain things*! O you who think yourselves independent because you have no judges on earth! Never say: *It suits me*; DISCITE JUSTITIAM MONITI ["know justice—you have been warned"]![13] What hand, at once severe and paternal, crushed France with all imaginable scourges, and sustained the empire by supernatural means in turning all the efforts of her enemies against themselves? Let no one speak to us of assignats, of the force of numbers, etc., for it is precisely the possibility of assignats and the force of numbers that is beyond nature. Moreover, it is by neither paper money nor the advantage of numbers that the winds conduct French ships and repulse those of their enemies; that winter makes for them ice bridges at the moment when they need them; that the sovereigns who hamper them die at the right moment; that they invade Italy without cannons, and that phalanges, reputed to be the bravest of all armies, throw

13 Vergil, *Aeneid*, book 6, line 620.

down their arms and pass under the yoke in the face of equal numbers.

Read the fine reflections of M. Dumas on the present war; you shall see perfectly *why*, but not at all *how* it took on the character we see. We must always go back to the Committee of Public Safety, which was a miracle, and whose spirit is still winning battles.

In fine, the punishment of the *French* breaks all the ordinary rules, as does the protection afforded *to France*: but these two miracles together multiply one another, and present one of the most astonishing spectacles that the human eye has ever seen.

As events unfold, we shall see further reasons and more wondrous reports. Moreover, I only see a part of those which a sharper vision could have discovered at this moment.

The horrible shedding of human blood occasioned by this great upheaval is a terrible means; however, it is a means as much as a punishment, and it can give rise to interesting reflections.

Chapter III: Of the Violent Destruction of the Human Species

The king of Dahomey, in the interior of Africa, was not so wrong, unfortunately, when he told an Englishman: "God made this world for war; all kingdoms, great and small, have practiced it in all ages, though on different principles."[1]

History unfortunately proves that war is the usual state of the human race in a certain sense, that is to say that human blood must flow without interruption somewhere or other on the globe; and that peace, for every nation, is but a respite.

The closing of the temple of Janus under Augustus can be cited;[2] we cite only one year of the warlike reign of Charlemagne (the year 790) when he did not make war.[3] We cite a short time after the peace of Ryswick in 1697, and another no less short after that of Karlowitz in 1699, when there was no war, not only throughout Europe, but even throughout the known world.

But these periods are nothing but exceptions. Moreover, who can know what is happening over the whole globe at one time or another?

The century now ending began, for France, with a cruel war which ended only in 1714 with the Treaty of Rastadt. In 1719, France declared war on Spain; the treaty of Paris put an end to it in 1727. The election of the king of Poland rekindled war in 1733; peace was made in 1736. Four years later, the terrible War of the Austrian Succession ignited, and lasted without

1 *The History of Dahomey*, by Archibald Dalzel, British Library, May 1796, vol. II, No. 1, p. 87.

2 [The doors of the temple ("Gates of Janus") were opened in times of war and closed in times of peace. From the time of Tullus Hostilius down to that of Augustus (about 600 years), the Gates of Janus were closed for a total of 8 years. Augustus boasted that they had only ever been closed twice until his reign, during which they had been closed three times.]

3 *Histoire de Charlemagne*, by M. Gaillard, vol. II, book I, ch. V.

interruption until 1748. Eight years of peace was beginning to heal the wounds of eight years of war when English ambition forced France to take up arms. The Seven Years' War is all too well known. After fifteen years of respite, the American Revolution drew France anew into a war the consequences of which all human wisdom could not foresee. The peace was signed in 1782; seven years later, the Revolution began; it continues to this day, and thus far has cost France perhaps three millions of men.

Thus, considering France alone, we have forty years of war out of ninety-six. If some nations have been more fortunate, others have been less so.

But it is not enough to consider one point in time and one point on the globe; we must briefly survey the long series of massacres that has soiled every page of history. We shall see war rage without interruption, like a continuous fever marked by frightful paroxysms. I ask the reader to follow this spectacle since the decline of the Roman Republic.

In a single battle, Marius exterminated two hundred thousand Cimbri and Teutons. Mithridates slaughtered eighty thousand Romans: Sulla killed ninety thousand men in a battle in Boeotia, where he himself lost ten thousand. Soon we see civil wars and proscriptions. Caesar alone killed a million men on the field of battle (before him Alexander had held this noxious honour): Augustus momentarily closed the temple of Janus; but opened it for centuries, establishing an elective empire. A few good princes allowed the state to breathe, but war never ceased, and under the rule of the *good* Titus, six hundred thousand men perished at the siege of Jerusalem. The destruction of men carried out under Roman arms is truly frightening.[4] The Late Empire presents nothing more than a series of massacres. To begin with Constantine, what wars and battles! Licinius lost twenty thousand men at Cibalis, thirty-four thousand at Adrianople, and one hundred thousand at Chrysopolis. The peoples of the north then begin to erupt. The Franks, the Goths, the Huns, the Lombards, the Alans, the Vandals, etc. attack the empire in succession and tear it down. Attila douses Europe in fire and blood. The Franks kill more than two hundred thousand men near Châlons; and the Goths, the following year, inflict upon it an even greater loss. In less than a century, Rome was taken and sacked three times; and in a revolt that broke out in Constantinople, forty thousand people were slaughtered. The Goths seized Milan and killed three hundred thousand inhabitants there. Totila massacred all the inhabitants of Tivoli and ninety thousand men in the sack of Rome. Mohammed appears; the sword and the Koran overrun two-thirds of the globe. The Saracens range from the Euphrates to the Guadalquivir. They

4 Montesquieu, *Esprit des Lois*, book XXIII, ch. XIX.

destroy from its foundation the immense city of Syracuse, losing thirty thousand men in a single naval combat near Constantinople, and Pelagius kills twenty thousand in a land battle. These losses were nothing to the Saracens; but the torrent runs up against the Frankish genius on the plains of Tours, where the son of the first Pepin, amid three hundred thousand corpses, attaches to his name the *terrible* epithet which still distinguishes him.[5] Islam finds in Spain an indomitable rival. Never, perhaps, has there been any more glory, more grandeur, and more carnage than in the eight-hundred-year struggle between Christians and Muslims in Spain. Several expeditions, and even several battles, cost twenty, thirty, forty, and up to eighty thousand lives.

Charlemagne ascends the throne, and wages war for half a century. Each year he decrees on which part of Europe he must visit death. Present everywhere and everywhere a conqueror, he crushes nations of iron just as Caesar crushed the effeminate men of Asia. The Normans begin that long series of ravages and cruelties that still make us shudder. Charlemagne's immense inheritance is rent asunder: ambition covers it with blood, and the name of the Franks disappears at the battle of Fontenay. All Italy is sacked by the Saracens, while the Normans, Danes, and Hungarians ravage France, Holland, England, Germany, and Greece. The barbarous nations are finally settled and tamed. This vein no longer yields blood; in an instant another is opened: the Crusades begin, Europe as a whole rushes upon Asia; the number of victims can be counted only in myriads. Genghis Khan and his sons subjugate and ravage the globe, from China to Bohemia. The French, who had taken up the cross against Muslims, do so against heretics in the cruel Albigensian crusade. The battle of Bouvines takes place, where thirty thousand men lose their lives. Five years later, eighty thousand Saracens perish at the siege of Damietta. The Guelphs and the Ghibellines begin that conflict which is to bloody Italy for so long. The flame of civil war ignites in England. Then the Sicilian Vespers. Under the reigns of Edward and Philip of Valois, France and England clash more violently than ever, and create a new era of carnage. The massacre of the Jews; the battle of Poitiers; the battle of Nicopolis: the victor falls under the blows of Tamerlane, who repeats Genghis Khan. The Duke of Burgundy has the Duke of Orleans assassinated, and the bloody rivalry of these two families begins. The battle of Agincourt. The Hussites douse a great part of Germany in fire and blood. Mohammed II reigns and fights for thirty years. England, pushed back to her frontiers, is torn apart by her own hand, the houses of York and Lancaster bathing her in blood. The heiress

5 [Charles Martel, "Martel" meaning "hammer".]

of Burgundy joins her estates to the house of Austria; and in this marriage contract it is written that men shall slaughter each other for three centuries from the Baltic to the Mediterranean. Discovery of the New World: the death sentence of three million Indians. Charles V and Francis I appear on the world stage: every page of their history is red with human blood. The reign of Suleiman. The battle of Mohacs. The siege of Vienna, the siege of Malta, etc. But it is from the shadow of a cloister that one of the greatest plagues on the human race emerges. Luther appears; Calvin follows him. The Peasants' Revolt; The Thirty Years' War; the civil war in France; the massacre of the Low Countries; the massacre of Ireland; the massacre of the Cévennes; St. Bartholomew's Day; the murder of Henry III, Henry IV, Mary Stuart, and Charles I; and finally, in our own time, the French Revolution, which takes its rise from the same source.

I shall not press on further into this terrible picture: our own century and its predecessor are too well known. Let us go back to the birth of nations; let us come down to our own day; let us examine peoples in all possible conditions, from the state of barbarism to the most refined civilization; we shall always find war. Owing to this cause—the principal one—and owing to all those that unite with it, the shedding of human blood is never suspended in the world: sometimes the effusion is spread over a larger surface, sometimes it is concentrated into a smaller one; so that the flow is nearly constant. But from time to time there come extraordinary events which increase it prodigiously, such as the Punic wars, the Triumvirates, the victories of Caesar, the irruption of the barbarians, the Crusades, the wars of religion, the Spanish Succession, the French Revolution, etc. If we had tables of massacres like meteorological tables, who knows if we would not discover a law after a few centuries of observation?[6] Buffon has proven quite conclusively that a large part of animals are destined to die a violent death. Apparently, he could have extended his demonstration to man; but the facts speak for themselves.

Yet there is reason to doubt that this violent destruction is, in general, so great a misfortune as is believed; at least, it is one of those evils which enters into an order of things wherein everything is violent and *against nature*, and which produces compensations. In the first place, when the

6 Consisting, for example, of the report made by the chief surgeon of the Imperial Army that out of 250,000 men employed by the Emperor Joseph II against the Turks from June 1, 1788 to May 1, 1789, 33,543 were killed by disease, and 80,000 by the sword (*Gazette nationale et* étrangère, 1790, No. 34). And we can see, from a rough calculation made in Germany, that in the month of October 1795 the present war has already cost France a million men, and the allies 500,000 (Extract from a German periodical, in the *Courrier de Francfort*, October 28, 1795, No. 296).

human soul has lost its resilience through softness, incredulity, and the gangrenous vices which follow the excess of civilization, it can only be retempered in blood. It is far from easy to explain why war produces different effects in different circumstances. What we see, quite clearly, is that the human race can be considered as a tree that an invisible hand relentlessly prunes, and which often benefits from this operation. In truth, if one touches the trunk, or if one prunes *carelessly*, the tree may perish: but who knows the limits of the human tree? What we know is that extreme carnage is often associated with extreme population, as was seen particularly in the ancient Greek republics, and in Spain under the domination of the Arabs.[7] Platitudes about war mean nothing: one need not be very intelligent to know that the more men are killed, the fewer at that moment remain; just as the more branches are cut, the fewer remain on the tree; but it is the results of the operation that must be considered. Now, to further extend the metaphor, we may observe that the clever gardener directs the pruning less to total vegetation than to the fruiting of the tree: it is fruits, and not wood and leaves, that he demands of the plant. Now, the true fruits of human nature—the arts, sciences, great enterprises, high conceptions, manly virtues—are above all due to the state of war. It is known that nations never reach the summit of greatness of which they are capable until after long and bloody wars. Thus, the shining moment for the Greeks was the terrible epoch of the Peloponnesian War; the age of Augustus immediately followed the civil war and the proscriptions; French genius was rough-hewn by the League and polished by the Fronde:[8] all the great men of Queen Anne's century were born in the midst of political upheavals. In a word, it is said that blood is the fertilizer of that plant we call *genius.*

I am not sure if we know what we are talking about when we say that *the arts are friends of peace*. It would be necessary at least to explain and circumscribe the proposition; for I see nothing less peaceful than the ages of Alexander and Pericles, of Augustus, of Leo X and Francis I, of Louis

7 Spain at that time contained up to forty million inhabitants; today it is only ten. — *In the old days Greece flourished in the midst of the cruellest wars, blood flowed in torrents, and the whole country was covered with men. "It seemed," says Machiavelli, "that in the midst of murders, proscriptions, and civil wars, our republic became more powerful, etc."* (Rousseau, *Social Contract*, book III, ch. X).

8 [The Holy League (or Catholic League) was a Catholic association opposing Protestantism in France during the Wars of Religion, resulting in the assassination of Henry III and the conversion of Henry IV to Roman Catholicism. The Fronde was a series of civil wars from 1648–53 sparked by Louis XIV's attempt to raise taxes, wherein the royal government prevailed over the feudal lords and sovereign courts, paving the way for absolutism.]

XIV and Queen Anne.

Could it be that the shedding of human blood might not have a great cause and great effects? Think about it: history and fable, the discoveries of modern physiology, and ancient traditions come together to supply material for these meditations. It would not be more shameful to grope around in the dark on this point than on a thousand others more foreign to man.

Nevertheless, let us thunder against war, and try to arouse disgust toward it in sovereigns; but let us not give in to the dreams of Condorcet, that philosophe so dear to the Revolution, who spent his life preparing the misfortune of the present generation, bequeathing perfection to our posterity. There is only one way to restrain the plague of war—to restrain the disorders that bring about this terrible purification.

In the Greek tragedy of Orestes, Helen, one of the characters in the play, is carried off by the gods to the just resentment of the Greeks and placed in the sky next to her two brothers to be, with them, a sign of salvation to navigators. Apollo appears in order to justify this strange apotheosis:[9] "The beauty of Helen," he says, "was only an instrument that the gods used to pit the Greeks and the Trojans against each other, and to shed their blood, in order to quench[10] on earth the iniquity of men become too numerous."[11]

Apollo spoke very well: it is men who gather the clouds, and then complain of storms.

It is the wrath of kings that arms the earth;
It is the wrath of heaven that arms kings.

I know well that in all these considerations we are continually beset by the wearisome picture of the innocent who perish with the guilty. But without dwelling on this question, which is the most profound of all, we can consider it solely in its relation to the universal dogma, as old as the world, *that the innocent suffer for the benefit of the guilty*.

It was from this dogma, it seems to me, that the ancients derived the usage of sacrifice that they practiced throughout the world, and judged useful not only for the living, but also for the dead:[12] a typical usage that habit makes us regard without astonishment, but the root of which is nonethe-

9 *Dignus vindice nodus* ["a difficulty worthy of a god's deliverance"]. Horace, *Ars Poetica*, 191. [Maistre incorrectly has "nobis" in place of "nodus"]

10 ὡς ἀπαντλοῖεν.

11 Euripides, *Orestes*, lines 1655–58.

12 They sacrificed, literally, *for the repose of souls*; and these sacrifices, says Plato, "are very effective, as whole cities say, and poets born of the gods, and prophets inspired by the gods." Plato, *Republic*, book II.

less difficult to reach.

Self-sacrifices, so famous in antiquity, derive from still the same dogma. Decius[13] had *faith* that the sacrifice of his life would be accepted by the Divinity, and that he could redress the balance for all the evils that menaced his country.[14]

Christianity has come to consecrate this dogma, which is entirely natural to man, although difficult to arrive at by reasoning.

Thus, there may have been in the heart of Louis XVI, and in that of the saintly Elizabeth, such an impulse, such an acceptance, capable of saving France.

One sometimes asks what the use of these terrible austerities is, practiced by certain religious orders, and which are also self-sacrifices; it would make as much sense to ask what the use of Christianity is, since it rests entirely on the same dogma enlarged—on innocence paying for crime.

The authority which approves these orders chooses certain men and *isolates* them from the world to make them *conductors*.

There is nothing but violence in the world; but we are tainted by modern philosophy which says that *all is good*, whereas evil has defiled everything, and in a very real sense *all is evil*, since nothing is in its place. The keynote of the system of our creation having been lowered, all other notes were lowered proportionally, according to the rules of harmony. *The whole creation groaneth*[15] and tends, with effort and pain, toward another order of things.

The spectators of great human calamities, above all, are led to these sad meditations; but let us not lose courage; there is no chastisement that does not purify; there is no disorder that ETERNAL LOVE does not turn against the principle of evil. It is comforting, amid general upheaval, to presage the plans of Divinity. We shall never see all during our sojourn, and often we

13 [It is unclear which Decius Maistre had in mind, likely Publius Decius Mus, Roman consul who, in 340 BCE, sacrificed himself in battle through the ritual of *devotio*.]

14 *Piaculum omnis deorum irae omnes minas periculaque ab diis, superis inferisque in se unum vertit* ["in a propitiatory sacrifice to appease all the wrath of the gods, one man took upon himself all menaces and dangers from deities supernal and infernal"]. (Livy, book VIII, 9 and 10)

15 Saint Paul to the Romans, VIII, 22 *et seq*. Charles Bonnet's system of palingenesis has some points of similarity with St. Paul's text, but this idea did not lead him to that of a previous degradation: however, they agree very well. [Bonnet's theory of palingenesis, based on the idea of the Great Chain of Being, is in some ways similar to Haeckel's theory of recapitulation, where an organism's gestational development "recapitulates" its evolutionary development.]

shall deceive ourselves; but in all possible sciences, except the exact sciences, are we not reduced to conjecture? And if our conjectures are plausible; if they find for themselves an analogy; if they are supported by universal ideas; if, above all, they are consoling and can make us better, what do they lack? If they are not true, they are good; or rather, since they are good, are they not true?

After having considered the French Revolution from a purely moral point of view, I shall turn my attention to politics, without forgetting, however, the main object of my work.

Chapter IV: Can the French Republic Last?

It would be better to ask this other question: *can the Republic exist*? We suppose so, but too quickly, and the *preliminary question* seems quite well founded; for nature and history unite in establishing that a large, indivisible republic is an impossibility. A small number of republicans confined within the walls of a city may, no doubt, have millions of subjects: this was the case at Rome; but a great, free nation cannot exist under a republican government. This is so clear in itself that theory could disregard experience; but experience, which decides all questions in politics no less than in physics, is here in perfect accord with theory.

What could have been said to the French to get them to believe in a republic of twenty-four million men? Two things only: (1) nothing prevents us from doing what has never been seen before; (2) the discovery of the representative system makes possible for us what was impossible for our predecessors. Let us examine the strength of these two arguments.

If we were told that a die, thrown a hundred million times, has only ever shown five numbers—1, 2, 3, 4 and 5—could we believe that there was a 6 on one of the faces? Unquestionably no; and this would be as apparent to us as it would be if we had seen that one of the six faces is blank, or that one of the numbers is repeated.

Very well! let us run through history, we shall see what men call *Fortune* throwing the die tirelessly for four thousand years: has it ever brought about a LARGE REPUBLIC? No. So this *number* was not on the die.

If the world had seen a succession of new governments, we would have no right to affirm that this or that form is impossible just because it has never been seen; but it is entirely otherwise: monarchies have always been known and republics have sometimes been known. If one then wants to go into the subdivisions, one can call *democracy* that government in which the mass exercises sovereignty, and *aristocracy* that in which sovereignty belongs to a more or less limited number of privileged families.

And that is all there is to it.

The analogy of the die is, therefore, perfectly fitting: the same numbers having always come out of the horn of Fortune, we are authorised by the theory of probability to maintain that there are no others.

Let us not confuse the essences of things with their modifications: the former are unalterable and always recur; the latter change and vary the spectacle a little, at least for the multitude; for every practiced eye easily penetrates the changing garb in which eternal nature cloaks itself according to time and place.

What, for example, is special and new in the three powers which constitute the government of England—the names of *Peers* and that of *Commons*, the dress of the Lords, etc.? But the three powers, considered in an abstract manner, are found everywhere alongside a wise and lasting liberty; they are found especially in Sparta, where before Lycurgus the government *was always in turmoil, inclining now to tyranny when the royals had too much power, and then to popular confusion when the common people came to usurp too much authority*. But Lycurgus placed between them the senate, "which was," as Plato says, "a salutary counter-weight … and a strong barrier holding the two extremities in equal balance, and putting the state of public affairs on a firm footing, because the senators … at one time ranged themselves on the side of the kings when there was a need to resist popular temerity, and, on the contrary, at another time strengthened the part of the people against the kings to keep them from usurping a tyrannical power."[1]

Thus, there is nothing new, and a large republic is impossible because there has never been a large republic. As to the representative system that some believe is capable of solving the problem; I feel compelled to make a digression which I hope I will be forgiven.

Let us begin by noting that this system is in no way a modern discovery, but a *product*, or, to put it better, a *part* of feudal government when it reached that point of maturity and equilibrium which rendered it, on balance, the most perfect the world had ever seen.[2]

Having formed the communes, the royal authority summoned them to the national assemblies; they could only appear there by their proxies; hence the representative system.

In brief, it was the same with the trial by jury. According to the hierarchy of tenures, vassals of the same order were summoned to the court of their respective suzerains; hence the maxim that every man ought to

1 Plutarch, *Life of Lycurgus*, French translation by Amyot.

2 "I do not think there has ever been a government on earth so well tempered, etc." (Montesquieu, *Esprit des lois*, Book XI, ch. VIII)

be judged by his peers (*pares curtis*):[3] the maxim which the English have retained in its broadest meaning, and which they have since developed; but the French on the other hand, less tenacious, or yielding perhaps to overwhelming circumstances, have not developed it to the same extent.

One would have to be quite incapable of penetrating into what Bacon called *interiora rerum* ["the interior of things"] to imagine that men could have raised up such institutions by anterior reasoning, or that they could have been the fruit of deliberation.

Moreover, national representation is not particular to England; it is found in every European monarchy—but it is alive in Great Britain; elsewhere it is dead or it slumbers. It does not enter into the plan of this little work to examine whether it has been suspended to the misfortune of humanity, and whether it would be advisable to approximate ancient forms. It is enough to observe from history (1) that in England, where national representation has obtained and retained more power than anywhere else, it is not mentioned before the middle of the thirteenth century;[4] (2) that it was not an invention, nor the result of deliberation, nor the result of the action of the people exercising their ancient rights; but an ambitious soldier, in order to satisfy his particular views, in reality created the balance of the three powers after the battle of Lewes, without knowing what he was doing, as always happens; (3) that not only was the convocation of the Commons in the National Council a concession of the monarch, but that in the beginning the king named the representatives of the provinces, cities, and boroughs; (4) that, even after the Commons had arrogated to themselves the right to name their representatives in Parliament during Edward I's sojourn in Palestine, they had only a consultative voice; that they presented their *grievances*, like the Estates-General in France, and the formula for the concessions emanating from the throne as a result of their petitions was constantly: *granted by the King and his spiritual and temporal lords, on the humble prayers of the Commons*; (5) finally, that the co-legislative power attributed to the House of Commons is still very new, since it scarcely goes back to the middle of the fifteenth century.

If we therefore understand by this term "national representation" a *certain* number of representatives sent by *certain* men, taken in *certain* towns or boroughs, by virtue of an ancient concession of the sovereign, we need

3 See the *Book of Fiefs*, following Roman law.

4 English democrats have tried to trace the rights of the Commons much further back, and they have found the people even in the famous WITENAGEMOTS; but they have had to gracefully give up such an unsustainable thesis. (Hume, vol. I, appendix I, p. 144; appendix II, p. 407; London, Millar, 1762)

not quarrel over words—such a government exists, and it is that of England.

But if one wishes that *all* the people be represented, that they should be represented only by virtue of a mandate,[5] and that *every* citizen, with a few physically and morally inevitable exceptions, should be capable of giving or receiving these mandates; and if it is claimed that the abolition of all hereditary distinction and offices is to be joined to such an order of things—then this representation is something which has never been seen, and which will never succeed.

America is here cited to us: I know of nothing so annoying as the praises heaped up on this babe-in-arms: let it grow.

But to render this discussion as clear as possible, it must be noted that the fathers of the French Republic must not only prove that *perfected* representation, as the innovators put it, is possible and good; but also that the people, by this means, can retain their *sovereignty* (again, as they put it), and form, in their totality, a republic. This is the crux of the matter; for if the *republic* is in the capital, and the rest of France is the *subject* of the republic, it is not accountable to the *sovereign people.*

The most recent commission charged with deciding on a method for of national representation has estimated the number of Frenchmen at thirty million. Let us grant this number and suppose that France keeps her conquests. Each year, according to the constitution, two hundred and fifty people will leave the legislative body and be replaced by two hundred and fifty others. It follows that if the fifteen million men that this population assumes were immortal, skilled as representatives, and nominated in order, then invariably each Frenchman would, in his turn, come to exercise national sovereignty every sixty thousand years.[6]

But since, in such an interval, men will surely die from time to time; and since, moreover, some men will be elected more than once; and since some in a host of men will always be disqualified, by nature and good sense, from national representation, the mind boggles at the prodigious number of sovereigns condemned to die without having reigned.

Rousseau held that *the national will cannot be delegated*; we are free to

5 It is often assumed, out of bad faith or inattention, that the *mandatory* alone can be a *representative*: this is a mistake. In the courts, the child, the madman, and the absent are represented every day by men who hold their mandate only from the law: now, the *people* eminently unite these three qualities; for it is always a *child*, always *mad*, and always *absent*. Why should its *guardians* not do without these mandates?

6 I am not taking into account the five places of Directors. For our purposes, the probability is so small that it can be considered zero.

agree or disagree, and to debate these academic questions for a thousand years. But what is certain is that the representative system directly excludes the exercise of sovereignty, especially in the French system, where the rights of the people are limited to naming electors; where not only are the people unable to give special mandates to their representatives, but the law takes care to sever all relations between them and their respective provinces, warning them that *they are not sent by those who sent them*, but by the *nation*; a splendid word, infinitely convenient because we can make of it what we wish. In a word, it is impossible to imagine legislation better calculated to destroy the rights of the people. Thus, that vile Jacobin conspirator was quite right in saying during a judicial inquiry: "I believe the present government a usurper of authority, a violator of all the rights of the people, whom it has reduced to the most deplorable slavery. It is the frightful system of the happiness of a few, founded on the oppression of the masses. The people are so muzzled, so bound in chains by this aristocratic government, that it is becoming more difficult than ever for them to break them."[7]

So! What does the empty privilege of representation matter to the *nation* when it is so indirectly involved, and when millions of individuals will never enjoy it? Are they any less estranged from sovereignty and government?

But they might say in rebutting the argument, what does it matter to the nation if the privilege of representation is empty, if the resultant system establishes public liberty?

This is not the question; the question is not whether the French people can be made *free* by the constitution given to them, but whether they can be *sovereign*. They change the question to escape the reasoning. Let us begin by ignoring the exercise of sovereignty; let us insist on the fundamental point that the sovereign will always be in Paris, and that all this claptrap about representation means nothing; that the *people* are thoroughly estranged from government; that they are more subject than under the monarchy, and that the term *large republic* is as self-defeating as *square circle*. Now, here is an arithmetic demonstration.

The question is therefore reduced to whether it is in the French people's interest to be *subject* to an executive directory and two councils instituted according to the 1795 constitution, rather than to a king reigning according to ancient forms.

There is much less difficulty in resolving a problem than in posing it.

It is therefore necessary to discard this word *republic* and speak only of

7 See the interrogation of Babeuf, June 1796.

government. I will not examine if it is fit to produce public welfare; the French know this well enough! Let us see only if, such as it is, and by whatever name it is called, it is permissible to believe in this government's permanence.

Let us first raise ourselves up to a height that befits the intelligent being, and from this elevated viewpoint, let us consider the origin of this government.

Evil has nothing in common with existence; it cannot create, since its power is purely negative: *Evil is the schism of being; it is not true.*

Now, what distinguishes the French Revolution, and what makes it a unique *event* in history, is that it is radically *bad*, no element of good comforts the eye of the observer; it is the highest degree of corruption known; it is pure impurity.

On which page of history shall we find so many vices acting at the same time, on the same stage? What an appalling assemblage of baseness and cruelty! What profound immorality! What forgetfulness of all shame!

The childhood of liberty has characteristics so striking that it is impossible to mistake them. In this age, love of country is a religion, and respect for the laws a superstition; character is strongly pronounced, morals are austere; all virtues shine forth at once; parties work toward the profit of the country, because the only dispute is over the honour of serving it; everything, even crime, bears the mark of greatness.

If we compare this picture with that offered by France, how can we believe in the persistence of a liberty that takes its rise from gangrene? Or, to speak more precisely, how can we believe that this liberty can be born (since it does not yet exist), and that from the heart of the most disgusting corruption can emerge this form of government possessed of more virtues than all others? When one hears these so-called republicans speak of liberty and virtue, one imagines a faded courtesan putting on the airs of a virgin with blushes of rouge.

A republican journal has reported the following anecdote about the morality of Paris:

> A case of seduction was pleaded before the Civil Tribunal; a 14-year-old girl astonished the judges with a degree of corruption matched only by the profound immorality of her seducer; more than half of the audience was comprised of young women and girls; of these, more than twenty were no more than thirteen or fourteen, with several beside their mothers; and instead of covering their faces, they laughed with relish at the necessary

> but disgusting details which made the men blush.[8]

Reader, may you remember that Roman[9] who, in the halcyon days of Rome, was punished for embracing his wife in front of his children; draw your own parallel and conclusion.

The French Revolution has, no doubt, gone through a number of phases; yet its general character has never varied, and even at birth it showed promise of all that it would become. There was a certain inexplicable delirium, a blind impetuosity, a scandalous contempt for all that is respectable among men: a new kind of atrocity that joked about its crimes; above all, an impudent prostitution of reasoning, and of all words meant to express ideas of justice and virtue.

It is difficult to convey a sense of the feeling one gets in looking at the acts of the National Constituent Assembly in particular. When I think back to the time of its meeting, I feel myself transported as the sublime English bard into a cerebral world; I see the enemy of the human race seated in the Manège,[10] and summoning all *evil spirits* to this new *pandemonium*; I distinctly hear *il rauco suon delle tartar trombe* ["the dreadful blast of the infernal trumpet"];[11] I see all the vices of France answer the call, and I am not so sure if I what write here is allegory.

And once again, note how crime serves as the whole basis for everything. This republican scaffolding, this word *citizen*, which they have substituted for the ancient forms of civility, they apply to the vilest of humans: it was in one of their legislative orgies that the brigands invented this new title. The republican calendar, which should be seen not only in its ridiculous aspect, was a conspiracy against religion; their era dates from the greatest crimes ever to have dishonoured humanity; they cannot date an act without covering themselves in shame, recalling the ignominious origin of a government whose very holidays make the blood run cold.

Must an enduring government emerge, then, from this bloody mire? Let us not draw a comparison with the ferocious and licentious manners of the barbarian peoples who have, however, become civilized: barbarous ignorance has undoubtedly presided over the establishment of a number of political systems; but learned barbarism, systematic atrocity, calculated corruption, and especially irreligion, have never produced anything. Greenness leads to maturity; decay leads to nothing.

8 *Journal de l'opposition*, 1795, No. 173, p. 705.

9 [Manius Manilius. See Plutarch, *Cato the Elder*, 17.7]

10 [The venue for the deliberations of the National Constituent Assembly, and later the National Convention.]

11 [Torquato Tasso, *Jerusalem Delivered*, book IV, verse 3.]

Moreover, have we ever seen a government, and above all a free constitution, begun in spite of its members, and without their consent? Yet this is the phenomenon that would be presented to us by this meteor known as the *French Republic*, if it could last. This government is believed to be strong because it is violent; but strength differs from violence as much as from weakness; and the astonishing way it operates at this time is, by itself, perhaps proof enough that it cannot endure long. The French nation does not *want* this government, it *suffers* it, and remains submissive either because it cannot shake it off, or because it fears something worse. The republic rests on these two columns which have no reality; we can say that it rests entirely on two negations. It is, therefore, very remarkable that the apologists, friends of the Republic, do not bother to demonstrate its worth, they sense that this is the chink in their armour; they say only, as boldly as they can, that it is possible; and passing as lightly over this thesis as over hot coals, they are concerned only to prove to the French that they would expose themselves to the greatest evils if they should return to their former government. On this point they are most eloquent; they never cease speaking of the dangers of revolutions. If pressed, they would grant that the revolution which created the present government was a crime, as long as you grant that a new one is unnecessary. They throw themselves before the French nation; they beg her to keep the Republic. One senses in all they say about the stability of government not the conviction of reason, but the dreams of desire.

Let us move on to the great anathema that weighs upon the republic.

Chapter V:
Of the French Revolution Considered in its Anti-Religious Character – Digression on Christianity

There is a *satanic* character in the French Revolution which distinguishes it from all we have seen, and, perhaps, from all we shall see.

Recall the great assemblies! Robespierre's speech against the priesthood, the solemn apostasy of the priests, the desecration of objects of worship, the inauguration of the goddess Reason, and this host of unheard-of scenes wherein the provinces tried to outdo Paris—all this exceeds the bounds of ordinary crime and seems to belong to another world.

And even now, when the Revolution has lost most of its furore, the great excesses have disappeared, but the principles remain. Have not the *legislators* (to use their term) made this declaration, unprecedented in history: *the nation shall not sponsor any worship*? Some men of our time have, in my view, appeared at certain moments to reach the point of hatred for Divinity; but this frightful act is not necessary to annul the greatest creative efforts: the mere neglect of (to say nothing of contempt for) the great Being is an irrevocable anathema on human works tainted by it. All imaginable institutions are either based on a religious idea, or they are merely transient. They are as strong and enduring as they are *deified*, if we can put it that way. Not only can human reason, or what is ignorantly called *philosophy*, not supply what is yet more ignorantly called "superstitious" foundations, but philosophy is, on the contrary, an essentially disruptive force. In a word, man can only represent the Creator by putting himself in harmony with Him. How senseless we are! — if we want a mirror to reflect the image of the sun, do we turn it toward the earth?

These reflections are addressed to everyone, to the believer as to the sceptic; it is a fact that I advance and not a thesis. Whether one laughs at these ideas or venerates them, whether true or false, they are no less the sole basis of all enduring institutions.

Rousseau, perhaps the most mistaken man this world has ever seen, has nevertheless hit upon this observation without having wanted to follow its consequences.

> The Judaic Law, which remains always in force; that of the child of Ishmael, which for ten centuries have governed half of the world, still proclaim today the great men who laid them down ... Proud philosophy or the blind spirit of party sees in them only lucky impostures.[1]

He had only to draw the conclusion, instead of telling us about *that great and powerful genius which presides over enduring institutions*: as if this poetry explained something!

When reflecting on the facts attested by the whole of history; when one considers that the chain of human institutions—from those which have marked the ages of the world down to the smallest social organization, from the empire to the brotherhood—has a divine basis, and that human power, whenever isolated, has only been able to give to its works a false and transitory existence; what shall we think of the new French system and the power that has produced it? For myself, I shall never believe in the fecundity of nothingness.

It would be a curious thing to successively delve into our European institutions and show how they are all *Christianised*; how religion mixes into everything, animates and sustains everything. Human passions may soil, even pervert primitive creations, but if the principle is divine, this is enough to give them a prodigious endurance. Among a thousand examples, we may mention that of military orders; we should certainly not disparage their members in affirming that the original religious object is no longer their first concern: no matter—they remain, and this endurance is a marvel. How many superficial wits laugh at this strange amalgam of monk and soldier! Better to rhapsodize about that hidden force by which these orders have survived the centuries, overcome formidable powers, and mustered the most astonishing resistances in history. Now, this force is the name on which these institutions rest; for nothing *is* but through *the One who is*. Amid the general upheaval we are witnessing, the want of education, in particular, arrests the anxious attention of the friends of order. More than once, they have been heard to say that the Jesuits must be restored. I shall not enter here into the merits of this order; but this wish does not suggest deep reflection. Do they mean that St. Ignatius is ready at

1 *Contrat social*, book I, ch. VIII.

hand to serve our aims? If the order is destroyed, some of the cooks among the brethren may be able to restore it in the same spirit that created it; but all the sovereigns of the world would not succeed.

This is a divine law as certain and as palpable as the laws of motion.

Whenever a man puts himself, according to his ability, in communion with the Creator, and produces any institution whatsoever in the name of the Divinity; whatever may be his individual weakness, his ignorance, his poverty, the obscurity of his birth, in a word, his absolute want of all human means, he participates in some way in that omnipotence of which he is the instrument; he produces works whose force and endurance astonish reason.

I beg every attentive reader to look closely around him; in even the least objects will he find these great truths demonstrated. It is not necessary to go back to the *son of Ishmael*, to Lycurgus, to Numa, to Moses, whose laws were all religious; a popular festival, a rustic dance, will suffice for the observer. He will see in some Protestant countries certain gatherings, certain popular celebrations which have no apparent purpose, and which come down from Catholic usages altogether forgotten. These kinds of festivities have in themselves nothing moral, nothing respectable; they derive, though very distantly, from religious ideas, and this is enough to perpetuate them. Three centuries have not been able to efface their memory.

But you, masters of the earth! princes, kings, emperors, powerful majesties, invincible conquerors! try only to bring the people on such-and-such a day each year to a specified place to dance. I ask very little of you, but I dare solemnly challenge you to succeed, just as the humblest missionary will succeed, and will be obeyed two thousand years after his death. Every year, in the name of *St.* John, *St.* Martin, *St.* Benedict, etc., the people gather around a rustic temple; they arrive, animated by a noisy and yet innocent glee; the religion sanctifies the joy, and the joy embellishes the religion: they forget their troubles; they think, on leaving, of the pleasure they will have the following year on the same day, and that day is for them fixed.

Next to this picture, place that of the masters of France, whom an unheard-of revolution has invested with every power, and who cannot organize a simple festival. They lavish gold, they call to their aid all the arts, and the citizen stays home, or heeds the call only to laugh at the organizers. Listen to the scorn of impotence! Listen to these memorable words of one of those *deputies of the people* speaking to the *Legislative* Body, in a sitting of the month of January 1796: "What then?" he exclaimed, "men foreign to our customs, to our usages, have succeeded in establishing ridiculous festivals for unknown events, in honour of men whose existence is itself a problem. What! they have been able to obtain the use of immense funds to repeat each day, with a dismal monotony, insignificant and often absurd ceremonies; and the men who have overthrown the Bastille and the throne, the men who have conquered Europe, will not succeed in preserving, in national festivals, the memory of the great events which immortalize our revolution!"

O delirium! O depth of human weakness! Legislators! meditate on this great confession; it teaches you what you are and what you can do. What more do you now need to judge the French system? If its deficiency is unclear, there is nothing certain in this world.

I am so convinced of the truths that I defend that when I consider the general decline of moral principles, the divergence of opinions, the undermining of sovereignties without foundation, the immensity of our needs, and the poverty of our means, it seems to me that any true philosopher must choose between these two hypotheses: either a new religion shall be born, or Christianity shall be rejuvenated in some extraordinary way. It is between these two suppositions that we must choose, according to the position we have taken on the truth of Christianity.

This conjecture will be scornfully rejected only by those short-sighted men who believe only what they see. What man of antiquity could have foreseen Christianity? And what stranger to this religion could have foreseen its success from its beginnings? How do we know that a great moral revolution has not already begun? Pliny, as proved by his famous letter,[2] had not the slightest idea of this giant, of which he saw only the infancy.

But what a host of ideas comes to assail me at this moment and raises me to the widest of considerations!

The present generation is witness to one of the greatest spectacles ever beheld by the human eye: it is the fight to the death between Christianity and sophistry. The lists are open, the two enemies have come to grips, and the world looks on.

As in Homer, we see *the father of gods and men* holding the scales which weigh two great stakes; soon one of the scales will come down.

For the biased man, and especially for the one whose heart has convinced his head, events prove nothing; the partisan having irrevocably taken a side either for or against, observation and reasoning are equally useless. But all you men of good faith who deny or doubt, perhaps this great epoch of Christianity will settle your uncertainty. For eighteen centuries it has reigned over a great part of the world, and particularly over the most

2 [Pliny the Younger, Roman governor of Bithynia, wrote to Trajan ca. 112 CE seeking counsel on dealing with the problem of Christians in the Empire who refused to sacrifice to the Roman gods.]

enlightened portion of the globe. This religion does not originate even in antiquity; reaching back through its founder, it is tied to another order of things, to a prototypical religion that preceded it. The one cannot be true without the other being so: the one boasts of promising what the other boasts of possessing; so that this religion, by a sequence that is a visible fact, goes back to the origin of the world.

> It was born on the day that days were born.[3]

There is no example of such endurance; and to confine ourselves just to Christianity, no institution in the world can be compared to it. To compare other religions to it is to quibble; several striking characteristics exclude all comparison: this is not the place to detail them; one word only is enough. Let us be shown another religion founded on miraculous facts and revealing incomprehensible dogmas, believed for eighteen centuries by a great part of the human race, and defended from age to age by the foremost men of the time, from Origen to Pascal, despite the utmost efforts of an enemy sect which has not ceased howling, from Celsus to Condorcet.

What a remarkable thing! when one thinks about this great institution, the most natural hypothesis which every probability suggests is that of a divine foundation. If the work is human, there is no way of explaining its success: in excluding a miracle, a miracle is required.

All nations, it is said, have mistaken copper for gold. Very well: but has this copper been thrown into the European crucible, and for eighteen centuries subjected to chemical observation? or, if it has survived this ordeal, has it done so to its credit? Newton believed in the Incarnation; but Plato, I think, thought little of Bacchus' miraculous birth.

Christianity has been preached by the ignorant and believed by the learned, and in this it resembles nothing else known.

In addition, it has survived every trial. It is said that persecution is a wind that nourishes and spreads the flame of fanaticism. Granted: Diocletian favoured Christianity; but according to this supposition Constantine should have stifled it, and this has not happened. It has resisted everything—peace, war, scaffolds, triumphs, daggers, temptations, pride, humiliation, poverty, opulence, the night of the Middle Ages and the great daylight of the ages of Leo X and Louis XIV. An all-powerful emperor,[4] master of the greatest part of the known world, once exhausted all the resources of his

3 [Racine, *La Religion*, book III, verse 36]

4 [Julian the Apostate, Roman emperor who, in the wake of Constantine's conversion to Christianity, attempted to restore Roman paganism as the state religion.]

genius against it; he spared nothing to revive ancient dogmas; he skilfully associated them with the Platonic ideas which were then in fashion. Hiding the rage which animated him under the mask of a purely external tolerance, he used against this enemy worship weapons which no human work has resisted; he exposed it to ridicule; he impoverished the priesthood to make it despised; he deprived it of all the support which man can give to his works: slanders, intrigues, injustice, oppression, ridicule, force, and skill; all was useless; the *Galilean* prevailed over Julian *the philosophe*.

Finally, the experiment is being repeated today under even more favourable circumstances; nothing is lacking that can make it decisive. So pay close attention, all you whom history has not instructed well enough. You say that the sceptre supported the tiara;[5] very well! there is no longer a sceptre on the world stage, it is broken, and the pieces thrown into the mud. You wondered at the extent to which a rich and powerful priesthood's influence could sustain the dogmas it preached; I do not believe in any power to make one believe; but let us pass over this point. There are no more priests; they have been driven out, slaughtered, degraded; they have been plundered: and those who have escaped the guillotine, the stake, the daggers, the fusillades, the drownings, the deportations, today receive the alms they once gave. You feared the force of custom, the ascendency of authority, the illusions of the imagination: nothing of that remains; there is no longer any custom; there is no longer a master: the mind of each man is his own. Philosophy having eroded the cement that united men, there are no longer any moral ties. The civil authority, favouring with all its strength the overthrow of the old system, gives to the enemies of Christianity all the support it once granted to Christianity itself: the human mind takes hold of every imaginable means to combat the old national religion. These efforts are applauded and paid for, and the contrary efforts are crimes. You have nothing to fear from the enchantment of the eyes, which are always the first to be deceived; pompous dress and vain ceremonies no longer impress men before whom everything has been mocked for seven years. The churches are closed, or open only to the cacophonous discussions and debauches of an unbridled people. The altars are overthrown; filthy animals have been paraded in the streets in bishops' vestments; chalices have served in abominable orgies; and on these altars which the old faith surrounded with dazzling cherubim, naked prostitutes have been mounted. Sophistry therefore has no more complaints to make; all human chances are in its favour; everything is done for it and everything against its rival. If it is victorious, it will not say, as Caesar did: *I came, I saw, I conquered*; but

5 [i.e., that the Crown supported the Papacy.]

it will finally have conquered: it can applaud and sit proudly on an overturned cross. But if Christianity emerges from this terrible test purer and more vigorous; if the Christian Hercules, strong in his own power alone, lifts the *son of the earth*, and crushes him in his arms, *patuit Deus* ["God has become manifest"]. — Frenchmen! make way for the most Christian King, carry him yourselves to his ancient throne; take up his oriflamme, and let his coinage, reaching again from one pole to the other, carry everywhere the triumphal motto:

> CHRIST COMMANDS, HE REIGNS,
> HE IS VICTOR.

Chapter VI: Of Divine Influence in Political Constitutions

Man can modify everything within the sphere of his activity, but he creates nothing: such is his law, in the physical as in the moral world.

Man can no doubt plant a seed, raise a tree, perfect it by grafting, and prune it in a hundred ways; but never has he imagined that he had the power to make a tree.

How can he have imagined that he had the power to make a constitution? Could it be through experience? Let us see what it teaches us.

All the known free constitutions in the world have been formed in one of two ways. Sometimes they have, so to speak, *germinated* in an imperceptible manner by the convergence of a host of circumstances which we call "fortuitous"; and sometimes they have a single author who appears as a phenomenon, and makes himself to be obeyed.

In these two assumptions, here are the signs by which God warns us of our weakness and the right He has reserved to Himself in the formation of governments:[1]

1. No constitution results from deliberation; the rights of the people are never written, or at least the constitutive acts or the written fundamental laws are never anything but declaratory statements of pre-existing rights, of which we can say nothing more than that they exist because they exist.[2]

2. God, having not judged it appropriate to use supernatural means in this business, circumscribes at least human action to the point that, in

1 [The points that follow are, with some differences, contained in the *Essay on the Generative Principle*, p. 5, which refers to this work.]

2 "It would take a fool to ask who gave liberty to the cities of Sparta, Rome, etc. These republics did not receive their charters from men. God and nature gave them to them." (Algernon Sidney, *Discourses Concerning Government*, vol. I, §2) The author is not suspect.

the formation of constitutions, circumstances do everything, and men are only circumstances. Quite commonly even, in pursuing a certain aim they attain another, as we have seen in the English constitution.

3. The rights of the *people*, properly so-called, often originate in the concession of sovereigns, and in this case, they may be traced historically; but the rights of the sovereign and the aristocracy, at least their essential, constitutive, and *basic* rights, if it is permissible to call them that, have neither date nor author.

4. Even the concessions of the sovereign have always been preceded by a state of affairs which necessitated them, and which did not depend on him.

5. Although written laws are nothing but declarations of pre-existing rights, it is nowhere near possible that they be written; there is always, in every constitution, something which cannot be written,[3] and which must remain in a dark and venerable cloud, on pain of overturning the state.

6. The more one writes, the weaker the constitution; the reason is clear. Laws are only declarations of rights, and rights are only declared when they are attacked; so that the multiplicity of written constitutional laws only proves the multiplicity of conflicts and the danger of destruction.

This is why the most vigorous constitution of secular antiquity was that of Sparta, wherein nothing was written.

7. No nation can give itself liberty if it does not have it.[4] By the time it begins to reflect on itself, its laws are made. Human influence does not extend beyond the development of rights which already exist but are ignored or contested. If imprudent men overstep these bounds with reckless reforms, the nation loses what it had without gaining what it wants. Hence the necessity of innovating only very rarely and always

3 The wise Hume often made this remark. I will cite only the following passage: "This [Parliament's right to challenge the king] touched upon that circumstance in the English constitution which is most difficult, or rather altogether impossible, to regulate by laws, and which must be governed by certain delicate ideas of propriety and decency, rather than to any exact rule or prescription." (Hume, *History of England*, ch. LIII, note B).

Thomas Payne is of a different opinion, as we know. He claims that a constitution does not exist until it can be put in his pocket.

4 *Un populo uso a vivere sotto un principe, se per qualche accidente diventa libero, con difficolta mantiene la liberta* ["A people accustomed to live under a prince, should they by some eventuality become free, will with difficulty maintain their freedom"]. (Machiavelli, *Discourses on Livy*, book I, ch. XVI).

with restraint and trepidation.

8. When Providence has decreed the more rapid formation of a political constitution, there appears a man clothed with an indefinable power: he speaks and makes himself to be obeyed: but these extraordinary men perhaps belong only to the ancient world and the youth of nations. Be that as it may, the distinctive characteristic par excellence of these legislators is that they are kings, or high nobles: there is and can be no exception in this regard. It was this that sullied the constitution of Solon, the most fragile of antiquity.[5] The days of Athens' greatness, which were soon passed,[6] were interrupted by conquest and tyranny, and Solon himself suffered to see the Pisistratids.[7]

9. These legislators, even with their marvellous power, have only ever gathered together pre-existing elements in the customs and character of peoples; but this gathering, this rapid formation attached to creation, is only performed in the name of the Divinity. The political and the religious merge together: there is hardly any distinction between the legislator and the priest; and his public institutions consist mainly *of ceremonies and religious holidays*.[8]

10. Liberty was always, in a sense, the gift of kings; for all free nations were constituted by kings. This is the general rule, and the exceptions that might be pointed out would fall under the rule if thoroughly scrutinized.[9]

5 Plutarch recognized this truth very well: "Solon," he says, "could not long maintain a city in union and concord, for he was born of common stock, and was not one of the richest of his city, and of only bourgeois means." (Plutarch, *Solon*, French translation by Amyot).

6 *Haec extrema fuit aetas imperatorum Atheniensium Iphicratis, Chabriae, Timothei; neque post illorum obitum quisquam dux in illa urbe fuit dignus memoria.* ["This was the end of the age of the Athenian emperors Iphicrates, Chabrias, and Timotheus; and after the death of those illustrious men, no general in that city was worthy of memorializing."] (Cornelius Nepos, *Life of Timotheus*. ch. IV) 114 years passed from the battle of Marathon to that of Leucade, won by Timothy. This is the glory of Athens sounding out.

7 [The dynasty of Peisistratos. Promising the poor a division of Eupatrid lands, Peisistratos attained power over Athens by subterfuge. He was twice overthrown, and twice returned to power; his sons reigned after him, and the tyrant Cleisthenes, whose reforms subverted Eupatrid power forever, after them.]

8 Plutarch, *Life of Numa*.

9 *Neque ambigitur quin Brutus idem, qui tantum gloriae, superbo exacto rege, meruit, pessimo public id facturus fuerit, si libertatis immaturae cupidine priorum regum alicui regnum extorsisset, etc.* ["Nor is there any doubt but that the very

11. There never existed a free nation which did not have, in its natural constitution, seeds of liberty as old as itself; and no nation has ever successfully attempted to develop, by its fundamental written laws, rights other than those which existed in its natural constitution.

12. No assembly of men whatever can constitute a nation; and any such enterprise exceeds in madness the greatest absurdities and extravagances to which all the *Bedlams* in the world could give birth.[10]

To prove this proposition in detail after what I have said, would, it seems to me, be disrespectful to the wise, and do too much honour to the ignorant.

13. I have spoken of one principal characteristic of true legislators; here is another which is quite remarkable, and upon which a book could easily be written. It is that they are never called *learned*, that they do not write, that they act by instinct and impulse rather than by reasoning, and that they have no other instrument with which to act than a certain moral force that bends men's wills as the wind bends a wheat field.

I might say some interesting things in showing that this observation is only the corollary of a general truth of the highest importance, but I fear digressing too far: I prefer to dispense with the intermediary arguments and to go straight to the conclusions.

The same difference exists between political theory and constitutional laws as between poetics and poetry. The illustrious Montesquieu is to Lycurgus, in the scale of genius, what Batteux is to Homer or Racine.

This is not all: these two talents positively exclude each other, as we have seen in the example of Locke, who stumbled badly when he decided to give laws to the Americans.

I have seen a great admirer of the Republic seriously lament that the French had not found in Hume's works a piece entitled *Plan for a Perfect Republic.* — *O caecas hominum mentes* ["O the blind minds of men"]! If you see an ordinary man with good sense, but who has never shown any sort of outward sign of superiority, you cannot be sure that he has not the makings of a legislator. There is no reason to say yes or no; but in the case

same Brutus, who earned such glory by driving out the arrogant king, would have wrested rule from any of the earlier kings if a premature desire for liberty, etc."] Livy, II, 1. The whole passage is quite worthy of consideration.

10 *E necessario che uno solo sia quello che dia il modo, e della cui mente dipenda qualunque simile ordinazione* ["It is essential that there should be but one person upon whose mind and method depends any similar process of organization"]. (Machiavelli, *Discourses on Livy*, book I, ch. IX)

of Bacon, Locke, Montesquieu, etc., say no without hesitation; for the talent he does have proves that he does *not* have the other.[11]

The application to the French constitution of the principles I have just expounded is obvious; but it is well to consider it from a particular point of view.

The greatest enemies of the French Revolution must frankly admit that the commission of eleven which produced the last constitution has, by all appearances, more sense than its work, and that it has done all it could. It had at its disposal disobedient materials which forbade it from following principles; and the division of powers alone, although divided only by a wall,[12] is still a fine victory over the prejudices of the moment.

But it is not only a question of the intrinsic merit of the constitution. It does not enter into my plan to look for particular defects which assure us that it cannot last; besides, everything has been said on this point. I will only indicate the theoretical error which has served as the basis for this constitution, and which has misled the French from the outset of their revolution.

The Constitution of 1795, like its predecessors, is made for *man*. But there is no such thing as *man* in the world. In my life, I have seen Frenchmen, Italians, Russians, etc.; thanks to Montesquieu, I know even *that one can be Persian*, but as for *man*; I declare that I have never met him in my life; if he exists, he is unbeknownst to me.

Is there a single country in the world where you can find a Council of Five Hundred, a Council of Elders, and Five Directors? This constitution may be presented to all human associations, from China to Geneva. But a constitution which is made for all nations is made for none: it is a pure abstraction, an academic work made to impress upon the mind a hypothetical ideal, and which must be addressed to *man* in the imaginary realm he inhabits.

What is a constitution? Is it not the solution to the following problem?

Given the population, morals, religion, geographical situation, political relations, wealth, good and bad qualities of a certain nation, to find the laws that suit it.

Yet this problem is not even addressed in the Constitution of 1795, which considers only *man*.

11 "Plato, Zenon, Chrysippus, produced books; but Lycurgus, deeds." (Plutarch, *Life of Lycurgus*) There is not a single sound idea in morals and politics that has escaped the good sense of Plutarch.

12 Under no circumstances may the two Councils meet in the same room, *Constitution de 1795*; title V, article 60.

Every imaginable reason converges to establish that this work does not bear the divine seal. — It is just a *schoolboy's exercise*.

And so, already at this moment, how many signs of decay!

Chapter VII: Signs of Deficiency in the French Government

The legislator resembles the Creator; he is not always working; he gives birth, and then he rests. All true legislation has its *Sabbath*, and intermittency is its distinctive characteristic; so that Ovid has stated a first-rate truth when he said:

> *Quod caret alterna requie durabile non est*
>
> ["What lacks alternating periods of rest will not endure"].

If perfection were the endowment of human nature, each legislator would speak only once; but while all our works are imperfect, and as political institutions are corrupted the sovereign must support them with new laws, yet human legislation approaches its model by that intermittency of which I just spoke. Its repose honours it as much as its original action: the more it acts, the more human—that is, the more fragile—its works.

Look at the works of the three French national assemblies; what a prodigious number of laws!

From July 1, 1789, to October 1791, the National Assembly passed	2,507
The Legislative Assembly, in eleven and a half months, passed	1,712
The National Convention, from the first day of the Republic until 4 Brumaire, Year IV (October 26, 1795), passed in 57 months	11,210
Total	15,479[1]

1 This calculation, which was made in France, is taken from a foreign gazette of February 1796. This number of 15,479 in less than six years, already seemed to me

I doubt if the three houses of French Kings have spawned such a collection. When one reflects on this infinitude of laws, one experiences two quite different sentiments in succession: the first is that of admiration, or at least astonishment; with Mr. Burke, one is astonished that this nation, whose laxity is a proverb, has produced such persistent workers. Such an edifice of laws is a work of Atlantean proportions whose very aspect astounds. But astonishment suddenly turns to pity when one considers the deficiency of these laws; and we see only children killing each other to raise a grand house of cards.

Why so many laws? Because there is no legislator.

What have the so-called legislators made in six years? Nothing; for to *destroy* is not to *make*.

We cannot tire of contemplating the incredible spectacle of a nation giving itself three constitutions in five years. A legislator does not grope around; in the manner of a legislator, he says *fiat*, and the machine springs into action. Despite the various efforts made here by the three assemblies, everything has gone from bad to worse, since the work of the legislators has constantly and increasingly lacked the assent of the nation.

Certainly, the Constitution of 1791 was a fine monument to folly; yet it must be admitted that it had captivated the French; and it is with a pure heart, though very foolishly, that the majority of the nation swore an oath *to the nation, the law, and the king*. The French even pledged themselves to this constitution to the point that, long after it was no longer in question, it was a rather common expression among them that *to return to the real monarchy, it would be necessary to pass through the Constitution of 1791*. Which is essentially to say that to return to Europe from Asia, it is necessary to pass through the moon; but I am only speaking of the facts.[2]

quite honest when I found in my notes the assertion, in one of those scintillating sheets (*Quotidienne*, November 30, 1796, No. 218), of a very agreeable journalist who was absolutely sure that the French Republic has two million and a few hundred thousand laws that are printed, and eighteen hundred thousand that are not. — For my own part, I agree.

2 A man of intellect who had his reasons for praising that constitution, and who absolutely wants it to be *a monument to written reason*, nevertheless agrees that, to pass over the horror of both chambers and the restriction of the *veto*, it still contains *several other principles of anarchy* (20 or 30 for example). See *Coup-d'oeil sur la Révolution française, par un ami de l'ordre et des lois, by M. M.* (General Montesquieu) Hamburg, 1794, p. 28 and 77.

But what follows is still more curious. *This constitution,* says the author, *sins not in what it contains, but what it lacks*. Montesquieu, *Coup-d'oeil*, p. 27. Meaning the Constitution of 1791 would be perfect if it were made: this is the Apollo of the

Condorcet's constitution was never put to the test and was not worth the trouble; yet the one preferred to his, the work of a few cutthroats, pleased their fellows; and thanks to the Revolution, this phalanx is not insignificant in France; so that, on the whole, of the three constitutions, the one which counts the fewest defenders is today's. In the primary assemblies that accepted it (according to the government), several members naively wrote: *Accepted for want of better*. This is, in fact, the general disposition of the nation: it has submitted from weariness, from despair of finding better: in the excess of misfortunes which overwhelmed it, the nation believed that it could breathe under this frail shelter; it preferred a bad port to an angry sea; but nowhere can be found conviction and heartfelt consent. If this constitution was made for the French, the invincible force of experience would win it new partisans every day: now, precisely the opposite is happening; every minute democracy finds a new deserter; it is apathy, it is fear alone, which maintains the throne of the pentarchs;[3] and the most clear-minded and disinterested travellers who have traversed France say in unison: *It is a republic without republicans.*

But if, as has so often been preached to kings, the power of governments resides entirely in the love of its subjects; if fear alone is an insufficient means of maintaining sovereignty, what must we think of the French Republic?

Open your eyes, and you will see that she does not *live*. What a huge contraption! what a multiplicity of springs and cogs! what a fracas of clashing pieces! what an enormous number of men employed to repair the damage! Everything announces that nature accounts for nothing in these movements; for the basic character of natural creations is the power attached to an economy of means: everything being in its place, there are no jerks, no gyrations: with friction low, there is no noise, but an august silence. So it is in physics; perfect weighting, equilibrium, and exact symmetry of parts even give to rapid movement the appearance of rest so satisfying to the eye.

There is, therefore, no sovereignty in France; everything is artificial, everything is violent, everything announces that such an order of things cannot last.

Modern philosophy is at once too materialist and too presumptuous to perceive the real mainsprings of the political world. One of its follies is to believe that an assembly can constitute a nation: that a *constitution*, that is to say, all the fundamental laws proper to a nation and that give it this or

Belvedere, less the statue and the pedestal.

3 [The five directors of the Directory.]

that form of government, is a piece of handiwork like any other, requiring nothing but wit, knowledge, and experience; that one can learn for himself the *trade of constituting*, and that the spirit can move men at any moment to say to other men: *Make us a government*, as one might say to a workman: *Make us a fire pump or a loom.*

Nevertheless, here is a truth as certain in its way as a mathematical proposition; it is that *no great institution results from deliberation*, and human works are fragile in proportion to the number of men involved and the degree to which science and reasoning have been employed *a priori.*

A written constitution such as that which governs the French today is only an automaton, which possesses only the outward appearance of life. Man, by his own powers, is at most a *Vaucanson*; to be a *Prometheus*, one must ascend to heaven; for *the legislator cannot command obedience either by force or by reasoning.*[4]

At this moment, it can be said that the experiment is concluded; for when we say that the French constitution is *working* we inattentively mistake the constitution for the government. The latter, which is a highly advanced despotism, works only too well; but the constitution exists only on paper. It is observed or violated according to the interests of the governors: the people count for nothing; and the outrages which their masters inflict on them under the forms of respect are well suited to cure them of their errors.

The life of a government is something as real as the life of a man; one feels it; or better, one sees it, and no one can deceive himself on this point. I entreat all Frenchmen who have a conscience to ask themselves whether they must do themselves a certain violence in giving their representatives the title of *legislators*; if this title of etiquette and *courtesy* does not demand of them a slight effort, about the same as when, under the ancien régime, they were pleased to call the son of the king's secretary a *count* or *marquis*?[5]

All honour comes from God, said Homer of old;[6] he speaks like St. Paul, to the letter, yet without having plagiarized him. What is certain is that it is not given to man to communicate that indefinable characteristic called *dignity*. To sovereignty alone belongs *honour* par excellence; it is from the sovereign, as from a vast reservoir, that it devolves in number, weight, and measure on classes and individuals.

4 Rousseau. *Contrat social*, book II, ch. VII. It is necessary to constantly keep an eye on this man, and to surprise him when he distractedly lets the truth slip out.

5 [The office of secretary to the king carried with it hereditary nobility but could also be purchased by commoners.]

6 *Iliad*, 1, 178.

I have noticed that a member of the legislature, having spoken of his RANK in print, was mocked by the newspapers, because in fact there is no *rank* in France; but only *power*, which depends solely on force. The people see in a deputy only the seven-hundred-and-fiftieth part of a power to do much harm. The deputy is not respected because he is a *deputy*, but because he is respectable. No doubt everyone would like to have delivered M. Siméon's speech on divorce; but everyone would like him to have given it before a legitimate assembly.

It may be an illusion on my part; but this *salary*, which a vainglorious neologism calls an *indemnity*, seems to me a prejudice against French representation. The Englishman, free by law and independent in his fortune, who comes to London to represent the nation at his own expense, has something imposing about him. But these French *legislators* who charge the nation five or six million livres to make laws for it; these *decree merchants*, who exercise national sovereignty for four bushels[7] of wheat per day, and who live off their legislative power; these men, in truth, are not particularly impressive; and when one comes to wonder what they are worth, the imagination cannot but evaluate them in terms of wheat.

In England, these two magical letters M.P., conjoined to a little-known name, suddenly exalt it and give it the right to a distinguished marriage. In France, a man who would aspire to a deputy's place to marry up has probably made quite the miscalculation.

This is because any representative, any instrument whatsoever of a false sovereignty, can excite only curiosity or terror.

Such is the incredible weakness of isolated human power that it does not belong to it even to consecrate a dress code. How many reports have been made to the legislature on the costume of its members? Three or four at least, but always in vain. Representations of these beautiful costumes are sold in foreign countries, while in Paris public opinion ridicules them.

An ordinary costume, contemporary with a great event, can be consecrated by this event; then the character which marks it exempts it from the world of mere fashion: while fashions change, it remains the same; and respect surrounds it forever. This is roughly how costumes of great dignity are formed.

For those who examine everything, it may be interesting to observe that, of all the revolutionary finery, only the sash and the plume—which belong to chivalry—have achieved a certain constancy. They remain, though withered, like trees whose nourishing sap is gone, but which have not yet lost their beauty. The *public official*, laden with these dishonoured sym-

7 [Maistre gives "eight myriagrammes".]

bols, resembles the thief who stands out in the clothes of the man whom he has just stripped.

I do not know if I read well, but I read everywhere the deficiency of this government.

Pay close attention—the conquests of the French have created the illusion of their government's durability; the splendour of military success has dazzled even great minds, who do not at first perceive how unrelated these successes are to the stability of the Republic.

Nations have conquered under all possible governments; and even revolutions, by exalting morale, may bring victory. The French will always have military success under a firm government which has the wit to despise them even in praising them, and to throw them at the enemy like bullets, promising them epitaphs in the newspapers.

Even now, it is still Robespierre who wins battles; it is his iron despotism that leads the French to slaughter and victory. It is by squandering gold and blood; it is by straining all means that the masters of France have obtained the success that we have witnessed. A supremely brave nation, exalted by some kind of fanaticism and led by skilful generals, will always conquer, but will pay dearly for its conquests. Did the Constitution of 1793 receive the seal of durability from its three years of victories? Why should it be otherwise for that of 1795? and why should victory give to the one a character which it could not impress upon the other?

Besides, a nation's character is always the same. Barclay, in the sixteenth century, sketched very well the military character of the French. *It is a nation,* he says, *supremely brave, and presenting on its home front an invincible mass; but when it spills over its borders, it is no longer the same. Hence it has never been able to maintain empire over foreign peoples, and its strength is its own misfortune.*[8]

No one feels more strongly than I that the present circumstances are extraordinary, and that it is quite possible that what we are seeing is unprecedented; but this question is irrelevant to the object of this work. It is enough for me to point out the falsity of this reasoning: *the republic is victorious; therefore it will last.* If it were absolutely necessary to prophesy, I would rather say: *war keeps it alive, so peace will kill it.*

The author of a system of physics would no doubt applaud himself if he had in his favour all the facts of nature, as I can quote in support of my reflections all the facts of history. I examine in good faith the movements

8 *Gens armis strenua, indomitae intra se molis; at ubi in exteros exundat, statim impetus sui oblita: eo modo nec diu externum imperium tenait, et sola est in exitium sui potens.* J. Barclaius, Icon *Animorum*, ch. III.

with which history furnishes us, and I see nothing that favours this chimerical system of deliberation and political construction by prior reasoning. At best we could cite America; but I have answered this in advance, saying that the time to cite it is not yet. I will, however, add a few reflections.

1. British America had a King but did not observe him: the splendour of monarchy was foreign to her, and the sovereign was to her a kind of supernatural power which does not strike the senses.
2. She possessed the democratic element present in the constitution of the mother country.
3. She also possessed those elements brought by a host of her first settlers born amid religious and political troubles, and almost all republican in spirit.
4. The Americans built with these elements, on the plan of the three powers that they inherited from their ancestors, and not from a *tabula rasa*, like the French.

But all that is truly new in their constitution; all that results from popular deliberation, is the most fragile thing in the world; we could not gather together more symptoms of weakness and decay.

Not only do I doubt the stability of the American government, but the particular establishments of British America do not inspire me with any confidence. The cities, for example, animated by a scarcely respectable jealousy, could not agree on the place where the Congress should sit; none wished to yield this honour to the other. As a result, it was decided that a new city should be built as the seat of government. A most advantageous location was chosen on the banks of a great river; it was decided that the city should be called *Washington*; the site of all public buildings has been marked out; hands have been set to work, and the plan of the *queen-city* is already circulating all over Europe. Essentially, there is nothing here beyond human powers; one may well build a city: nevertheless, there is too much deliberation, too much *humanity* in this affair; and one can wager a thousand to one that the city will not be built, or that it will not be called *Washington*, or that the Congress will not reside there.

Chapter VIII: Of the Old French Constitution – Digression on the King and on His Declaration to the French of the Month of July 1795[1]

Three different theories about the old French constitution have been argued: some have claimed that the nation had no constitution; others have claimed the opposite; others have taken, as happens in all important questions, a moderate position: they have claimed that the French had a constitution, but that it was not observed.

The first view is untenable; the other two do not really contradict each other.

The error of those who have claimed that France had no constitution arises from the great error concerning human power, prior deliberation, and written laws.

If a man of good faith, having in himself only good sense and uprightness, should ask what the old French constitution was, we can answer him boldly: "It is what you felt when you were in France; it was that mixture of liberty and authority, of law and opinion, which made the foreigner, the subject of a monarchy traveling in France, believe that he was living under a government other than his own."

But if we wish to consider the matter more thoroughly, we shall find in the corpus of French public law those characteristics and laws which elevate France above all known monarchies.

A peculiar characteristic of this monarchy is that it possesses a certain theocratic element which is particular to itself, and which has made it

1 The Declaration of Verona by Louis XVIII made many concessions to the republican cause including religious tolerance, sweeping reform of abuses, the reconstitution of the Estates-General with expanded voting rights and the right of petition, but also demanded punishment for regicides and the re-establishment of hereditary monarchy and state religion. It was poorly received by republicans who saw it as insufficiently progressive.

endure for fourteen hundred years: there is nothing so national as this element. The bishops, successors of the druids in this respect, have only perfected it.

I do not believe that any other European monarchy has employed, for the good of the state, a greater number of priests in the civil government. I think back from the peaceful Fleury to these Saint-Ouens, these Saint-Legers, and so many others so distinguished in political sense during their benighted times; true Orpheuses of France, who tamed tigers and led them in chains; I doubt whether a parallel series could be shown elsewhere.

But while the priesthood was one of the three pillars in France which supported the throne and played such an important role in the nation's councils, courts, ministry, and embassies, its influence was, at best, little perceived in the civil administration; and even when a priest was Prime Minister, there was not a *government of priests* in France.

All the influences were well balanced, and everyone was in his place. From this point of view, it was England that most closely resembled France. If she ever banishes from her political vocabulary these words: *Church and state*,[2] her government shall perish like that of her rival.

It was the fashion in France (because everything is fashionable in this country) to say that one was enslaved: but why then did one find in the French language the word of *citoyen* (even before the Revolution seized upon it much to its dishonour),[3] a word that cannot be translated into other European languages? The younger Racine addressed this beautiful verse to the King of France, in the name of his city of Paris:

> Under a citizen king, every citizen is king.

To praise the patriotism of a Frenchman, they said: *C'est un grand citoyen.* It would be hopeless to try to convey this expression in our other languages; *Gross bürger* in German,[4] *gran cittadino* in Italian, etc., would not be tolerable.[5] But we must go beyond generalities.

Several members of the old magistracy have brought together and devel-

2 [Maistre gives this phrase in English.]

3 [During the French Revolution, the term *citoyen* replaced that of *monsieur, madame*, or *mademoiselle* as an honorific.]

4 Bürger, *verbum humile apud nos et ignobile* ["a word lowly and ignoble to us"]. J. A. Ernesti, in *Dedicat. Opp. Ciceronis*, p. 79.

5 Rousseau made an absurd note on this word *citoyen*, in his *Contrat social*, book I, ch. VI. Unembarrassed, he accuses a very learned man [Bodin] of having made on this point an awkward blunder; whereas Jean-Jacques makes an awkward blunder in each line; he shows an ignorance as much of languages as he does of metaphysics and history.

oped the principles of the French monarchy in an interesting book which appears to deserve all the confidence of the French.[6]

These magistrates appropriately begin with the royal prerogative, and certainly there is nothing more magnificent.

"The constitution attributes to the King the legislative power; from him emanates all jurisdiction. He has the right to render justice, and to have it administered by his officers; to give pardon, to bestow privileges and rewards; to establish offices, to confer nobility; to convoke and to dissolve national assemblies whenever his wisdom so inclines him; to make peace and war, and to summon the army." (p. 28)

No doubt, these are great prerogatives; but let us see what the French constitution has put on the other side of the balance.

"The King reigns only by the law and *has no power to do anything at will.*" (p. 364)

"There are laws that kings have confessed themselves (according to the famous expression) *happily powerless to violate*; they are *the laws of the realm*, as opposed to circumstantial or non-constitutional laws, called *royal laws.*" (pp. 29 and 30)

"Thus, for example, the succession to the crown is by male primogeniture, according to a rigid form."

"Marriages of princes of the blood, made without the authority of the King, are null and void." (p. 262)

"If the reigning dynasty is extinguished, it is the nation that gives itself a king." (pp. 263 *et seq.*)

"Kings, as supreme legislators, have always spoken affirmatively in publishing their laws. Nevertheless, there is also a consent of the people, but this consent is only the expression of the will, the gratitude, and the acceptance of the nation."[7] (p. 271)

"Three orders, three chambers, three deliberations; this is how the nation is represented. The result of the deliberations, if it is unanimous, exhibits the will of the Estates-General." (p. 332)

"The laws of the realm can only be made in general assembly of the whole realm, with the common consent of the people of the three estates. The prince may not derogate from these laws; and if he dares meddle with

6 *Développement des principes fondamentaux de la monarchie française*, 1795.

7 If one carefully examines this intervention of the nation, one will find *less* than a co-legislative power, and *more* than mere consent. This is an example of those things which must be left in a certain obscurity, and which cannot be subjected to human determination: it is the *most divine* part of the constitution, if it is permissible to say. It is often said: *One has only to make a law to know where one stands.* Not always; there are *reserved cases.*

them, all he has done can be undone by his successor." (pp. 292, 293)

"The necessity of the consent of the nation to the establishment of taxes is an incontestable truth, recognized by kings." (p. 302)

"The will of two orders cannot bind the third, except with its consent." (p. 302)

"The consent of the Estates-General is necessary for the validity of any perpetual alienation of the domain." (p. 303) — "And the same supervision is recommended to them to prevent any partial dismemberment of the realm." (p. 304)

"Justice is administered in the king's name by magistrates who examine the laws to see if they are not contrary to the fundamental laws." (p. 343) Part of their duty is to resist the misguided will of the sovereign. It was concerning this principle that the famous Chancellor l'Hôpital addressed the Parliament of Paris in 1561: *The magistrates must not be intimidated by the transient wrath of sovereigns, nor by the fear of disgrace; but must always keep before them their oath to obey the ordinances, which are the true commandments of kings.*" (p. 345)

We see Louis XI, arrested by the double refusal of his parliament, abandoning an unconstitutional alienation. (p. 343)

We see Louis XIV solemnly recognize this right of free verification (p. 347) and order his magistrates *to disobey him on pain of disobedience* if he should address to them commands contrary to law (p. 345). This order is not a play on words: the King forbids obedience to the man; he has no greater enemy.

Furthermore, this superb monarch ordered his magistrates to consider all letters-patent null which bear evocations or commissions for the judgment of civil and criminal cases, *and even to punish the bearers of these letters.* (p. 363)

The magistrates exclaim: *Happy land, where servitude is unknown!* (p. 361) And it is a priest distinguished by his piety and knowledge (Fleury) who writes, in expounding the public law of France: *In France, all individuals are free: there is no bondage: there is freedom of domicile, travel, commerce, marriage, choice of profession, acquisitions, disposition of property, and succession.* (p. 362)

"Military power must not interfere in the civil administration." *Provincial governors have nothing to do with the army; and they may only use it against the enemies of the state, and not against the citizen who is subject to the justice of the state.* (p. 364)

"Magistrates are irremovable, and these important offices can only be vacated by the death of the holder, his voluntary resignation, or a legal forfeiture."[8] (p. 356)

"The King, in cases which concern him, pleads against his subjects in his tribunals. It has happened that he has been ordered to pay a tithe on the fruits of his gardens, etc." (pp. 367 *et seq.*)

If the French examine themselves in good faith and with the passions quieted, they will feel that this is enough, *and perhaps more than enough*, for a nation too noble to be a slave, and too spirited to be free.

Shall we say that these beautiful laws were not observed? In this case, it was the fault of the French, and there is no more hope of liberty for them, for when a people does not know how to take advantage of its own fundamental laws, it is no use looking for others: it is a sign that it is not suited to liberty or that it is irredeemably corrupt.

But in rebutting these sinister ideas, I will cite, on the excellence of the French constitution, a testimony irrefutable from every point of view: that of a great politician and an ardent republican—that of Machiavelli.

> "There have been," he says, "many kings and very few of them good. I mean among the absolute sovereigns, among whom are not to be reckoned the kings of Egypt when that country, in the remotest ages, was governed by laws; nor those of Sparta; nor those of France in modern times, the government of this kingdom being, to our knowledge, the one most tempered by laws."[9]
>
> "The kingdom of France," he says elsewhere, "is happy and tranquil because the King is subject to an infinitude of laws which guarantee the security of the people. The one who constituted this government[10] wanted Kings to dispose of the army and treasury at their will; but in other cases, they were subjugated under the laws."[11]

8 Why bother declaiming so strongly against the venality of the offices of the magistracy? Venality should be considered only as a means to hereditary benefit, and thus the problem is reduced to knowing whether, in a country like France, or in one such as France has been for two or three centuries, justice could be administered better than by hereditary magistrates? The question is very difficult to resolve; the enumeration of inconveniences is a misleading argument. What is bad in a constitution, what must even destroy it, is, in fact, still as much a part of it as what is best in it. I am reminded of the passage in Cicero: *Nimia potestas est tribunorum, quis negat,* ["the power of the tribunes is excessive, who would deny it?"] etc. *De Legibus*, III. 10.

9 *Discourses on Livy*, book I, ch. LVIII.

10 I should like to know him.

11 *Discourses on Livy*, I, XVI.

Who would not be struck to see from what point of view this powerful mind contemplated the fundamental laws of the French monarchy three centuries ago?

The French have been spoiled on this point by the English. They told them, without believing it, that France was a slave; as they told them that Shakespeare was better than Racine; and the French believed them. Even the honest judge Blackstone, towards the end of his Commentaries, with a smirk, placed on an equal footing France and Turkey: about which one must say, like Montaigne: *the impudence of this coupling cannot be ridiculed too much.*

But these English, when they made their revolution, such as it was, did they suppress kingship or the House of Lords to give themselves liberty? Not at all. Rather, they drew the declaration of their rights from their ancient constitution resurrected.

There is no Christian nation in Europe that is not by right *free* or *free enough*. There is none which does not have, in the purest examples of its legislation, all the elements of the constitution which suits it. But we must, above all, avoid the enormous mistake of believing that liberty is something absolute, not admitting of more or less. Remember the two jars of Jupiter; instead of good and evil, let us call them repose and freedom. Jupiter casts the lot of nations; *more to one and less to the other*: man counts for nothing in this distribution.

Another most catastrophic error is to attach oneself too rigidly to ancient monuments. They must undoubtedly be respected; but above all, we must consider what jurists call the *last state*. Every free constitution is by nature variable, and variable in proportion as it is free;[12] to want to bring it back to its rudiments without losing something is a fool's errand.

All this serves to establish that the French sought to surpass human power; that these disorderly efforts are leading them into slavery; that they only needed to know what they possessed, and that if they are suited to a greater degree of freedom than the one they enjoyed seven years ago (which is not at all clear), they have in their hands, in all the monuments of their history and their legislation, all that is necessary to make them the honour and the envy of Europe.[13]

12 "All human governements, particularly those of mixed frame, are in continual fluctuation." Hume, *History of England*, Charles I, ch. L.

13 A man whose personality and opinions I respect equally (M. Mallet du Pan), and who does not share my opinion on the old French constitution, has taken the trouble of developing part of his ideas in an interesting letter, for which I am infinitely grateful. He objects, among other things, that *the book of the French magistrates, quoted in this chapter, would have been burned under the reign of Louis*

But if the French are made for monarchy, and if it is only a question of establishing the monarchy on its true footings, what error, what fatality, what disastrous prejudice could estrange them from their legitimate King?

Hereditary succession is, in a monarchy, something so precious that every other consideration must yield before it. The greatest crime that a French royalist can commit is to see in Louis XVIII anything but his King, and to diminish the favour with which the King must be surrounded by discussing unfavourably the qualities or actions of the man. The Frenchman who would not blush to look back on the past in search of real or imagined wrongs would be very vile and guilty! The accession to the throne is a new birth: we count only from that moment.

If there is a commonplace in morality, it is that power and greatness corrupt man, and the best kings were those whom adversity has tested. Why, then, would the French deprive themselves of the advantage of being governed by a prince trained in the terrible school of misfortune? How many reflections the last six years must have provided him! how far he is from intoxication with power! how inclined he must be to reign gloriously by any means! by what holy ambition he must be penetrated! What prince in the world could have more motives, more desires, more means to bind the wounds of France!

Have the French not tested the blood of the Capets long enough? They know from eight centuries' experience that this blood is good; why change? The chief of this great family showed himself in his declaration to be loyal, generous, deeply infused with religious truth; no one begrudges him his abundance of natural intelligence and knowledge. There was a time, perhaps, when it was well that the King be illiterate; but in this century, when we believe in books, a literate King is an advantage. What is more important is that he cannot be presumed to hold to any of those exaggerated ideas capable of alarming the French. Who could forget that Koblenz

XIV and Louis XV, as an attempt against the fundamental laws of the monarchy and against the rights of the monarch. — I believe it: just as M. Delolme's book would have been burned in London (perhaps along with the author), under the reign of Henry VIII or his rude daughter.

When one has taken a position on great questions, with full knowledge of the cause, he rarely changes his opinion. Nevertheless, though I distrust my prejudices as much as I should; yet I am sure of my good faith. It will be noted that I have not cited any contemporary authority in this chapter, for fear that the most respectable might appear suspect. As for the magistrates who authored the *Développement des principes fondamentaux, etc.*, if I have used their work, it is because I prefer not to do what has been done, and because these gentlemen have mentioned certain records, and this was exactly what I needed.

was displeased with him? This does him great honour. In his declaration, he pronounced the word *liberty*; and if anyone objects that this word was not more emphasized, it may be answered that a King must not speak the language of revolution. A solemn discourse addressed to his people must be distinguished by a certain sobriety of designs and expression that has nothing in common with the haste of a private individual. When the King of France has said that *the French constitution subjects the laws to the forms it has consecrated, and the sovereign himself to observance of the laws in order to protect the legislator's wisdom against seductive traps and to defend the subjects'* liberty *against the abuses of authority,* he has said everything, since he has promised *liberty through the constitution.* The King must not speak like a Parisian tribune. If he has discovered that it is wrong to speak of liberty as something absolute, that it is, on the contrary, something admitting of more and less; and that the art of the legislator is not to make the people *free*, but *free enough*, he has discovered a great truth, and he must be praised rather than blamed for his restraint. A famous Roman, at the moment when he restored liberty to a people most suited to it, and most anciently free, advised this people: *libertate modice utendum* ["to use their liberty with restraint"].[14] What should he have said to the French? Surely the King, in speaking soberly of liberty, was thinking less of his own interests than of those of the French.

The constitution, the King continues, *prescribes the conditions for the establishment of taxes, in order to assure the people that the taxes which they pay are necessary for the health of the state.* The King, therefore, has no right to impose them arbitrarily, and this avowal alone excludes despotism.

It entrusts the highest body of the magistracy with the registration of laws, so that they may see to their execution and enlighten the monarch's conviction if it should be deceived. Here is the registration of laws given into the hands of the higher magistrates; here is the right of remonstrance consecrated. Now, wherever a great body of hereditary—or at least irremovable—magistrates have the constitutional right to warn the monarch, to enlighten his conviction, and to complain of abuses, there is no despotism.

It places the fundamental laws under the safeguard of the King and the three orders in order to prevent revolution, the greatest calamity that can afflict peoples.

There is, therefore, a constitution, since the constitution is only the collection of fundamental laws, and the King cannot touch these laws; if he should try, the three orders would have the *veto* over him, as each of them has over the other two.

14 Livy, XXXIV, 49.

And one would surely be misguided in accusing the King of having spoken too vaguely, for this vagueness is precisely the proof of high wisdom. The King would have acted very imprudently if he had laid down limits preventing himself from advancing or retreating: he was inspired in reserving to himself a certain latitude of execution. The French will agree one day: they will admit that the King has promised all that he could.

Was Charles II better off for having adhered to the propositions of the Scots? He was told, as was Louis XVIII: "We must live in the present; we must be flexible": *it is a folly to sacrifice a crown to save the hierarchy.* He believed it and acted very badly. The King of France is wiser: how are the French so obstinate as to refuse him justice?

If this prince had been foolish enough to propose a new constitution to the French, then one could have accused him of presenting a perfidious vagueness; for in so doing he would have said nothing: if he had proposed a work of his own, there would have been an outcry against him, and this outcry would have been well founded. By what right, in effect, could he have made himself to be obeyed once he abandoned the old laws? Is not arbitrariness a common domain to which everyone has an equal right? There is not a single young man in France who would not point out the defects of this new work and propose corrections. Let the matter be thoroughly examined, and it will be seen that as soon as the King had abandoned the old constitution, he would have had but one more thing to say: *I will do whatever you wish.* It is to this indecent and absurd phrase that the King's most beautiful orations would have been reduced, once translated into clear language. Are we to be taken seriously when we blame the King for not having proposed to the French a new revolution? Since the insurrection began the dreadful misfortunes of his family, he has seen three constitutions accepted, sworn to, and solemnly consecrated. The first two lasted but a moment, and the third does not exist except in name. Should the King have proposed five or six to his subjects and let them take their pick? Certainly, the three attempts cost them dear enough, so that no sensible man should venture to propose another. But this new proposition, which would be folly on the part of an individual, would be, on the part of the King, a folly and a crime.

However he had conducted himself, the King could not please everyone. There would have been complaints in not publishing any declaration; there were complaints in publishing such as he did; there would have been complaints in any other case. Mired in doubt, he did well to stick to principles and to offend only passion and prejudice in saying that *the French constitution would be for him the ark of the covenant.* If the French examine this declaration with cool heads, I am much mistaken if they should not find there something for which to respect the King. In the terrible circumstances in which he found himself, nothing would have been more attractive than the temptation to compromise his principles to reconquer the throne. So many people have said and believed that the King lost in persisting in old ideas! It would have seemed so natural to listen to proposals for accommodation! Above all, it would have been so easy to accede to these proposals, preserving the ulterior motive to return to the old prerogative, without disloyalty, but relying solely on the force of things, to where it required much frankness, much nobility, and much courage to say to the French: "I cannot make you happy; I can, I must reign only through the constitution; I shall not touch the ark of the Lord; I am waiting for you to come to your senses; I await your apprehension of this truth so simple, so evident, and that you nevertheless persist in rejecting; that is to say, *with the same constitution, I can give you a completely different regime*."

Oh! how wise was the King when he said to the French that *their ancient and wise constitution was for him the holy ark, and that he was forbidden to touch it with a reckless hand*. He adds, however, *that he wishes to restore to it all purity which time had corrupted, and all vigour which time had weakened*. Once again, these words are inspired; for here one clearly reads what is in man's power as separate from what belongs only to God. There is not in this statement, too little contemplated, a single word which should not recommend the King to the French.

It is to be hoped that this impetuous nation, which knows to return to the truth only once it has exhausted error, should at last wish to see a very palpable truth; it is that it is the dupe and the victim of a small number of men who place themselves between it and its legitimate sovereign, from whom it can expect only good deeds. Let us put forth a worst-case scenario. *The King will allow the sword of justice to fall on some parricides; he will punish by humiliation some nobles who have displeased him*: so? what does it matter to you, a good labourer, an industrious artisan, a peaceful citizen, whoever you may be, to whom heaven has given obscurity and happiness? Recall, then, that you, with your fellows, form almost the whole nation; and that the whole people suffer all the evils of anarchy only because a handful of reprobates vilifies the King whom they themselves fear.

Never will a people have let slip a better chance if they continue to reject their King, since they expose themselves to being ruled by force, instead of crowning their legitimate sovereign themselves. What a gesture it would be to this prince! with what efforts of zeal and love would the King seek to reward his people's fidelity! The national will would always be before his eyes to animate him in the great enterprises, in the dutiful work which the regeneration of France requires of its chief, and every moment of his life would be consecrated to the happiness of the French.

But if they persist in rejecting their King, do they know what their fate will be? The French today are sufficiently matured by misfortune to grasp a hard truth; amid the spasms of their fanatical freedom, the detached observer is often tempted to exclaim, like Tiberius: *O homines ad servitutem natos* ["O men born for slavery"]! There are, as we know, many kinds of courage, and surely the Frenchman does not possess them all. Intrepid before the enemy, but not before authority, even the most unjust. Nothing equals the patience of this people who call themselves free. In five years, it was made to accept three constitutions and the revolutionary government. Tyrants succeeded one another, and always the people obeyed. Never have we seen them succeed in any effort to escape from their impotence. Their masters have gone so far as to smite them with mockery. They told them: *You think that you do not want this law, but rest assured, you want it. If you dare to refuse it, we will shoot you with grapeshot to punish you for not wanting what you want.* — And so they did.

It is no matter that the French nation is no longer under the terrible yoke of Robespierre. Certainly, she may well *congratulate* herself, but cannot boast of having escaped this tyranny; and it is not clear whether the days of her servitude were more shameful for her than those of her enfranchisement.

The history of 9 Thermidor[15] is brief: *A few scoundrels killed a few scoundrels.*

If not for this family feud, the French would still be groaning under the sceptre of the Committee of Public Safety.

And at this very moment, do a small number of seditious men not still speak of putting one of the Orléans family on the throne?

The French now lack only the reproach of putting the son of a tortured man on a pedestal instead of the brother of a martyr. And yet, nothing promises them that they will not suffer this humiliation if they do not hasten to return to their legitimate sovereign.

They have given such proof of patience that there is no kind of degradation that does not await them. The great lesson—I do not say for the French people, who more than any other people in the world will always accept and never choose their masters, but for the small number of good Frenchmen whom circumstances will render influential—is to neglect nothing in wresting the nation from these degrading fluctuations by de-

15 [The parliamentary revolt on 9 Thermidor, year II (July 27, 1794) against Robespierre, in response to his attacks against the Committee of Public Safety and Committee of General Security for the excesses of the Terror.]

livering it into the arms of its King. He is a man, no doubt, but do they hope to be governed by an angel? He is a man, but today we are sure he knows this, and that counts for very much. If the wish of the French was to restore him to the throne of his fathers, he would be wedded to his nation, which would find everything in him: goodness, justice, love, gratitude, and incontestable talents matured in the unforgiving school of misfortune.[16]

The French have appeared to pay little attention to the words of peace which he has addressed to them. They did not praise his statement, they even criticized it, and have probably forgotten it; but one day they will do him justice: one day posterity will call this statement a model of wisdom, frankness, and royal style.

The duty of every good Frenchman at this moment is to work tirelessly to direct public opinion in favour of the King, and to present all his acts whatsoever in a favourable light. It is here that the royalists must examine themselves with the utmost severity and must harbour no illusions. I am not a Frenchman, I know nothing of their intrigues, I am not personally acquainted with them. But suppose that a French royalist told me: "I am ready to shed my blood for the King; however, without derogating from the loyalty I owe him, I cannot help but blame him, etc." I should answer to this man what his conscience will doubtless tell him more authoritatively than I: *You are lying to the world and to yourself; if you were capable of sacrificing your life for the King, you would sacrifice your prejudices for him. Besides, he does not need your life, but your prudence, your measured zeal, your passive devotion, even* (to silence all conjectures) *your very indulgence; keep your life, which he does not need at this moment, and render him the service he does need. Do you believe that the most heroic are those who thunder forth in the gazettes? The most obscure, on the contrary, can be the most effective and the most sublime. This is not a matter of your pride; please your conscience and Him who gave it to you.*

Like those threads that a child at play could snap but nevertheless, when joined, form a cable that can support a great vessel's anchor, so a host of insignificant critiques can muster a formidable army. How much service would we render to the King of France in combating those prejudices which have somehow developed, and linger on? Have men who profess the age of reason not reproached the King for his inaction? Have others not arrogantly compared him to Henry IV, observing that this great prince could find weapons other than intrigues and declamations to regain his throne? But since we are being witty, why not reproach the King for not having conquered Germany and Italy like Charlemagne and for not living

16 I shall postpone until chapter X the interesting discussion on amnesty.

nobly there while waiting for the French to listen to reason?

As for the more or less numerous party which utters great cries against the monarchy and the monarch, hate is not nearly the entirety of the feeling that animates it, and it seems that this mixed sentiment is worth analysing.

There is no man of intelligence in France who does not despise himself to some extent. National ignominy weighs on all hearts (for never was a people despised by more despicable masters); we need to console ourselves, and good citizens do this in their own way. But the vile and corrupt man, stranger to all elevated ideas, avenges himself for his past and present abjection by contemplating, with that ineffable pleasure that comes from baseness, the spectacle of humiliated greatness. To raise himself up in his own eyes, he looks down on the King of France, and he is pleased with his stature in comparing himself to this overturned colossus. Imperceptibly, by a feat of his own disordered imagination, he comes to look upon this great fall as his own work; he invests himself alone with all the power of the republic; he rebukes the King; he arrogantly calls him *a pretended Louis XVIII*; and, lashing out at the monarchy in his furious pamphlets, if he succeeds in frightening a few *Chouans*, he elevates himself to among La Fontaine's heroes: *I am thus a thunderbolt of war.*

We must also take into account the fear that howls against the King, lest his return should bring another rifle shot.

People of France, let yourself not be seduced by the sophisms of private interest, vanity, or cowardice. Listen not to the reasoners any longer: there has been only too much reason in France, and *reasoning has banished reason.* Deliver yourself without fear and reservation to the infallible instinct of your conscience. Do you want to raise yourself up in your own eyes? Do you want to acquire the right to self-esteem? Do you want to perform a sovereign act? Recall your sovereign.

I am perfectly foreign to France, which I have never seen, and can expect nothing from its King, whom I will never know—if I make mistakes, the French can at least read them without anger, as altogether impartial errors.

But what are we, weak and blind human beings! and what is this quavering light that we call *reason*? When we have mustered all the probabilities, questioned history, satisfied all doubts and all interests, we may still embrace only a deceptive cloud instead of the truth. What decree has He pronounced, this great Being before whom nothing is great; what decrees has He pronounced on the King, his dynasty, his family, France, and Europe? Where and when will the shocks come to an end, and with how many misfortunes must we yet buy tranquillity? Is it to build[17] that He has overthrown, or are his rigours without reprieve? Alas! a dark cloud covers the future, and no eye can pierce this darkness. However, all things announce that the established order of things in France cannot last, and that invincible nature must restore the monarchy. So, whether our wishes are fulfilled or inexorable Providence has decided otherwise, it is curious and even useful to examine, never losing sight of the history and nature of man, how these great changes work, and what role the multitude may play in an event whose date alone seems doubtful.

17 [Maistre's original manuscript has *détruire* here, corrected subsequently to *construire*.]

Chapter IX: How Will the Counter-Revolution Happen, If It Comes?

In forming theories on the counter-revolution, too often we make the mistake of reasoning as if this counter-revolution should and could only be the result of popular deliberation. *The people fear,* it is said; *the people want, the people will never consent; it is not acceptable to the people, etc.* What a pity—the people count for nothing in revolutions, or at least they enter into them only as a passive instrument. Four or five people, perhaps, will give to France a King. Letters from Paris will announce to the provinces that France has a King, and the provinces will cry out: *Long live the King*! In Paris itself, all the inhabitants, less perhaps a twentieth, will learn, on waking, that they have a King. *Is it possible*? they will exclaim; *what a rarity! Does anyone know by what gate he will enter? It would be good, perhaps, to rent windows in advance, for one will suffocate with the crowds.* If the monarchy is restored, the people will no more decree its restoration than they decreed its destruction, or the establishment of the revolutionary government.

I beg that one think well upon these reflections, and I recommend them especially to those who believe counter-revolution[1] impossible, because there are too many Frenchmen attached to the Republic, and a change would cause too many to suffer. *Scilicet is superis labor est* ["surely this is the work of the gods"]![2] We can certainly dispute whether the Republic has the support of the majority, but it matters not at all: enthusiasm and fanaticism are not enduring states. Human nature soon tires of this degree of enthusiasm; so that even supposing that a people, and especially the French people, may want something for a long time—it is at least certain that they will not be able to want it for a long time passionately. On the

1 [Maistre's original manuscript has *révolution* here, corrected subsequently to *contre-révolution*.]

2 [Vergil, *Aeneid* IV, 379]

contrary, the fever having broken, despondency, apathy, and indifference always follow great outbursts of enthusiasm. This is the case with France, which desires nothing more passionately than repose. If we suppose that the Republic has the support of the majority in France (which is no doubt false), what does it matter? When the King presents himself, surely voices will not be counted, and no one will stir; first of all, because he who prefers the Republic to monarchy prefers repose to the Republic; and furthermore, because those opposed to royalty will not be able to unite.

In politics as in mechanics, theories are misleading if they fail to take into consideration the different qualities of the materials that make up *the machines*. At first glance, for example, this proposition seems true: *The prior consent of the French is necessary for the restoration of the monarchy*. Yet nothing is more false. Let us put aside theories, and account for the facts.

A courier, having arrived at Bordeaux, Nantes, Lyon, etc., brings news that *the King has been acknowledged in Paris; that some faction or other* (whether named or not) *has seized power, and has declared that it possesses it only in the name of the King: that a courier has been despatched to the sovereign, who is expected forthwith, and that all around, the white cockade is worn.*[3] Rumour seizes upon this news, and saddles it with a thousand impressive circumstances. What shall be done? To give the Republic a sporting chance, I grant it a majority, and even a corps of republican troops. These troops may, from the first, assume a lively attitude; but that very day they will want to eat, and will begin to detach themselves from the power that no longer pays them. Every officer who does not enjoy any regard, and who feels the bite in any case, sees quite clearly that the first to cry *long live the King!* shall be a great man: self-esteem sketches for him, with a seductive pencil, the image of a general in the armies of *His Most Christian Majesty*, shining with decorations and looking down from the height of his grandeur at those men who would formerly have summoned him before the municipal court. These ideas are so simple, so natural, that they can escape no one: every officer feels it; and it follows that they suspect one other. Fear and distrust produce deliberation and detachment. The soldier, no longer inspired by his officer, grows even more discouraged; the bond of discipline receives this inexplicable blow, this magic blow that suddenly undoes it. One man turns his eyes to the royal paymaster who approaches; another takes advantage of the opportunity to re-join his family: command or obedience are impossible; they no longer form one body.

It is quite another story among the townspeople: they come, they go; they dispute, they question: everyone fears the one he has need of; doubt

3 [Emblem of the Jacobites.]

consumes hours, and minutes are decisive: everywhere audacity runs up against prudence; the old man lacks determination, the young man counsel: on one side are terrible perils, on the other a certain amnesty and likely favours. Moreover, where are the means to resist? where are the trustworthy leaders? There is no danger in repose, and the slightest move may be an irreparable mistake: we must wait. We wait; but the next day we receive notice that such-and-such a fortified town has opened its gates; all the more reason not to rush into anything. Soon we learn that the news was false; but two other cities which believed it to be true have set the example, believing what they had heard, they have just submitted, and have defined the course of the first, which had not thought of such a thing. The governor of this place presented to the King the keys to *his good city of*… He is the first officer who had the honour to receive the King in a citadel of his realm. The King created him marshal of France on the spot; an immortal honour has covered his escutcheon with *numberless fleurs-de-lis*; his name is forevermore the most celebrated in France. Every minute the royalist movement is strengthened; soon it becomes irresistible. LONG LIVE THE KING! cries love and fidelity, at the height of joy: LONG LIVE THE KING! replies the republican hypocrite, at the height of terror. So what? there is only one cry. — And the King is crowned.

Citizens! this is how counter-revolutions are made. God, having reserved to Himself the formation of sovereignties, warns us of this by never confiding to the multitude the choice of their masters. He employs them in those great movements which decide the fate of empires only as a passive instrument. They never get what they wish: they always accept, never choose. We may even notice that it is an *affectation* of Providence (if I may say so) that the people's efforts to attain an object are precisely the means Providence uses to take it from them. Thus, the Roman people gave themselves masters in thinking that they were resisting the aristocracy in the wake of Caesar. This is the image of all popular insurrections. In the French Revolution, the people have continually been enslaved, abused, ruined, and mutilated by all factions; and the factions in their turn, playthings one and all, despite all their efforts, have continually drifted towards the threatening rocks on which they will at last founder.

But if one wishes to know the probable result of the French Revolution, it suffices to examine by what all the factions have been united; all have desired the debasement, even the destruction, of the universal Church and the monarchy; *whence it follows* that all their efforts will only result in the exaltation of Christianity and the monarchy.

All men who have written or reflected on history have admired this secret force that sports with human plans. He was one of us, that great captain of antiquity, who honoured this force as an intelligent and free power, and who undertook nothing without recommending himself to it.[4]

But it is especially in the establishment and overthrow of sovereignties that the working of Providence shines forth in the most striking manner. Not only do the people enter en masse into these great movements, but they do so like wood and ropes employed by a machinist; but even their leaders are such only to the untrained eye: in fact, they are ruled just as they rule the people. Those men who, taken together, seem to be the tyrants of the multitude, are themselves tyrannized by two or three men, who are tyrannized by one. And if this single individual could and would tell his secret, we would see that he does not himself know how he seized power; that his influence is a greater mystery to himself than to others, and that circumstances which he could neither foresee nor bring about have done everything for him and without him.

Who would have told the proud Henry VI that a peasant girl[5] would snatch from him the sceptre of France? The vapid explanations given of this great event do not deprive it of its wonder; and although it has been dishonoured twice—first by the absence and then by the prostitution of talent[6]—it has nonetheless remained the only subject in French history truly worthy of the epic muse.

Do we believe that the *arm* which once used such a weak instrument *will be shortened*, and that the Supreme Author of empires should accept the advice of the French to give them a King? No, He will yet choose, as He has always done, *the weakest to confound the strongest*. He does not need foreign legions, He does not need the *coalition*; and as He has maintained the integrity of France in spite of the counsels and the force of so many princes, *who are before His eyes as if they were not*, when the time has come, He will restore the French monarchy in spite of its enemies; He will drive out these noisy insects *pulveris exigui jactu* ["by sprinkling a little dust"]:[7] the King will come, he will see, and he will conquer.

Then we will be astonished at the profound impotence of those men who appeared so powerful. Today, it behoves the wise men to warn of this judg-

4 *Nihil rerum humanarum sine Deorum numine geri putabat Timoleon; itaque suae domi sacellum* Αὐτοματίας *constituerat, idque sanctissime colebat* ["Timoleon thought that nothing in human affairs is beyond the will of the gods; and so he set up a shrine at his home, and worshiped at it most scrupulously"]. Cornenlius Nepos, *Life of Timoleon*, ch. IV.

5 [Joan of Arc, who prophesied that not Henry but Charles VII, whom she aided, would be crowned king at Reims.]

6 [By Chapelain and Voltaire, respectively.]

7 [Vergil, *Georgics*, IV, line 87]

ment, and to be sure, before experience has proved it, that the rulers of France possess only artificial and fleeting power, the very excess of which proves its nothingness; *that they were neither planted nor sown; that their trunk has not struck roots into the earth, and that a gentle breeze shall carry them off like straw.*[8]

It is, therefore, in vain that so many writers insist on the difficulties in restoring the monarchy; it is in vain that they frighten the French with the consequences of a counter-revolution; and when they conclude from these difficulties that the French, fearing them, will never suffer the restoration of the monarchy, they reason very poorly; for the French will not deliberate—perhaps it is from the hand of a maid that they shall receive a King.

No nation can give itself a government: only when this or that right exists in its constitution[9] and is unrecognized or suppressed, can certain men, aided by certain circumstances, brush aside the obstacles and make recognized the rights of the people: human power extends no further.

What's more, although Providence is by no means embarrassed by the cost to the French of having a King, it is nonetheless important to observe that the writers who frighten the French with the misfortunes that would accompany the restoration of the monarchy are certainly in error or bad faith.

8 Isaiah, 40:24.

9 I mean its *natural* constitution; for its *written* constitution is only paper.

Chapter X:
Of the Pretended Dangers of a Counter-Revolution

I. General Considerations.

It is an all-too-common fallacy of this age to insist on the dangers of a counter-revolution in order to establish that we must not return to the monarchy.

A great number of works intended to persuade the French to hold to the Republic are but a development of this idea. The authors of these works insist on the evils inseparable from revolutions; then, observing that the monarchy cannot be restored in France without a new revolution, they conclude that the Republic must be maintained.

This stupendous fallacy, whether derived from fear or the desire to deceive, merits careful discussion.

Words are the source of almost all errors. It has become customary to give the name *counter-revolution* to any movement which must kill the Revolution; and because this movement will be contrary to the other, one would have to conclude that it is its exact inverse.

But would one perhaps argue that the return from illness to health is as painful as the transition from health to illness? and that the monarchy, overthrown by fiends, must be restored by their ilk? Ah! would that those who peddle this fallacy do it justice in their heart of hearts! They know well enough that the friends of religion and the monarchy are incapable of any of the excesses with which their enemies are defiled; they know well enough that in a worst-case scenario, and taking into account all human frailties, the oppressed party has a thousand times more virtue than their oppressors! They know well enough that the first party knows not how to defend or avenge itself: often enough they are openly mocked for it.

In order to accomplish the French Revolution, it was necessary to overthrow religion, outrage morality, violate all propriety, and commit every crime: for this diabolical work it was necessary to employ so many vicious men that perhaps never before have so many vices acted in concert to do any evil whatsoever. On the contrary, to restore order, the King will summon all virtues; he will wish to do so, no doubt; but, by the very nature of things, he will be forced to do so. His most pressing interest will be to combine justice with mercy; worthy men will come of their own volition to place themselves in posts where they can be useful; and religion, lending its sceptre to politics, will give it the strength that it can draw only from this august sister.

I have no doubt that a host of men should ask to be shown the basis of these magnificent hopes; but do we, therefore, believe that the political world works haphazardly, that it is not organized, directed, and animated by the same wisdom that manifests in the physical world? The guilty hands which overthrow a state necessarily produce tears of pain; for no free agent can oppose the plans of the Creator without attracting, in the sphere of his own activity, evils proportionate to the magnitude of the crime; and this law belongs more to the goodness of the Supreme Being than to His justice.

But when man works to restore order, he associates himself with the Author of order; he is favoured by *nature*, that is, by the ensemble of secondary forces which are the ministers of Divinity. His action has something of the divine in it, being at once gentle and imperious; it forces nothing, and nothing resists it: in arranging, it restores health: as it acts, we see disquiet calmed, that painful agitation which is the effect and the symptom of disorder; just as, under the hand of the skilled surgeon, it is apparent by the cessation of pain that the dislocated joint has been put right.

Frenchmen, it is to the sound of infernal songs, the blasphemies of atheism, the cries of death, and the prolonged moans of slaughtered innocence; it is by the light of the fires, on the debris of throne and altar, anointed with the blood of the best kings and of an innumerable host of other victims; it is in contempt of morality and the public faith; it is in the midst of every crime that your seducers and tyrants have founded what they call *your liberty*.

It is in the name *du Dieu TRÈS-GRAND ET TRÈS-BON*,[1] following the men He loves and inspires, and under the influence of His creative power, that you will return to your old constitution, and that a king will give you the only thing you should wisely desire, *liberty through the monarch*.

What deplorable blindness makes you persist in struggling painfully against that power which annuls all your efforts to warn you of its pres-

1 [The French rendering of the Latin ecclesiastical formula *Deo Optimo Maximo* ("to God most Good and Great").]

ence? You are powerless only because you have dared to separate yourself from it, and even to oppose it; the moment you act in concert with it, you will participate in some way in its nature; all obstacles will be levelled before you, and you will laugh at the childish fears that disturb you today. All parts of the political machine having a natural tendency towards the place assigned to them, and this tendency, which is divine, will favour all the efforts of the King; and order being the natural element of man, you shall find the happiness that you vainly seek in disorder. The Revolution has made you suffer because it was the work of every vice, and the vices are very justly the executioners of man. For the contrary reason, the return to monarchy, far from producing the evils that you fear for the future, will put an end to those that are consuming you today; all your efforts will be positive; you will destroy only destruction.

Rid yourselves, for once, of these distressing doctrines which have dishonoured our century and lost France. You have already learned to recognize the preachers of these fatal dogmas for what they are; but the impression they have made on you has not been effaced. In all your plans for creation and restoration, you forget naught but God: they have separated you from Him: it is only by an effort of reasoning that you raise your thoughts to the inexhaustible source of all existence. You want to see only man—his actions so weak, so dependent, so circumscribed; his will so corrupt, so wavering—and the existence of a superior cause is for you only a theory. Yet it presses in on you, it surrounds you: you feel it, and the whole universe announces it to you. When it is told you that without it you shall have the power only to destroy, this is no vain theory you are sold, it is a practical truth founded on the experience of all ages, and on the knowledge of human nature. Examine history, and you will see no political creation—what am I saying! you will see no institution whatsoever, if it has any strength and duration, which does not rest on a divine idea; it matters not what its nature is, for there is no entirely false religious system. So speak to us no more of the difficulties and misfortunes that alarm you in the consequences of what you call *counter-revolution*. All the misfortunes you have suffered are your own doing; why should you not have been maimed by the ruins of the edifice which you have toppled over on to yourselves? Reconstruction is another order of things; you have only to return to the path that can lead you there. It is not by the path of nothingness that you will create anything.

Oh! how guilty are those deceitful or fainthearted writers who permit themselves to frighten the people with this vain scarecrow called *counter-revolution*! who, while agreeing that the Revolution was a terrible scourge, nevertheless maintain that it is impossible to go back. Shall we say that the evils of the Revolution have passed, and that the French have arrived at a safe harbour? The reign of Robespierre has so crushed this people, so beaten down its imagination, that it considers as endurable and almost as happy any state of affairs other than uninterrupted slaughter. During the height of the Terror, foreigners remarked that all letters from France recounting the frightful scenes of this cruel age ended with these words: *At present it is tranquil*; that is to say, *the executioners are resting; they are recovering their strength; in the meantime, everything is fine*. This feeling survived the infernal regime that produced it. The Frenchman, paralysed by terror and discouraged by foreign policy errors, has shut himself up in an egoism which allows him to see only himself and his own time and place: a hundred places in France play host to murder; no matter, for it is not he who has been pillaged or massacred; if any one of those attacks has been committed on his street, near his house, what does it matter? The moment has passed; *now all is quiet*: he will double his locks and think no more of it: in a word, every Frenchman is happy enough on any given day when he is not being killed.

Nevertheless, the laws are without force, and the government recognizes its impotence to execute them: the most infamous crimes multiply in all quarters: the revolutionary demon proudly raises its head, the constitution is no more than a spider's web, and the regime permits itself horrible outrages. Marriage is no more than a legal prostitution; there is no more paternal authority, no more fear of crime, no more refuge for indigence. Hideous suicides announce to the government the despair of the unfortunates who accuse it. The people are demoralized in the most frightening manner; and the abolition of religion, together with the total absence of public education, is preparing for France a generation the very thought of which makes one shudder.

Cowardly optimists! here is the order of things you fear to see change! Throw off, throw off your wretched lethargy! Instead of showing the people the imaginary evils which a change must produce, use your talents to make them desire the sweet and health-giving upheaval which will restore the King to his throne, and order to France.

Show us, men too preoccupied, show us these terrible evils that so menace you as to disgust you with the monarchy; do you not see that your republican institutions have no roots, and that they are only *placed* on your soil, as opposed to their antecedents, which were *planted* there? It took the axe to fell these; others will yield to a gust of wind and leave no trace. It is, no doubt, altogether different to deprive a parliamentary president of his hereditary rank, which was his property, than it is to remove from his bench a temporary judge who has no rank. The Revolution has caused so much suffering because it has destroyed so much; because it has brusquely and harshly violated all propriety, prejudice, and custom; all plebeian tyranny being reckless, insulting, and ruthless in its nature, that which brought about the French Revolution had to push these characteristics to excess; the universe has never seen a baser and more absolute tyranny.

Opinion is man's sore point: he cannot help but cry out when he is wounded here; this is what made the Revolution so painful, because it trampled underfoot all nobility of opinion. Now, when the restoration of monarchy should cause the same number of men the same real privations, there would always be an immense difference in that it would not destroy any dignity; for there is no dignity in France, for the same reason that there is no sovereignty.

But even if we considered only physical privations, the difference would be no less striking. The usurping power has immolated the innocent; the King will pardon the guilty: the one has abolished legitimate property, the other will consider whether to abolish illegitimate property. The one has taken for its motto: *diruit, aedificat, mutat quadrata rotundis* ["it destroys, it builds, it changes square things into round"].[2] After seven years of effort, it has not yet been able to organize a primary school or a country festival: even its supporters mock its laws, its public offices, its institutions, its feasts, and even its vestments: the other, building on a foundation of truth, will not fumble about; an obscure force will preside over its actions; it will act only to restore: for all orderly action torments only evil.

Furthermore, it is a great error to imagine that the people have something to lose in the restoration of the monarchy; for the people have won in the general upheaval nothing but an idea: *they are all entitled to any position*, it is said; what is the significance? The significance lies in knowing what these positions are worth. These positions, over which so much fuss is made, and which are offered to the people as a great conquest, in fact count for nothing in the tribunal of public opinion. The military class itself, honourable in France above all others, has lost its lustre; it has no more nobility of opinion, and peace will lower it still further. The military are threatened with the restoration of the monarchy, and yet no one has a greater interest in its restoration than they. There is nothing so evident as the King's necessity of maintaining them at their post; and dependence upon them will, sooner or later, change this necessity of politics into the necessity of affection, respect, and gratitude. By an extraordinary combination of circumstances, there is nothing in the military that could shock the most royalist opinion. No one has the right to despise them, since they

2 [Horace, *Epistle I*, 100]

fight only for France: there is between them and the King no barrier of prejudice capable of hindering their mutual respect; he is a Frenchman first and foremost. Let them remember James II, during the battle at *La Hogue*,[3] applauding from the seashore the valour of those Englishmen who finished by dethroning him: could they doubt that the King was proud of their valour and saw them in his heart as the defenders of the integrity of his kingdom? Did he not publicly applaud this valour, regretting (it must be said) *that it was not employed for a better cause*? Did he not congratulate the brave men of Condé's army *for having conquered the hatreds that the deepest artifice had worked so long to nourish*?[4] The French soldiers, after their victories, have only one need: it is that legitimate sovereignty comes to legitimize their character; at present they are feared and despised. The most profound unconcern is their wage, and their fellow-citizens are the men most indifferent of all in the world to the triumphs of the army; they often go so far as to hate those victories which nourish the warlike temper of their masters. The restoration of the monarchy will suddenly grant to the military a high place in public opinion; talents will be on the way to eliciting a real dignity, an ever-increasing lustre which will be warrior's due, and which they shall hand down to their children; this pure glory, this tranquil brilliance, will be worth the honourable mentions, and the ostracism of forgetfulness which has succeeded the scaffold.

If we examine the question from a more general point of view, we will find that monarchy is, without fear of contradiction, the government that gives the greatest distinction to the largest number of people. In this kind of government, sovereignty possesses enough brilliance to communicate a part of it, with the necessary gradations, to a host of agents whom it distinguishes to a greater or lesser degree. Sovereignty is not as palpable in a republic as in monarchy; it is a purely moral concept, and its greatness is incommunicable: also, in republics, public offices are nothing outside the city where the government resides; and they are nothing insofar as they are occupied by members of the government; then it is the man who honours the office, not the office that honours the man; he does not shine forth as an *agent*, but as a *portion* of the sovereign.

We can see in the provinces that obey republics that public offices (except those reserved for members of the sovereign) raise men very little in the eyes of their peers, and are of almost no significance at all in public opin-

3 [During the Nine Years' War, when the Dutch and English fleet destroyed the French ships beached at La Hogue in 1692.]

4 Letter from the King to the Prince of Condé, January 3, 1797, printed in all the newspapers.

ion; for by its nature, a republic is the government which gives the most rights to the smallest number of men who are called the *sovereign*, and which takes the most away from all others who are called *subjects*.

The nearer a republic approaches pure democracy, the more striking this observation will be.

Recall that innumerable host of offices (even disregarding all those bought and sold) that the former government of France presented to universal ambition. The secular and regular clergy, the sword, the robe, finance, the administration, etc., doors open to all talents and all kinds of ambition! What incalculable gradations of personal distinction! Of this infinite number of places, none was, by law, placed above the aspirations of the ordinary citizen;[5] there were even an enormous quantity that were valuable properties, which really made the holder a *notable*, and belonged exclusively to the Third Estate.

That the highest positions were more difficult for the ordinary citizen to obtain was a very reasonable thing. There is too much movement in the state, and not enough subordination, when *all* have a claim to *everything*. Order demands that, in general, offices be graduated just as the condition of the citizens, and that talents, and sometimes even simply patronage, should surmount the barriers separating the different classes. In this way, there is emulation without humiliation, and movement without destruction; the distinction attached to an office is even produced, as the word implies, only by the greater or lesser difficulty of obtaining it.

If we object that these distinctions are bad, we change the nature of the question; but I say, if your offices do not elevate those who possess them, do not boast of giving them to everyone; for you shall not give them anything. If, on the contrary, offices are and must be distinctions, I repeat what no man of good faith can deny—that monarchy is the government which, by offices alone, and independently of the nobility, *distinguishes* the greatest number of men from the rest of their fellow citizens.

Moreover, one must not be the dupe of that ideal equality which is equality in words only. The soldier who has the privilege of speaking to his officer in a grossly informal tone is not, by that, his equal. An aristocracy of position, which could not at first be perceived in the general upheaval, is beginning to take shape; even the nobility is again taking up its indestructible influence. The army and navy are already commanded, in part, by gentlemen, or by pupils whom the old regime had ennobled by admitting

5 The famous law which excluded the Third Estate from military service could not be enforced; it was simply ministerial clumsiness which passion has deemed a fundamental law.

them to a noble profession. The Republic has even won its greatest successes by them. If the perhaps unfortunate delicacy of the French nobility had not sundered it from France, it would already command everywhere; and it is quite common to hear *that if the nobility had been willing, they would have been given all the offices.* Certainly, at the time of writing (January 4, 1797) the Republic would like to have on its ships the nobles whom it had massacred at Quiberon.[6]

The people, or the mass of citizens, have nothing to lose; and on the contrary, they have everything to gain from the restoration of the monarchy, which will bring back a host of real, lucrative, and even hereditary distinctions in place of the fleeting and undignified jobs that the Republic brings.

I have not insisted on the monetary compensation attached to these positions, since it is well known that the Republic pays poorly if it pays at all. It has produced only scandalous fortunes: vice alone has been enriched in its service.

I shall end this article with observations which (it seems to me) clearly prove that the danger we see in the counter-revolution lies precisely in delaying this great change.

The Bourbon family cannot be touched by the chiefs of the republic; it exists; its rights are visible, and its silence speaks louder, perhaps, than any possible manifesto.

It is an obvious truth that the French Republic, even since it has apparently softened its maxims, cannot have real allies. By its nature, it is the enemy of all governments; it tends to destroy them all; so that all have an interest in destroying it. Politics may no doubt give allies to the Republic;[7] but these alliances are unnatural, or, if you like, *France* has allies, but the *French Republic* has none.

Friends and enemies will always agree to give to France a King. The success of the English Revolution in the last century is often cited; but what a

6 [The disastrous battle of Quiberon saw 6,332 counter-revolutionary Chouans and émigrés captured on July 20, 1795. Of these, 430 were nobles, many of them veterans of Louis XVI's fleet, executed by Lazare Hoche after a promise to treat them as prisoners of war.]

7 *Scimus, et hanc veniam petimusque damusque vicissim;*
Sed non ut placidis coeant immitia, non ut
Serpentes avibus geminentur, tigribus agni.

["We know this, and this indulgence we seek and offer in turn;
But not so that the wild may rut with the tame, nor that
Serpents be united with birds, lambs with tigers."
Horace, *Ars Poetica*, 11–13]

This is what certain cabinets ought to say to the Europe that questions them.

difference! The monarchy was not overthrown in England. The monarch alone had disappeared to make way for another. The very blood of the Stuarts was on the throne; and it was from this that the new King acquired his right. This King of himself was a strong prince, with all the power of his House and his family connections. The government of England, moreover, posed no threat to other governments: it was a monarchy as before the Revolution: nevertheless, it would not have taken much for James II to regain his sceptre; had he only a little more good fortune or skill, it would not have escaped him; although England had a King; although religious prejudices united with political prejudices to exclude the Pretender; although the very location of this kingdom defended it against invasion; nevertheless, until the middle of this century, the danger of a second revolution weighed upon England. Everything depended, as we know, on the Battle of *Culloden*.[8]

In France, on the other hand, the government is not monarchical; it is, in fact, the enemy of all neighbouring monarchies; it is not a prince who commands; and if ever the state is attacked, there is no reason to think that the foreign relatives of the pentarchs[9] would raise troops to defend them. France will therefore be in habitual danger of civil war; and this danger will have two constant causes, for it shall have constantly to fear the just rights of the Bourbons, and the clever policy of the other powers, which might try to profit from circumstances. While the French throne is occupied by the legitimate sovereign, no prince in the world could think of seizing it; but while it is vacant, every royal ambition may covet and clash with it. Moreover, power is within anyone's grasp since it is face down in the dirt. An orderly government excludes an infinity of plots; but under the dominion of a false sovereignty, there are nothing but chimerical plots; all passions are unleashed, and all hopes are permitted. The cowards who rebuff the King for fear of civil war are preparing the very fuel for it. It is because they foolishly desire *repose and the constitution* that they will have neither repose nor the constitution. There is no perfect security for France in her current state. Only the King, and the legitimate King, in raising from his throne the sceptre of Charlemagne, can extinguish or disarm all hatreds, foil all sinister plots, order ambitions by ordering men, calm agitated minds, and suddenly raise that magical enclosure around power which is its real guardian.

8 [Where the Scottish Jacobite army of pretender Charles Edward Stuart was finally defeated in 1746, and their struggle to restore the deposed Stuart dynasty came to an end.]

9 [See note 3, p. 101]

There is still a thought which must constantly be kept before the eyes of those Frenchmen who are part of the establishment, and who, in their position, can influence the restoration of the monarchy. The most esteemed of these men must not forget that, sooner or later, they will be carried away by the force of circumstances; that time flies, and that hope of glory escapes them. That which they enjoy is a comparative glory: they have stopped the massacres; they have tried to dry the nation's tears: they shine because they have succeeded the greatest villains ever to defile the globe; but when a hundred causes together have raised the throne, *amnesty*, in the full sense of the term,[10] will be theirs; and their names, forever obscure, will remain enshrouded in oblivion. Let them never lose sight of the immortal halo that must surround the names of the monarchy's restorers. Each insurrection of the people against the nobles only ever results in the creation of new nobles; we see already how these new races will be formed, whose circumstances shall hasten their glory; and who, from the cradle, will be able to claim everything.

II. Of National Property.

The French are frightened of the restitution of national property; the King is accused of having not dared, in his declaration, to broach this delicate subject. One could say to a very large part of the nation: *what does it matter to you?* and perhaps this would not be such a bad response. But, so as not to appear to evade difficulties, it is better to observe that, with regard to national property, the visible interest of France in general, and even the well-understood interest of the buyers of these properties in particular, accords with the restoration of the monarchy. The brigandage exercised over these properties strikes even the most insensitive conscience. No one believes in the legitimacy of these acquisitions; and even he who speaks the most eloquently in favour of the present legislation hastens to sell to secure his profit. We dare not fully enjoy them; and the cooler opinions on them become, the less we dare spend on these funds. The buildings will languish, and no one will dare build new ones for a long time: growth will be weak; French capital will wither away considerably. There is much of this trouble already, and those who have reflected on the abuses of *decrees* must understand that this is like a decree heaped upon perhaps a third of the most powerful kingdom in Europe.

In the heart of the legislative body, we have often seen striking depictions

10 ["L'amnistie", ultimately from the Greek ἀμνηστῐᾱ, having the secondary meaning of "amnesty", but the primary meaning of "forgetfulness, a passing over".]

of the deplorable state of this property. Trouble will never cease until the public conscience no longer doubts the soundness of these acquisitions; but who can foresee when?

To consider only the possessors, the first danger for them comes from the government. Do not be deceived, it matters not which government: the most unjust one imaginable will ask no more than to fill its coffers while making itself the fewest possible enemies. Yet we know under what conditions the buyers have acquired their properties: we know what nefarious manoeuvring, what scandalous *premiums* they have involved. The original and continued corruption of these acquisitions is apparent to all eyes; so the French government cannot but know that in pressuring these buyers it will have public opinion on its side, and that it will seem unjust only to the buyers; besides, in popular governments, even legitimate ones, injustice has no shame; we can judge what will happen in France, where the government, as variable as its staff and lacking identity, never thinks that it is breaking its word in reversing what it has done.

It will, therefore, plunder national property as soon as possible. Strong in its conscience, and (let us not forget) in the jealousy of all paupers, it will torment the possessors, either by new sales modified in some way, or by general calls for price supplements, or by extraordinary taxes; in a word, the possessors will never have a moment's peace.

But everything is stable under a stable government; so that it is even important to the buyers of national property that the monarchy be restored, so they can know where they stand. It is quite misplaced to reproach the King for not having spoken clearly on this point in his declaration: he could not have done so without extreme imprudence. When the time comes, a legal solution on this point may not be the best approach.

But here we must recall what I said in the preceding chapter; the conveniences of this or that class of individuals will not stop the counter-revolution. All I pretend to prove is that it is in the interest of that small number of men who can influence this great event not to wait for the accumulated abuses of anarchy to make it inevitable and bring it to fruition suddenly; for the more the King is needed, the crueller the fate of all those who have gained from the Revolution.

III. Of Vengeance.

Another scarecrow used to make the French fear the return of their King is the vengeance which must accompany this return.

This objection, like the others, is above all made by intelligent men who do not believe in it; nevertheless, it is well to discuss it for the benefit of those who honestly believe it to be well-founded.

Many royalist writers have rejected, as an insult, this desire for vengeance which is supposed on their part; one alone will speak for all: I quote him for my own pleasure and for that of my readers. I shall not be accused of choosing from among cold and indifferent royalists.

> Under the dominion of an illegitimate power, the most horrible vengeance is to be feared; for who would have the right to oppose it? The victim can only call to his aid the authority of laws that do not exist, and a government which is only the product of crime and usurpation.
>
> It is quite otherwise with a government resting on sacred, ancient, and legitimate bases; it has the right to stifle the most just vengeance, and at a moment's notice, to punish with the sword of justice anyone who delivers himself more to the feeling of nature than to those of his duties.
>
> A legitimate government alone has the right to proclaim an amnesty and the means to enforce it.
>
> Then it is shown that the most perfect, the purest of royalists, the one whose parents and properties have been the most grievously outraged, must be punished with death under a legitimate government if he should dare to avenge his own injuries when the King ordered them to be forgiven.
>
> It is, therefore, under a government based on our laws that amnesty can be certainly granted and severely observed.
>
> Ah! no doubt it would be easy to dispute to what extent the right of the King may extend amnesty. The exceptions prescribed by the first of his duties are quite evident. All who were stained with the blood of Louis XVI have no hope of pardon but from God; but who would then dare to trace with a sure hand the limits of the King's amnesty and clemency? My heart and my pen equally dare not. If anyone dares to write on such a subject, it will doubtless be that rare and perhaps unique man, if he exists, who himself has never failed of his duty during this horrible revolution; and whose heart, as pure as his conduct, has never needed pardon.[11]

Reason and sentiment could not be expressed with more nobility. We should pity the man who does not recognize in this piece the accent of conviction.

11 *Observations sur la conduite des puissances coalisées*, by the count d'Antraigues; avant-propos, pp. XXXIV *et seq.*

Ten months after the date of this writing, the King pronounced, in his declaration, this phrase so well-known and so worthy of being known: *who would dare to avenge himself when the King grants pardon*?

He excluded from amnesty only those who voted the death of Louis XVI, the co-operators, the direct and immediate instruments of his execution, and the members of the revolutionary tribunal who sent to the scaffold the Queen and Madame Elizabeth. Seeking even to restrict the anathema to the first, as far as conscience and honour permitted, he did not place into the rank of parricides those about whom it might be believed that *they associated with the assassins of Louis XVI only with the intention of saving him*.

Even with regard *to those monsters whom posterity will name only with horror*, the King has contented himself with saying, with as much restraint as justice, that *the whole of France calls down upon their heads the sword of justice*.

By this phrase, he is not deprived of the right to grant pardon to individuals: it is for the guilty to see what they can place in the balance to make amends for their crime. Monck used Ingoldsby to stop Lambert. We can do even better than Ingoldsby.[12]

I will observe, moreover, without claiming to minimize the horror which is justly due the murderers of Louis XVI, that in the eyes of divine justice, not all are equally guilty. In the realm of morality as well as of physics, the strength of fermentation is determined by the fermenting mass. The seventy judges of Charles I were far more masters of themselves than the judges of Louis XVI. There were, certainly, some very wilful culprits among them, who cannot be detested enough; but these great culprits had the craft to excite such terror; they had made such an impression on less vigorous minds that I doubt not that several deputies were deprived of a part of their free will. It is difficult to form a clear idea of the indefinable and supernatural delirium which seized the assembly at the time of Louis XVI's judgment. I am persuaded that many of the guilty, remembering this disastrous period, think of it like a bad dream; that they are tempted to doubt what they have done, and that they are less able to explain it to themselves than we are to them.

Those guilty men, angry and surprised to be so, should try to make their peace.

12 [Strategically outmanoeuvred by George Monck, John Lambert was deserted by his army, and after being arrested, escaped from the Tower of London in 1660 and tried to halt the Restoration. Shortly after, he was captured by the regicide Richard Ingoldsby, who received a pardon for his efforts.]

Moreover, this concerns them alone; for the nation would be base indeed if it regarded the punishment of such men as an inconvenience of the counter-revolution; but for the faint of heart, it may be observed that Providence has already begun the punishment of the guilty: more than sixty regicides, among them the most guilty, have died a violent death; others will no doubt perish, or vacate Europe before France has a King; very few will fall into the hands of justice.

The French, perfectly calm about judicial revenge, must also be so about private vengeance: they have received the most solemn promises in this regard; they have the word of their King; they are not permitted to fear.

But as one must speak to all men and overcome all objections; and as one must answer even those who do not believe in honour and faith, one must prove that private vengeance is not possible.

The most powerful ruler has only two arms; he is only strong by the instruments he employs, and what public opinion presents to him. Now, although it is clear that after the supposed restoration the King will seek only to pardon, let us, to consider a worst-case scenario, make the exact opposite supposition. How would he go about it if he wished to exercise arbitrary vengeance? Would the French army as we know it be a very flexible instrument in his hands? Ignorance and bad faith are pleased to represent this future King as a Louis XIV, who, like Homer's Jupiter, had only to nod his head to convulse France. We hardly dare prove how false this supposition is. The power of sovereignty is altogether moral; it commands in vain if this power is not with it; and it must be possessed in its fullness to be abused. The King of France who ascends the throne of his ancestors will surely have no desire to begin with abuses; and if he had, it would be in vain, because he would not be strong enough to satisfy this desire. The red bonnet, in touching the royal forehead, has made all trace of holy oil disappear: the charm is broken; prolonged profanations have destroyed the divine sway of national prejudices; and for a long time yet, while cold reason will make bodies to kneel, minds will remain upright. We pretend to fear that the new King of France will clamp down on his enemies: the poor unfortunate! can he even recompense his friends?[13]

The French, therefore, have two infallible guarantees against the alleged vengeance of which they are frightened, the King's interest, and his impotence.[14]

13 We are reminded of Charles II's joke on the pleonasm of the English formula, Amnesty and Amnesia: *I understand,* he says; *amnesty for my enemies, and oblivion for my friends.*

14 Events have justified all these common-sense predictions. Since this work

The return of the émigrés furnishes the opponents of the monarchy with still another inexhaustible subject of imaginary fears; it is important to dispel this vision.

The first thing to note is that there are true propositions which are true only in one age; yet one is accustomed to repeat them long after time has rendered them false and even ridiculous. The revolutionary party might have feared the return of the émigrés shortly after ratifying the law that proscribed them; nevertheless, I do not affirm that they were right; but what does it matter? this is a purely idle question which it would be quite useless to address. The question is to know if, *at this moment*, the return of the émigrés is something dangerous for France.

The nobility sent two hundred eighty-four deputies to the Estates-General of fatal memory which produced all that we have seen. According to a work done on several bailiwicks, we have never found more than eighty electors for a deputy. It is not absolutely impossible that some bailiwicks had a higher number; but one must also take into account individuals who have voted in more than one bailiwick.

All things considered, we can estimate at 25,000 the number of heads of noble families who are represented in the Estates-General; and multiplying by five, a number we know is commonly attributed to each family, we have 125,000 noble heads. Let us take 130,000 to be even more charitable: let us then subtract the women; 65,000 remain. Let us subtract from this number, (1) the nobles who never left; (2) those who have returned; (3) the elderly; (4) the children; (5) the ill; (6) the priests; and (7) all those who have perished in war, by torture, or by natural causes—a number will remain which is not easy to precisely determine, but which, from every possible point of view, cannot alarm France.

A prince, worthy of his name, led to war five or six thousand men at most; this corps, which was not even composed of nobles alone, has shown admirable valour under foreign colours; but if we isolate it, it would disappear. In the end, in military terms, clearly émigrés are nothing and can do nothing.

There is one more consideration which relates more particularly to the spirit of this work, and which deserves to be developed.

has been completed, the French Government has discovered and published documents concerning two conspiracies, which are to be judged in a somewhat different manner: one Jacobin, and the other royalist. In the Jacobin sheet it was written: *death to all our enemies*; and in the royalist: *pardon to all those who shall not refuse it*. To prevent the people from drawing the consequences, it was said that the parliament should annul the royal amnesty; but this stupidity exceeds the *maximum*; surely it will not gain any currency.

In this world there is no chance, and even in a secondary sense there is no disorder, in that disorder is ordered by a sovereign hand that bends it according to a rule and forces it to contribute toward a goal.

A revolution is only a political movement that must produce a certain effect in a certain time. This movement has its laws; and in observing them attentively within a certain period of time, certain enough conclusions can be drawn for the future. Now, one of the laws of the French Revolution is that émigrés can attack it only to their own misfortune and are totally excluded from any work they undertake.

From the first chimeras of counter-revolution to the lamentable expedition of Quiberon, none of their efforts were successful—they have even mockingly turned against them. Not only are they unsuccessful, but all that they undertake is marked with such a character of impotence and deficiency that public opinion has at last become accustomed to regard them as men who persist in defending a proscribed party; which casts them into a disrepute that even their friends perceive.

And this disrepute will surprise few men who think that the principal cause of the French Revolution was the moral degradation of the nobility.

M. de Saint-Pierre has observed somewhere in his *Etudes de la Nature* that if we compare the countenance of French nobles with that of their ancestors, the painting and sculpture of whom has conveyed their features to us, we see evidence that these races have degenerated.

We can believe him on this point better than on polar fusions and the shape of the earth.[15]

In each state, even in monarchies, there is a certain number of families which may be called *co-sovereigns*; for in these governments, the nobility is but an extension of sovereignty. These families are the repositories of the sacred fire; it is extinguished when they cease to be *chaste*.

There is a question as to whether these families, once extinguished, can be perfectly replaced. We must at least not believe, if we want to speak precisely, that sovereigns can *ennoble*. There are new families which, so to speak, spring into the administration of the state; that draw themselves out of the mass of equals in a striking manner and arise from among the others like vigorous saplings amid a thicket. Sovereigns can sanction these natural ennoblements, but this is the limitation of their power. If they oppose too many of them, or if they allow too many *on their own authority*, they work for the destruction of their states. False nobility was one of the

15 [In his theory of tides, Saint-Pierre claimed that the shifting altitude ("annual fusions") of the polar ice caps could change the shape of the earth and its motion on the ecliptic.]

great plagues of France: other less brilliant empires are wearied and dishonoured by it while awaiting other misfortunes.

Modern philosophy, which loves to speak of *chance*, speaks above all of the *chance of birth*; this is one of its favourite texts: but there is no more chance on this point than on any other: there are noble families just as there are sovereign families. Can a man make a sovereign? At most he can serve as an instrument to dispossess a sovereign and deliver his states to another sovereign already a prince.[16] Moreover, there has never been a sovereign family which can be assigned a plebeian origin. If such a phenomenon should appear, it would mark a new epoch in the world.[17]

Keeping proportion in view, it is the same with nobility as with sovereignty. Without going into greater detail, let us observe that if the nobility renounces the national dogmas, the state is lost.[18]

The part played by some nobles in the French Revolution is a thousand times, I do not say more *horrible*, but more *terrible* than anything we have seen during this revolution. There has been no more frightening, more decisive sign of the awful judgment of the French monarchy.

Perhaps we may ask what these faults have in common with the émigrés who hate them. I answer that the individuals who make up nations, families, and even political bodies, are in solidarity: this is a fact. Secondly, I reply that the causes of the émigré nobility's suffering are quite anterior to its emigration. The difference which we perceive between these or those French nobles, is, in the eyes of God, only a difference of longitude and latitude: it is not because one is here or there, that one is what one must be; *and not all who say, Lord! Lord! will enter the kingdom*. Men can only

16 And even the way in which human power is used in these circumstances is quite apt to humiliate it. It is here, especially, that one can address to man these words of Rousseau: *Show me your power, I will show you your weakness.*

17 It is often said that *if Richard Cromwell had had his father's genius he would have made the protectorate hereditary in his family*. Very well said!

18 An Italian scholar has made a singular remark. After observing that the nobility is a natural guardian and almost a depositary of the national religion, and that this character is more striking as one ascends towards the origin of nations and things, he adds: *Talché dee esser un grand segno che vada a finire une nazione ove i nobili disprezzano la religione natia* ["So it must be a great sign that a nation is at an end when the nobles despise the native religion"]. (Vico, *The New Science*, book II)

When the priesthood is part of the state's political apparatus, and its highest offices are generally occupied by the high nobility, the result is the strongest and most durable of all possible constitutions. Thus sophism, which is the universal solvent, has produced its masterpiece in running roughshod over the French monarchy.

judge by the exterior; but this noble at Koblenz is able to reproach himself more sternly than that noble on the left in the so-called *constituent* assembly. Lastly, the French nobility can blame only itself for all its misfortunes; and when it is persuaded thus, it will have taken a great step forward. The exceptions, more or less numerous, are worthy of the world's respect; but one can only speak in general. Today the unfortunate nobility (who can suffer only an eclipse) must bow its head and resign itself. One day it must willingly embrace *children whom it has not held to its bosom*; meanwhile, it must no longer make exterior efforts; perhaps it would even be desirable that it should never be seen in a menacing attitude. In any case, emigration was an error, and not an injustice: the greater number believed they were obeying honour.

> *Numen abire jubet; prohibent discedere leges.*[19]
>
> ["The god bids him depart; the laws forbid him to leave."]

God must prevail.

There are many other things to be said on this point; let us keep to the obvious. *Émigrés* can do nothing; we may even add that they are nothing; for every day, despite the government, their number diminishes by a continuation of that invariable law of the French Revolution, which wills that everything be done in spite of men, and against all probabilities. Long misfortunes having softened the émigrés, every day they approximate their fellow-citizens; bitterness disappears; on both sides we begin to recall our common fatherland; we offer up a hand, and even on the field of battle we recognize our brothers. The strange amalgam we have seen for some time has no visible cause; for these laws are invisible, but no less real. Thus, it is obvious that the number of émigrés is of no account, that they are of no account in force, and that soon they will be of no account in hatred.

As for the more vigorous passions of a small number of men, we can neglect them.

But there is still an important reflection that I must not pass over in silence. Some imprudent speeches uttered by young men, thoughtless or embittered by misfortune, are relied upon to frighten the French at the return of these men. To put all suppositions against me, I grant that these discourses really do announce definite intentions: do we think that those who harbour them will be able to execute them after the restoration of the monarchy? We would be badly deceived. From the very moment when the legitimate government is restored, these men would have no power but to

19 [Ovid, *Metamorphoses*, XV, 28]

obey. Anarchy is required for revenge; order sharply excludes it. A man who, at this moment, speaks only of punishment, will then be surrounded by circumstances that will force him to will only what the law wills; and, for his own interest, he will be a quiet citizen, and will leave vengeance to the courts. We are always dazzled by the same sophism: *One party cracked down harshly while in power; therefore, the opposing party will do so when it comes to power*. Nothing is more false. In the first place, this sophism supposes that there are the same vices on both sides; which there assuredly are not. Without insisting too much on the virtues of the royalists, I am sure, at least, that I have with me the world's conscience when I simply affirm that there are fewer virtues on the side of the republicans. Besides, their prejudices alone, separated from their virtues, would assure France that, on the part of the royalists, she can suffer nothing of the same sort as she experienced from their enemies.

Experience has already furnished a prelude on this point to calm the French: on more than one occasion, they have seen that the party which had suffered everything on the part of its enemies has not known how to avenge itself when it held them in its power. A small number of retaliations, which have provoked such a great uproar, prove the same proposition; for it has been seen that only the most scandalous denial of justice could bring about these retaliations, and that no one would have taken justice into his own hands if the government could or would have done it.

What's more, there is great evidence that the King's most pressing interest will be to prevent revenge. In putting the evils of anarchy behind him, he will not want to bring it back; the very idea of violence will make him blanch, and this crime will be the only one he will not allow himself to pardon.

Besides, France is so very tired of convulsions and horrors, it does not want any more blood; and since public opinion is, at this moment, strong enough to suppress the party that would wish for it, one can judge of this opinion's strength at a time when it has government endorsement. After such prolonged and terrible evils, the French will rest with delight in the arms of the monarchy. Any attack on this tranquillity would truly be a crime of *lèse-nation*, which the courts, perhaps, may not have time to punish.

These reasons are so convincing that no one can be mistaken: furthermore, we must not be duped by those writings in which we see a hypocritical philanthropy pass judgement on the horrors of the Revolution, and then rely on these excesses to establish the necessity of preventing a second. In fact, they condemn this Revolution only in order not to excite a universal outcry against themselves; but they love it, they love its authors and its results; and of all the crimes it has begat, they hardly even condemn those they could have done without. There is not one of these writings in which we do not find obvious proofs that the authors are inclined to the party that they shame.

Thus, the French, perennial dupes, are duped on this occasion more than ever: they are generally afraid for their safety, and they have nothing to fear; and they sacrifice their happiness to please a few scoundrels.

But if the most obvious theories cannot convince the French, and if they still cannot bring themselves to believe that Providence is the guardian of order, and that it is altogether not the same thing to act with or against it, let us at least judge what Providence shall do by what it has done; and if reasoning slips our minds, let us at least believe in history, which is experimental politics. In the last century, England has offered nearly the same spectacle that France has in our own. There the fanaticism of liberty, agitated by that of religion, penetrated souls far more deeply than it did in France, where the cult of liberty rests on nothing whatsoever. Moreover, what a difference in the character of the two nations, and in that of the actors who played a part on the two stages! Where are, I do not say the Hampdens,[20] but the Cromwells of France? And yet, in spite of the burning fanaticism of the republicans, in spite of the attentive firmness of the national character, in spite of the too understandable terrors of numerous guilty parties, and especially of the army, did the restoration of the monarchy in England cause schisms similar to those begotten by a regicide revolution? Show us the atrocious vengeance of the royalists. Some regicides perished under the authority of the law; apart from that, there was neither fighting nor private revenge. The return of the King was marked only by a cry of joy which resounded throughout England; all enemies embraced each other. The King, surprised at what he saw, emotionally exclaimed: *Is it not my fault if I have been rejected so long by such a good people!* The illustrious Clarendon, a witness to and impartial historian of these great events, tells us that "a man could not help but wonder where those people dwelt who had done all the mischief, and kept the King from enjoying the comfort and support of such excellent subjects for so many years."[21]

That is to say, the *people* no longer recognized the *people*. It could not be put any better.

20 [A dynasty of parliamentarians, with ship money tax protestor John Hampden (b.1594) the first to attain political significance. For the relevance of ship money to the English Civil War, see introduction to Filmer's *Patriarcha*, Imperium Press, 2021.]

21 Hume, book X, ch. LXXII, 1660.

But this great change, whence came it? From nothing, or, better still, from nothing visible: a year before, no one thought it possible. It is not even known whether it was brought about by a royalist; for it is an insoluble problem to know when Monck began to serve the monarchy in good faith.

Was it not, at least, the royalist forces that imposed this on the opposing party? Not at all: Monck had only six thousand men; the republicans had five or six times more: they held all the offices, and militarily possessed the whole kingdom. Nevertheless, Monck was not put in the position of having to fight a single battle; everything was done without effort and as if by magic: it will be the same in France. The return to order cannot be painful because it will be natural, and because it will be favoured by a secret force whose action is entirely creative. We will see precisely the opposite of all that we have seen. Instead of these violent commotions, these painful divisions, these perpetual and desperate oscillations—a certain stability, an indefinable repose, a universal well-being, will announce the presence of sovereignty. There will be no shocks, no violence, not even any grave punishments except those which the true nation will approve: even crime and usurpations will be treated with a measured severity, with a calm justice that belongs only to legitimate power: the King will bind the wounds of the state with a restrained and paternal hand. In short, here is that great truth by which the French cannot be too deeply permeated: the restoration of the monarchy, which one calls the *counter-revolution*, will not be a *contrary revolution*, but the *contrary of revolution*.

Chapter XI:
Fragment of a History of the French Revolution, by David Hume[1,2]

Eadem mutata resurgo.

["I rise again, changed, but the same."]

The Long Parliament declared, by a solemn oath, that it could not be dissolved (p. 181). To ensure its power, it never ceased to work on the minds of the people; sometimes it inflamed their minds by artful speeches, (p. 176); and sometimes it arranged for petitions to be sent from all parts of the realm in support of the Revolution (p. 133). Abuse in the press was carried to extremes: numerous clubs all around produced noisy tumults; fanaticism had a language all its own; it was a new jargon, invented by the fury and hypocrisy of the times (p. 131). Every day produced some new harangue on past grievances (p. 129). All the old institutions were overthrown one after the other (pp. 125, 188). The S*elf-denying* ordinance and the *new model* bill utterly disorganized the army and gave it a new form and a new composition which forced a host of former officers to resign their commissions (p. 13). All crimes were placed on the shoulders of the royalists (p. 148): and the art of deceiving and frightening the people was carried to the point that they succeeded in making them believe that the royalists had mined the Thames (p. 177). No King! No nobility! universal equality! this was the general cry (p. 87). But amid this popular efferves-

1 I quote the English edition of Basel, 12 volumes, at Legrand, 1789.

2 [Along with the rest of this chapter, Maistre's tongue-in-cheek title underscores the striking parallels between the French Revolution and the events surrounding the English Civil War. In a later edition produced long after Maistre's death (Vitte, 1884), the title of this chapter was changed to *Fragment d'une Histoire de la Révolution anglaise, par David Hume*. In the present edition, Hume has been quoted verbatim where possible, and where Maistre has condensed and paraphrased, his French has been translated.]

cence, a separate party—the *Independents*—could be discerned, which finished in shackling the Long Parliament (p. 374).

Against such a storm, the goodness of the King proved useless; even the concessions made to his people were calumniated as having been made in bad faith (p. 186).

It was by these preliminaries that the rebels had prepared the doom of Charles I; but a simple assassination would not have fulfilled their designs; this crime would not have been national; the shame and danger would have fallen only on the murderers. It was necessary to conceive another plan; it was necessary to astonish the world with an unprecedented procedure, to adorn it with the outward trappings of justice, and to cover cruelty with audacity; in a word, it was necessary to fanaticize the people with notions of perfect equality, to secure the obedience of the majority, and gradually to form a general coalition against royalty (vol. X, p. 91).

The annihilation of the monarchy was the preliminary to the death of the King. By this vote of non-addresses, so it was called, the king was, in reality, dethroned, and the whole constitution formally overthrown.

Soon the blackest and most ridiculous calumnies were attributed to the King and spread about, to kill that respect which is the safeguard of thrones. The rebels neglected nothing to blacken his reputation; they accused him of having given fortresses over to England's enemies, of shedding the blood of his subjects. It was by slander that they prepared for violence (p. 94).

During the King's imprisonment at Carisbroke Castle, the usurpers of power dedicated themselves to heaping up all kinds of misery on the head of this unfortunate prince. He was deprived of his servants; he was not allowed to communicate with his friends; no society, no diversion was permitted to assuage the melancholy of his thoughts. He expected to be murdered or poisoned at any moment;[3] for the idea of a trial did not enter into his thoughts (pp. 59, 95).

While the King suffered cruelly in his prison, Parliament contrived to publish that he was very well, and that he was in a very good humor (*ibid).*[4]

The great source whence the king derived consolation amidst all his calamities, was undoubtedly religion; a principle, which, in him, seems to have contained nothing fierce or gloomy, nothing which enraged him against his adversaries, or terrified him with the dismal prospect of futurity. While every thing around him bore a hostile aspect; while friends,

3 This was also the sentiment of Louis XVI. See his historical eulogy.

4 We recall having read in Condorcet's paper a piece on the King's good appetite on his return from Varennes.

family, relations, whom he passionately loved, were placed at a distance, and unable to serve him; he reposed himself with confidence in the arms of that being, who penetrates and sustains all nature, and whose severities, if received with piety and resignation, he regarded as the surest pledges of unexhausted favour (pp. 95–96).

The men of law acted poorly in this circumstance. Bradshaw, who was of this profession, did not blush at presiding over the tribunal which condemned the King; and Coke offered himself up as public prosecutor for the people (p. 123). The tribunal was composed of officers of the rebel army, members of the lower house, and middle-class men of London; almost all were of low birth (p. 123).

Charles did not doubt that he would die; he knew that a king is rarely dethroned without perishing; but he believed he would die of murder rather than from a solemn trial (p. 122).

In his prison he was already dethroned: all ostentation of his rank had been removed from him, and those who attended to him had received orders to treat him without any mark of respect (p. 122). He soon grew accustomed to suffer the casual treatment and even the insolence of these men, as he had suffered in his other misfortunes (p. 123).

The King's judges styled themselves *representatives of the people* (p. 124). Of the people ... the unique source of all legitimate power (p. 127), and the indictment stated: *That, abusing the limited power entrusted to him, he had traitorously and maliciously attempted to raise an unlimited and tyrannical power atop the ruins of liberty.*

After the charge was finished, the president directed his discourse to the king, and told him, *that the court expected his answer*. The king, though long detained a prisoner, and now produced as a criminal, sustained, by his magnanimous courage, the majesty of a monarch. With great temper and dignity, he declined the authority of the court, and refused to submit himself to their jurisdiction (p. 125). It is confessed, that the king's behaviour, during this last scene of his life, does honour to his memory (p. 127); and that, in all appearances before his judges, he never forgot his part, either as a prince or as a man. Firm and intrepid, he maintained, in each reply, the utmost perspicuity and justness both of thought and expression (p.128): Mild and equable, he rose into no passion at that unusual authority, which was assumed over him. His soul, without effort or affectation, seemed only to remain in the situation familiar to it, and to look down with contempt on all the efforts of human malice and iniquity.

The people remained in that silence and astonishment, which all great passions, when they have not an opportunity of exerting themselves, naturally produce in the human mind. The soldiers, being incessantly plied with prayers, sermons, and exhortations, were wrought up to a degree of fury, and imagined, that in the acts of the most extreme disloyalty towards their prince, consisted their greatest merit in the eye of heaven (p. 130).

Three days were allowed the king between his sentence and his execution. This interval he passed with great tranquillity, chiefly in reading and devotion. All his family, that remained in England, were allowed access to him, who received from him wise counsel and great marks of tenderness (p. 130). Every night, during this interval, the king slept sound as usual; though the noise of workmen, employed in framing the scaffold, and other preparations for his execution, continually resounded in his ears. The morning of the fatal day, he rose early; and calling Herbert, one of his attendants, he bade him employ more than usual care in dressing him, and preparing him for so great and joyful a solemnity. Bishop Juxon, a man endowed with the same mild and steady virtues, by which the king himself was so much distinguished, assisted him in his devotions, and paid the last melancholy duties to his friend and sovereign (p. 132).

The scaffold was deliberately placed in front of the palace to show more strikingly the victory won by the justice of the people over the royal majesty. When the King was mounted on the scaffold, he found him surrounded by an armed force so considerable that he could not flatter himself that he was heard by the people, so that he was obliged to address his last words to the few people who were with him. He forgave his enemies; he did not accuse anyone; he made vows for his people. *SIRE,* said the prelate, who was assisting him, *one more step! It is difficult, but it is short, and it must lead you to Heaven. I am going,* replied the King, *to change a perishable crown against an incorruptible crown and unalterable happiness.*

The street before Whitehall was the place destined for the execution: For it was intended, by choosing that very place, in sight of his own palace, to display more evidently the triumph of popular justice over royal majesty. When the king came upon the scaffold, he found it so surrounded with soldiers, that he could not expect to be heard by any of the people: He addressed, therefore, his discourse to the few persons who were about him; particularly colonel Tomlinson, to whose care he had lately been committed, and upon whom, as upon many others, his amiable deportment had wrought an entire conversion. He justified his own innocence in the late fatal wars, and observed, that he had not taken arms, till after the parliament had inlisted forces; nor had he any other object in his warlike operations, than to preserve that authority entire, which his predecessors had transmitted to him. He threw not, however, the blame upon the parliament; but was more inclined to think, that ill instruments had interposed, and raised in them fears and jealousies with regard to his intentions. Though innocent towards his people, he acknowledged the equity of his execution in the eyes of his Maker; and observed, that, an unjust sentence, which he had suffered to take effect, was now punished by an unjust sentence upon himself. He forgave all his enemies, even the chief instruments of his death; but exhorted them and the whole nation to return to the ways of peace, by paying obedience to their lawful sovereign, his son and successor. When he was preparing himself for the block, bishop Juxon called to him: "There is, Sire, but one stage more, which, though turbulent and troublesome, is yet a very short one. Consider, it will soon carry you a great way; it will carry you from earth to heaven; and there you shall find, to your great joy, the prize, to which you hasten, a crown of glory." "I go," replied the king, "from a corruptible to an incorruptible crown; where no disturbance can have place." At one blow was his head severed from his body. A man in a vizor performed the office of executioner: Another, in a like disguise, held up to the spectators, the head, streaming with blood, and cried aloud, *This is the head of a traitor!* (pp. 132, 133)

This prince deserved the title of *good* rather than of *great*. From time to time, he harmed his own majesty by inappropriately deferring to the opinion of people of a capacity inferior to his own. He was better suited to reign over a regular and peaceful government than to evade or repulse the assaults of a popular assembly (p. 136); but if he lacked the courage to act, he always had the courage to suffer. He was born, much to his misfortune, in difficult times; and if he had not enough skill to extricate himself from such a cumbrous position, he may easily be excused, since even after the event, when it is commonly easy to see all errors, it is still by no means clear what he should have done (p. 137). Exposed without help to the clash of the most hateful and implacable passions, he could not make the slightest error without calling down upon himself the most fatal consequences; a position whose difficulty surpasses the force of the greatest talent (p. 137).

Some historians have rashly questioned the good faith of this prince: But, for this reproach, the most malignant scrutiny of his conduct, which, in every circumstance, is now thoroughly known, affords not any reasonable foundation. On the contrary, if we consider the extreme difficulties, to which he was so frequently reduced, and compare the sincerity of his professions and declarations; we shall avow, that probity and honour ought justly to be numbered among his most shining qualities (p. 137).

The death of the King put the seal on the destruction of the monarchy. The commons ordered a new great seal to be engraved, on which that assembly was represented, with this legend, ON THE FIRST YEAR OF FREEDOM, BY GOD'S BLESSING, RESTORED, 1648. The forms of all public business were changed, from the king's name, to that of the keepers of the liberties of England (p. 142). The court of *King's Bench* was called the court of *Public Bench*. The king's statue, in the Exchange, was thrown down; and on the pedestal these words were inscribed: EXIT TYRANNUS, REGUM ULTIMUS: *The tyrant is gone, the last of the kings.* (p. 143).

Charles, in dying, left to his people an image of himself (Εἰκὼν Βασιλικὴ)[5] in that famous work, a masterpiece of elegance, purity, neatness, and simplicity. It is not easy to conceive the general compassion excited towards the king, by the publishing, at so critical a juncture, a work so full of piety, meekness, and humanity. Many have not scrupled to ascribe to that book the subsequent restoration of the royal family (p. 146).

It is seldom, that the people gain any thing by revolutions in government; because the new settlement, jealous and insecure, must commonly be supported with more expence and severity than the old (p. 100).

But on no occasion was the truth of this maxim more sensibly felt, than in the present situation of England. Complaints against the oppression of ship-money, against the tyranny of the star-chamber, had rouzed the people to arms: And having gained a complete victory over the crown, they found themselves loaded with a multiplicity of taxes, formerly unknown; and scarcely an appearance of law and liberty remained in the administration. Every office was entrusted to the most ignoble part of the nation. A base populace exalted above their superiors: Hypocrites exercising iniquity under the vizor of religion (p. 100). The loan of great sums of money, often to the ruin of families, was exacted from all such as lay under any suspicion of favouring the king's party, though their conduct had been ever so inoffensive. Never, in this island, was known a more severe and arbitrary government, than was generally exercised, by the patrons of liberty in both kingdoms (p. 112, 113).

The first act of the Long Parliament had been an oath by which it declared that it could not be dissolved (p. 181).

The confusions, which overspread England after the murder of Charles I proceeded as well from the spirit of refinement and innovation, which agitated the ruling party, as from the dissolution of all that authority, both civil and ecclesiastical, by which the nation had ever been accustomed to be governed. Every man had framed the model of a republic; and, however new it was, or fantastical, he was eager in recommending it to his fellow citizens, or even imposing it by force upon them. Every man had adjusted a system of religion, which, being derived from no traditional authority,

5 [*The Pourtrature of His Sacred Majestie in His Solitudes and Sufferings*—the spiritual autobiography published in the name of Charles, in the aftermath of his execution.]

was peculiar to himself; and being founded on supposed inspiration, not on any principles of human reason, had no means, besides cant and low rhetoric, by which it could recommend itself to others. The *levellers* insisted on an equal distribution of power and property, and disclaimed all dependance and subordination.[6] The millenarians[7] or fifth-monarchy-men required, that government itself should be abolished, and all human powers be laid in the dust, in order to pave the way for the dominion of Christ, whose second coming they suddenly expected. The Antinomians even insisted, that the obligations of morality and natural law were suspended, and that the elect, guided by an internal principle, more perfect and divine, were superior to the beggarly elements of justice and humanity. A considerable party declaimed against tithes and hireling priesthood, and were resolved, that the magistrate should not support by power or revenue any ecclesiastical establishment: leaving to each man the liberty to support the one which would suit him the best. What's more, all religions were tolerated, except Catholicism. Another party inveighed against the law and its professors; and on pretence of rendering more simple the distribution of justice, were desirous of abolishing the whole system of English jurisprudence, which seemed interwoven with monarchical government (p. 148). Ardent republicans repudiated their baptismal names, substituting for them names of an extravagance matching the spirit of the Revolution (p. 242). They decided that, marriage being no more than a contract, it should be celebrated before civil magistrates (p. 242). Finally, there is a tradition in England that they pushed their fanaticism to the point of suppressing the word *kingdom* in the Lord's Prayer, saying: *thy commonwealth come.* As for the idea of an organ of the state, in imitation of Rome, dedicated to *propagation* of the faith, that belongs to Cromwell (p. 285).

The less fanatical republicans thought themselves no less above all laws, all promises, all oaths. All bonds of society were loosed, and the most dangerous passions became even more venomous, relying on still more anti-social and speculative maxims (p. 148).

The royalists, consisting of the nobles and more considerable gentry, being degraded from their authority and plundered of their property, were inflamed with the highest resentment and indignation against those ignoble adversaries, who had reduced them to subjection. From inclination and principle, they zealously attached themselves to the son of their unfor-

6 *We want a government where distinctions arise only from equality itself; where the citizen is submissive to the magistrate, the magistrate to the people, and the people to justice.* Robespierre. See the *Moniteur* of February 7, 1794.

7 We must not pass lightly over this similarity.

tunate monarch, whose memory they respected, and whose tragical death they deplored.

On the other hand, the Presbyterians, founders of the republic, whose credit had first supported the arms of the parliament, were enraged to find that, by the treachery or superior cunning of their associates, the fruits of all their successful labours were ravished from them. This discontent pushed them towards the royalist party, but still without proving decisive; they had still many prejudices to overcome, many fears and jealousies to be allayed, ere they could cordially entertain thoughts of restoring the family, which they had so grievously offended, and whose principles they regarded with such violent abhorrence.

After having murdered their sovereign with so many appearing circumstances of solemnity and justice, and so much real violence and even fury, these men thought to give themselves a regular form of government. They named a council of state, thirty-eight in number, to whom all addresses were made, who gave orders to all generals and admirals, who executed the laws, and who digested all business before it was introduced into Parliament (pp. 150, 151). The administration was divided between several committees which had seized all (p. 134), and rendered account to none (pp. 166, 167).

The usurpers of power, both by the turn of their disposition, and by the nature of the instruments which they employed, were better qualified for acts of force and vigour than for the slow and deliberate work of legislation; nevertheless, the assembly as a whole assumed the air of handling nothing but legislation for the country. According to them, they were working on a new plan of representation, and as soon as they should have settled the nation, they professed their intention of restoring the power to the people, from whom, they acknowledged, they had entirely derived it (p. 151).

In the meantime, the parliament judged it necessary to enlarge the laws of high-treason beyond those narrow bounds within which they had been confined during the monarchy. They even comprehended verbal offences, nay intentions, though they had never appeared in any overt act against the state. To affirm the present government to be an usurpation, to assert that the parliament or council of state were tyrannical or illegal, to endeavour subverting their authority or stirring up sedition against them; these offences were declared to be high-treason. The power of imprisonment, of which the petition of right had bereaved the king, it was now found necessary to restore to the council of state; and all the jails in England were filled with men whom the jealousies and fears of the ruling party had represented as dangerous (p. 163).

It was a great delight for the new masters to strip the landed nobility of their titles; and when the brave Montrose was executed in Scotland, *James Graham* was the only name his judges vouchsafed to give him (p. 180).

Besides the customs and excise, ninety thousand pounds a month were levied on land for the subsistance of the army. The sequestrations and compositions of the royalists, the sale of the crown lands, and of the dean and chapter lands, though they yielded great sums, were not sufficient to support the vast expences, and, as was suspected, the great *depredations*, of the parliament and of their creatures (pp. 163, 164).

Even the royal palaces were pulled in pieces, and the materials of them sold. All the king's furniture was put to sale: His pictures, disposed of at very low prices, enriched all the collections in Europe: The cartoons, when complete, were only appraised at 300 pounds, though the whole collection of the king's curiosities was sold at above 50,000 (p. 388).

In the end, the republicans, so-called representatives of the people, had little popularity and credit. These men had not that large thought, nor those comprehensive views, which might qualify them for acting the part of legislators. Selfish and hypocritical, they made small progress in that important work which they professed to have so much at heart, the settling of a new model of representation, and fixing a plan of government. The nation began to apprehend that they intended to establish themselves as a perpetual legislature, and to confine the whole power to 60 or 70 persons, who called themselves *the parliament of the commonwealth of England*. And while they pretended to bestow new liberties upon the nation, they found themselves obliged to infringe even the most valuable of those which, through time immemorial, had been transmitted from their ancestors. Not daring to entrust the trials of treason to juries, who, being chosen indifferently from among the people, would have been little favourable to the commonwealth, the parliament erected a high court of justice, which was to receive indictments from the council of state (p. 206, 207). This court was composed of men devoted to the ruling party, without name or character, determined to sacrifice everything to their own safety or ambition.

As for the royalists taken prisoner in battle, they were put to death by sentence of a court martial (p. 207).

The only solid support of the republican independent faction, which, though it formed so small a part of the nation, had violently usurped the government of the whole, was a numerous army of near fifty thousand men (p. 149). Such is the influence of established government, that the commonwealth, though founded in usurpation the most unjust and unpopular, had authority sufficient to raise every where the militia of the counties; and these, united with the regular forces, bent all their efforts against the King (p. 199). At Newbury (in 1643) the militia of London, especially, equalled what could be expected from the most veteran forces. The officers preached to their soldiers, and the new republicans marched into battle singing fanatical hymns (p. 13).

A numerous army served equally to retain everyone in implicit subjection to established authority, and to strike a terror into foreign nations. The power of peace and war was lodged in the same hands with that of imposing taxes. The military genius of the people had, by the civil contests, been roused from its former lethargy; and excellent officers were formed in every branch of service. The confusion into which all things had been thrown had given opportunity to men of low stations to break through their obscurity, and to raise themselves by their courage to commands which they were well qualified to exercise, but to which their birth could never have entitled them (p. 209). We see a man of fifty (Blake) suddenly passed from land service to the navy, wherein he distinguished himself in the most brilliant manner (p. 210). During the variety of ridiculous and distracted scenes, which the civil government exhibited in England, the military force was exerted with vigor, conduct, and unanimity; and never did the kingdom appear more formidable to all foreign nations (p. 248).

A government totally military and despotic is almost sure, after some time, to fall into impotence and languor: but when it immediately succeeds a legal constitution, it may, at first, to foreign nations appear very vigorous and active, and may exert with more unanimity that power, spirit, and riches, which had been acquired under a better form. This is the spectacle that England presented at this time. The moderate temper and unwarlike genius of the two last princes, the extreme difficulties under which they laboured at home, and the great security which they enjoyed from foreign enemies, had rendered them negligent of the transactions on the continent; and England, during their reigns, had been, in a manner, overlooked in the general system of Europe; but the republican government suddenly restored its prestige (p. 263). Notwithstanding the late wars and bloodshed, and the present factions, the power of England had never, in any period, appeared so formidable to neighbouring kingdoms (p. 209), and to all foreign nations (p. 248), as it did at this time, in the hands of the commonwealth. The weight of England, even under its most legal and bravest princes, was never more sensibly felt than during this unjust and violent usurpation (p. 263).

The parliament, elated by the numerous successes which they had obtained over their domestic enemies, thought that every thing must yield to their fortunate arms; it treated with the greatest haughtiness second-rate powers; and for real or pretended offenses, it declared war or exacted solemn satisfaction (p. 221).

This famous parliament, which had filled all Europe with the renown of its actions, and with astonishment at its crimes, was, nevertheless, enslaved by one man (p. 128); All Europe stood astonished to see a nation so turbulent and unruly who, for some doubtful *encroachments on their privileges*, had dethroned and murdered an excellent prince, descended from a long line of monarchs, now at last subdued and reduced to slavery by one who, a few years before, was no better than a private gentleman, whose name was not known in the nation, and who was little regarded even in that low sphere to which he had always been confined (p. 236).[8] But the conduct of this same tyrant in foreign affairs, though imprudent and impolitic, was full of vigour and enterprise, and drew a consideration to his country which, since the reign of Elizabeth, it seemed to have totally lost. He seemed to ennoble, instead of debasing, that people whom he had reduced to subjection; and their national vanity, being gratified, made them bear with more patience all the indignities and calamities under which they laboured. (pp. 280, 281).

It seems now proper to look abroad to the general state of Europe, and to consider the measures which England, at this time, embraced in its negotiations with the neighbouring princes. (p. 262).

Richelieu was then prime minister of France. It was he who, through his emissaries, had furnished fuel to the flame of rebellion when it first broke out in Scotland; but after the conflagration had diffused itself, the French court, observing the materials to be of themselves sufficiently combustible, found it unnecessary any longer to animate the British malcontents to an opposition of their sovereign. On the contrary, they offered their mediation for composing these intestine disorders; and their ambassadors, from decency, pretended to act in concert with the court of England in exile (p. 264).

In the end, however, Charles received but few civilities, and still less support, from the French court (p. 170, 266).

One morning, the princess Henrietta was obliged to lie abed for want of a fire to warm her. To such a condition was reduced, in the midst of Paris, a queen of England, and daughter of Henry IV of France (p. 266)!

Finally, they treated Charles with such affected indifference that he

8 So little were these men endowed with the spirit of legislation, that they confessed, or rather boasted, that they had employed only four days in drawing this instrument which placed Cromwell at the head of the republic. *Ibid.*, p. 245.
The Constitution of 1793 may be cited on this subject, *made in a few days by a few juveniles*, as has been said in Paris after the fall of its builders.

thought it more decent to withdraw, and prevent the indignity of being desired to leave the kingdom. (p. 267).

Spain was the first power to recognize the republic, although its royal family was related to that of England. It sent an ambassador to London, and received one from the parliament (p. 268).

Sweden being at the height of its greatness, the new republic anxiously sought alliance with it, and obtained it (p. 263).

The King of Portugal had dared to close his ports to the republican admiral; but soon dreading so dangerous a foe to his newly acquired dominion, and sensible of the unequal contest, in which he was engaged, made all possible submissions to the haughty republic, and was at last admitted to negociate the renewal of his alliance with England.

The people in the United Provinces were much attached to Charles' interests. Besides his connection with the family of Orange, which was extremely beloved by the populace, all men regarded with compassion his helpless condition, and expressed the greatest abhorrence against the murder of his father; a deed to which nothing, they thought, but the rage of fanaticism and faction could have impelled the parliament. But though the public in general bore great favour to the King, the States were uneasy at his presence. They dreaded the parliament, so formidable by their power, and so prosperous in all their enterprises. They apprehended the most precipitate resolutions from men of such violent and haughty dispositions. And after the murder of Dorislaus, they found it still more necessary to satisfy the English commonwealth by removing the king to a distance from them (p. 169).

Cardinal Mazarine, by whom all the councils of France were directed, was artful and vigilant, supple and patient, false and intriguing; all circumstances of respect were paid to the daring usurper, who had imbrued his hands in the blood of his sovereign, a prince so nearly related to the royal family of France. Mazarin was seen writing to Cromwell expressing *his regret that his urgent affairs should deprive him of the honour, which he had long wished for, of paying, in person, his respects to the greatest man in the world* (p. 307).

This same Cromwell was seen to be treated on an equal footing with Louis XIV, and in a treaty between the two nations, the protector's name was inserted before the French king's in that copy which remained in England (p. 268, note).

Finally, the Prince Palatine, during the civil wars, had much neglected his uncle and paid court to the parliament: he accepted of a pension of 8,000 pounds a year from them, and took a place in their assembly of divines (p. 263, note).

Within England itself, there were great numbers at that time who made it a principle always to adhere to any power which was uppermost, and to support the established government (p. 239). At the head of this system was the illustrious and gallant Blake, who said to his sailors, *it is still our duty to fight for our country, into what hands so ever the government may fall* (p. 279).

Against an order of things so well established, the royalists embarked on enterprises which were nothing if not ill-considered, and which turned against them. The government had spies everywhere, and it was not difficult to obtain intelligence of a confederacy so generally diffused, among a party who valued themselves more on zeal and courage than on secrecy and sobriety (p. 259). The royalists, observing this general ill will towards the establishment, could no longer be retained in subjection; but fancied that everyone who was dissatisfied, like them, had also embraced the same views and inclinations. They did not consider that the old parliamentary party, though many of them were displeased with Cromwell who had dispossessed them of their power, were still more apprehensive of any success to the royal cause; whence, besides a certain prospect of the same consequence, they had so much reason to dread the severest vengeance for their past transgressions (p. 259).

The situation of these unfortunate royalists in England was deplorable.

In London, one could not ask for better grounds than these imprudent conspiracies to justify the most tyrannical severities (p. 260). The royalists were imprisoned; an edict was issued, with the consent of the council, for exacting the tenth penny from that whole party; in order, as was pretended, to make them pay the expenses to which their mutinous disposition continually exposed the public. The royalists were obliged anew to redeem themselves by great sums of money; and many of them were reduced by these multiplied disasters to extreme poverty. Whoever was known to be disaffected, or even lay under any suspicion, though no guilt could be proved against him, was exposed to the new exaction (pp. 260, 261).

Near one half of the goods and chattels, and at least one half of the lands, rents, and revenues of the kingdom, had been sequestered. To great numbers of royalists, all redress from these sequestrations was refused: To the rest, the remedy could be obtained only by paying large compositions and subscribing the covenant, which they abhorred. Besides pitying the ruin and desolation of so many ancient and honourable families; indifferent spectators could not but blame the hardship of punishing with such severity, actions, which the law, in its usual and most undisputed interpretation, strictly required of every subject (pp. 66, 67). The severities, too, exercised against the episcopal clergy, naturally affected the royalists, and even all men of candor, in a sensible manner. By the most moderate computation, it appears, that above one half of the established clergy had been turned out to beggary and want, for no other crime than their adhering to the civil and religious principles, in which they had been educated; and for their attachment to those laws, under whose countenance they had at first embraced that profession (p. 67).

The royalists had been instructed by the King to remain quiet, and to cover themselves under the appearance of republicans (p. 254).

For himself, poor and neglected, the King wandered about Europe, changing his place of refuge according to the circumstances, and consoling himself for his present calamities with the hope of a better future (p. 152).

The condition of that monarch, to all the world, seemed totally desperate (p. 341), all the more so because, seeming to seal his fate, all the commons signed without hesitation an engagement not to alter the present government (p. 325).[9] His friends had been baffled in every attempt for his service: the scaffold had often streamed with the blood of the more active royalists: the spirits of many were broken with tedious imprisonments: the estates of all were burdened by the fines and confiscations which had been levied upon them: no one durst openly avow himself of that party: And so small did their number seem to a superficial view, that, even should the nation recover its liberty, which was deemed no wise probable, it was judged uncertain what form of government it would embrace (p. 342). But amidst all these gloomy prospects, *fortune*,[10] by a surprising revolution, was now paving the way for the king to mount, in peace and triumph, the throne of his ancestors (p. 342).

When Monck began to put his great project into execution, the nation had fallen into complete anarchy. He advanced with his army, which was near 6,000 men: the scattered forces in England were above five times more numerous. In all counties through which Monk passed, the prime gentry flocked to him with addresses; expressing their earnest desire, that he would be instrumental in restoring the nation to peace and tranquillity, and to the enjoyment of those liberties, which by law were their birthright, but of which, during so many years, they had been fatally bereaved (p. 352). Men were dispatched to confirm the general in his inclination to a free parliament, the object of all men's prayers and endeavours. (p. 353). The tyranny and the anarchy, which now equally oppressed the kingdom; the experience of past distractions, the dread of future convulsions, the

9 In 1659, a year before the restoration!!! I bow to the will of the people.

10 No doubt!

indignation against military usurpation, against sanctified hypocrisy: all these motives had united every party and formed a tacit coalition between royalists and Presbyterians. The latter agreed that they had gone too far, and the lessons of experience finally united them with the rest of England to desire the king's restoration, the only remedy for all these fatal evils (pp. 333, 353).[11]

Monck, however, pretended not to favour these addresses (p. 353). How early he entertained designs for the king's restoration, we know not with certainty (p. 345). When he arrived in London, he told the parliament that he had been employed as the instrument of Providence for effecting their restoration (p. 354). He added that it was for the present parliament to summon a new assembly, free and full, who, meeting without oaths or engagements, might finally give contentment to the nation, and that it was sufficient for public security if the fanatical party and the royalists were excluded; since the principles of these factions were destructive either of government or of liberty. (p. 355).

He even served the Long Parliament in a violent measure (p. 356). But as soon as soon as intelligence was conveyed of his decision on a new convocation, joy and exultation displayed itself throughout the kingdom. The royalists, the Presbyterians, forgetting all animosities, mingled in common joy and transport, and vowed never more to gratify the ambition of false and factious tyrants by their calamitous divisions (p. 358). All these motives had united every party, except the most desperate (p. 353).[12]

Determined republicans, particularly the late King's judges, did not forget themselves on this occasion. By themselves or their emissaries, they represented to the soldiers that all those brave actions which had been performed during the war, and which were so meritorious in the eyes of the parliament, would no doubt be regarded as the deepest crimes by the royalists, and would expose the army to the severest vengeance: that in vain did that party make professions of moderation and lenity: the king's death, the execution of so many of the nobility and gentry, the sequestration and imprisonment of the rest, were in their eyes crimes so deep, and offences so personal, as must be prosecuted with the most implacable resentment (p. 366).

But the agreement of all parties formed one of those popular torrents

11 In 1659; four years earlier, the royalists, according to this same historian, made a serious miscalculation in imagining that the enemies of the government were the friends of the King. See above, p. 242.

12 In 1660—but in 1655, *they feared the restoration of the monarchy much more than they hated the established government* (p. 259).

where the most indifferent, or even the most averse, are transported with the general passion, and zealously adopt the sentiments of the community to which they belong. The enthusiasts themselves seemed to be disarmed of their fury; and between despair and astonishment gave way to those measures which, they found, it would be impossible for them by their utmost efforts to withstand (p. 363). The Presbyterians, the royalists, being united, formed the voice of the nation, which, without noise, but *with infinite ardour*, called for the king's restoration.[13] *The kingdom was almost entirely in the hands of the republicans*;[14] and some zealous leaders among them began to renew the demand of those *conditions* which had been required of the late king in the treaty of Newport: but the general opinion seemed to condemn all those rigorous and jealous capitulations with their sovereign. Harassed with convulsions and disorders, men ardently longed for repose, and were terrified at the mention of negotiations or delays which might afford opportunity to the seditious army still to breed new confusion. The passion too for liberty having been carried to such violent extremes, and having produced such bloody commotions, began, by a natural movement, to give place to a spirit of loyalty and obedience; and the public was less zealous in a cause which was become odious, on account of the calamities which had so long attended it. After the legal concessions made by the late King, the constitution seemed to be sufficiently secured (p. 364).

The Parliament, whose functions were about to expire, had voted that no one should be elected who had himself, or whose father had, borne arms for the late King (p. 365); for they well knew that to call a free parliament, and to restore the royal family, were visibly, in the present disposition of the kingdom, one and the same measure (p. 361). But little regard was anywhere paid to this ordinance (p. 365).

Such was the general disposition, when…

Caetera DESIDERANTUR.

13 But the year before, THE PEOPLE signed, *without hesitation*, an agreement to maintain the republic. Thus, it takes only 365 days at most, for the heart of this sovereign to change from *hatred* or *indifference* to *infinite ardour*.

14 Note well!

POST SCRIPTUM

The new edition of this work[1] was nearing completion when some Frenchmen, worthy of complete confidence, assured me that the book *Développement des vrais-principes*, etc., which I cited in chapter VIII contains maxims of which the King does not approve.

"The magistrates," they tell me, "authors of the book in question, reduce our Estates-General to the faculty of presenting grievances, and attribute to the parlements the exclusive right of verifying the laws, even those which have been rendered at the request of the Estates; that is to say, they elevate the magistracy above the nation."

I avow that I had not perceived this monstrous error in the work of the French magistrates (which is no longer at my disposal); it seemed to me that this error was even excluded by some texts of this work, quoted on page 113 of mine; and we have seen in the note on page 116 that the book in question can give rise to objections of a very different kind.

If, as I am assured, the authors have departed from true principles in regard to the legitimate rights of the French nation, I am not surprised that their work, excellent in other respects, should have alarmed the King; for even those who have not had the honour of meeting him know by a host of irrefutable testimonies that these sacred rights have no proponent more loyal than him, and that no one could offend him more than by attributing to him contrary systems.

I repeat that I have read the book *Développement*, etc. with no systematic view. Separated from my books for a long time; obliged to use not those books I sought, but those I found; often reduced to citing from memory or notes taken formerly, I needed a collection of this sort to gather my ideas. It was recommended to me (I must say) from its effectiveness against the enemies of royalty; but if it contains errors which have escaped me, I sincerely disavow them. A stranger to all systems, to all parties, to all hatreds, in character, reflection, and position, I will assuredly be more than satis-

1 This is the third in five months, including the counterfeit French edition that has just appeared. The latter faithfully copied the innumerable errors of the first and has added others.

fied with every reader who reads me with intentions as pure as those that have dictated my work.

What's more, if I wished to examine the nature of the different powers of which the old French constitution was composed; if I wanted to go back to the source of these ambiguities, and present clear ideas on the essence, function, rights, grievances, and wrongs of the parlement, I would go beyond the bounds of a postscript, even those of my work; and, moreover, I would be doing something perfectly useless. If the French nation returns to its King, as every friend of order must desire, and if it has regular national assemblies, the various powers will come to take their natural place, without contradiction and without commotion. In all suppositions, the exaggerated claims of the parlements, the discussions and quarrels to which they have given birth, seem to me to belong entirely to ancient history.

END.

Study on Sovereignty

Book I: Origins of Sovereignty

Chapter I: Of the Sovereignty of the People[1]

Non illi imperium.
["Not for him is the empire."]

Vergil, Aeneid, I, 138.

They say that the people are sovereign; but over whom? Over themselves, apparently. The people are, therefore, subject. There is surely some equivocation here if not an error, for the people who *command* are not the people who *obey*. To state the general proposition "*the people are sovereign*" is, therefore, enough to feel that it needs commentary.

We shall not have to wait long for this commentary, at least in the French system. The people, it will be said, exercise their sovereignty by means of their Representatives. This is starting to become clear. The people are a sovereign that cannot exercise sovereignty. Each individual male of this people has the right of command, in his turn, only for a certain time. For

1 <The manuscript of this *study* bears the dates of Lausanne, 1794, 1793, 1796.> This work was written in the book before you and never read again. Some pieces have passed into other writings. St. Petersburg, 16 (28) January 1815. (Author's note)

example, if we suppose 25 million men in France and 700 eligible deputies every two years, we understand that if these 25 million men were immortal, and deputies appointed in turn, each Frenchman would periodically be king roughly every three thousand five hundred years. But since, in this space of time, we must be allowed to die every now and then, and since voters are authorized to choose as they please, the mind reels at the dreadful number of kings condemned to die without having reigned.

But since we must examine this question more seriously, let us first observe that on this point, as on so many others, it might well be that we have not made ourselves clear. And so, let us begin by posing the question properly.

There have been heated disputes over whether sovereignty comes from God or from men, but I do not know if it has been observed that the two propositions can both be true.

It is quite true, in a lower and coarse sense, that sovereignty is based on human consent: for if any people suddenly agreed not to obey, sovereignty would disappear, and it is impossible to imagine the establishment of sovereignty without imagining a people that consent to obey. If, then, the adversaries of the divine origin of sovereignty mean only this, they are right, and it would be quite useless to dispute. Since God did not judge it expedient to employ supernatural instruments for the establishment of empires, it is certain that everything must have been done by men. But to say that sovereignty does not come from God because He has seen fit to use men to establish it, is to say that He is not the Creator of man because we all have a father and a mother.

All *theists*[2] in the world will no doubt agree that whosoever violates the laws opposes the divine will and is guilty before God even though he only violates human ordinances, for it is God who has made *man* sociable; and since He has *willed* society, He has also *willed* the sovereignty and laws without which there is no society.

Thus, laws come from God in the sense that He wills that the laws be obeyed, and yet these laws also come from men, since they are made by men.

In the same way, sovereignty comes from God, since He is the Author of everything except evil, and in particular He is the Author of society, which cannot subsist without sovereignty.

And yet this same sovereignty also comes from men in a certain sense—

2 Although this word, in its primitive sense, is synonymous with *deist*, use has, however, rendered it the opposite of *atheist*, and it is in this sense that I use it. It is a necessary word, the word *deist* excluding belief in all revelation.

that is, as this or that mode of government is established and declared by human consent.

Proponents of divine authority cannot, therefore, deny that human will plays any role in the establishment of governments, and the proponents of the contrary system cannot, in their turn, deny that God is, par excellence and in an eminent way, the Author of these same governments.

It seems, then, that these two propositions—*sovereignty comes from God*, and *sovereignty comes from men*—do not absolutely contradict each other; no more than these two others—*the laws come from God*, and *the laws come from men*.

It is enough, then, in order to understand ideas, to put them in their place and not to confound them. With these precautions we are sure not to go astray, and it seems that we should listen favourably to the writer who says, "I come not to tell you that sovereignty comes from God or from men; let us examine together only what is divine and what is human in sovereignty."

Chapter II:
The Origin of Society

One of man's strange obsessions is to create difficulties for the simple pleasure of resolving them. The mysteries that surround him on all sides are not enough for him, he still repudiates clear ideas and reduces everything to a problem by some convolution of pride—I know not what—that makes him regard believing what everyone else believes as below himself. Thus, for example, there has been a long debate about the origin of society; and in place of the entirely simple solutions that naturally present themselves to the mind, metaphysics has been deployed to construct airy hypotheses rejected by common sense and experience.

When the question is put as to the causes of society's origin, it is patently assumed that there was a time where mankind existed before society; but this is precisely what needs proving.

Doubtless, it cannot be denied that the earth is generally meant for the man's habitation; now, the multiplication of man having entered into the Creator's designs, it follows that the nature of man is to be united in great societies over the whole surface of the globe: for the nature of a being is to exist as the Creator willed it. And this will is manifested perfectly by the facts.

The isolated man is not, therefore, *the man of nature*; when a small number of men were spread over a large area of land, mankind itself was not yet what it was to become. There were then only families, and these families thus scattered were still, *individually* or by their future union, nothing but peoples in embryo.

And if, long after the formation of great societies, some tribes lost in the desert still present to us the phenomenon of the human species in its infancy, they are still children-peoples who are not yet what they ought to be. What would one think of a naturalist who should say that man is an animal thirty to thirty-five inches long, without strength and intelligence, and uttering nothing but inarticulate cries? Yet this naturalist, by bestowing on the physical and moral nature of man only the characteristics of infancy, would be no more ridiculous than the philosopher seeking the political nature of this same being in the *rudiments* of society.

Any question about the nature of man must be resolved by history. The philosopher who wants to prove to us, by *a priori* reasoning, what man ought to be, does not deserve to be listened to: he substitutes expediency for experience, and his own decisions for the will of the Creator.

Let me suppose that we can prove that a savage in America is happier and has fewer vices than a civilized man: could we conclude that the latter is a degraded being, or, if you will, further from *nature* than the former? Not at all. It is just like saying that the nature of the individual man is to remain a child because at this stage of life he is free from the vices and misfortunes which must besiege him in his manhood. History constantly shows us men united into more or less numerous societies, ruled by different sovereignties. Once they have multiplied beyond a certain point, they cannot exist otherwise.

Thus, strictly speaking, there has never been for *man* a time before society, because before the formation of political societies, man is not altogether man, and it is absurd to look for the characteristics of any being in the germ of that being.

Thus, society is not the work of man, but the immediate result of the will of the Creator who willed that man should be what he always and everywhere has been.

Rousseau and all the thinkers of his temper imagine, or try to imagine, a people *in the state of nature* (this is their expression), properly deliberating on the advantages and disadvantages of the social state and finally determining to pass from one to the other. But there is not a shadow of common sense in this. What were these men doing before this *National Convention* in which they finally resolved to give themselves a sovereign?[1] They lived apparently without laws, without government; but for how long?

It is an essential error to represent the social state as an elective state based on the consent of men, on deliberation, and on a primitive contract, which is a thing impossible. When we talk about the state of *nature* as opposed to the social state, we talk nonsense deliberately. The word *nature* is one of those general terms which, like all abstract terms, is abused. In its widest sense, this word really signifies only the set of all laws, forces, and springs *which constitute* the universe; and *the particular nature* of this or that being signifies the set of all qualities which make it what it is, and without which it would be something else and could no longer fulfill the

1 [On September 3, 1791, the Constitution of 1791 was ratified, making the people, in the form of the nation, the sovereign (title III, article 1).]

designs of its maker. Thus, the union of all the parts comprising a machine meant to tell the time forms the nature or the essence of the *watch*; and the *nature* or essence of the *balance wheel* is to have such and such a shape, dimension, and position, otherwise it would no longer be a balance wheel, and could not fulfill its functions. The *nature* of a viper is to crawl, to have scaly skin and hollow, movable fangs that discharge a deadly venom; and the *nature* of man is to be an intelligent, religious, and sociable animal. An unswerving experience teaches us this; and I see nothing that opposes it. If someone wants to prove that the nature of the viper is to have wings and a melodious voice, and that of the beaver to live isolated at the top of the highest mountains, it is up to him to prove it. In the meantime, we will believe in what is, what must be, and what has always been.

"The social order," says Rousseau, "is a sacred right that serves as a basis for all others. Yet this right does not come from *nature*: it is, therefore, based on convention." (*Contrat social*, ch. IV)

What is *nature*? What is a *right*? And how is an *order* a *right*? ... But let us pass over these difficulties: the questions would never end with a man who abuses all terms and defines none. We at least have the right to ask him for proof of this great assertion: "*the social order does not come from nature*". – "I must," he himself said, "establish what I have just advanced." This is, indeed, what should be done; but the way in which he does it is truly curious. He spends three chapters proving that the social order does not come from familial society, nor from force, nor slavery (ch. II, III, IV), and he concludes (chapter 5) *that we must always return to a first convention.* This manner of demonstration is convenient, and all that is missing is the majestic formula of the geometers: "*which was to be demonstrated*".[2]

It is also strange that Rousseau has not even tried to prove the only thing that had to be proven: for if the social order comes from nature, there is no social pact.

"Before examining," he says, "the act by which a people elects a king,[3] it would be well to examine the act by which a people is a people: for this act, being necessarily prior to the other, is the true foundation of society." (*Ibid.* ch. V) – "It is the eternal mania of philosophers," Rousseau says elsewhere, "to deny what is, and to explain what is not."[4] Let us add, on our side: it is the eternal mania of Rousseau to make fun of philosophers,[5] without

2 [i.e. "QED".]

3 Why a king? He would have to say a sovereign.

4 *Nouvelle Heloise*, vol. 4.

5 See *Emile*, vol. 3, the portrait that Rousseau made of so striking a truth about these gentlemen. He only forgets to add: *Et quorum pars magna fui* ["and in which I played a great part" Vergil, Aeneid, book 2, line 6].

suspecting that he too was a *philosopher* in the full sense that he attributed to word: for example, from cover to cover, the *Social Contract* denies the nature of man, which *is*, in order to explain the *social pact*, which *is not*.

This is how one reasons when one separates man from the Divinity. Instead of tiring oneself out in the search for error, it would cost little to turn one's eyes towards the source of beings; but a manner of philosophizing so simple, so sure, and so consoling, is not to the taste of the writers of this unfortunate age, whose true malady is an abhorrence of common sense.

Could it not be said that man, this property of the Divinity,[6] is cast upon the earth by a blind cause; that he could be this or that, and that it is by virtue of his choice that he is what he is? Certainly, in creating *man*, God had in mind an end: so the question is thus reduced to knowing whether man has become a *political animal*, as Aristotle said, *through* or *against* the divine will. Although this question, stated plainly, is a true sign of madness, it is nevertheless stated indirectly in a host of writings, the authors of which very often even decide in favour of the latter. The word *nature* has made a host of errors to be pronounced. Let us repeat that the nature of a being is only the aggregation of qualities attributed to this being by the Creator. Mr. Burke has said, with a depth that cannot be sufficiently admired, that art is man's nature: yes, without a doubt, man with all his affections, all his knowledge, all his arts, is truly *the natural man*, and the web of the weaver is as *natural* as that of the spider.

The *state of nature* for man is, therefore, to be what he is today and what he has always been, that is to say, *sociable*: all the archives in the world establish this truth. Because we have found in the forests of America a new country about which everything has not yet been said, and wandering hordes we call *savages*, it does not follow that man is not naturally sociable: the savage is an exception, and, therefore, proves nothing; he has fallen from the *natural state*, or has not yet arrived at it. And note well that the savage does not even form an exception, strictly speaking: for this species of men lives in society and knows sovereignty just as we do. His Majesty the Cacique[7] is covered with a greasy beaver skin instead of a coat of Siberian fox; he dines royally on his enemy prisoner instead of sending him back on his own recognizance, as in our degraded Europe. But after all, there is among the savages a society, a sovereignty, a government, and laws of some sort. As for the true or false stories of human beings found in the woods and living absolutely like animals, we are, no doubt, excused from examining theories based on these kinds of facts or tales.

6 This beautiful expression is Plato's. See the *Phaedo*.

7 [The term originally refers to a tribal chief in the Spanish West Indies.]

Chapter III:
Of Sovereignty in General

If sovereignty is not anterior to the *people*, these two ideas are at least collateral since it takes a sovereign to make a *people*. It is as impossible to imagine a human society, a people, without a sovereign, as a hive and a swarm of bees without a queen: for by virtue of the eternal laws of nature, the swarm exists either in this way or not at all. Society and sovereignty were thus born together; it is impossible to separate these two ideas. Picture to yourself an isolated man: there is, then, no question of laws or of government, since he is not quite fully a man and there is not yet any society. Put the man in contact with his fellows: from that moment you suppose a sovereign. The first man was king over his children;[1] each isolated family was governed in the same way. But as soon as the families joined together, they needed a sovereign, and this *sovereign* made a *people* by giving them laws, since there is no society but by the sovereign. Everyone knows this famous verse:

> The first who was king was a fortunate soldier.[2]

Perhaps nothing falser has ever been said; on the contrary, it must be said that: *the first soldier was paid by a king.*

There was a *people*, a civilization of some kind, and a sovereign as soon as men joined together. The word *people* is a relative term which has no meaning separate from the idea of sovereignty: for the idea of a *people* implies that of an aggregation around a common centre, and without sovereignty there can be no political cohesion or unity.

We must, therefore, exile to the world of fantasy the ideas of choice and

1 In observing that there can be no human association without some sort of domination, I do not intend to establish an exact parity between paternal authority and sovereign authority: everything has been said on this point. [cf. Filmer's *Patriarcha*]

2 [Lefranc de Pompignan, *Didon* (act III, scene III); Maistre quotes Voltaire, who borrowed this line for his *Mérope* (act I, scene III).]

deliberation in the establishment of society and sovereignty. This operation is the immediate work of nature or, to put it better, of its Author.

If men have rejected such simple and obvious ideas, they are to be pitied. Let us accustom ourselves to seeing in human society only the expression of the divine will. The more these false teachers have tried to isolate us and detach the branch from its STEM, the more we must attach ourselves to it, on pain of desiccation and decay.

Chapter IV:
Of Particular Sovereignties and Nations

The same power which decreed social order and sovereignty has also decreed different modifications of sovereignty according to the differing character of nations.

Nations are born and die like individuals; nations have *fathers*, in the literal sense, and *founders* ordinarily more famous than their fathers, although the greatest merit of these founders is to penetrate the character of the infant-people and place it in circumstances wherein it may most fully develop its powers.

Nations have a general *soul* and a true moral unity which makes them what they are. This unity is especially manifested through language.

The Creator has marked out over the globe the limits of nations, and St. Paul has spoken philosophically to the Athenians when he said to them: *And [He] hath made of one blood all nations of men for to dwell on all the face of the earth, and hath determined the times before appointed, and the bounds of their habitation* (Acts, XVII, 26). These bounds are visible, and we always see each people tending to fill completely one of the enclosed spaces between these bounds. Sometimes invincible circumstances hurl two nations into one another and force them to mingle: then their constituent principles interpenetrate, and the result is a *hybrid* nation which may be more or less powerful and famous than if it were of *pure* stock.

But several national precepts thrown into the same receptacle may cause mutual harm. The seeds are squeezed and smothered; the men who compose them, condemned to a certain moral and political mediocrity, will never attract the eyes of the world despite a great number of individual merits, until a great jolt, starting one of these seeds germinating, allows it to engulf the others and assimilate them to its own substance. *Italiam! Italiam!*[1]

1 <The keen vision of one J. de Maistre is not required to recognize with him the disadvantages of the excessive fragmentation of Italy. But the constant adversary of the Revolution, the honest and Christian politician, would with all his energy

Sometimes one nation subsists amid a much more numerous one, refusing to amalgamate because there is not enough affinity between them, and retains its moral unity. Then, if some extraordinary event comes to disorganize the dominant nation, or prompts a great movement, we will be very surprised to see the other resist the general impetus and produce a contrary movement. Hence the miracle of the Vendée. The other malcontents of the kingdom, though in much greater numbers, could not have accomplished anything of this kind, because these discontented men are only *men*, whereas the Vendée is a *nation*. Salvation can even come from this, for the *soul* that presides over these miraculous efforts, like all active powers, has an expansive force that makes it tend constantly to enlarge, so that it can, in gradually assimilating what resembles itself and pressing out the rest, finally acquire enough supremacy to achieve a prodigy. Sometimes the national unity is strongly pronounced in a very small tribe; as it cannot have a language of its own, to console itself it appropriates that of its neighbours by an accent and particular forms. Its virtues are its own, its vices are its own; in order not to have the ridiculous ones of others, it makes them its own; without physical strength, it will make itself known. Tormented by the need to act, it will be conqueror in its own way. Nature, by one of those contrasts that it loves, will place it, playfully, beside frivolous or apathetic peoples who will make it noticed from afar. Its brigandage will be cited in the realm of opinion; at last, it will make its mark, it will be cited, it will succeed in putting itself in the balance with great names, and it will be said: *I cannot decide between Geneva and Rome.*[2]

have disapproved of the methods of a Cavour and a Garibaldi. There was a way to unite the forces and resources of the brilliant peninsula while respecting its rights.> [Count Camillo Benso di Cavour—described by Benjamin Disraeli as "utterly unscrupulous"—sometime Prime Minister of Piedmont-Sardinia, convinced King Charles Albert to revert to constitutional monarchy and to go to war against Austria, leading to the king's abdication; he also exacerbated the waning influence of the Catholic Church by ordering the closure of half of the monastic houses within Sardinian territories. Garibaldi, general, popular hero, and intense anticlerical and social reformer, was privately supported and publicly opposed by Cavour in his expedition against Sicily, later winning Naples and ostensibly leading a private expedition against the Papal States, but with the secret complicity of the Italian government.]

2 [For Maistre, in the world-historical struggle between the forces of secularism and those of religion, Geneva and Rome stand for the latter; yet Protestant Geneva is only nominally on the same side as Catholic Rome. In his *Oeuvres*, Maistre characterizes Protestantism as "le *sans-cullottisme* de la religion", and in *Considerations on France*, p. 73, states that Protestantism and the French Revolution partake of a common source.]

When we speak of the *spirit* of a nation, the expression is not as metaphorical as we think.

From the differing character of nations arises the different modifications of governments. We can say that each has its own character, for even those that belong to the same class and bear the same name present different shades to the eye of the observer.

The same laws cannot suit different provinces, which have different customs, live in opposite climates, and cannot bear the same form of government…

The general objects of every good institution must be modified in each country by the relationships which spring as much from the local situation as from the character of the inhabitants; and it is on the basis of these relationships that we must assign to each people a particular system of institutions which is the best, not perhaps in itself, but for the state for which it is intended…

There is only one good government possible in a state: and as a thousand events can change the relations of a people, not only can different governments be good for different peoples, but for the same people in different times! …

There has always been much discussion about the best form of government, without considering that each of them is the best in some cases, and the worst in others! …

We must not, therefore, believe that "*all forms of government are appropriate to all countries; liberty, for example, not being the fruit of all climates, is not within the grasp of all peoples.*" The more we meditate on this principle established by Montesquieu, the more one senses its truth. The more we challenge it, the more this leads to establishing it by new proofs…

When, therefore, we ask what the best government is absolutely, we formulate a question as insoluble as it is indeterminate; or, if you will, it has as many good solutions as there are possible combinations in the absolute and relative positions of peoples.

From these certain principles arises a consequence which is no less certain: that the social contract is a chimera. For if there are as many different governments as there are different peoples; if the forms of these governments are forcibly prescribed by the power which has given to each nation this or that moral, physical, geographical, and economic composition, it is no longer permissible to speak of a *pact*. Each mode of sovereignty is the immediate result of the Creator's will, like sovereignty in general. For one nation, despotism is as natural and legitimate as democracy is for another,[3]

3 Will it be said that, even in this hypothesis, there is always a pact according

and if a man established for himself these unshakable principles[4] in a book expressly written to establish that "*one must always go back to a convention*",[5] if he wrote in one chapter that "man was born free,"[6] and in another that "liberty, not being a fruit of all climates, is not made for all peoples";[7] this man would be, without contradiction, one of the most ridiculous in the world.

No nation having been able to give itself the character and composition that render it fit for such and such a government, all have agreed not only to believe this truth abstractly, but to believe that the divinity intervened directly in the establishment of their particular sovereignty.

The Holy Scriptures show us the first king of the chosen people, elected and crowned by an immediate intervention of the divinity;[8] the annals of all the nations of the world assign the same origin to their particular governments. Only the names are changed. All of them, after having traced the succession of their princes to a more or less remote period, finally arrive at those mythological times whose true history would instruct us far better than any other. All of them show us the cradle of sovereignty surrounded by miracles; always divinity intervenes in the foundation of empires; always the first sovereign, at least, is a favourite of Heaven: he receives the sceptre from the hands of the divinity. The divinity communicates with him, inspires him, engraves on his forehead the sign of its power, and the laws that he dictates to his fellow men are only the fruit of his celestial communications.

These are fables, it will be said. In truth, I do not know anything about that, but the fables of all peoples, even modern peoples, enfold many realities. The Holy Ampulla,[9] for example, is only a hieroglyph; one only need know how to read. The power of healing attributed to certain princes or certain dynasties of princes is also due to this universal dogma of the divine origin of sovereignty. Let us not be surprised, then, that the ancient

to which each contracting party is bound to maintain the government as it is? In this case, for despotism or absolute monarchy, the pact will be precisely that which Rousseau ridicules at the end of his pitiful chapter on slavery. "I make with you a convention entirely at your expense and entirely for my benefit, that I will observe so long as I please, and that you will observe so long as I please." (*Contrat social*, 1. I, ch. IV)

4 *Contrat social*, 1. I, ch, IX, 11; 1. III, ch. I, II, III.

5 *Contrat social*, 1. I, ch. V.

6 *Contrat social*, 1. I, ch. I.

7 *Contrat social*, 1. III, ch. VIII.

8 [1 Kings 10:1]

9 [See note 46, p. 25, in the *Essay on the Generative Principle*.]

founders have spoken so much of God. They felt that they had no right to speak in their own name. It is of them, moreover, that it was necessary to say without exaggerating "*est Deus in nobis, agitante calescimus ipso* ["there is a god within us, when he stirs, we become inflamed" Ovid, *Fasti*, VI, lines 5–6]".[10] The philosophers of this age have complained much of the alliance between the empire and the priesthood, but the wise observer cannot refrain from admiring the obstinacy of men in intertwining these two things; the further back we go towards antiquity, the more religious legislation we find. All that nations relate to us about their origin proves that they are agreed in regarding sovereignty as divine in its essence: otherwise they would have told quite different tales. They never speak to us of a *primordial contract*, of voluntary association, of popular deliberation. No historian cites the *primary assemblies* of Memphis or Babylon. It is a true folly to imagine that universal prejudice is the work of sovereigns. A particular interest may well abuse the general belief, but it cannot create it. If that of which I speak had not been based on the prior assent of peoples, not only could it not have been forcibly adopted, but the sovereigns could not have imagined such a fraud. In general, every universal idea is natural.

10 [The transcription is wrong—the actual line is *est deus in nobis; agitante calescimus illo*.]

Chapter V:

An Examination of Some Ideas of Rousseau on the Legislator

Rousseau has written a chapter on *the legislator* where all ideas are confounded in the most intolerable way. In the first place, this word *legislator* can have two different meanings: usage gives this name to the extraordinary man who promulgates constitutional laws, and to the much less admirable man who publishes civil laws. It seems that Rousseau understands the word in the first sense, since he speaks of the one "who dares to undertake to institute a people and who constitutes the Republic". But, soon after, he says that "*the legislator is in all respects an extraordinary man*, IN THE STATE". Here there is already a state; the people is thus constituted, so it is no longer a question of *instituting* a people, but, at most, of reforming it.

Then Lycurgus, the modern legislators of the republics of Italy, Calvin, and the decemvirs are cited mercilessly and all at once.

Calvin can thank Rousseau for having placed him next to Lycurgus; he certainly needed such an introduction, and without Rousseau he would never have chanced to find himself in such good company.

As for the decemvirs, Rome was 300 years old and possessed all its fundamental laws when three deputies went to seek civil laws for it in Greece; and I do not see that we must regard the decemvirs as above the human sphere[1] for having said:

> *SI IN JUS VOCAT, ATQUE EAT, SI CALVITUR*
> *PEDEMVE STRUIT, MANUM ENDO JACITO*[2]

1 "The legislator is in every respect an extraordinary man in the state… His business … has nothing in common with human dominion. (*Contrat social*, ch. VII)

2 [Maistre has run the first two statutes of the twelve tables together: (1) *Si in jus vocat, atque eat; ni it, antestamino: igitur eum capito* ("If the plaintiff summons him to trial, he shall go; if he does not go, the plaintiff shall call a witness: only then

> ["If the plaintiff summons him to trial, he shall go ...
> if he attempts evasion
> or takes flight, the plaintiff shall lay a hand on him"]

...and a thousand other things, assuredly very beautiful, on legacies, wills, funerals, roads, gargoyles, and gutters, but which are nevertheless a little below the creations of Lycurgus.

Rousseau confounds all these ideas, and generally affirms that the legislator is neither magistrate nor sovereign. "His business," he says, "is a superior function that has nothing in common with human dominion." If Rousseau means to say that a private individual can be consulted by a sovereign and can propose to him good laws that may be accepted, this is one of those truths so trivial and so sterile that it is useless to take it up. If he intends to maintain that a sovereign cannot make civil laws, as the decemvirs did, this is a discovery of which he has all the honour, no one having ever suspected it. If he intends to prove that a sovereign cannot be a legislator in the full sense of the term and cannot give to peoples truly constitutional laws by creating and perfecting their public law, I appeal to universal history.

But universal history never troubles Rousseau, for when it condemns him (which almost always happens), he says that it is wrong. "Whoever drafts the laws," he says, "therefore, does not have *or ought not to have* any legislative right." (*Ibid.*)

Here we must remain silent: Rousseau himself speaking as legislator, there is nothing left to say. However, he also quotes history, and it is not unprofitable to examine how he acquits himself.

"Rome," he says, "in its greatest age... was brought to the brink of destruction for having placed into the same hands (the decemvirs) legislative authority and sovereign power." (*Ibid.*)

In the first place, legislative power and sovereign power being the same thing according to Rousseau, it is as if he had said that the decemvirs united sovereign power and sovereign power.

In the second place, since, according to Rousseau himself, "the decemvirs never claimed for themselves the right to pass any law on their own authority," and since, in effect, the laws they drew up were sanctioned by the assembly of centuries, it is, again, as if he had said that the decemvirs had the legislative authority and did not have the legislative authority.

In short, the simple truth, not according to Rousseau, but according to Livy, is that the Romans, having had the imprudence to abolish all their

shall the plaintiff seize him"). (2) *Si calvitur, pedemve struit, manum endo jacito* ("If he attempts evasion or takes flight, the plaintiff shall lay a hand on him").]

magistracy and to unite all the powers on the heads of the decemvirs,[3] thus created true sovereigns who lost their heads like all *impromptu* sovereigns, and abused their power. This is, again, one of those banal truths that everyone knows, and which is absolutely foreign to what Rousseau wished to prove. Let us pass on to Lycurgus.

"When Lycurgus," he says, "gave laws to his country, he began by abdicating the throne." (*Ibid.*) These words obviously signify that this famous legislator, *being a king*, abdicated kingship *at the moment* when he wished to give laws to his country, and to put himself in a position to do so. Now, up to this point we had believed that Lycurgus, strictly speaking, was never king, that he was only believed to be king for a moment, that is to say, from the death of his brother to the moment when his sister-in-law's pregnancy was declared; that, in truth, he had governed for eight months—but as regent and tutor (*Prodicos*) of the young Charilaüs; that, in showing his nephew to the Spartans and telling them "Spartan Lords, a king is born to us," he had done unto the legitimate heir only a strict act of justice which could not bear the name *abdication*. We had believed, moreover, that Lycurgus thought nothing *of giving laws to his country*; that since that memorable epoch, fatigued by the intrigues and hatred of his brother's widow and his partisans, he travelled to the isle of Crete, to Asia Minor, Egypt, and even, according to a Greek historian, to Spain, Africa, and even to the great Indies; and that it was only upon his return from these long voyages that he undertook his great work, overcome by the repeated prayers of his compatriots and by the oracles of the gods. This is what Plutarch tells us; but Rousseau would have been able to say, like Molière, "*we have changed all that*".

Behold how well this great political mind knew history!

3 *Placet creari decemviros sine provocatione, et ne quis eo anno alius magistratus esset* ["It was determined to create decemvirs, from whom there should be no appeal, and that there be no other magistracy that year"]. (Livy, 1, III)

Chapter VI:
Continuation of the Same Subject

After having seen what the legislator *must not be* according to Rousseau, let us see *what he must be* according to him.

> To discover the best rules of society which are appropriate to nations would require *a superior intelligence* that saw all the passions of men and yet experienced none; who had nothing to do with our nature and yet knew it thoroughly; whose happiness was independent of us, and yet who was willing to look after ours."[1]

This intelligence is already found. He is mad indeed who looks for it on earth, or who does not see it where it is.

> It would take *gods* to give laws to men.[2]

Not at all, it takes only one.

> Whoever dares to undertake to found a people must feel that he is in a position to change human nature, so to speak; to transform every individual who, by himself, is a perfect and solitary whole, into part of a greater whole, from which this individual in a manner receives his life and his being; to alter man's constitution in order to reinforce it; to substitute a partial and moral existence for the physical and independent existence we have all received from nature; it is necessary, in a word, that he take from man his own forces in order to give him those which are alien to him, and of which he can make no use without the help of others.[3]

1 *Contrat social*, 1, VIII, ch. VII: The Legislator.
2 *Contrat social*, 1, VIII, ch. VII.
3 *Contrat social*, 1, VIII, ch. VII.

The *founder of a people* is a man whose distinctive quality is a certain *practical* good sense altogether incensed by metaphysical subtleties. Lycurgus would not have understood a word of the tirade we have just read and would have recommended the author to the powerful Aesculapius.[4] What is the *transformation* of an *individual* whose essence and end are determined by the Supreme Being? What is a *perfect and solitary whole*? Where, when, and how has this wonder existed? What is *man's constitution*? What is the strengthening of a constitution by its *alteration*? What is the *physical and independent* existence of an essentially spiritual, moral, and dependent being? Thank God that it is not on these cobwebs that good sense builds empires.

> Thus, in the work of legislation, we find two things that are incompatible: an enterprise beyond human strength, and, to execute it, an authority which comes to nothing.[5]

On the contrary, the founder of a nation has, for the execution of his enterprise, an authority which is everything. For "he was born to command, nature having given him grace and an efficacy in enticing men to obey him willingly because he is loved by the gods, and a god rather than man."[6]

Rousseau then shows perfectly how and why all legislators have had to speak in the name of the divinity; then he adds these remarkable words:

> But it does not belong to any man to make the gods speak, nor to be believed when he proclaims himself their interpreter. The great soul of the legislator is the true miracle that must prove his MISSION. Any man can engrave stone tablets, or buy an oracle, or feign a secret exchange with some divinity, or train a bird to speak into his ear, or find other crude means to impose upon the people. One who does no more than this may perhaps even cobble together a band of fools, but he will never found an empire, and his extravagant work will soon perish with him.[7]

Such is the character of Rousseau; he often hits upon particular truths and expresses them better than anyone; but these truths are barren in his hands: he almost always concludes badly, because his pride constantly drives him from the roads beaten by common sense and throws him into eccentricity. No one carves his materials better than he, and no one builds

4 [Greek god of medicine.]
5 *Contrat social*, 1, VIII, ch. VII.
6 Plutarch, *in Lycurgus*, French translation by Amyot.
7 *Contrat social*, I, II, ch. IV.

more poorly. Everything is good in his works, except his systems.

After the brilliant and even profound piece just read, we expect interesting conclusions on the organization of peoples. Here is the result:

> "It is not necessary from all this to conclude, with Warburton, that politics and religion have among us a common object, but that, in the origin of nations, the one serves as an instrument for the other."

Desinit in piscem ["Finishes as a fish"].[8] Warburton,[9] who understood himself, never said that politics and religion had *the same goal among us*, which means nothing. But he was able to say with great justification that the goal of politics will not be achieved if religion does not serve as its base.

8 [From the opening of Horace's *Ars Poetica*. The full quote makes clear Maistre's reaction: *Humano capiti cervicem pictor equinam iungere si velit, et varias inducere plumas, undique conlatis membris, ut turpiter atrum desinat in piscem mulier formosa superne, spectatum admissi risum teneatis, amici.* ("If a painter should wish to join a horse's neck to a human head, and to spread a variety of plumage over all manner of limbs, so that what begins as a beautiful woman above should finish as a fish below, could you hold back your laughter, my friends, were you met with such a sight?")]

9 [William Warburton, literary critic, theologian, and Bishop of Gloucester, was author of *Alliance between Church* and *State and The Divine Legation of Moses*. The latter was a conservative defence of Christian belief against deism, and well known by Maistre.]

Chapter VII: Founders and the Political Constitution of Peoples

When one reflects on the moral unity of nations, it cannot be doubted that it is the result of a single cause. What wise Bonnet, in refuting a fantasy of Buffon,[1] said of the animal body can be said of the body politic: every seed is necessarily *one*, and it is always from one man that each people takes its dominant trait and its distinctive character.

To know, then, why and how a man literally *engenders* a nation, and how he communicates to it that moral temperament, that character, that general soul which must, through the centuries and an infinite number of generations, survive in a sensible way and distinguish one people from all others—this is a mystery, like so many others, upon which we can meditate profitably.

The genealogies of nations are written in their languages. Like peoples, idioms are born, grow, mingle, interpenetrate, associate, fight, and die.

Some languages have perished in the fullest sense of the word, like Egyptian: others, like Greek and Latin, are dead only in one sense, and live on through writing.

There is one, Hebrew, perhaps the oldest of all, whether considered in itself or as a dialect of *Syriac*, which still lives on in Arabic, with the passage of fifty centuries unable to efface its traits.

The mixture of idioms produces the same confusion as that of peoples, but we are not completely lost in this labyrinth, and the penetrating eye of the Sir William Jones can trace back, through a host of dialects most foreign to our ears, to three primitive nations from which all the others are descended.[2]

1 [See also note 15, p. 76. Bonnet's 1764 work *Contemplation of Nature* was written in part with the aim of refuting Georges Louis Leclerc, comte de Buffon's theories of spontaneous generation and epigenesis.]

2 *Asiatic researches*, in 4e. Calcutta, 1792, vol. 3. [Sir William Jones was among

But the development of these lofty speculations does not belong to this work. I return to my subject, observing that the government of a nation is no more its own work than is its language. Just as, in nature, the seeds of countless plants are destined to perish unless the wind or the hand of man places them where they can be fruitful—in the same way, there are in nations certain qualities, certain forces which exist only in potential until they receive their impetus from circumstances alone or from those made use of by a living hand.

The founder of a people is precisely this skilful hand; endowed with an extraordinary penetration, or, what is more probable, an infallible instinct (for often genius is not aware of what it is doing, and this is why it differs from intelligence), he divines those hidden forces and qualities which form his nation's character, the means of fertilizing them, of putting them into action, and of making the greatest possible use of them. We never see him write or argue; his manner is inspired: and if he sometimes takes up the pen, it is not to expound, but to command.

One of the grand errors of this age is to believe that the political constitution of peoples is a purely human work; that one can make a constitution like a watchmaker makes a watch. Could anything be more false? What is yet more false is the idea that this great work can be executed by an assembly of men. The Author of all things has but two ways of giving a government to a people: almost always He reserves to Himself its formation more directly by tending to it, so to speak, making it germinate imperceptibly like a plant, by the concurrence of an infinity of circumstances that we call fortuitous; but when He wants to lay all at once the foundations of a political edifice and to show the universe a creation of this kind, it is to rare men, it is to the true elect that He confides His powers: placed at intervals through the course of the ages, they rise like obelisks on the path of time, and as the human race ages, they appear less often. To make them fit for these extraordinary works, God invests them with extraordinary power, often unknown to their contemporaries, and perhaps to themselves. Rousseau himself has uttered the right word when he said that the work of the founder of peoples was a MISSION. It is a truly childish idea to turn these great men into charlatans, and to attribute their success to I know not what *tricks* invented to impose themselves on the multitude. They quote the pigeon of Mahomet, the nymph Egeria, etc.;[3] but if the founders of nations,

the first to posit a relationship between the Sanskrit, Latin, and Greek languages, which would yield the discovery of Indo-European.]

3 [The reference to Mohammed's pigeon is possibly from *The New and Complete Pigeon Fancyer* by Daniel Girton (1735), which claims that Mohammed owned a

who were all prodigious men, should present themselves before us; if we but knew their genius and their power, instead of talking foolishly about usurpation, fraud, and fanaticism, we would fall down at their knees, and our deficiency would perish before the sacred sign that shone forth from their brows.

> Empty artifice forms a transitory bond; only wisdom makes it endure. The still surviving Judaic law, that of the child of Ismael, which for ten centuries have governed half the world, still proclaims today the great men who laid it down; and while proud philosophy or the blind spirit of party sees in them only lucky impostures, the true political mind admires that great and powerful genius which presides over enduring institutions.[4]

What is certain is that the civil constitution of peoples is never the result of deliberation.

Almost all great legislators have been kings, and even nations destined for republicanism have been constituted by kings; it is they who preside over the political establishment of peoples and who create their first fundamental laws. Thus, all the small republics of Greece were first governed by kings, and free under monarchical authority.[5] Thus, in Rome and Athens, kings preceded the republican government and were the true founders of liberty.

The most famous nation of high antiquity, the one that most attracted the curiosity of ancient observers, that was the most visited, the most studied—Egypt—was never governed but by kings.

The most famous legislator in the world, Moses, was more than a king; Servius and Numa were kings; Lycurgus was so close to royalty that he had all its authority. He was a Philip of Orleans, with the ascendancy of genius, experience, and virtue. In the Middle Ages, Charlemagne, St. Louis, and Alfred can still be ranked among the constituent legislators.

white Barb pigeon which would whisper sayings from God into his ear. Egeria was divine consort and counsellor of Numa Pompilius, dictating to him the laws and religious rituals of Rome.]

4 *Contrat social*, 1, II, ch. IV.

5 *Omnes Graeciae civitates a principio reges habuere, non tamen despoticos, ut apud gentes barbares, sed secundum leges et mores patrios, adeo ut regum potentissimus fuerit qui justissimus erat et legum observantissimus* ["In the beginning, all Greek cities were ruled by kings, yet not by despots as among the barbarian peoples, but according to hereditary laws and customs, to the extent that it was the great power of kings which was most just and respectful of the laws"]. (Dionysius of Halicarnassus, book 5)

Finally, the greatest legislators have been sovereigns; and Solon is, I believe, the only example of a private individual who forms a somewhat striking exception to the general rule.

As for the small republics of modern Italy, these political atoms deserve little attention. No doubt they began like those of Greece; besides, one should never concern oneself with anything but the general case: it is Rousseau's talent (and one should not envy him it) to build systems on exceptions.

Observe all the world's constitutions, ancient and modern: you will see that the experience of the ages may, from time to time, have held forth some institutions destined to perfect governments according to their primitive constitutions, or to prevent abuses capable of altering them. It is possible to assign the date and authors of these institutions; but you will notice that the true roots of the government have always been there, and that it is impossible to show their origin for the quite simple reason that they are as old as the nations, and that, not being the result of agreement, there can be no trace of a convention which never existed.

No important and truly constitutional institution ever establishes anything new; it only declares and defends previous rights: hence one never knows the constitution of a country on the basis of its written constitutional laws, because these laws are made at different times only to declare rights forgotten or contested, and because there is always a host of things that are unwritten.[6]

There is certainly nothing so remarkable in Roman history as the establishment of the tribunes; but this institution does not establish any new right for the people, who only gave themselves magistrates to protect their ancient and constitutional rights against the attacks of the aristocracy. Everyone gained by it, even the patricians. Cicero has furnished excellent reasons for it which clearly prove that the establishment of these famous magistrates only gave form to the disorderly action of the people and allowed them the protection of their constitutional rights.[7] In effect, the Ro-

6 I believe, for example, that the most erudite man would be extremely reluctant to mark out the precise limits of the power of the *Roman Senate*.

7 *Nimia potestas est tribunorum plebis. Quis neget? Sed vis populi mullo saevior multoque vehementior, quae, ducem, quod habet, interdum lenior est, quam si nullum haberet. Dux enim suo periculo progredi cogitat: populi impetus periculi sui rationem non habet* ["The power of the tribunes of the plebs is excessive. Who would deny it? But the power of the people is much harsher and crueller, which, because it has a leader, it is sometimes calmer than if it had none. For a leader considers that he advances at his own peril: the ardour of the people has no thought for its own peril"]. (Cicero, *de Legibus*, I. 3, ch. X)

man people, like all the little nations of Greece I mentioned earlier, was always free, even under its kings. It was a tradition in this country that the division of the people into thirty *curiae* went back to Romulus, and that he himself had, with the assembly of the people, brought forth some of those laws which were called for this reason *leges curiatae* ["curiate laws"]. His successors made several more of this kind with the solemn formula: IF IT PLEASE THE PEOPLE.[8] The right of war and peace was divided between the senate and the people in a quite remarkable manner.[9] Finally, Cicero tells us that the people were sometimes called to the judgment of kings:[10] which is not surprising, for the democratic principle existed in the Roman Constitution, even under the kings; otherwise it could never have been established.[11] Tarquin was not expelled because he was king, but because he was a tyrant;[12] the royal power was given to two annual consuls; the revolution

8 *Romulum traditur populum in 30 partes divisisse, quas paries curias appellavit: propterea quod tunc reipublicae curam per sententias partium carum expediebat: et ita leges quasdam et ipse curiatas ad populum tulit. Tulerunt et sequentes reges, ut rogarent* SI PLACERENT LEGES ["According to tradition, Romulus divided the people into thirty parts, which parts he called curiae: for the reason that he had improved the administration ("curam") of the commonwealth by the advice of these parts: and so he put certain laws to the people. So did subsequent kings, that they should propose LAWS, IF IT PLEASE (the people)"]. (Pomponius, in 1. I. Dig., *de origine juris*)

9 *Plebi permisit de bello, si rex permisisset, decernere: non tamen in his populo absolutam voluit esse potestatem nisi in iis accessisset senatus auctoritas* ["If the king should allow, it was permitted to the plebs to decree concerning war: yet in these matters their power was not absolute, unless the authority of the senate had assented to this"]. (Dionysius of Halicarnassus, *Roman Antiquities*. 1, II) — These are the three powers which, I believe, are found wherever your freedom is at least an enduring freedom.

10 *Provocationem ad populum etiam a regibus fuisse docet* ["It is taught that final appeal even from kings was to the people"]. (Cicero, *de Republica. Apud Senecam*, epist. 108; Brottier, sur *Tacite*, Ann. II, 22)

11 *Romulus in urbe sua democratiam moderatam instituit… quare leges eius primigeniae, democratiae indoli ac naturae conveniunt* ["Romulus founded in his city a moderate democracy… because his primitive laws were naturally and innately fitted to democracy"]. (V, Jos. Toscano J. C. *Neapolitani juris publici romani arcana, sive de causis romani juris*, 1. 1, §2 and 3, p. 52, 70)

12 *Regale civitatis genus probatum quondam, postea, non tam regni, quam regis vitiis, repudiatum est* ["The monarchy, which was at first preferred, was afterward changed, not so much through the fault of monarchy, but of a monarch"]. (Cicero, *de Legibus*, L. III, c. 7) — *Regium imperium initio conservandae libertatis atque augendae reipublicae fuit* ["Royal power from the first tended to preserve freedom and enrich the state"]. (Sallust, *The War with Catiline*. VII)

went no further. The people did not acquire new rights; it returned only to liberty because it was made for liberty, because it was born with it and had enjoyed it originally. Its leaders (for the people never do anything) did justice to the tyrant, not to establish a new constitution, but to restore the old one, which the tyrant had temporarily violated.

Let us take another example from modern history.

Just as the foundations of Roman liberty long precede the establishment of the tribunate, and even the expulsion of kings, those of English liberty must be sought well before the Revolution of 1688. Freedom has been able to slumber in this nation; but it has always existed, it has always been possible to say of the government: *Miscuit res olim dissociabiles, principatum et libertatem* ["it blended things long irreconcilable, sovereignty and liberty", Tacitus, *Agricola*, III, 2]. There is even a very important observation to be made that the English monarchs to whom the Constitution of this kingdom owes the most—ALFRED, HENRY II and EDWARD I—were precisely conquering kings, that is to say, the most capable of violating it with impunity; and as an English historian very well observed, it is an insult to these great men to maintain, as some have done, that England had neither Constitution nor true liberty before the expulsion of the Stuarts.[13] In fine, as nations *are born*, literally, so are governments born with them. When we say that a people has given itself a government, it is as if we say that it has given itself a character and a colour. If we sometimes do not know how to distinguish the foundations of a government in its infancy, in no way does it follow that they do not exist. See these two embryos: can your eye see any difference between them? Yet, one is Achilles, and the other is Thersites.[14] Let us not take developments for creations.

The different forms and degrees of sovereignty have made us think that it was the work of peoples that had modified it at their pleasure; but nothing could be further from the truth. All peoples have the government that suits them, and none has chosen it. It is remarkable that it is nearly always to its misfortune that a people tries to give itself one, or, to put it more exactly, that too large a portion of the people aim at this object; for, in this disastrous experiment, it is too easy for the people to deceive itself as to its true interests; to pursue doggedly what cannot suit it, and, on the contrary,

13 Minford's *History of Greece*, vol. 2 — A distinguished member of the Opposition (Mr. Gray) said very well in the sitting of the English Parliament of February 11, 1794, that "the bill of rights did not establish new principles for the English Constitution; but only declared what are its true principles." (*Courier de Londres*, 1794, No. 13)

14 [The bow-legged, lame soldier who rebuked Agamemnon out of turn. *Iliad*, book II, lines 211–277.]

to reject what suits it best; and we know how terrible are errors of this kind. This is what made Tacitus say, with his simple profundity, that "there is less hazard *in accepting* a sovereign than *in seeking one.*"[15]

Moreover, as any exaggerated proposition is false, I do not intend to deny the possibility of political improvements brought about by a few wise men. It would be as sensible to deny the power of moral education and gymnastics for the physical and moral improvement of man; but this truth, far from undermining my general thesis, on the contrary, confirms it in establishing that human power can create nothing, and that everything depends on the primordial aptitude of peoples and individuals.

Hence, a free constitution is assured only when the different pieces of the political edifice are born together and, so to speak, beside one another. Men never respect what they have constructed: this is why an elective king does not possess the moral strength of an hereditary *sovereign*, because he is not *noble* enough, that is, he does not possess that kind of grandeur independent of men which is the work of time.

In England, it is not the Parliament that made the King, nor the King that made the Parliament. These two powers are collateral: they have established themselves, no one knows when or how, and the insensible and powerful sanction of opinion has finally made them what they are.[16]

Take, if you like, any republican government; a great Council will ordinarily be found in which, strictly speaking, sovereignty resides. Who established this Council? Nature, time, circumstances, that is, God. Several men have been put in their place, as elsewhere a single man has been. This country needed a sovereignty divided between several heads; and because

15 *Minore discrimine sumitur princeps quam quaeritur*. (Tacitus, *Histories*, 1, 56)

16 The truth can be found even in the Jacobin tribune. Félix Lepelletier, one of them, said on February 5, 1794, in speaking of the government of England, "The members of the *very high* Chamber hold their titles and their powers from the king; those of the *very low* Chamber have received theirs from a number of towns or communities where one class of privileged individuals alone has the right of suffrage. The mass of the people had no part in the creation of the kingdom in England nor in the present organization of Parliament. (See *le Moniteur*, 1794, No. 137)

The honourable member was wrong to confound the *peers* with the *peerage*, which holds from the king neither its existence nor its rights; he is wrong to confound the *representatives* with *representation*, which owes nothing to anyone, any more than the peerage. Other than this, he is right. No, undoubtedly, the English government (no more than others) is in no way the work of the people; and the criminal or extravagant conclusions which the Jacobin orator soon draws from this principle cannot alter the truth.

it had to be so, it was so established: this is all we know.

But as the general deliberations, intrigues, and interminable delays which result from a sovereign Council do not generally agree with the secret, prompt, and vigorous measures of a well-organized government, the force of things would demand the establishment of still some other power different from this General Council; and this necessary power you will find everywhere in these kinds of government, yet without being able to assign to it an origin. In a word, the mass of the people counts for nothing in all political creations. They respect the government only because it is not their work. This feeling is engraved upon their hearts in deep grooves. They bend under sovereignty because they feel that it is something sacred that they can neither create nor destroy. If, by dint of corruption and perfidious suggestions, it comes to an end, erasing within them this preservative feeling, if they have the misfortune to believe themselves called en masse to reform the state, all is lost. That is why, even in free states, it is so important that the men who govern be separated from the mass of the people by that personal regard which stems from birth and wealth: for if public opinion does not put a barrier between itself and authority, if power is not beyond its reach, if the governed host can believe itself the equal of the few who govern, there is no more government: thus the aristocracy is sovereign or governing in its essence; and the principle of the French Revolution runs headlong up against the eternal laws of nature.

Chapter VIII:
The Weakness of Human Power

In all political and religious creations, whatever their object and importance, it is a general rule that there is never any proportion between cause and effect. The effect is always immense in relation to the cause, so that man knows that he is but an instrument, and that he himself can create nothing.

The French *National Assembly*, which had the guilty folly of calling itself *Constituent*, seeing that all the legislators in the world had decorated the frontispiece of their laws with a solemn homage to the Divinity, felt obliged to also make a profession of faith, and I know not what involuntary spasm of a dying consciousness tore these paltry lines from the pretended legislators of France.[1]

> The National Assembly recognizes and declares, in the presence and under the auspices of the Supreme Being, etc.[2]

In the presence: no doubt, to their misfortune; but *under the auspices*: what madness! It is not a turbulent multitude, agitated by vile and furious passions, that God has chosen for the instrument of His will, in the exercise of the greatest act of his power on earth: the political organization of peoples. Wherever men gather and become restless, wherever their power unfolds with a crash and pretension, there the creative force is not to be found: *non in commotione Dominus* ["but the LORD was not in the earthquake"].[3] This power is announced only by the *gentle wind*.[4] It has been oft-repeated in recent times that freedom *is born* among storms: never, never. It *defends* itself, it is *strengthened* during storms, but it is born in silence, in peace, in

1 Constitution of 1789. Preamble of the Declaration of Human Rights.

2 When one speaks of the Constituent Assembly, it is hardly necessary to recall that one always abstracts from the respectable minority whose healthy principles and inflexible resistance have earned the admiration and respect of the world.

3 1 Kings XIX, 11.

4 1 Kings XIX, 12.

darkness; often even the father of a constitution does not know what he is doing in creating it; but the centuries that pass prove his mission, and it is Paul-Emile[5] and Cato who proclaim the greatness of Numa.

The more human reason trusts in itself, the more it seeks to draw all its strength from itself, the more absurd it is, the more it reveals its impotence. Hence the greatest scourge in the world has always been, in all ages, what we call *philosophy*, since philosophy is nothing but human reason acting alone, and human reason reduced to its own forces is nothing but a brute whose whole power is reduced to destroying.[6]

An elegant historian of antiquity has made a remarkable observation on what were called in his day, as now, the philosophers. "So far am I," he says, "from regarding philosophy as the teacher and blessed perfector of life, that I judge no men more in need of instruction in how to live than several of those engaged in discussing it. For I see that a great part of those who speak most eloquently of propriety and restraint in the schools are the very same men who live plunged headlong into all manner of vice."[7]

When, in olden days, Julian *the philosopher* called his colleagues to court, he made a cesspool of it. The good Tillemont, writing the history of this prince, thus names one of his chapters: "Julian's Court is filled with philosophers and condemned men;" And Gibbon, who is not suspect, naively observes that "it is awkward not to be able to contradict the accuracy of this title."[8]

Frederick II, philosopher in spite of himself, who paid these people to praise him, but who knew them well, thought no better of them; common sense forced him to say what everyone else knows, that "if he wanted to lose an empire, he would make it governed by philosophers."

Thus, it was not a theological exaggeration, it was a simple truth rigorously expressed, this sentence of one of our prelates who, fortunately for himself, died when he could still believe in a renewal: "In its pride, philosophy has said: '*It is to me that wisdom, science, and dominion belong; it is to me that the conduct of men belongs, since it is I who enlighten.* In order

5 [Lucius Aemilius Paullus, twice consul, in 219 and 216 BCE.]

6 <It is evident from what follows that the author does not deny reason the power to know the truth by itself, but he does deny it the power to lead man to happiness when it is reduced to its individual strengths.>

7 *Tantum abest ut ego magistram esse putem vitae philosophiam beataeque vite perfectricem, ut nullis magis existimem opus esse magistris vivendi quam plerisque qui in ea disputanda versantur video enim magnam partem eorum qui in schola de pudore et continentia praecipiunt argutissime, eosdem in omnium libidinum cupiditatibus vivere.* (Cornelius Nepos, *Fragmenta apud Lactantium, Inst. Div.* 15, 10)

8 [*Decline and Fall of the Roman Empire*, Vol. 2, ch. XXIII, note 48.]

to punish it, to cover it with disgrace, it was necessary that God should condemn it to reign for a moment.'"

Indeed, it has reigned over one of the most powerful nations in the world; it reigns, it will doubtless reign long enough that it cannot complain that it wanted for time; and never was there a more deplorable example of the absolute deficiency of human reason reduced to its own forces. What spectacle did the French legislators present us? Aided by all human knowledge, lessons from all philosophers ancient and modern, and the experience of all ages, masters of opinion, expending immense wealth, having allies everywhere, in a word, fortified in every human power, they have spoken on their own behalf; the world is witness to the result: human pride has never had more means; and, putting aside its crimes for a moment, never has it been more ridiculous.

Our contemporaries shall believe as they will, but posterity shall doubt not that the most senseless of men were those who ranged themselves around a table and said: "we will deprive the French people of their ancient Constitution and will give to it another" (this one or that, no matter). Although this derision is common to all parties that have desolated France, yet the Jacobins present themselves as destroyers first rather than builders, and they leave in the imagination a certain impression of grandeur as a result of the immensity of their successes. One can even doubt that they had seriously planned to organize France into a Republic, for the Republican Constitution they made is nothing but a kind of comedy played to the people to distract it for a moment, and I cannot believe that the least enlightened of its authors could have believed in it for a moment.

But the men who appeared on the scene in the early days of the Constituent Assembly really thought themselves legislators: quite seriously and visibly, their ambition was to give France a political constitution, and they believed that an assembly could decree, by majority vote, that such and such a people would no longer have such and such a government, but some other. Now, this idea is of the utmost extravagance; and from all the *Bedlams* in the world the like has never emerged. So from these men springs only the idea of feebleness, ignorance, and *disappointment*. No feeling of admiration or terror equals the kind of angry pity inspired by this constituent *Bedlam*. The palm of villainy belongs by right to the Jacobins; but posterity will unanimously award the Constitutionalists that of folly.

True legislators have all felt that human reason could not stand alone, and that no purely human institution could last. Hence they have, so to speak, interlaced politics and religion, so that human weakness, bolstered by supernatural support, could be reinforced by it. Rousseau admires the Judaic law and that of the child of Ishmael, which have survived for so many centuries: this is because the authors of these two famous institutions were at once high priests and legislators: because in the Koran as in the Bible, politics is made divine; because human reason, crushed by religious ascendancy, cannot infuse its atomizing and corrosive poison into the machinery of government: so that the citizens are believers whose fidelity is exalted to faith, and obedience to enthusiasm and fanaticism.

Great political institutions are perfect and enduring as far as the union of politics and religion is perfect. Lycurgus distinguished himself on this fundamental point, and all the world knows that few institutions can compare to his for duration and wisdom. He imagined nothing, he proposed nothing, he ordered nothing but on the faith of oracles. All his laws were, so to speak, religious precepts; through him Divinity intervened in the councils, in treaties, in war, in the administration of justice, to the point that "he entered into a design to remove the kings of the Spartans, but sensed that he could not do so without the help of the gods, because the Spartans were accustomed to refer all things to the oracles; first, he tried to corrupt Delphi, etc."[9] And so, when Lysander wished to destroy kingship at Sparta, he first tried to corrupt the priests who gave the oracles, because he knew that the Spartans did not undertake anything important without consulting them.[10]

The Romans were another example of the strength of the religious bond introduced into politics. Everyone knows that famous passage of Cicero where he says that the Romans had superiors in everything, except in the fear and worship of God.

"O conscript fathers," he said, "let us flatter ourselves as we will, yet we surpass not the Spanish in numbers; nor the Gauls in vigour; nor the Carthaginians in cunning; nor the Greeks in skill; nor, lastly, the Italians and Latins in that natural and domestic sensibility native to the peoples of this country—but in piety, religion, and that singular wisdom wherein we have seen that all things are ruled and governed by the will of the gods, we surpass all peoples and nations."[11] Numa had given to Roman politics that

9 *Iniit consilia reges Lacedaemoniorum tollere, sed sentiebat id se sine ope deorum facere non posse, quod Lacedaemonii omnia ad oracula referre consueverant, primum Delphos corrumpere est conatus, etc.* (Corn. Nep. *in Lysander*, 3)

10 Plutarch, *in Lycurgus*, French translation by Amyot.

11 [*Quam volumus licet, patres conscripti, ipsi nos amemus, tamen nec numero Hispanos nec robore Gallos nec calliditate Poenos nec artibus Graecos nec denique hoc ipso huius gentis ac terrae domestico nativoque sensu Italos ipsos ac Latinos, sed pietate ac religione atque hac una sapientia, quod deorum numine omnia regi gubernarique perspeximus, omnis gentis nationesque superavimus.* (Cicero, *De Haruspicum Responso*, 9.19). Cicero makes a similar point in *De natura deorum*, 2.8.]

religious character which was the sap, the soul, the life of the Republic, and which perished along with it. It is a constant fact among all learned men that the oath was the true cement of the Roman Constitution: it is by oath that the unruliest plebeian, bowing his head before the council which demanded his name, displayed under the flags the docility of a child. Livy, who had seen the birth of philosophy and the death of the Republic (in the same age), sometimes pines for those happy times when religion assured the welfare of the state. At the point where he tells the story of that young man who came to inform the consul of a fraud committed by the keeper of the auspice chickens, he adds: "this young man was born before men were taught to despise the gods."[12]

It was especially in the comitia that the Romans manifested the religious character of their legislation: the assemblies of the people could not take place until the presiding magistrate had taken the *Auspices*. Their scruples in this respect were boundless, and the power of the *Augurs* was such that they were known to annul the comitia's deliberations several months after the fact;[13] with that famous word *alio die*, the *augur* broke up the whole assembly of the people.[14] Any magistrate superior or equal to the one who presided over the comitia was also entitled to take the Auspices. And if he declared that *he had looked aloft to the heavens* (*se de coelo servasse*) and had discerned thunder or lightning,[15] the comitia were dismissed.

It was in vain that *abuses* were feared, which were even palpable on certain occasions.

It was in vain that the least astute plebeian saw in the doctrine of the augurs an infallible weapon in the aristocracy's hands to impede the projects and deliberations of the people: the ardour of party spirit slackened before respect for Divinity. The magistrate was believed *even if he had forged the auspices,*[16] because it was thought that an object of this importance should be left to the magistrate's conscience, and that it was better to expose oneself to deception than to offend religious custom.

In the same age when it was written that *an augur could scarcely look another augur in the face without laughing,* Cicero, whom a plotter had flattered by securing the office of augur for him, wrote to his friend: "*I*

12 *Juvenis ante doctrinam deos spernentem natus.* (Livy, X, 40)

13 Cicero, *De natura deorum*, II, 4.

14 Cicero, *De divinatione*, II, 12.

15 *Jove fulgente cum populo agi nefas esse* ["It is forbidden to do business with the people when Jupiter was casting lightning"]. (Cicero, *in Vatinium* 8, *De divinatione*, II, 18) Adam's *Roman Antiquities*, Edinburgh, 1792, p. 99

16 *Etiam si auspicia ementitus esset.* (Cicero, *Phillipicae*, II, 23)

admit it, only that could have tempted me,"[17] so deeply rooted in the Roman imagination was the regard attached to this kind of priesthood.

It would be useless to repeat what has been said a thousand times, and to show what the religion of Romulus had in common with that of other nations; but in this people, religion had aspects that distinguish it from others and that it is well to observe.

The Roman legislator or magistrate in the *Forum* was, so to speak, surrounded by the idea of Divinity, and this idea even followed him into the military camp. I doubt if it would have occurred to another people to turn the principal part of a camp into a temple where military symbols mixed with statues of the gods became veritable deities and changed these trophies into altars.

This is what the Romans did. Nothing can express the respect with which opinion surrounded the praetorium of a camp (*principia*). There rested the eagles, the flags, and the images of the gods. There was found the general's tent where the laws were proclaimed, there the council was held, and the signal for battle given. Roman writers speak of this place only with a certain religious veneration,[18] and for them the violation of the praetorium was a sacrilege. Tacitus, recounting the revolt of two legions near Cologne, says that Plancus, sent by the emperor and the senate to the mutinous legions, and on the point of being massacred, found no other means of saving his life than to embrace the eagles and flags, *placing himself under the aegis of religion*.[19] Then he adds: "had the standard-bearer Calpurnius not protected him from extreme violence, the blood of a legate of the Roman people would have stained the altars of the gods in a Roman camp, a thing most rare even among the enemy."[20]

The more one studies history, the more one becomes convinced of the indispensable necessity of this alliance of politics and religion.

17 *Epistulae ad Atticum*.

18 Stace calls it: "the sanctuary of the council and the dreadful dwelling of the flags." *Ventum ad concilii penetrale domumque verendam signorum* ["Having come to the inner chamber of the council, the venerated home of the standards"]. (Statius, X, 120)

19 *Caedem parant, Planco maxime... neque aliud periclitanti subsidium quam castra primae legionis: illic signa et aquilas amplexus, religione sese tutabatur* ["They were on the point of killing them, Plancus especially... there was no other help for this peril than the camp of the first legion: there, clinging to the standards and eagles, *he protected himself under the banner of religion*"]. (Tacitus, *Annals*, I, 39)

20 *Ac ni aquilifer Calpurnius vim extremam arcuisset... legatus populi romani romanis in castris sanguine suo altaria deum commaculavisset*. (Tacitus, *Annals*, I, 39)

Abuses of this kind mean nothing; we must be careful when we reason about the abuse of necessary things and take care not to make men wish to destroy the thing to get rid of the abuse, without thinking that this word *abuse* refers only to the disordered use of a good thing that must be preserved. But I will not persist in considering an issue that would take me too far afield.

I wished only to show that human reason, or what is called philosophy, is as useless for the happiness of states as for that of individuals; that all great institutions, moreover, have their origin and their conservation elsewhere, and that human reason is mingled with these only to pervert and destroy them.

Chapter IX:
Continuation of the Same Subject

Paine, in his poor work on the rights of man, has said that "the constitution precedes the government; that it is to government what the laws are to the courts; that it is visible, material, article by article, or else it does not exist: so that the English people have no constitution, their government being the fruit of conquest, and not a production of the will of the people."[1]

It would be difficult to accumulate more errors in fewer lines. Not only can the people not give itself a constitution; but no assembly, a small number of men in relation to the total population, can ever accomplish such a work. It is precisely because there was in France an all-powerful *Convention* which wanted a Republic that there will be no enduring republic. The Tower of Babel is the naive image of a host of men who assemble to create a constitution. "And the CHILDREN OF MEN said, Go to, let us build us a city and a tower, whose top may reach unto heaven; and let us make us a name, lest we be scattered abroad upon the face of the whole earth."[2]

But the work is called *Babel*, that is to say, *confusion*; everyone speaks *his own language*; no one understands each other, and *dispersion* is inevitable.

There never was, there never will be, there cannot be a nation constituted *a priori*. Reasoning and experience unite to establish this great truth. What eye is capable of encompassing all at once the circumstances which must fit a nation to this or that constitution? How, especially, can a number of men be capable of this effort of intelligence? Unless we deliberately blind ourselves, we must admit that this is impossible; and history, which must decide all these questions, comes again to the aid of theory. A small number of free nations have shone forth in the world: not one is found constituted in the manner of Paine. Every particular form of government is a divine work, like sovereignty in general. A constitution in the philosophical sense is, therefore, only the mode of political existence attributed to each nation by a higher power; and, in an inferior sense, a constitution is only

1 Paine's *Rights of man*, London, 1791, p. 57. [Maistre is summarizing Paine.]

2 [Genesis 11:4]

the set of more or less numerous laws that declare this mode of existence. It is not necessary for these laws to be written: it is, rather, to constitutional laws that the axiom of Tacitus applies more particularly: *Pessimae reipublicae plurimae leges* ["the more numerous the laws, the more corrupt the state"]: the more wisdom nations have, the more public spirit they possess, the more perfect their political constitution, and the fewer written constitutional laws they have, for these laws are only props, and a building needs props only when it is out of balance or is violently shaken by an external force. The most perfect constitution of antiquity is, without contradiction, that of Sparta, and Sparta has left us not a line of its public law. It boasted that it had written its laws only in the hearts of its children. Read the history of Roman laws, I mean of those which belong to public law:[3] you will observe, first, that the true roots of the Roman Constitution do not grow out of written laws. Where is the law that fixed the respective rights of the king, the patricians, and the people? Where is the law that, after the expulsion of the kings, divided power between the senate and the people, assigned to each its just portion of sovereignty, and fixed upon the consuls, successors of the kings, the precise limits of the executive power with which they had just been clothed? You will not find anything of the sort.

In the second place, you will see that in the early days of the Republic there are almost no laws, and that they multiply to the extent the state bends towards ruin.

Two powers are present: the senate and the people. These two powers are placed there by what is called *nature*: this is all that can be known about the primitive basis of the Roman Constitution.

If these two combined powers had, at the time of the expulsion of the Tarquins, placed on the throne an hereditary king with whom they would have stipulated the maintenance of their constitutional rights, according to all laws of probability the Constitution of Rome would have lasted much longer; but the annual consuls did not have enough power to maintain equilibrium. When sovereignty is shared between two powers, the *balancing* of these two powers is necessarily a *combat*; if you introduce a third power with the necessary strength, it will immediately establish a tranquil equilibrium by gently inclining sometimes to one side and sometimes to the other. This is what could not take place in Rome by the very nature of things: so it was always by alternating jolts that the two powers were maintained, and the whole of Roman history presents the spectacle of two

3 Gian Vincenzo Gravina, *Origines juris civilis*; Joannes Rosinus, *Antiquitatum romanarum corpus absolutissimum* annotated by Thomas Dempster of Muresk; — Alexander Adam's *Roman Antiquities*, p. 191 et suiv.

vigorous athletes who grapple and roll, by turns victor and vanquished. These various jolts necessitated laws, not to establish new bases for the Constitution, but to maintain the ancient ones alternately shaken by two different ambitions; and if the two parties had been wiser, or contained by a sufficient power, these laws would have not necessary.

Let us return to England. Its written liberties can be reduced to six articles: (1) the Magna Carta; (2) the statute called *Confirmatio chartarum*; (3) the *Petition of Rights*, which is a declaration of all the rights of the English people, made by the Parliament and confirmed by Charles I at his accession to the throne; (4) *Habeas corpus*; (5) The Bill of Rights presented to William and Mary upon their arrival in England, to which the Parliament gave the force of law on February 13, 1688; (6) lastly, the act passed at the beginning of the century, known as the Act of *Settlement*, because it fixes the crown in the reigning house; the civil and religious liberties of England are there newly consecrated.[4]

It is not in virtue of these laws that England is free, but it possesses these laws because it is free. A people born for freedom could alone demand the Magna Carta; and the Magna Carta would be useless to a people foreign to liberty.

"Our constitution," said a member of the House of Commons very aptly, in the sitting of the English Parliament of May 10, 1793, "was not the result of an assembly; it was the offspring of experience. Our ancestors only had an eye to those theories which could be reduced to practice. The Constitution was not formed at once, it was the work of time; it emerged from a concurrence of circumstances, from a collision of parties, and contention for power."[5] There is nothing more true; and these truths belong not only to England; they apply to all nations and all political constitutions in the world.

What Paine and so many others see as a defect is, therefore, a law of Nature. The *natural* constitution of nations is always prior to the *written* constitution, and can dispense with it: there never was, and never could there be a written constitution made all at once, especially by an assembly; and the fact that it would be written all at once is enough to prove it false and unenforceable. Every constitution, properly so called, is a *creation* in the full sense of the term, and all *creation* exceeds the power of man. The written law is but the declaration of the prior and unwritten law. Man cannot give himself rights, he can only defend those granted to him by a higher power, and these rights are *good customs*, good because they are not writ-

4 See Blackstone's *Commentary on the civil and criminal laws of England*, ch. I.

5 M. Grey. See *le Craftsman*, No. 1746.

ten, and because we cannot assign to them either a beginning or an author.

Let us take an example from religion. The *canons*, which are also exceptional laws of a sort, cannot create dogmas since a dogma would be false precisely because it would be new. The very people who believe that one can innovate in a true religion will be forced to agree that dogma or belief must precede the canon: otherwise, a universal outcry would refute the innovators. The canon or written dogma is produced by *heresy*, which is a religious insurrection. If the belief had not been attacked, it would have been useless to declare it.

Similarly, in matters of government, men create nothing. Every constitutional law is only a declaration of a prior right or *political dogma*. And it is never produced except by the opposition of a party who disregards or attacks this right: so that a law which pretends to establish a new mode of government *a priori* is an act of extravagance in the full sense of the term.

Chapter X:
Of the National Soul

Human reason reduced to its own resources is perfectly useless, *not only for the creation, but also for the conservation of any religious or political association*, because it produces nothing but disputes, and because for man to conduct himself well, he needs not problems but beliefs. His cradle must be surrounded by dogmas, and when his reason awakens, he must find all his opinions formed, at least on all things relating to his conduct. There is nothing so important to him as *prejudices*. Let us not take this word in its bad aspect. It does not necessarily mean false ideas, but only, in the strict sense of the word, opinions adopted before any examination. Now, these kinds of opinions are the man's greatest need, the true elements of his happiness, and the Palladium of empires. Without them there can be no worship, no morality, no government. There must be a state religion as there is a state policy; or, rather, it is necessary that the religious and political dogmas be mingled and fused together to form a *universal* or *national reason* strong enough to repress the aberrations of individual reason which is, of its nature, the mortal enemy of any association whatever, because it produces only divergent opinions.

All known peoples have been happy and powerful to the extent that they have faithfully obeyed this national reason, which is nothing but the annihilation of individual dogmas and the absolute and general reign of national dogmas, that is to say, of useful prejudices. Let every man rely on his individual reason in the matter of worship, and you will immediately see the birth of anarchy of belief or the annihilation of religious sovereignty. Similarly, if everyone thinks himself judge of the principles of government, you will immediately see the birth of civil anarchy or the annihilation of political sovereignty. Government is a true religion: it has its dogmas, its mysteries, and its ministers; to annihilate it or to subject it to the discussion of each individual is the same thing; it lives only through national reason, that is, through political faith, which is a *creed*. Man's primary need is that his nascent reason be bent under this double yoke, that it be extinguished, that it lose itself in the national reason, so that it changes its individual existence into another common existence, like a river that rushes into the ocean exists everywhere in the mass of waters, but without name and without a distinct reality.[1]

What is *patriotism*? It is this national reason of which I speak, it is individual *abnegation*. Faith and patriotism are the two great thaumaturges of this world. Both are divine: all their deeds are miracles, speak not to them of scrutiny, choice, or discussion; they will say that you blaspheme; they know two words only: *submission* and *belief*: with these two levers they raise the world; their very errors are sublime. These two children of Heaven prove their origin in the eyes of all by creating and conserving; but if they come together, join forces, and seize upon a nation together, they exalt it, they make it divine, they multiply its forces a hundredfold. We shall see a nation of five or six million men seat upon the barren rocks of Judea the most superb city of superb Asia,[2] withstand shocks that would have pulverized nations ten times more numerous, brave the torrent of centuries, the sword of conquerors, and the hatred of nations, to astonish the masters of the world by its resistance,[3] in fine, to survive all conquering nations, and still, after forty centuries, to hold forth its lamentable remains to the eyes of the surprised observer.

We shall see another people, emerging from the deserts of Arabia, become, in the twinkling of an eye, a prodigious colossus; to range over the world, a scimitar in one hand, and the Koran in the other, shattering empires in its triumphal march, redeeming the evils of war through its institutions. Great, generous, and sublime, it shall shine forth at once with reason and imagination, it shall bear the sciences, the arts, and poetry amid the night of the Middle Ages; and from the Euphrates to the Guadalquivir, twenty prostrate nations will lower their heads under the peaceful sceptre of Harun-al-Rashid.

But this sacred fire which animates nations, is it you who can light it, insignificant man? Can you give a common soul to several million men?

1 Rousseau has said that one must not speak of religion to children, and that their reason must be relied upon in choosing one. This maxim can be placed side by side with this other: "The constitution of man is the work of nature; that of the state is the work of art." (*Contrat social*) It would take little more to establish that this Jean-Jacques, so superficial, under a vain appearance of depth, had not the slightest idea of human nature and of the true bases of politics.

2 *Hierosolyma longe clarissima urbium orientis, non Judaeae modo* ["Jerusalem, by far the most famous city of the East, not of Judea alone"]. (Pliny, *Historia naturalis*, 5, 14)

3 Josephus, de *Bello Judaico*, 6, 9.

Can you make only one will of all these wills? join them together under your laws? gather them around a single centre? impress your thought upon men yet unborn? make future generations to obey you, and create those venerable customs, those conserving *prejudices*, fathers of the laws and stronger than the laws? — Hold your tongue.

Chapter XI: Application of the Preceding Principles to a Particular Case

The National Convention recently dealt with the great question of public education. The reporter, speaking on behalf of the Committee of Public Instruction, told the so-called legislators, in the session of October 24, 1794:

> Turgot often expressed the wish to have, for one year, the absolute power to carry out, without obstacles and without delay, all that he had conceived in favour of reason, liberty, and humanity.
>
> You lack nothing that Turgot had, and everything he lacked, you have. The resolution you are going to take will be an epoch in the history of the world.[1]

Many bad things have been said of Turgot in the belief that these things were good. This wish to possess absolute power *for a year* to carry out *without obstacles and without delay* the prodigies he imagined—this wish, I say, could doubtless have arisen in an excellent heart; but doubtless it has also announced a head radically spoiled by philosophy. If he had possessed the power he desired, he would have built only houses of cards, and his extravagant work would not have outlasted him.

But let us leave Turgot and think only of the National Convention. Here it is, clothed with omnipotence: it is a matter of establishing a system of national education; the way is clear before the legislators: nothing encumbers them; let us see how they shall do it. It is a shame that the Jacobins were destroyed: by this misstep, the National Convention deprived itself of powerful co-operators, for they, *in their wisdom*, also took care of national education, and God knows what wonders they would have worked! An

1 Lakanal, on behalf of the Committee of Public Instruction. (*Moniteur*, 1794, No. 37, 165)

orator of the society said to it on October 24, 1794: "In directing all members of the society towards the desire to make one another happy, we will succeed in forming A NATION OF GODS."[2]

It must be confessed, we have come very near happiness: for Rousseau having prattled that a Republic such as he conceived it was made only for *a people of gods*,[3] and this government being, however, the only legitimate form, since legitimate monarchy is itself a republic,[4] it follows, unfortunately, that with the Jacobins no longer there to form *a nation of gods*, we must give up on ever seeing a legitimate government.

What is more, should the National Convention be comprised only of *angels*, this would be a great deal, and I think it would be wrong to ask for more: it remains only to see how they shall do it.

First, we may note that this important work has not begun under happy auspices. The two chairmen had scarcely begun the exposition of their project when the fathers of families cried in the stands: "before teaching us how our children are to be raised, we must know how we shall give them bread."[5]

But no doubt it would be hard to base our judgment on an exclamation which may only be an outburst of a passing, bad humour. So let us examine the plans of the National Convention.

These plans are altogether simple. "You shall have as many masters as are required: they shall teach your children what you want, and you will give them so much a year." There is the whole secret; but you have to go into the details to form an idea of the enterprise at large.

It has been noted that a population of 1,000 yields 100 children, 50 of each sex. 24 million men therefore require 24,000 male teachers and as many female teachers. To the first, a pension of 1,200 francs will be given, and only 1,000 to the second.[6]

These teachers of both sexes must be lodged; but this is easy, they will give them the former presbyteries, now useless since the *august* representatives of the *premier nation of the world* have solemnly declared that the French *nation* does not pay for any religion.[7]

2 Boissel to the Jacobins. (Session of October 24, 1794. *Moniteur*, No. 39, p. 171)

3 *Contrat social*, 1. lll, ch. V.

4 *Contrat social*, 1. II, ch. VI, note.

5 *Moniteur*, 1794, No. 46, p. 200.

6 Sessions of October 27 and November 15, 1794. (*Moniteur*, No. 40, p. 178; No. 57, p. 246)

7 "Already your laws have freed the nation from the enormous expense of religion." (Cambon, in the name of the Finance Committee, session of November 3, 1794. *Moniteur*, No. 46, p. 201) — "The government *cannot* adopt, let alone *salary*

In truth, many of these presbyteries are destroyed or sold or used for other purposes; but in these sorts of cases, we will buy other houses, and it is right that the whole nation bear these expenses, like those of repairs.[8]

As far as possible, male and female teachers shall be lodged in the same building; when the layout of the presbyteries absolutely prevents this, it will be necessary to have two buildings.[9]

But all these expenses concern only primary schools; it is obvious that we need others where more advanced knowledge is taught: and in effectively the same session where the plan for the former schools was examined they strongly insisted on the very pressing question of the organization of cantonal schools.[10]

This is not all: the sciences, properly speaking, no doubt require special instruction. Here is the masterpiece of the legislators. In the capital, scientists of the first order shall be chosen. These shall instruct the students who will come from the departments to reflect the sacred fire whose hearth is in Paris.

The office of the Committee of Public Instruction does not conceal that this expense will be "the Republic's greatest in peacetime."[11] So it would be quite desirable to enter into the necessary details.

Let us try to supply them: a rough sketch suffices for the object of this work.

For 24,000 male teachers in the primary schools, at 1,200 fr. per head	28,800,000 fr.
For 24,000 female teachers, at 1,000 fr.	24,000,000 fr.
For 24,000 school buildings, we would first have to approximate the number of complete reconstructions required occasionally from wear and tear or violent cause; but let us not be too finicky, and value at 100 fr. only the annual repairs of each building, including in this sum the price of the reconstructions for 24,000 buildings	2,400,000 fr.

any religion." (Grégoire, session of December 21, 1794. *Moniteur*, No. 93, p. 388)

8 [See the sessions cited above.]

9 [See the sessions cited above.]

10 *Moniteur*, No. 58, p. 250.

11 Session of October 24, 1794 (*Moniteur*, No. 40, p. 178)

For the cantonal schools, let us count ten municipalities per canton; this is, I believe, all that can be allowed. Since France has 42,000 municipalities,[12] we will have 4,200 teachers; and the importance of their functions requiring a higher salary, let us grant them 1,800 fr.	7,500,000 fr.
And since female teachers are also necessary in this canton for the persons of this sex whose parents could and would wish to give them a more advanced education, let us grant these teachers 1,500 fr.	6,300,000 fr.
For the repairs of the 4,200 houses that I assume will be a little more decorated, to the tune of 200 fr. annually, including reconstructions of the same	840,000 fr.

As for the écoles normales,[13] let us place only one in each departmental capital: we cannot assume less unless we want to concentrate all education in the capital, which would render the institution almost useless. Let us again exclude all French conquests to arrive at the lowest calculation. We have no certain basis for the number of professors; but in fine, either the écoles normales will be of no account, or they will have at least one professor of mathematics, one of chemistry, one of anatomy, and one of medicine. I could add French law, learned languages, veterinary medicine, etc.; but I limit myself to what is strictly necessary.

Six professors of écoles normales, multiplied by 83, the supposed number of departments, yield 498, and being unable to allocate a salary of less than a thousand crowns to such distinguished scholars as we suppose	1,494,000 fr.

12 We could make a stronger assumption, since the Finance Committee grants 50,000 parishes to France. (Cambon, on behalf of this Committee, sitting of November 2, *Moniteur*, No. 45, p. 195)
The Committee of Eleven, which has just proposed to the National Convention a fourth perfect Constitution, grants 44,000 municipalities (*Journal de Paris* of June 24, 1795) but we can do without accuracy.

13 [Training colleges for teachers.]

For the repairs of 83 buildings of écoles normales, which will necessarily be distinguished edifices, let us allot 400 fr. per year, and for each of these buildings, including reconstructions	332,000 fr.
Total (!)	71,666,000 fr.

This is a first taste of the government's proposed spending. Let us add some observations:

1. A host of presbyteries have been sold or employed for uses indispensable to the new regime or have been destroyed by the fury of a blind and frenzied people; it will be necessary to supply this *deficit*, and it will be an enormous expense.
2. The insufficiency of the presbyteries is well known: a host of these houses will not be capable of containing two schools; it will, therefore, be necessary to find a second building.
3. The most beautiful of these houses being rather mediocre, however, the male and female teachers, as well as the young men and women, will be almost pell-mell; and primary education perhaps extending up to 15 or 16 years of age, and even longer, if one delayed in organizing the écoles normales, the primary schools would soon be *public houses* in every sense of the word.
4. The Committee of Public Instruction has considered the population of France en masse and without any distinction: equity requires, however, that the population of the cities be distinguished from that of the countryside. Paris, for example, will have 600 professors and as many primary school teachers. If the sum of 1,200 fr. and 4,000 fr. suffices in the village, clearly it will not suffice in Paris, or even in a city of the second or third order; a new increase of a very considerable expense.
5. When governments organize machines as complicated as those in question, the most penetrating eye cannot form an idea of the expenses they will require: only the main ones can be seen, but soon the *molti pochi*[14] of the Italian proverb presents itself everywhere, and one is quite surprised to see the expense doubled. This is especially true at a time when "*all public servants at once demand an increase in fees.*"[15]

14 [*Molti pochi fanno un assai*, similar to the English "many a little makes a mickle."]

15 Cambon, on behalf of the Finance Committee. (Session of October 1794. *Moniteur*, No. 32, p. 142)

> 6. But this frightful expenditure, which exceeds the revenue of five or six crowned heads—will it at least deliver a national education for the French? By no means: for, despite the complaints of some Jacobins who lacked the means to be heard, parents will remain free to raise their children at home or elsewhere, as they may see fit. Soon, in the dictionary of the vainest nation in the world, the primary schools, despised like dirt, will be blemished with some epithet that will drive away what will always be called *good company*, in spite of *liberty* and *equality*; even decency and morals will unite with vanity to debase *national education* in public opinion, and this whole great institution will be but a great ridicule.

To this picture, which has nothing exaggerated or chimerical in it, and in which we have made suppositions most favourable to the philosophical *great work*, I oppose another, the comparison of which seems to me striking.

The whole world has heard of the Jesuits, and a large part of the present generation has seen them; they would survive still if some governments had not allowed themselves to be influenced by the enemies of this Order, which was certainly a great mistake; but we must not be astonished that old men prattle idly on the eve of their death.

Ignatius of Loyola, a simple Spanish gentleman, a soldier without fortune and learning, driven by an interior movement of religion, resolved in the sixteenth century to establish an Order entirely devoted to the education of youth and the extirpation of the heresies that rent the Church apart in that age. He willed it with that creative will for which nothing is impossible; he immediately found ten men who willed likewise, and these ten men brought about what we have seen.

Considering the Constitution of this Order only as a political work, it is, in my opinion, one of the most beautiful conceptions of which the human mind can boast. No founder attained his goal better, none succeeded more perfectly in the annihilation of individual wills in order to establish the general will and that common reason which is the generating and conserving principle of every institution, large or small: for the *esprit de corps* is but the diminished *public spirit*, just as patriotism is but the enlarged *esprit de corps*.

If one wishes to form an idea of the inner strength, activity, and influence of this Order, it suffices to reflect on the implacable and truly furious hatred with which philosophism and its eldest son Presbyterianism have honoured it: for these two enemies of Europe were precisely those of the Jesuits, who fought them to the end with unparalleled vigour and perseverance.

Since Bellarmine,[16] whom a robust Protestant of the last century agreeably called "the luscious favourite of the dreadful Roman beast"[17] to Father Berthier,[18] the great flogger of the Encyclopedists; the combat between the Jesuits and innovators of all kinds has not relented for a moment; we shall not find an institution that has better fulfilled its purpose.

We can believe Rabaut de Saint-Etienne,[19] fanatical Constituent, *philosophe* in the full sense of the term, preacher paid by his sect[20] to stir up the people of Paris. In the history of the French Revolution that he sketched out, he speaks of the Jesuits as a power, and makes clear that the Revolution is due in large part to the abolition of this Order. "The most violent," he says, "and the most capable enemies of the freedom to write, the Jesuits, had disappeared; and no one since then has dared to display the same despotism and perseverance."

"Once the minds of the French were turned toward instructive readings, they turned their attention to the mysteries of government."[21]

And the enemies of *superstition* have spoken on this point, as have those of *despotism*.

"There is, however," exclaimed Frederick II, "a new advantage which we have just won against Spain. The Jesuits have been driven out of this kingdom… what is not to be expected from the century following ours? The axe is at the root of the tree. The edifice (of superstition), undermined at its foundations, shall collapse."[22]

16 [Robert Bellarmine, an Italian Jesuit and Catholic cardinal who argued, on the basis of a proto-Rousseauvian notion of the "state of nature", for government founded on the consent of the people. He was vigorously opposed by Robert Filmer in the latter's *Patriarcha*.]

17 *Immanis illae belluae romanae delicium bellissimum*. See Johannis Sauberti, *De sacrificiis veterum conlectanea historicophilologica*. Lugd. Bat., 1699, ch. II, p. 20.

18 [Guillaume-François Berthier, a Jesuit professor and writer who opposed the encyclopédistes, earning him their rancour, particularly that of Voltaire.]

19 It was this Rabaud that Mr. Burke had condemned to a cold bath for having said, in a speech to the National Assembly, that it was necessary to destroy everything in France, even names. But the Committee of Robespierre, who found this judgment too mild, reformed it, as we know.

20 [Maistre's term for the continuum leading from Protestantism to Jacobinism. See introduction, p. x]

21 *Précis de l'histoire de la Révolution française*, Book 1, p. 17 (1792).

22 The King of Prussia to Voltaire. (*Oeuvres* of the latter, edited by Kell, vol. 86, p. 248) The judgments of the King of Prussia on philosophers are the most curious thing in the world. When he surrenders himself to his hatred for Christianity,

Thus, the Jesuits were, in the judgment of Frederick II, the *root* of this *tree* and the *foundations* of this *edifice*. What luck for them!

A Protestant doctor,[23] who recently published in Germany a *General History of the Christian Church*, did not exaggerate in asserting that "without the Jesuits, the religious revolution of the sixteenth century would have extended its action much further, and would have ended in no longer finding any barrier"; that "if this Order, on the contrary, had existed earlier, there would have been no reform, and that perhaps an insurmountable universal monarchy, unknown to history, would have been established."[24]

Let us pass, smiling, over *insurmountable universal monarchy*. What seems at least infinitely probable is that if the Jesuits had survived to our time, they alone would have prevented this Revolution which an armed Europe could not suppress.

It was an ex-Jesuit who, in 1787, prophesied the French Revolution in the most extraordinary manner; who named to Louis XVI all his enemies, who developed them with frightening precision, and ended with these memorable words: "*Sire, your throne is posed on a volcano.*"[25]

The lamentable fate of this unfortunate prince has only too well justified the prediction. Louis XVI was dethroned by philosophism allied to pure Presbyterianism for the destruction of France.

Let us note, too, that the spirit of this institution was so strong, so energetic, so *lively*, that it survived the death of the Order. Like those living animals whose limbs, amputated by the knife of the physiologist, seem

which was in his country a veritable disease, a rage, he then speaks of these gentlemen as his colleagues: he makes common cause with them, and he says: WE. But when the outbreak is over and it is no longer a question of theology, he speaks of them and to them with the utmost contempt: for no one knew them better than he did. This observation is justified in every page of his correspondence.

23 Heinrich Philipp Konrad Henke.

24 See *Algemeine Geschichte des christlichen Kirche*, von D. Heinr. Phil. Cour. Henke, profes. der theol. zu Helmstadt, Braunsweig, 1794, t. 2, dritter theil, p. 69. Professor, affirming in the same sentence: (1) that the Reformation would have extended its action much further: "*wurde die kirche reform ihre wirkungen wiel weiter ausgebreit*;" and (2) that it would have ended in no longer finding any barrier: "*und zulest gar keinem widerstand mehr gefunden haben*," no doubt means that it would have overthrown more dogmas and would have persuaded more people: otherwise, there would be a palpable tautology. In this supposition it cannot be overly regretted that the Jesuits should have prevented a greater purge of Christianity.

25 See the Memoir *Discours a lire au conseil en presence du roi, par un ministre patriote, sur le projet d'accorder l'etat civil aux protestants*, 1787 (final pages). The work is by the ex-Jesuit Bonnaud.

to share the life which they possessed in common, and still present to the astonished eye the phenomena of living nature, the Jesuits, scattered members of a disorganized body, have reproduced before our eyes all the characteristics of association: the same firmness in their systems, the same attachment to national dogmas, the same antipathy for innovators. The dreadful persecution by the French clergy they suffered in recent times has not been able to force any of these men, weakened by age and want, to bend. Equally faithful to the Church and to this inhuman government which while taking their millions refused them sustenance, neither terror nor seduction had the strength to create among them a single apostate, and the languishing remains of this marvellous Order could still furnish twenty-one victims for the massacre in the month of September 1792.[26]

If it were a question of judging the Jesuits, I would be content with the judgment of that same Frederick writing under the dictates of common sense, in one of those moments when humour and prejudice did not influence his judgment:

"Remember, I beg you," he wrote to Voltaire, "Father Tournemine, your nurse, with whom you have sucked the sweet milk of the Muses; and reconcile yourself with an Order which has sustained you and which, last century, has furnished France with men of the greatest merit."[27]

It is reason itself that has written this passage. I could add to this testimony that of another warrior whom you would hardly expect to hear cited on this subject.

> The Jesuits had the great talent to elevate the souls of their disciples through self-esteem, and to inspire them with courage, selflessness, and self-sacrifice.[28]

26 See *Histoire du clergé pendant la Révolution française*, by Father Barruel, chaplain to the Princess of Conti, 2nd edition, Antwerp, 1794, p. 369.

27 Letter of October 1777, p. 391.

28 Vie du général Dumouriez, 1795, vol. I, p. 2. The general tells us (October 1777 letter) that he would have become a Jesuit if the *best of fathers* had not made him read Bayle's *Analysis* and other good works; but it is a great question whether this father, like so many others, was not mistaken. If his son had only spent six months in the novitiate of the Jesuits, he would never have confided a certain secret to an envoy of the National Convention. But if he had made his vows in the Order, I do not doubt that with his talents, his activity, and his ambition, he would have acquired a great and immaculate reputation, perhaps in the sciences, perhaps in the apostolate, who knows? He was a man to convert Kalmyk Tartars or Zealanders or Patagonians; in fine, in one way or another, he would have had his life written: which is probably much better than writing it himself.

This is something, as we see; but it is less a question of examining here the merit of the Jesuits than the force of their instruction, which I compare to the fact that philosophy, aided by all human power, has attempted to do this in much the same way.

In order to take over universal education, St. Ignatius did not beg sovereigns, with an *uncivilized air*, to give him absolute *power for a year*: he established an Order of men who put all the sovereigns in his party; he did not ask for millions, but we hastened to offer millions to his children; his bank was general persuasion, and his society was rich because it succeeded everywhere; but even these riches, which have been spoken of as the equal of Tamerlane's, were still a magical edifice bound up with the spirit of the Order and which disappeared with it. Shamelessly squandered in the treasury's coffers, these riches, so powerful in the hands of their possessors, gave birth to not a single useful establishment in Europe.

It was a curious thing to hear these *philosophes*, veritable prodigies of pride and impotence, declaim bitterly against the pride of these Jesuits, whom the same century viewed as masters of education throughout Catholic Europe, advisors of all the rulers in this part of the world, eloquent preachers before kings, men of good company among the noble, humble missionaries in the workshops of the people, enlightened children with children, mandarins and astronomers in China, martyrs in Japan, and legislators in Paraguay.

Certainly, it would not have been all that much to intoxicate with pride those pygmies who announced with every fanfare that they had donated a *garland of roses*, founded an *incentive prize*, or rewarded some academic verbiage with a pension of twenty-five louis.

Where are the *clock makers of Ferney* now, whom Voltaire ridiculously called his *colony*, and with which he entertained us to boredom? Had he been able to gather on the banks of the Orinoco or Mississippi two or three hundred savages, to make them disgusted with human flesh in the name of philosophy and to teach them to count to twenty, I exaggerate not—he would have choked to death on pride, demanding an apotheosis.

"D'Alembert (and Voltaire) were close with Frederick, and Diderot was close with Catherine; and Russia remains peopled with barbarians, and Prussia remains peopled with slaves."

And so, from what mouth has this anathema come? From that of a member of the National Convention speaking to this assembly on national education in the name of the Committee of Public Instruction.[29]

29 Lakanal, in the name of the Committee of Public Instruction. (Session of October 24, 1794, *Moniteur*, No. 37, p. 164)

One might believe that we were hearing a criminal of the old regime being tortured to betray the secret of his *band*.

La Bruyère, mocking human power in the last century, said to it, "*I do not demand that you make me a beautiful woman; make me a toad*."[30]

A *toad*! It is too difficult to make a beautiful woman, and we must not be so demanding. I will only say, "Human power, proud philosophy, do what you will, but do something chosen, from the vast sphere of possibilities, which will seem to you the easiest; choose from among your followers the most skilful, the most active, the most zealous for your glory; may he show us your power by some useful institution; we do not ask that it run for centuries; we will be content, provided *his work lasts a little longer than himself*."

But philosophy will never be honoured by a useful establishment; and since this concerns education, we can boldly defy the all-powerful legislators of France to found, I do not say a durable government, but only a primary school which has the approbation of universal reason, that is to say, of the principle of duration.[31]

30 *Characteristics*, book II, chapter on free thinkers.

31 The revolutionary genius has just given birth to a curious work to favour the views of these legislators; it is *an instruction for the use of youth, drawn from the example of animals*. (*Moniteur*, November 15, 1794, 57, 246)
O whoever you are, illustrious author! worthy organ of human reason, receive my homage: no one was more worthy than you to serve the views of the worshipers of the *Goddess Reason* and of those who said: "The nation salaries no religion." The generation they have infected no longer belongs to human nature.

Chapter XII: Continuation of the Same Subject

"When I think," said the King of Prussia, whom I always quote with pleasure, "that a *fool*, an *imbecile* like St. Ignatius found a dozen proselytes to follow him, and that I could not find three philosophers, I have been tempted to believe that reason is good for nothing."[1]

Although this passage may be written in *paroxysm*, yet it is precious; the great man was on the right path. No doubt, in a certain sense, reason is good for nothing: we have the scientific knowledge necessary for the maintenance of society; we have made conquests in mathematics and in what is called natural science; but as soon as we leave the circle of our needs, our knowledge becomes useless or doubtful. The human mind, always at work, *propagates* systems that succeed one another without interruption: we see them born, shine forth, wither, and fall like the leaves of trees; the season is longer, that is the only difference.

And throughout the moral and political world, what do we know, and what can we do? We *know* the morality we have received from our fathers as a set of useful dogmas or prejudices adopted by national reason. But on this point we owe nothing to the individual reason of any man. On the contrary, whenever this reason has interfered, it has perverted morality.[2]

In politics, we *know* that we must respect the powers established we know not how or by whom. When time brings about abuses capable of altering the principles of governments, we *know* that these abuses must be removed, but without touching the principles, which requires great dexterity; and we *can* undertake these salutary reforms until the principle of life being totally spoiled, the death of the body politic is inevitable.[3]

1 *Oeuvres de Voltaire*, vol. 86, 3rd in the correspondance. Letter 162.

2 Several writers have amused themselves by collecting the most frightful maxims scattered in the works of only French philosophers; but nobody, I believe, did it in a more striking way than an anonymous writer in the old *Journal de France*, 1791 or 1792. This search escaped me.

3 Rousseau, in making a vulgar comparison, advances, on the subject of political

It would be a very interesting work that would examine the powers of our reason and tell us exactly what we *know* and what we can do. Let us only repeat that individual reason[4] produces nothing and conserves nothing for the general welfare: like this impure insect that soils our apartments, always solitary, always concealed, it produces nothing but annoying trivialities; swollen with pride, it is only venom, it works only to destroy, it refuses every association with works; and if a being like itself should chance *upon its web*, it rushes upon it and devours it.

But national reason resembles that other insect which Asia has presented to Europe; innocent and peaceful, it is only at ease with its fellow-creatures and lives only to be useful; carnage is foreign to it; all its substance is a treasure, and the precious cloth that it leaves us on dying forms the *girdle* of beauty and the mantle of kings.

That famous Frederick was surprised and indignant at being unable to find *three philosophes* to follow him. O great prince, how little you know of the true principle of all associations and all human institutions! Ah! By what right could your reason subjugate that of another and force it to

maladies, an incredible error which is good to read in passing, to make still better known his manner of reasoning, and to clarify even better this theory. "It does not belong to men," he says, "to prolong their lives; but it is for them to prolong that of the state." (*Contrat Social*, 3, II)
What! there is no medicine, no hygiene, no surgery! Diet and temperament are abuses; you need not bleed the patient for pleurisy! Mercury is useless to philosophers, and in the aneurysm we need not bind the artery! Here, for example, is a new discovery. Rousseau, however, would not have been embarrassed: as he was the foremost in the world in defending one error with another; he would have supported fatalism rather than back down.

4 <To those who know what esteem J. de Maistre professed for true philosophers, even pagan ones, it is obvious that, in these outbursts against individual reason, the author is in no way at odds with Lamennais [Hugues-Félicité-Robert de Lamennais, who argued for religion in his *Essai sur l'indifférence en matière de religion on the basis of tradition and the general reason of mankind rather than on individual reason*]. It is not a question here of the grounds for certainty, but only of the impotence of individual reason to procure general happiness, when it isolates itself and separates itself from national reason and from religion, when it shuts itself up in itself without taking any account of the truths recognised by the whole of mankind, and of religious teachings. Between the traditionalism of Lamennais, which denies all power and all certainty to individual reason, and the superb rationalism of those men who, disdaining the rest of the human race, flatter themselves to discover by their reason alone all that is important to know in order to ensure the happiness of the world, there is a happy medium, and it is in this medium that stands J. de Maistre.>

march to the same tune? You have never known how to rise above the idea of force; and when you had collected some materials that you might have held together with your arms of iron, you thought they could do without cement. No, this is not how to create. You have disappeared from this theatre which you have illuminated and bloodied; but your contemporaries are still there.

Make no mistake: the successes of philosophy might dazzle inattentive eyes; it is important to appreciate them. If one asks these men what they have done, they will speak to you of their influence on opinion: they will tell you that they have destroyed *prejudices* and especially *fanaticism*, for that is their great word; they will celebrate in magnificent terms the kind of magistracy that Voltaire exercised over his century during his long career; but these words *prejudice* and *fanaticism*, in the final analysis, signify the belief of several nations. Voltaire has chased this belief out of a host of heads, that is to say, he has destroyed it, and this is precisely what I am saying. No less can be said of philosophy, so that a man given over to his individual reason is dangerous in the moral and political order precisely in proportion to his talents: the more genius, activity, and perseverance he has, the more disastrous his existence. He only multiplies a negative power and sinks into nothingness.

A pen friendly to religion, when it addresses reproaches to philosophy, is suspicious to a great number of readers who persist in seeing fanaticism wherever they do not see incredulity or *indifferentism*.

And so it will not be useless to borrow the phrase of a writer who exclaims in his own words, "O Providence, IF YOU EXIST, answer! Who shall be able to absolve you?"[5] … This man is surely not fanatical. See in what terms he confronts the philosophers:

> And you, foolish philosophes, who, in your presumptuous knowledge, pretend to rule the world; apostles of *tolerance* and humanity; *you who have prepared our* GLORIOUS *Revolution*, who have boasted of the progress of light and reason:
>
> Come out of your tombs; come out into the midst of these corpses, and explain to us how, in this so highly vaunted century, thirty tyrants who commanded murder could find three hundred thousand executioners to commit it? Your writings are in their (the tyrants') pockets; your maxims are on their lips; your pages shine in their *reports* to the tribune; and it was in the name of virtue that the most frightful robberies were committed; it was in the name of humanity that two million men

5 *Accusateur public*, No. 2, p. 22, lines 19 and 20.

> perished; it was in the name of liberty that a hundred thousand Bastilles were raised: there is not one of your writings which would not be on the desk of our forty thousand Revolutionary Committees. They would put aside their Diderot for a moment to sign off on drownings! The sole fruit of your tirades was to teach crime to cover itself with polite language to carry out more dangerous blows. Injustice and violence were called *sharp forms*; rivers of blood, *perspiration from the body politic* … Did you think, so-called sages, that the seed of philosophy could sprout up on barren, arid, and uncultivated land? And in your frenzied paradoxes and your metaphysical abstractions, did you count men's passions for nothing? etc.[6]

Rousseau has painted the portrait of the philosophes without suspecting that he was painting his own: it would be useless to cite here that striking piece which everyone knows;[7] but there is one phrase which deserves particular attention: "*If you count their voices*," said he, "*each speaks for himself*." Behold, all at once, the condemnation of philosophy and the charter of philosophy inflicted on Rousseau by Rousseau himself. What is philosophy *in the modern sense? It is the substitution of individual reason for national dogmas*; and it is for this that Rousseau has worked all his life, his indomitable pride having constantly thrown him into dispute with all sorts of authority. Rousseau is, therefore, a *philosophe*, since he *has only his own voice* which has not the slightest right over that of others.

There is a book entitled *De Jean-Jacques Rousseau considéré comme auteur de la Révolution*, 2 vols.[8] This book and the bronze statue that the National Convention awarded to Rousseau are perhaps the greatest opprobrium that has ever dishonoured the memory of any writer.

Voltaire, however, challenges Rousseau for the frightful honour of having made the French Revolution, and he has great authorities in his favour.

6 *Accusateur public*, No. 2, p. 22, lines 19 and 20.

7 *Emile*, book II [the quote is actually from book IV].

8 This book is at once a laughable and deplorable proof of French impetuosity and of the precipitation of judgment which is the peculiar character of this nation. The Revolution is not ended, nothing presages its end. It has already produced the greatest of misfortunes, it announces yet greater ones; and while all those who may have contributed in some way to this terrible overthrow should hide themselves underground, here is Rousseau enthusiast presenting him as the author of this Revolution, to recommend him to the admiration and recognition of men; and while the author is writing his book, the Revolution is giving birth to every crime, every imaginable misfortune, and is covering an unfortunate nation with perhaps ineffaceable dishonour.

It was to him that Frederick II wrote: "The edifice of superstition, undermined at its foundations, shall collapse, and the nations will transcribe in the annals that Voltaire was the promoter of this Revolution of public opinion which took place in the eighteenth century."[9]

It was he who wrote to Frederick: "We are losing taste but are acquiring thought; there is especially a M. Turgot who would be worthy of speaking to Your Majesty. The priests are in despair: here is the beginning of a great revolution; while we dare not yet declare ourselves openly; we secretly undermine the palace of imposture founded 1775 years ago."[10]

It is of him that Rabaud de Saint-Etienne said: "All the principles of liberty, all the seeds of the Revolution are contained in his writings; he had predicted it, and he made it."[11]

In fact, the glory of having made the Revolution belongs exclusively neither to Voltaire nor to Rousseau. The whole philosophical sect claims its share; but it is just to regard them as leaders of the chorus: the one undermined politics by corrupting morality, and the other undermined morality by corrupting politics. Voltaire's corrosive writings have for sixty years gnawed away at the very Christian cement of this superb edifice, whose fall has made Europe to tremble. It is Rousseau whose moving eloquence has seduced the crowd, on which imagination has more hold than reason. He has everywhere breathed a contempt of authority and the spirit of insurrection. It was he who drew up the code of anarchy, and who, amid some isolated and sterile truths that everyone knew before him, laid down the disastrous principles of which the horrors we have seen are just the immediate consequences. Both were solemnly borne to the Pantheon in virtue of the National Convention's decree, which has condemned their memory to the ultimate punishment.

At present, we are ecstatic about the influence of Voltaire and his ilk: we are told of the *power* they exercised over their century. Yes, they were powerful, like poisons and fires.

Wherever individual reason predominates, there can be nothing great: for all that is great rests on a belief, and the clash of individual opinions left to themselves produces only scepticism, which destroys everything. Universal and particular morality, religion, laws, venerated customs, useful prejudices—nothing subsists, everything melts away before it: it is the universal solvent.

Let us return always to simple ideas. Any *institution* is but a political edi-

9 The King of Prussia to Voltaire. (*Oeuvres* of the latter, vol. 86, 248)

10 Voltaire to the King of Prussia, August 3, 1775. (*Oeuvres*. vol. 87, 185)

11 *Précis de l'Histoire de ta Révolution*, book I, p. 45.

fice. In the physical and the moral order, the laws are the same; you cannot seat a great edifice on narrow foundations, nor a durable edifice on a moving or transient base. If, in the political order, we wish to build on a grand scale and build for centuries, we must rely on an opinion, on a belief *broad* and deep: for if the opinion does not dominate the majority of minds and is not deeply rooted, it will provide only a *narrow* and transient base.

Now, if we look for the great and solid basis of all first or second order possible institutions, we always find religion and patriotism.

And if we reflect still more attentively, we shall find that these two things coincide; for there is no true patriotism without religion; patriotism can only manifest in centuries of belief, and it always declines and dies with religion. As soon as man separates himself from divinity, he becomes corrupt and corrupts everything he touches. His action is false, and he acts only to destroy. To the extent that this powerful bond weakens in a state, all the conserving virtues are weakened; all characters are degraded, and even good deeds are petty. A murderous egoism incessantly harries public spirit and drives it back before it, like the enormous glaciers of the high Alps, which can be seen advancing gradually but frightfully on the domain of life and crushing the useful vegetation in their path.

But as soon as the idea of divinity is the principle of human action, this action is fruitful, creative, and invincible. An unknown force makes itself felt on all sides, animating, warming, vivifying all. With whatever errors, with whatever crimes ignorance and human corruption have defiled this august idea, it nonetheless retains its incredible influence. Amid massacres, men multiply, and nations display a dizzying vigour. "In former times," said Rousseau, "Greece flourished amid the cruellest wars: blood flowed there, and the whole country was covered with men."[12] Without a doubt; but it was at that time a century of wonders and oracles; the century of *faith* after the manner of the men of this time, that is to say, the century of exalted patriotism. When one has said of the Great Being that He exists, one has not yet said anything: it must be said that He is *Existence*. "But He, being One, has with only one 'Now' completely filled 'Forever.'"[13] A drop of this immeasurable ocean of existence seems to detach itself and fall upon the man who speaks and acts in the name of the deity: his action astonishes and gives an idea of the creation. The centuries pass by, and his work remains. All among men that is great, good, agreeable, true, and enduring, comes from the *Existence, the source of all existences*; *apart from this* there

12 *Contrat social*, 3, X. Note.

13 Plutarch, *Moralia*, dissertation on the Epsilon at Delphi [trans. by Frank Cole Babbit, Loeb Classical Library Vol. V, 1957].

is only error, putrefaction, and nothingness.

Chapter XIII: Necessary Clarification

I must forestall an objection. In reproaching human philosophy for the evils it has done us, are we not at risk of going too far and being unjust towards it by throwing ourselves into the inverse excess?

No doubt, we must beware of enthusiasm; but it seems that in this regard there is a certain rule for judging philosophy. It is useful when it does not range beyond its sphere, that is to say, beyond the circle of the natural sciences: in this domain, all its endeavours are useful, all its efforts deserve our gratitude. But as soon as it sets foot in the moral world, it must recall that it is no longer at home. It is general reason that holds the sceptre in this area; and philosophy, that is to say, individual reason, becomes harmful, and consequently guilty, if it dares to contradict or to call into question the sacred laws of this sovereign, that is to say, the national dogmas: thus, when it moves into the empire of this sovereign, its duty is to act in unison with it. By means of this distinction, the validity of which I think cannot be contested, we know what to hold about philosophy: it is good when it keeps within its domains, or when it does not enter into the scope of an empire superior to its own except as an ally and even as a subject; it is detestable when it enters as a rival or an enemy.

This distinction serves to judge the century in which we live, and the one that preceded it: all the great men of the seventeenth century were, above all, remarkable for a general character of respect for, and submission to, all the civil and religious laws of their country. You will find in their writings nothing rash, nothing paradoxical, nothing contrary to the national dogmas which were, for them, givens, maxims, sacred axioms that they never called into question.

What distinguishes them is an exquisite common sense whose prodigious merit is felt only by men who have escaped the influence of false modern taste. Since they always address the conscience of their readers and this conscience is infallible, it seems that one has always thought what they thought, and sophistic minds complain that *nothing new* is found in their works, while their merit is precisely to clothe in brilliant colours those general truths which are common to all countries and places, and on which rests the happiness of empires, families, and individuals.

What is today called *a new idea, a bold thought, a great thought,* would have, in the dictionary of writers of the last century, almost always been called *criminal audacity, delirium,* or *outrage*: the facts show on what side reason is found.[1]

1 It is worth noting that in our modern times philosophy has become as powerless as it has audacious: the mathematical imagination of the famous Boskowich [Dalmatian polymath, nicknamed *the Croatian Leibniz,* who developed a precursor to atomic theory] expresses this as follows:

In philosophicis et potissimum physico-mathematicis disciplinis... si superius XVII saeculum et primos hujusce VXIII annos consideremus, quam multis, quam praeclaris inventis foecundum exstitit id omne tempus? Quod quidem si cum hoc praesenti tempore comparetur, patebit sane eo nos jam devenisse ut fere permanens quidam habeatur status, nisi etiam regressus jam coeperit. Qui enim progressus in iis quae Cartesius in algebrae potissimum applicatione ad geometriam, Galileus ac Hugenius in primis in optica, astronomia, mechanica invenerunt? Quidea quae Newtonus protulit pertinentia ad analysim, ad geometriam, ad mechanicam, ad astronomiam potissimum, quae ipse, quae Leibnitzius, quae universa Bernouillorum familia in calculo infinitesimali vel inveniendo vel promovendo prodiderunt? ... At ea omnia centum annorum circiter intervalle prodiderunt; initio quidem plura confertim, tum sensim pauciora. Ab annis jam triginta (he wrote in 1755), *vix quidquam adjectum est et si quid est ejusmodi, sane cum prioribus illis tantis harum disciplinarum incrementis comparari nulle modo potest. An non igitur eo jam devenimus, ut incrementis decrescentibus, brevi debeant decrementa succedere, ut curva illa linea quae exprimit hujus litteraturae statum ac vices, iterum ad axem deflexa delabatur et praeceps ruat?* (Roger Joseph Boskowich. S. J. *Vaticinium quoddam geometricum,* in the supplement to Benedetto Stay, *Philosophiae recentioris,* book II, vol. I, p. 408)

["In the philosophical, and especially in the physico-mathematical disciplines... if we examine the preceding 17th century and the first years of the 18th century, how fruitful was this whole period in so many illustrious discoveries? Now, if our present age be compared, it will be quite obvious that we have reached a point of stasis, if we have not already begun to slide backward. For what progress has there been, especially in what Descartes has discovered in the application of algebra to geometry, Galileo and Huygens in optics, astronomy, and mechanics? What of those things that Newton has revealed in analysis, geometry, mechanics, and especially in astronomy, and what of those that he himself, Leibniz, and the whole Bernoulli family have published in either discovering or advancing infinitesimal calculus? ... But they have published all these things in about a century—most, in fact, in a short space of time, then gradually more sparsely. For thirty years now,"] (he wrote in 1755) ["hardly anything of the sort has been added and if anything has, it is in no way comparable to those earlier developments, but incremental

I know that philosophy, ashamed of its frightful successes, has made up its mind strenuously to disavow the excesses to which we are witness; but this is not how one escapes the censure of the wise. Happily for humanity, disastrous theories are seldom found in men with the strength to put them into practice. But what does it matter to me that Spinoza lived quietly in a village in Holland? What does it matter to me that Rousseau, weak, timid, and sickly, never had the will or the power to excite revolt? What does it matter to me that Voltaire defended Calas in order to put himself in the newspapers? What does it matter to me that during the agonizing tyranny of France, the philosophes, trembling for their heads, shut themselves up in a prudent solitude? Once they laid down maxims capable of begetting all these crimes, these crimes are their work, since the criminals are their disciples. The most guilty of all, perhaps, has not feared to publicly boast that *after having obtained great success for reason, he took refuge in silence when reason could no longer be heard*;[2] but the success of *reason* was only the intermediate state through which it was necessary to pass to arrive at all the horrors we have seen. Philosophes! you shall never exonerate yourself by regretting the effect of which you are the cause. *You hate the crimes*, you say. *You have not slaughtered anyone*. Well then! *you have not slaughtered anyone*; that is the best that can be said of you. But you have made slaughter. It is you who have said to the people: "*The people, the sole author of political government, and the distributor of the power confided en masse or in different parts to its magistrates, is eternally entitled to interpret its contract, or rather its gifts, to modify its clauses, to annul them, and to establish a new order of things*."[3] It is you who have told them: "*Laws are always useful to those who possess and harmful to those who have nothing. Whence it follows that the social state is advantageous to men only as far as they all have something, and none of them has too much*."[4] It was you who told them, "*You are sovereign: you can change the laws at will, even the best fundamental laws, even the social compact, and if it please to harm yourselves, who has the right to stop you?*"[5] All the rest is only a consequence. The execrable Lebon,[6] the executioner of Arras, the monster who *halted*

to these disciplines. Have we not already reached the point where, with progress retreating, regress should follow soon after, so that the curve representing the state and condition of the literature should, with the line having bent downward, again slip beneath the axis and fall headlong below?"]

2 Notice on the life of Sieyès [author of *What Is the Third Estate?*] by himself.

3 Mably, cited in Nedham's translation, vol. I, p. 21.

4 *Contrat social*, 1, IX [note].

5 *Contrat social*, 2, XII; 3, VIII.

6 [Joseph Le Bon, a sometime priest in the order of the Oratory who, on mis-

the blade of the guillotine from falling on the heads of his victims just to read the news to the unfortunates stretched upon the scaffold, and had them slaughtered thereafter,[7] replied when he was questioned at the bar of the National Convention by the only men in the world who had no right to find him guilty: "*I had executed,*" he says, "*terrible laws, laws that made you blanch. I was wrong … I can be treated as I treated others. When I met men of principle, I let myself be led by them.* IT IS ABOVE ALL THE PRINCIPLES OF J.-J. ROUSSEAU THAT HAVE KILLED ME."[8]

He was right. The tiger who tears does what he must: the real culprit is the one who unmuzzles him and sets him upon society. Do not think that you are absolved by your affected *threnodies* on Marat and Robespierre. Listen to a truth: wherever you are, and wherever there are unfortunates who believe you, there will be such monsters, for every society contains scoundrels who are waiting to tear it apart, to be rid of the restraint of the laws. But without you, Marat and Robespierre would have done no harm, because they would have been held back by the restraint you have broken.

sions into the departments of the Somme, dealt brutally with offences against revolutionaries, and was later executed in the wake of the Thermidorian reaction.]

7 *Nouvelles politiques nationales et étrangères*, 1795, No. 272, p. 1088.

8 Session of July 6, 1795. *Quotidienne* or *Tableau de Paris*, No. 139, p. 4.

Book II: Of the Nature of Sovereignty

Chapter I: The Nature of Sovereignty in General

Every kind of sovereignty is, by nature, absolute; whether it is placed on one or more heads, whether it is divided, howsoever the powers are organized: there will always be, in the final analysis, an absolute power that can do evil with impunity, which will, from this point of view, be *despotic* in the full sense of the term, and against which there will be no other bulwark than that of insurrection.

Wherever powers are divided, the conflicts of these different powers may be considered as the deliberations of a single sovereign, whose reason balances the *pros* and *cons*. But as soon as the decision is made, the effect is the same in either case, and the will of any sovereign whatsoever is always invincible.

However we define and place sovereignty, always it is one, inviolable and absolute. Take, for example, the English government: the kind of political trinity which constitutes it does not prevent sovereignty from being one, there as elsewhere; the powers balance each other; but as soon as they agree, there is only one will that cannot be thwarted by any other legal will, and Blackstone was right to say that united the King and Parliament can do anything.

Thus, the sovereign cannot be judged: if he could be, the power that has this right would be sovereign, and there would be two sovereigns, which implies a contradiction. Sovereign authority can no more be modified than alienated: to *limit it* is to *destroy it*. *It is absurd and contradictory that the sovereign should recognize a superior*;[1] the principle is so incontestable that where sovereignty is divided, as in England, the action of one power over the other is limited to resistance. The House of Commons may refuse a tax proposed by a minister; the House of Lords may refuse its assent to a bill proposed by the other house, and the King, in his turn, may refuse his consent to the bill proposed by the two houses. But if you give the King the power to judge and punish the lower house for having refused a tax out of caprice or malice, if you attribute to him the right to force the consent of the Lords when it seems to him that they have rejected a bill approved by the Commons for no reason at all; if you invest one or both of the Chambers with the right to judge and punish the King for having abused the executive power, there is no more government: the power that judges is everything, the one that is judged is nothing, and the Constitution is dissolved.

The French *Constituent* Assembly was never more estranged from political principles than when it dared decree the case where the king would be supposed to have abdicated kingship.[2] These laws dethroned the king formally; they decreed at once that there would be a king and that there would not, or, in other words, that sovereignty would not be sovereign.

This incompetence would not be excused by observing that in the system of the Assembly the king was not sovereign. This would be an objection if the Assembly of Representatives were itself sovereign; but under this Constitution the National Assembly is no more sovereign than the King; it is the nation alone which possesses sovereignty, but this sovereignty is only metaphysical. The *palpable* sovereignty is entirely in the hands of the representatives and the king, that is to say, the representatives and the hereditary representative. Therefore, until the moment when the people see fit to recover sovereignty by insurrection, it is entirely in the hands of those who exercise it: so that all the powers are, with respect to each other, either independent or nothing.

The more we examine this question, the more convinced we shall be that sovereignty, even partial sovereignty, cannot be judged, displaced, or punished by virtue of a law: for no power can possess coercive force over itself, any power *amenable* to another power is necessarily subject to this power, since this latter makes laws that dominate the former. And if it has been able to make these laws, what shall prevent it from making others, from multiplying the cases of felony and supposed abdication, from creating crimes according to need, and finally, from judging without laws? This

1 *Contrat social*, 3, XVI.

2 French Constitution of 1791, ch. II, section 1.

famous *division of powers*, which has so agitated French heads, does not really exist in the French Constitution of 1791.

In order for there to have been a real division of powers, the king would have had to have been invested with a power capable of balancing that of the Assembly, and even of judging the representatives in certain cases, as he could be judged in others; but the king lacked this power, so that all the labours of the legislators only succeeded in creating a single power without counter-weights, that is to say, a *tyranny*, if one makes liberty to consist in the division of powers.

It was all very much worth *tormenting* Europe, spending perhaps four million men, crushing a nation under the weight of all possible misfortunes, and defiling it with crimes *unknown to hell!*

But let us return to sovereign unity: if we reflect carefully on this subject, we will perhaps find that the *division of powers*, of which so much has been said, never falls on sovereignty properly so called, which always belongs to *one* body. In England, the true sovereign is the king. An Englishman is not subject to Parliament; and no matter how powerful, however respectable this illustrious body may be, no one thinks to call it *sovereign*. Let us examine all the possible governments which have the right or the pretension to call themselves *free*: we shall see that *powers* which seem to possess a portion of sovereignty are really only counterweights or moderators that regulate and slow the march of the true sovereign. Perhaps a serviceable definition of the English Parliament would be: "the *necessary Council of the King*"; perhaps it is something more; perhaps it is enough to believe that it is. What is, is good; what is believed is good; everything is good, except the so-called creations of man.

In certain aristocratic governments, or those mixed with aristocracy and democracy, the nature of these governments is such that the sovereignty must belong by right to one body, and in fact to another: and equilibrium consists in the fear or the habitual anxiety that the first inspires in the second. Ancient and modern times provide examples of these kinds of governments.

Too many details on this particular topic would be uncalled-for here; it suffices for us to know that all sovereignty is necessarily *one* and necessarily *absolute*. The great problem, then, is not to prevent the sovereign from *willing invincibly*, which implies contradiction; but to prevent it from *willing unjustly*.

The Roman jurisconsults have been much criticized for having said that the prince is *above the laws* (*princeps solutus est legibus*). It would have been more charitable toward them to observe that they meant only the civil laws, or, more precisely, the formalities that they established for different civil acts.

But even if they had meant that the prince could violate moral laws with impunity, that is to say, without being able to be judged, they would only have advanced a truth, no doubt sad, but incontestable.

While I may be forced to agree that we have the *right* to massacre Nero, I would never admit that we have the right to judge him: for the law whereby he should be judged would be made either by him or by another, which would imply either a law made by a sovereign against himself, or a sovereign above the sovereign: two suppositions equally inadmissible.

In considering governments where powers are divided, it is easier to believe that the sovereign can be judged, because of the action of each of these powers which affects the other and which, acting with force on certain extraordinary occasions, leads insurrections of a second order which are far less inconvenient than proper or popular insurrections. But we must beware of the paralogism into which we might easily fall if we consider only one of the powers. We must consider them as a whole and wonder if the sovereign will that results from their united wills can be stopped, thwarted, or punished.

We shall first discover that every sovereign is despotic, and that there are only two courses to take regarding it: obedience or insurrection.

It may be argued, in truth, that although all sovereign wills are equally absolute, it does not follow that they are equally blind or vicious, nor that republican or mixed governments are superior to monarchy precisely in that their sovereign determinations are generally wiser and more enlightened.

This is, indeed, one of the principal considerations that must serve as an element in the important examination of the superiority of one government over another.

Secondly, we shall discover that it is no different to be *subject* to one sovereign than to another.

Chapter II: Of Monarchy

It can be said, in general, that all men are born for monarchy. This government is the oldest and the most universal.[1] Before the time of Theseus, there was no question of a republic in the world; democracy especially was so rare and so fleeting that it is permissible to ignore it. Monarchical government is so natural that men identify it with sovereignty without realizing it; they seem to be tacitly agreed that there is no true *sovereign* wherever there is no king. I have given some examples which it would be easy to multiply.

This observation is especially striking in all that has been said for or against the question which forms the subject of the first book of this work. Opponents of divine origin always rail against *kings* and speak only of *kings*. They do not want to believe that the authority of kings comes from God; but it is not a question of *royalty* in particular: it is a question of *sovereignty* in general. Yes, all sovereignty comes from God; in whatever form it exists, it is not the work of man. It is one, absolute, and inviolate by its nature. Why, then, is it a question of royalty, as if the inconveniences relied upon to oppose this system are not the same in every kind of government? This is because, once again, monarchy is the *natural government*, and is confounded with sovereignty in ordinary discourse by disregarding other governments, just as the exception is neglected by stating the general rule.

I shall observe on this subject that the vulgar division of governments into three species—monarchical, aristocratic, and democratic—rests en-

1 *In terris nomen imperii [Regium] id primum fuit.* ["That ('King') was the first title of imperium in the world."] (Sallust, *De coniuratione Catilinae*, 2). *Omnes antiquae gentes regibus quondam paruerunt.* ["All ancient nations once submitted to kings."] (Cicero, *de Legibus*, III, 2). *Natura commenta est regem.* ["Nature invented kingship."] (Seneca, *de Clementia*, 1). In the new world, which is also a world new, the two peoples who had made rather large steps towards civilization, the Mexicans and the Peruvians, were ruled by kings; and even among the savages the rudiments of monarchy were found.

tirely upon a Greek prejudice that seized upon the schools in the Renaissance, and which we have not figured out how to undo. The Greeks always saw the whole world in Greece; and as the three kinds of government balanced each other well enough in this country, the statesmen of this nation imagined the general division of which I speak. But if we want to be exact, rigorous logic does not enable us to establish a genre on an exception: and, to speak with precision, we should say: "Men in general are ruled by kings. However, we see nations where sovereignty belongs to many, and these governments can call themselves aristocracy or democracy according to THE NUMBER of persons who form THE SOVEREIGN."

Men must always be reminded of history, which is the first master in politics, or rather, the only one. When we say that man is born for liberty, we utter a phrase devoid of sense.

If a being of a higher order took up the *natural history* of man, certainly it is in the history of facts that he would look for instruction. Once he knows what man is, and what he has always been, what he does and what he has always done, he would write; and no doubt he would reject as madness the idea that man is not what he ought to be and that his state is contrary to the laws of creation. The mere enunciation of this proposition is sufficient to refute it.

History is experimental politics, that is to say, the only good politics; and just as in physics a hundred volumes of speculative theories disappear before a single experiment, so in political science no system can be admitted if it is not the more or less probable corollary of well-attested facts.

If one asks what the government most natural to man is, history is there to respond: *it is monarchy*.

This government has its disadvantages, no doubt, like all others; but all the declamations that fill modern books on these kinds of abuses are pitiful. It is pride that begets them, not reason. As soon as it is rigorously demonstrated that peoples are not all made for the same government, that each nation has its own which is best for it; above all, that "freedom [...] is not within the grasp of all peoples, and the more we meditate on this principle established by Montesquieu, the more we feel its truth,"[2] we no longer understand what is meant by dissertations on the vices of monarchical government. If their aim is to make these abuses more vividly felt by the unfortunates who are destined to endure them, this is a most barbarous pastime; if it is to induce them to revolt against a government made for them, it is an unspeakable crime.

But the subjects of monarchies are not reduced to saving themselves

2 *Contrat social*, 3, VIII.

from despair by philosophical meditations; they have something better to do, which is to suffuse themselves with the excellence of this government, and to learn to envy nothing of the others.

Rousseau, who throughout his life has not been able to forgive God for not having made him born a duke and a peer, has shown much anger against a government that is based on distinctions. He complains chiefly of hereditary succession which exposes peoples "to risk having children, monsters, and imbeciles for rulers to avoid having to dispute over the choice of good kings."[3]

We have no need to answer this chambermaid's objection, but it is useful to observe how infatuated this man was with his own false ideas of human action. "When one king dies," he said, "another is needed; elections leave dangerous intervals; they are stormy … intrigue and corruption are introduced. It is difficult for one to whom the state has been sold not to sell it in turn, etc… What has been done to prevent these evils? Crowns have been made hereditary in some families, etc."

Would it not be said that all monarchies were at first elective, and that nations, *considering* the infinite disadvantages of this government, afterwards decided *in their wisdom* on hereditary monarchy?

We know how this supposition accords with history; but this not the point. What is important to repeat is that no people ever gave themselves a government; that every idea of convention and deliberation, and that all sovereignty is a creation, is chimerical.

Certain nations are destined for, perhaps *condemned to* elective monarchy: Poland, for example, was subject to this form of sovereignty. It made an effort in 1791 to change its constitution for the better. See what this produced: we could have predicted the outcome without fail. The nation was too much in agreement; there was too much reasoning, too much prudence, too much philosophy in this great enterprise; the nobility, by a generous devotion, renounced its right to the crown. The third estate entered into the administration; the people were relieved, they acquired rights without insurrection; the immense majority of the nation, and even of the nobility, gave themselves over to the new project; a humane and philosophical king supported it with all his influence; the crown was fixed in an illustrious house already *related* to Poland, and the personal qualities of its chief recommended him to the veneration of Europe. What do you think? Nothing was more *reasonable*: this was itself the impossibility. The more a nation is agreed on a new constitution, the more wills united to sanction the change, the more united are the workers to raise the new edi-

3 *Contrat social*, 3, VI.

fice, above all, the more there are written laws calculated *a priori*, the more it will be proved that what the multitude wants will not happen. It was the arms of Russia, it is said, that overthrew the new Polish constitution. So what! no doubt, there must always be a cause, what does it matter whether this one or another?

If a Polish stable boy or a cabaret servant claiming to be sent from heaven had undertaken this same work, no doubt, he might have been unsuccessful; but, after all, it would have ranked among things possible, for in that case there would have been no proportion between cause and effect, an invariable condition in political creations, so that man feels that he can concur only as an instrument, and that the mass of men born to obey never stipulate the conditions of their obedience.

If some philosopher is saddened by the harsh condition of human nature, the father of Italian poetry may console him.[4]

Let us pass on to examine the principal characteristics of monarchical government.

Mirabeau has said somewhere in his book on the Prussian monarchy: "A king is an idol that is put there, etc." Putting aside *the reprehensible form of this thought*, he is certainly right. Yes, no doubt, the king is there at the centre of all the powers, as the sun is there at the centre of the planets: he rules and animates.

Monarchy is a *centralized* aristocracy. In all times and places, the aristocracy commands. Whatever form is given to governments, birth and wealth are always placed in the first rank, and nowhere do they rule more harshly than where their empire is not founded on law. But in a monarchy, the king is the centre of this aristocracy: it is, indeed, the aristocracy that commands as everywhere; but it commands in the king's name, or if you like, the king is illumined by the light of the aristocracy.

"It is a sophism very familiar to royalist political theorists," says Rousseau, "to give liberally to this magistrate (the king) all the virtues which he would need, and to suppose that the prince is always what he ought to be."[5]

I do not know what royalist writer made this strange supposition: Rous-

4 *Vuolsi cose colà dove si puote*
Ciò che si vuole e più non dimandare.
(Dante, *Inferno*, ch. III)
["It is thus willed there where is power
To do that which is willed; and farther ask not."
(tr. Charles Eliot Norton)]

Man, do you want to sleep soundly? Put your foolish head on this pillow.

5 *Contrat social*, 3, VI.

seau should have cited him. As he read very little, it is probable that he assumed this assertion, or that he took it from some dedicatory epistle.

But, in always avoiding exaggerations, we can be assured that the government of one is that where the vices of the sovereign have the least influence on the governed peoples.

Recently, at the opening of the republican Lyceum in Paris, a quite remarkable truth was spoken:

"In absolute governments,[6] the faults of the master can scarcely throw away everything at once, because his will alone cannot do everything; but a republican government is obliged to be essentially reasonable and just, because the general will, once misled, drags everything along with it."[7]

This observation is most just: the king's will is far from being able to do everything in the monarchy. It is supposed to do everything, and that is the great advantage of this government, but in fact it serves little more than to centralize advice and enlightenment. Religion, laws, customs, opinion, and class and corporate privileges constrain the sovereign and prevent him from abusing his power; it is even quite remarkable that kings are much more often accused of lacking will than of abusing it. It is always the prince's council that rules.

But the *pyramidal* aristocracy which administers the state in monarchies has particular characteristics which deserve our full attention.

In all countries and in all possible governments, high offices will always belong (with some exceptions) to the aristocracy, that is to say, to nobility and wealth, most often united. Aristotle, in saying that this *must be so*, enunciates a political axiom that simple common sense and the experience of all ages do not permit us to doubt. This privilege of the aristocracy is really a natural law.[8]

Now it is one of the great advantages of monarchical government that by it the aristocracy loses, as far as the nature of things permits, all that can be offensive to the lower classes. It is important to understand the reasons for this.

6 We must say *arbitrary*: for every government is absolute.

7 Speech delivered at the opening of the republican Lycée on December 31, 1794, by M. de la Harpe. (*Journal de Paris*, 1795, No. 114, 461)

8 Αριστίνδην και πλουτίνδην δει αἵρεισθαι τιυς ἄρχοντας. "The high magistrates belong to the nobility and to wealth." (Aristotle, *Politics*, II). *Optimam rempublicam esse duco ... quae sit in potestatem optimorum* ["I regard the best government as [...] one which is in the power of the aristocracy."]. (Cicero, *de Legibus*, III, 17). — "princes of the assembly, famous in the congregation, MEN OF RENOWN." [Maistre's French rendering has "ET QUI ONT UN NOM" — "AND WHO WERE CALLED BY NAME"] (Numbers 16:2).

1. This kind of aristocracy is legal; it is an integral part of government, everyone knows this, and it does not awaken in anyone's mind the idea of usurpation and injustice. In republics, on the contrary, the distinction between persons exists as in monarchies, but it is harsher and more insulting because it is not the work of the law, and because popular opinion regards it as a habitual insurrection against the principle of equality admitted by the Constitution.

There was perhaps as much distinction of persons, as much arrogance, properly as much *aristocracy* in Geneva as in Vienna. But what a difference in cause and effect!

2. Since the influence of the hereditary aristocracy is inevitable (the experience of all ages leaves no doubt on this point), the best that can be imagined in order to deprive this influence of what may be too wearisome for the pride of the lower classes is that it should not establish an insurmountable barrier between families in the state, and that none of them should be humiliated by a distinction that it can never enjoy.

Now this is precisely the case with a monarchy based on good laws. There is no family the merit of whose head cannot enable it to pass from the second rank to the first, independently even of this flattering aggregation, where, before it has acquired in time the influence which it is in fact due, all or at least a host of the offices in the state are accessible to merit, which take the place of and narrow hereditary distinctions.[9]

This movement of general ascension that pushes all families towards the sovereign and that constantly fills all the voids left by those who die out; this movement, I say, fosters a salutary emulation, stokes the flame of honour, and turns all individual ambitions towards the good of the state.

3. And this order of things will seem even more perfect if we consider that the aristocracy of birth and office, already made very gentle by the right that belongs to any family and to any individual to enjoy in turn the same distinctions, still loses all that may be too offensive to the lower classes, by the universal supremacy of the monarch before whom no citizen is more powerful than another; the man of the people, who finds himself insignificant compared to a great lord, compares himself to the sovereign, and this title of *subject* which submits them both to the same power and to the same justice is a kind of equality which dulls the inevitable pain of self-respect.

In these last two respects, aristocratic government yields to monarchy. In the latter, one unique family is separated from all the others by opinion, and is considered, or may be considered, as belonging to another nature.

9 *Lettres d'un royaliste savoisien*, letter 4, p. 193.

The greatness of this family humiliates no one because no one compares himself to it. In the first case, on the contrary, sovereignty residing on the heads of several men no longer makes the same impression on the mind, and the individual whom chance has made a member of the sovereign is great enough to excite envy, but not to stifle it.

In a government of many, sovereignty is not A UNITY, and although the parts that make it up theoretically represent UNITY, they are far from making the same impression on the mind. The human imagination does not grasp this whole which is only a metaphysical being; on the contrary, it takes pleasure in detailing each unit of the general whole, and the subject respects the less a sovereignty whose elements taken separately are not sufficiently above him.

Hence sovereignty in these kinds of governments does not have the same *intensity*, nor consequently the same moral force.

Hence also offices, that is to say, power delegated by the sovereign, obtain in a government of one an extraordinary consideration quite particular to monarchy.

In a government of many, the offices occupied by the members of the sovereign enjoy the consideration attached to this quality. It is the man who honours the office, but among the subjects of these governments, offices elevate their occupants very little above their fellows, and bring them no nearer to the members of the government.

In monarchy, offices, reflecting a brighter light on the people, dazzle more: they furnish an immense career for all manner of talents and fill the void that would otherwise stand between the nobility and the people. In general, the exercise of delegated power always raises the civil servant out of the class in which he was fixed by birth, but the exercise of high office in particular raises the new man to the first rank and prepares him for nobility.

If the individual placed by the caprice of birth in the second rank does not want to content himself with the possibility of passing into the first, and with the supplementary means furnished by the offices for doing so depending only on time, as far as the nature of things permits, it is clear that this man is ill, and, consequently, we have nothing to say to him.

All in all, it can be argued without exaggeration that monarchy involves *as much* and perhaps even *more liberty* and *equality* than any other government, which does not mean that *polyarchy* does not contain a large number of men freer than is generally the case in monarchies, but that monarchy does or can give more liberty and equality to a greater number of men, which should be well noted.

As for the vigour of this government, no one recognized it better than

Rousseau. "All respond," he says, "to the same motive, all the springs of the machine are in the same hands, everything marches towards the same goal; there are no opposing movements that destroy each other, and one cannot imagine any constitution in which less effort produces a greater action. Archimedes, sitting tranquilly on the shore and pulling a great ship afloat without difficulty, represents for me a skilful monarch governing his vast States from his study and moving all while appearing unmoved."

The word *skilful* is superfluous in this piece. Monarchical government is precisely that which best does without the skill of the sovereign, and this is perhaps just the first of its advantages. Rousseau's comparison could be put to greater use by making it more exact. The glory of Archimedes was not in pulling Hieron's galley behind him, but in imagining the machine capable of executing this movement, and monarchy is precisely this machine. Men did not create it, because they do not create anything; it is the work of the *eternal Geometer* who needs not our consent to arrange his plans, and the greatest merit of the engine is that a mediocre man can put it into play.

This word KING is a talisman, a magical power which gives all forces and talents central direction. If the sovereign has great talents, and if his individual action can immediately contribute to the general movement, doubtless this is good, but instead of his *person*, his *name* suffices.

As long as the aristocracy is healthy, as long as the name of king is sacred to it, and as long as it loves royalty with passion, the State is unshakeable, whatever the qualities of the king. But as soon as it loses its greatness, its pride, its energy, its faith, the spirit is withdrawn, the monarchy is dead, and its cadaver is left to the *worms*.

Tacitus said of republican governments: "*Some nations, weary of kings, preferred laws to them.*"[10] He was thus opposing the rule of laws to that of a man, as though the one excluded the other. This passage could furnish an interesting dissertation on the differences between ancient and modern monarchy. Tacitus, secretly irritated with the government of one, doubtless may have exaggerated, but it is also true that all the monarchies formed in Europe after the fall of the Roman Empire have a particular character which distinguishes them from monarchies outside Europe; Asia especially, eternally the same, has never known anything but the government of one, modified in a way suited to her, but which does not suit us. The Greek monarchy itself is not our own, and the government of the Roman emperors not being a monarchy properly so called, but rather

10 *Quidam, statim aut postquam regum pertaesum, leges maluerunt.* (Tacitus, *Annales*, III, 26).

a military and elective despotism, most of the reflections made on these kinds of governments do not apply to European monarchy.

Perhaps it would be possible to explain in metaphysical terms why the ancient monarchies were differently constituted than ours; but this would be to fall into the all-too-common fault of talking about everything in terms of everything. The difference of which I speak is a fact that it suffices to recall.

Without insisting on nuance, I will only point out one characteristic feature, namely that antiquity did not contest the right of kings to condemn to death—all the pages of history present judgments of this nature that historians report with no sign of disapproval. It is still the same in Asia where no one contests this right of sovereigns.

Among us, ideas are different. If a king, on his private authority, kills a man, European wisdom will not counsel retaliation or rebellion, but all the world will say, "*this is a crime*." On this point there are not two ways of thinking, and opinion is so strong that it protects us sufficiently.

In general, even agreeing that all powers eminently reside on the heads of his kings, the European does not believe that they have the right personally to exercise any branch of judicial power: and, as a matter of fact, they do not meddle with it. Abuses in this regard prove nothing; universal conscience has always protested. This is the great character, the physiognomy of our governments. Each monarchy in Europe has its own particular traits, and, for example, it would not be surprising to find a little *Arabism* in Spain and Portugal, but all these monarchies have a family resemblance which brings them together, and it can be said of them with the greatest truth:

> *... Facies non omnibus una;*
> *Nec diversa tamen, qualem decet esse sororum.*
>
> ["They do not all have one visage;
> Yet are alike as sisters should be."]

I will be careful not to deny that Christianity has modified all these governments for the better, nor that the public law of Europe has been infinitely perfected by this salutary law, but we must also bear in mind our common origin and the general character of the northern peoples who have taken the place of the Roman Empire in Europe.

"The government of the Germans," Hume has rightly said, "and that of all the northern nations, who established themselves on the ruins of Rome, was always extremely free; and those fierce people, accustomed to independence and inured to arms, were more guided by persuasion than authority, in the submission which they paid to their princes. The military despotism, which had taken place in the Roman empire, and which, previously to the irruption of those conquerors, had sunk the genius of men, and destroyed every noble principle of science and virtue, was unable to resist the vigorous efforts of a free people; and Europe, as from a new epoch, rekindled her ancient spirit, and shook off the base servitude to arbitrary will and authority, under which she had so long laboured. The free constitutions then established, however impaired by the encroachments of succeeding princes, still preserve an air of independence and legal administration, which distinguish the European nations; and if that part of the globe maintain sentiments of liberty, honour, equity, and valour superior to the rest of mankind, it owes these advantages chiefly to the seeds implanted by those generous barbarians."[11]

These reflections are strikingly true. It is in the midst of the forests and ice of the North that our governments were born. It is there that the European character was born, and however much it has been modified since then under the different latitudes of Europe, we are still all brothers, *durum genus* ["a hardy race"]. The fever that is currently afflicting all the nations of this part of the globe is a great lesson for statesmen: *et documenta damus qua simus origine nati* ["and we give proof from what stock we are sprung"].

It is in Asia that it is said: *It is better to die than to live; it is better to sleep than to wake; it is better to be seated than to walk etc.*

Reverse these maxims—you have the European character. The need to act and eternal restlessness are our two characteristic features. The frenzy for enterprise, discovery, and travel exists only in Europe.[12] I do not know what indefinable force agitates us without respite. Movement is the moral as well as the physical life of the European; for us, the greatest evil is not poverty, nor servitude, nor sickness, nor even death; it is rest.

One of the greatest results of this character is that the European can only with great difficulty bear to be an absolute stranger to government. The inhabitant of Asia does not seek to penetrate that dark cloud which envel-

11 Hume's History of England, book I, appendix i: *The anglo-saxon government and manners*.

12 A modern theosophe has remarked, in a work that everyone may read with pleasure as a masterpiece of elegance, that all the great *navigators were Christians* (Homme de désir, 1790, p. 70, §40). He could have said the same about Europeans. [Homme de désir, by gnostic mystic-philosopher Louis-Claude de Saint-Martin. He taught that ecclesiastical organization was to disappear in place of a spiritualized Christianity whose authority was derived from a supra-rational faculty whence we derive knowledge of God.]

ops or forms the majesty of the monarch. For him his master is a god, and he has no other relationship with this superior being than that of prayer. The laws of the monarch are oracles. His graces are heavenly gifts, and his anger is a calamity of invincible nature. The subject who honours himself by calling himself a *slave* receives from him a benefit like a dew, and the rope like a thunderclap.

Observe, however, how supreme wisdom has balanced these terrible elements of oriental power. This absolute monarch can be deposed; his right to ask for the head that displeases him is not contested, but often his own is demanded. Sometimes the laws deprive him of his sceptre and his life; sometimes sedition seizes him on this high throne and casts him down into the dust. How, then, are the weakness that prostrates and the energy that strangles found in the same souls? There is no other answer than that of Dante.

So wills the One who can do all he wills.

But he has wanted to do otherwise for us. Seditions are for us rare events; and the wisest of the nations of Europe, in making the inviolability of its sovereigns a fundamental principle, have merely sanctioned general opinion in this part of the world. We do not want sovereigns to be judged, we do not want to judge them. Exceptions to this rule are rare; they occur only in bouts of fever, and as soon as we are cured, we call them *crimes*. Providence has said to all the sovereigns of Europe: "*You shall not be judged*"; but it immediately adds: "*You shall not judge*"—this is the price of this inestimable privilege.

Tacitus, in describing with his vigorous brush the abasement of the Romans under the sceptre of the emperors, supports this universal recklessness which is the first fruit of servitude *and that changes public affairs into something foreign.*[13]

It is precisely this recklessness that is not in the character of modern Europeans. Always anxious, always alarmed, the veil that hides the workings of government from them disheartens them; submissive subjects, rebellious slaves, they want to ennoble obedience and, as the price of their submission, they demand the right to complain and to enlighten power.

Under the name of the *Fields of Mars* or of *May*, of *Parliaments*, of *States*, of *Cortes*, of *Establishments*, of *Diets*, of *Senates*, of *Councils*, etc., all the peoples of modern Europe have been involved to a greater or lesser extent in administration under the empire of their kings.

The French, who exaggerate everything, have drawn several equally fatal

13 *Incuria reipublicae velut alienae.* (Tacitus) [the original has "*inscitia rei publicae ut alienae*" – "men were ignorant of public affairs as being alien to them"]

theoretical conclusions from this factual truth, the first of which is "that the King's National Council had once been and must again be a co-legislator".[14]

I do not wish to examine here whether Charlemagne's Parliament was really a legislator; great publicists have made the question very problematical; but let us suppose that the affirmative has been proved: because the assemblies of Charlemagne's time would have been *co-legislators,* should we conclude that they must be so today? No, undoubtedly not, and the opposite conclusion would be far more sensible. In politics, we must always keep in mind what jurisconsults call the last state, and although we must not take this word in too narrow a sense, we must not give it too much latitude either.

When the Franks conquered the Gauls, they formed a hybrid people by mixing with them; but it is easy to see that this people was at first more Frankish than Gallic, and that the combined action of time and climate must have made it more Gallic than Frankish every day, so that we would be unwise and illiterate indeed to look (at least word for word) for the public law of modern France in the capitularies of the Carolingians.

If we rid ourselves of all prejudice and party spirit, if we renounce exaggerated ideas and all the theoretical daydreams born of French fever, European common sense will agree on the following propositions:

1. The king is sovereign; no one shares sovereignty with him, and all powers emanate from him.
2. His person is inviolable; no one has the right to depose or judge him.
3. He has no right to condemn to death, nor even to any corporal punishment. The power to punish originates in him, and that is enough.
4. If he imposes exile or prison in cases where reasons of state should forbid judicial review, he cannot be too reserved, nor act too much on the advice of an enlightened council.
5. The king cannot judge in civil matters; the magistrates alone, in the name of the sovereign, can rule on property and agreements.
6. Subjects have the right, by means of certain bodies, councils, or assemblies of different composition, to inform the king of their needs, to denounce abuses to him, and to make their *grievances* and their *most humble* remonstrances known to him legally.

14 I am speaking, as is clear, only of monarchical systems that deviated more or less from what was called the *ancien régime.*

It is in these sacred laws, all the more truly constitutional because they are written only in the heart, particularly in the paternal communication between the prince and his subjects, that we find the true character of the European monarchy.

Whatever the exalted and blind pride of the eighteenth century may say, this is all we need. These elements, combined in different ways, produce an infinity of nuances in monarchical governments: it is conceivable, for example, that the men charged with bearing to the foot of the throne the representations and grievances of the subjects may form *bodies* or *assemblies*; that the members who compose these assemblies or bodies may differ in number, in quality, in the nature and extent of their powers; that the mode of elections, the interval and duration of sessions, etc., vary the number of combinations still further: *facies non omnibus una* ["their faces were not all alike…"]; but you always find the general character, that is, always chosen men legally bearing to the father the complaints and wishes of the family: *nec diversa tamen* ["…nor yet unlike"].

Let us completely reject the judgement of passionate or over-systematic men and let us turn only to that precious common sense which makes and preserves all that is good in the universe. Take the most educated, most wise, most religious European, even the greatest friend of royalty, and ask him: "Is it just, is it expedient that the king should govern solely through his ministers? That his subjects should have no legal means of communicating with him as a body, and that abuses should continue until an individual is enlightened and powerful enough to put things to rights, or until an insurrection brings them to justice?" He will answer you without hesitation, "No". Now, what is really constitutional in any government is not what is written on paper; it is what is written in the universal conscience. What generally displeases us, what ill-suits our ancient, unquestionable, universal character and usages, is ministerial government or the vizierate. Oriental immobility accommodates itself very well to this form of government, and even refuses to accept any other; but the *bold race of Japheth* does not want it, because this form indeed does not suit it. On all sides there are cries of despotism, but public opinion often is misled, and takes one thing for another. People complain about the excess of power; it seems to me that it is rather the displacement and weakening of power that offends. As soon as the nation is condemned to silence and the individual alone can speak, it is clear that each individual taken separately is less strong than those in power; and as man's first ambition is to obtain power, and his greatest fault is to abuse it, it follows that all the individuals in the nation are weaker than the those in power, it follows that all the depositories of delegated power, being unconstrained and not directly answerable to opinion, seize the sceptre and divide it into small fragments proportional to the importance of their offices, so that everyone is king except the king. These reflections explain how, in most monarchies, one can complain both of despotism and of the weakness of government. These two complaints contradict each other only on the face of it. The people complain of despotism because they are not strong enough against the disordered action of the delegated power, and they complain of the weakness of government because they no longer see a centre; because the king is not king enough, because the monarchy has changed into a tiresome aristocracy; because every subject who does not participate or who participates but little in this aristocracy always sees a king next to him, and deplores his nullity, so that the government is both hated as despotism and despised as weak.

The remedy for such great evils is not hard to find: it is only a matter of reinforcing the authority of the king and restoring to him his quality of a father by re-establishing the ancient and legitimate correspondence between him and the large family. As soon as the nation possesses some means of making its voice heard legally, it becomes impossible for vice and incapacity to seize offices or to hold them for long, and direct correspondence with the king restores to monarchical government that paternal character necessary to monarchy in Europe.

How many errors power has committed! And how it has ignored the means of preserving itself! Man is hungry for power; he is infinite in his desires, and, always dissatisfied with what he has, he loves only what he has not. We complain about the despotism of princes; we should complain about that of *man*. We are all born despots, from the most absolute monarch in Asia to the child who smothers a bird in his hand for the pleasure of seeing that there is in the world a being weaker than himself. There is no man who does not abuse power, and experience proves that the most abominable despots, if they were to seize the sceptre, would be precisely those who howl against despotism. But the author of nature has set limits to the abuse of power: he has willed it to destroy itself as soon as it has passed these natural limits. He has engraved this law everywhere; and, in the physical world as in the moral world, it surrounds us and speaks to us at every moment. Observe this gun: up to a certain point, the more you extend it, the more you increase its effect: but if you pass this limit by a hair, you will see it diminish. Observe this telescope: up to a certain point, the more you increase its dimensions, the more effect it will produce; but beyond that, invincible nature turns the efforts you make to perfect the instrument against you. This is the straightforward image of power. To conserve itself it must restrain itself, and always it must avoid that point where its ultimate effort brings its final moment.

Assuredly, I do not like *popular* assemblies any more than anyone else; but French madness must not disgust us with the truth and wisdom that are to be found in the golden mean. If there is one incontestable maxim, it is that in all seditions, in all insurrections, in all revolutions, *the people always begin by being right, and always end by being wrong*. It is false that every people should have its *national assembly* in the French sense; it is false that every individual should be eligible for the national council; it is false even that he should be able to be an elector with no distinction of rank or fortune; it is false that this council should be a co-legislator; it is false, finally, that it must be composed in the same way in different countries. But because these exaggerated propositions are false, does it follow that no one has the right to speak for the common good in the name of the community, and that we are forbidden to be right because the French have performed a great act of madness? I do not understand this consequence. What observer would not be frightened by the current state of mind throughout Europe? Whatever the cause of such a general impulse, it exists, and it threatens all sovereignties.

Certainly, it is the duty of statesmen to seek to ward off the storm; and it will certainly not be achieved by timid immobility or recklessness. It is for the wise men of all nations to reflect deeply on the ancient laws of monarchies, on the *good customs* of each nation, and on the general character of the peoples of Europe. It is in these sacred sources that they will find remedies appropriate to our ills, and the wise means of regeneration infinitely removed from the absurd theories and exaggerated ideas which have done us so much harm.

The first and perhaps the only source of all the ills we experience is contempt for antiquity, or, what amounts to the same thing, contempt for experience: whereas *there is nothing better than what is proven*, as Bossuet said very well. The laziness and proud ignorance of this century are much better suited to theories which cost nothing and which flatter pride than to the lessons of moderation and obedience which must be painfully sought from history. In all the sciences, but especially in politics, whose many and changing events are so difficult to grasp as a whole, theory is almost always contradicted by experience. May Eternal Wisdom shed his rays on men destined to fix the destiny of others! May the peoples of Europe also close their ears to the voice of the sophists, and, turning their eyes away from all theoretical illusions, fix them only on those venerable laws which are rarely written down, of which it is impossible to assign either dates or the authors, and which the peoples have not made, but which have made the peoples.

These laws come from God: the rest is human!

Chapter III: Of Aristocracy

Aristocratic government is a monarchy whose throne is vacant. *Sovereignty there is in regency.*

The regents who administer sovereignty are hereditary, so that it is perfectly separate from the people, and in this respect aristocratic government approaches monarchical. It cannot, however, attain the vigour of the latter, but in wisdom it has no equal. Antiquity has left us no model of this government. In Rome, in Sparta, aristocracy no doubt played a very great role as in all governments, but it did not reign alone.

In general, it can be said that all non-monarchical governments are aristocratic since democracy is only an elective aristocracy.

"The first societies", says Rousseau, "governed themselves aristocratically".[1] This is false, if by the words "*first societies*" Rousseau means the *first peoples, the first nations* proper, which were all governed by kings. All observers have remarked that monarchy was the most ancient government known.

And if he means to speak of the first gatherings that preceded the formation of peoples into bodies of nations, he speaks of what he does not know and what none can know. Besides, in that age there was no government properly speaking; man was not yet what he must become; this point has been sufficiently discussed in the first book.

> The savages of North America still govern themselves in this way today (aristocratically) and *are very well governed.*[2]

The savages of America are not quite *men*, precisely because they are *savages*; they are, moreover, beings visibly degraded physically and morally, and, on this point at least, I do not see that the ingenious author of *Philo-*

1 *Contrat social*, 3, V.

2 *Contrat social*, 3, V.

sophical Investigations on the Americans[3] has been answered.

It is false, too, that these savages are governed aristocratically. Tacitus gave a history of all the savage peoples when he said: "They choose kings out of nobility, generals out of virtue: and kings have not unlimited or arbitrary power."[4] Tacitus' book on the customs of the Germans and the *Journal historique d'un voyage en Amérique* by Father de Charlevoix present a host of analogies.[5] Among these peoples we find not aristocratic government, but the rudiments of a moderate monarchy.

Leaving aside the natural aristocracy which results from physical strength and talents, which is quite unnecessary to attend to, there are only two kinds of aristocracy, elective and hereditary, as Rousseau observes, but the same narrow notions, the same childish prejudices which led him astray about monarchy, made him no more reasonable about aristocratic government.

> The elective aristocracy is the best, it is aristocracy proper.[6]

This is not an error, a misunderstanding, a distraction; it is an absolute lack of reasoning; it is a shameful blunder.

Monarchy is sovereignty vested in one man alone; and aristocracy is that same sovereignty vested in a few men (more or less).

But since elective monarchy is the weakest and least tranquil of governments, and since experience has clearly shown the superiority of hereditary monarchy, it follows, by an incontestable analogy, that hereditary aristocracy is preferable to elective. Let us repeat with Tacitus that *it is better to receive a sovereign than to seek one.*[7]

> Election is the means by which probity, enlightenment, expe-

3 Cornelius de Pauw, ethnologist and author of *Recherches philosophiques sur les Américains*, considered the foremost expert on the Americas at the time, who offered an environmental theory for what he took to be the inferiority of indigenous North Americans.

4 *Reges ex nobilitate, duces ex virtute sumunt: nec regibus infinita aut libera potestas.* (Tacitus, Germania, VII)

5 *Si Germanorum Canadensiumque principum potestatem conferas, eamdem omnino reperies.* ["If you compare the power of German and Canadian leaders, you will discover that it is altogether the same."] (See P. de Charlevoix, letter 18; Brottier, *ad Tac. de Mor. Germ.* VII et passim) [Pierre François-Xavier Charlevoix, author of the cited work in 1744; "Brottier" refers to the 1771 edition of Tacitus.]

6 *Contrat social*, 3, V.

7 *Minore discrimine sumitur princeps quam quaeritur.* ["It is much less trouble to acquire a prince than to seek one."]

> rience, and all other reasons of preference and public esteem, are so many fresh *guarantees* that one will be wisely governed.[8]

This argument comports exactly with hereditary monarchy, and with monarchs created before they reached the age of reason.

> The power being transmitted to the children with the property of the father makes the government hereditary, and we see twenty-year old senators.[9]

Further on he will say, speaking of hereditary monarchy; "*There is a risk of having children as rulers*."[10] This is always the same sagacity; it must be observed, however, that the argument is worse with regard to hereditary aristocracy, since the inexperience of *twenty-year-old senators* is amply compensated for by the wisdom of the elders.

And since the occasion presents itself naturally, I shall observe that the mixture of children and men is precisely one of the beautiful aspects of aristocratic government; all roles are wisely distributed in the world—that of youth is to do good, and that of old age to prevent evil; the impetuosity of the young, who demand only action and creation, is very useful to the State, but they are too inclined to innovate, to demolish, and they would do much harm without old age, which is there to stop them. Old age in turn opposes even useful reforms; it is too rigid, it knows not how to adapt to circumstances, and sometimes a *twenty-year old senator* can be placed very appropriately next to one of eighty.

All in all, hereditary aristocratic government is perhaps the most advantageous to what is called the *people*; sovereignty is concentrated enough to impose itself on them; but as it has fewer needs and less splendour, it demands less of them: if it is sometimes timid, it is because it is never imprudent; between the people and the sovereign there may be malcontents, but their sufferings are not the work of the government; they are only a matter of opinion, and this is an inestimable advantage for the mass whose happiness is a surety.

The mortal enemy of experience thinks quite differently; according to him, hereditary aristocracy "*is the worst of all governments*."[11]

The dominant sentiment in all Rousseau's works is a certain plebeian anger which chafes at any kind of superiority. The energetic submission of the wise man nobly bends under the indispensable empire of social dis-

8 *Contrat social*, 3, V.

9 *Contrat social*, 3, V.

10 *Contrat social*, 3, VI: *de la Monarchie*.

11 *Contrat social*, 3, V.

tinctions, and he never appears greater than when he bows; but Rousseau had no such elevation: weak and surly, he spent his life hurling insults at the great, as he would have hurled them at the people if he had been born a great lord.

This character explains his political heresies; it is not truth that inspires him, but mood; wherever he sees greatness, and especially hereditary greatness, he foams at the mouth and loses the faculty of reason: this is what happens to him especially when speaking of aristocratic government.

To say that this kind of government is the worst of all is to say nothing: it must be proved. Venice and Bern first come to mind, and one is not a little surprised to learn that there is no worse government than that of these two states.

But history and experience never embarrass Rousseau; he begins by laying down general maxims which he does not prove, and then he says: *I have proved it*. If experience contradicts him, he is little bothered, or he wriggles out of it with a little dance. Berne, for example, embarrasses him not at all. Dare we ask why? It is "maintained by the extreme wisdom of the senate and forms an honourable and highly dangerous exception."[12]

But the Bernese Senate forms precisely the essence of the Bernese government. It is the head of the body politic; it is the principal part without which this government would not be what it is: it is therefore just as if Rousseau had said:

Hereditary aristocratic government is detestable; the esteem of the world accorded for several centuries to that of Berne in no way contradicts my theory, for what makes this government not bad is that it is excellent. — O profundity![13]

The judgement on Venice is no less curious: "Venice," he says, "has fallen into hereditary aristocracy, and so has long been a dissolved state."[14]

Certainly, Europe was not aware of this; but what everyone is aware of is that Venice has subsisted for a thousand years, and that its power cast a shadow over all its neighbours when it was shaken by the League of Cam-

12 *Contrat social*, 3, V.

13 Montesquieu paid special homage to the government of Berne. "There is at present," he says, "in the world a republic that no one knows about, and which in secrecy and silence increases its strength every day. It is certain that if it ever reaches the state of greatness for which its wisdom destines it, it will necessarily change its laws, etc.". (*Grandeur et décadence des Romains*, ch. X) Let us put aside the prophecies; I believe only in those of the Bible. But it seems to me that we owe a compliment to the government wise enough to be praised simultaneously by wisdom and folly.

14 *Contrat social*, 3, V, note.

brai and had the skill to escape this peril at the beginning of the sixteenth century.

The Venetian government has grown old, no doubt, like all the governments of Europe, but the youth of Milo of Croton[15] renders his old age venerable, and no one has the right to insult it.

Venice has shone with all manner of brilliance: in laws, in trade, in arms, in the arts and in letters; its monetary system is an example to Europe. It played a dazzling role in the Middle Ages.[16] If Vasco de Gama doubled the Cape of Storms, if commerce took another route, it is not the fault of the Senate; and if at this moment Venice is obliged to put prudence in place of force, once again, let us respect her old age: after thirteen hundred years of life and health, one can be ill, one can even die with honour.[17]

Declamations on the state inquisition, which Rousseau calls a *tribunal of blood*,[18] are scarecrows for weaklings. Have we not heard that the state inquisitors shed human blood for their own amusement? This imposing magistracy is necessary because it exists, and it must not be so terrible because it belongs to one of the gentlest, most cheerful, and most friendly peoples in Europe. The malicious and the thoughtless can only complain when it comes to themselves; but it is a constant fact, attested by all sensible travellers, that there is perhaps no country where the people are happier, more tranquil, more free than in Venice: the foreigner shares this freedom, and at this moment it is under the laws of this peaceful government that the honourable victims of the French Revolution enjoy the kindest and most generous hospitality.

If the state inquisitors have sometimes ordered severe executions, severity did not exclude justice, and it is often to spare blood that blood is shed.

15 [Milo of Croton, a sixth century BCE Greek wrestler and, according to Diodorus Siculus, military commander. He won many victories in the Olympiad and other competitions and was said to have been devoured by wild beasts when, hubristically demonstrating his strength, his hand was caught in a tree trunk.]

16 Count Carli, one of the ornaments of Italy, has said some curious things about the ancient splendour of Venice; we may consult his works, which are full of STUNNING erudition, *sed Graecis incognitas qui sua tantum mirantur* ["but (these things are) unknown to the Greeks, who admire only their own"].

17 *Sola Veneta est (respublica) quae aevum millenarium jactet: felix fati, sed et legum atque institutorum felix quibus velut vinculis firmata est adhuc contra lapsum. Maneat, floreat, favemus, et vovemus*. ["Venice is the sole republic that has lasted a thousand years: blessed in fate, but also in its laws and institutions which are like chains that have hitherto stayed it from collapse. We applaud it and wish that it should endure and flourish."] (Justus Lipsius, *Monita et exempla politica*, 2, I)

18 *Contrat social*, 4, V.

As for errors and injustices, they are everywhere; but the state inquisitors did not give the hemlock to Morosini[19] on his return from the Peloponnese.

Rousseau, in saying that Venice had *fallen* into hereditary aristocracy, proves that he knew very little about the growth of empires. If he had known, instead of *fallen*, he would have said *achieved*. While the Venetians were only unfortunate refugees, living in shacks on those islets destined one day to support so many palaces, it is quite clear that their constitution was not mature, strictly speaking; they had none, since they did not yet enjoy absolute independence, which had been contested for so long. But in 697 they already had a leader powerful enough to have given us to think that he was sovereign: now, wherever there is a leader, at least a non-despotic leader, there is an hereditary aristocracy between this leader and the people; this aristocracy formed itself imperceptibly like a language and matured in silence. Finally, at the beginning of the twelfth century, it took on a legal form, and the government was what it must be. Under this form of sovereignty, Venice filled the world with its fame. To say that this government *degenerated*[20] by thus attaining its natural dimensions is to say that the government of Rome *degenerated* when the institution of the tribunes, as I have noted concerning Cicero, gave legal form to the constitutional but disordered power of the people.

Moreover, if we are to believe Rousseau, it is not only Venice that had *fallen* into hereditary aristocracy. Berne suffered the same fate; its government was similarly *contracted*, and consequently it *degenerated*, the day the people made the mistake of abandoning *to the prince* the election of magistrates.[21] If one asks in what annals this important fact is to be found, and how Berne *fell* from democracy or elective aristocracy into hereditary aristocracy, no one can answer; no one has heard of this *fall* revealed at the end of time in the *Contrat Social*. This Rousseau is a strange man: some-

19 [Francesco Morosini, captain of the Venetian forces during the siege of Candia on Crete. He surrendered the city and was accused of cowardice and treason but was eventually acquitted of the charges. He was later rehabilitated and became Doge from 1688–1694.]

20 *Contrat social*, 3, X, note 1.

21 *Contrat social*, 3, X, note 2. When Rousseau sees the truth, he never sees it in its entirety, and in that case his decisions are more dangerous, for four fifths of the readers, than perfect blunders, for example, when he says that the government which is tightening, is corrupting, he is wrong and he is right he is right with regard to the democratic government which departs from its nature; he is wrong with regard to the aristocratic government which approaches it: in the latter case, it is a movement of organization in the former, it is a movement of dissolution.

times he contradicts history, and sometimes he invents it.

In treating of hereditary aristocratic governments, we must not pass over Genoa in silence. It may be that, from certain points of view, it cannot stand comparison with other governments of the same class; it may be that the people are less happy there than in Venice or Berne; nevertheless, Genoa has had its fine moments and its great men; and for the rest, every people always has the government and the happiness it deserves.

After having examined the action of hereditary aristocracy on countries of a certain extent, it is good to see it acting in a more restricted theatre and to study it within the walls of a city. Lucca and Ragusa present themselves first to the observer. It has been said that democracy is best suited to small states; it would be more accurate to say that only small states can support it; but hereditary aristocracy suits them perfectly: here are two small states, two isolated cities in the middle of an inconspicuous territory, peaceful, happy, and distinguished by a host of talents. Geneva, with its turbulent democracy, presents an interesting object of comparison. Let us throw these political *grains* into the balance and see without prejudice on which side there is more wisdom and stability.

It is proved, by theory and still more by experience, that hereditary aristocratic government is perhaps the most favourable to the mass of the people, that it has much consistency, wisdom, and stability, and that it adapts itself to countries of very different size. Like all governments, it is good wherever it is established, and it is a crime to disenchant its subjects with it.

Chapter IV: Of Democracy

Pure democracy does not exist anymore than absolute despotism. "If we take the term in the strict sense," Rousseau says very well, "there never has been a real democracy, and there never will be. It is against the natural order for the many to govern and the few to be governed."[1]

The idea of a whole people as sovereign and legislator is so shocking to common sense that Greek political scientists, who must have understood a little of freedom, have never spoken of democracy as a legitimate government, at least when they want to express themselves precisely. Aristotle, especially, defines democracy as the *excess of republic (politia)*, as despotism is the *excess of monarchy*.[2]

If there is no democracy properly so called, the same can be said of perfect despotism, which is likewise a being of pure abstraction. "It is an error to believe that there is any authority in the world despotic in all respects; there never has been and there never will be; the most immense power is always limited in some area."[3]

But in forming clear ideas, there is no reason why we should not consider these two forms of government as two theoretical extremes that all possible governments approach to a greater or lesser degree. In this strict sense, I believe I can define democracy as *an association of men without sovereignty*. "But when the whole people", says Rousseau, "decrees for the whole people, it is considering only itself; and if a relation is then formed, it is between two aspects of the entire object, without there being any division of the whole. In that case the matter about which the decree is made is, like

1 *Contrat social*, 3, IV.

2 This is the remark of an English author who has collected good material for a history of Athens. See Young's *History of Athens*. [William Young, his *History* published in 1786. cf. Aristotle's *Politics* 3.7 for the definitions of democracy and despotism.]

3 Montesquieu, *Grandeur et décadence des Romains*, ch. XXII.

the decreeing will, general. This act is what I call a LAW."[4] What Rousseau prominently calls *law* is precisely what can no longer bear the name.

There is a passage from Tacitus on the origin of governments that deserves attention. After having recounted, like others, the history of the Golden Age, where repeating that vice, by introducing itself into the world, necessitated the establishment of public force, he adds: "Then sovereignties were born, and, for many peoples, they have had no end. Other nations have preferred laws, either at first, or after they had become disgusted with kings."[5]

I have spoken elsewhere of the opposition of kings and laws;[6] what I observe here is that by thus opposing sovereignties to republics, Tacitus implies that there is no *sovereignty* in republics. His subject did not lead him to pursue this idea, which is very apt.

Since no people or individual can possess coercive power over itself, if there were a democracy in its theoretical purity, clearly there would be no sovereignty in this state: for it is impossible to understand by this word anything other than a restraining power which acts on the *subject* and which is placed outside of him. Hence this word *subject*, which is a relative term, is foreign to republics, because there is no sovereign properly so called in a republic, and there can be no *subject* without a *sovereign*, as there can be no *son* without a *father*.

Even in aristocratic governments, where sovereignty is much more palpable than in democracies, the word *subject* is avoided; and the ear finds lighter words which include no exaggeration.

In all the countries of the world there are voluntary associations of men who have come together for some purpose of interest or benevolence. These men have voluntarily submitted themselves to certain rules which they observe as long as they find it good: they have even submitted themselves to certain penalties that they suffer when they have contravened the statutes of the association: but these statutes have no other sanction than the very will of those who have formed them, and as soon as there are dissenters, there is not among them any coercive force to constrain them.

It suffices to enlarge the idea of these corporations to get a fair idea of true democracy. The ordinances that would emanate from a people constituted in this way would be regulations, not laws. The law is so little the

4 *Contrat social*, 2, VI.

5 *Postquam exui aequalitas, et, pro modestia ac pudore, ambitio et vis incedebat, provenere dominationes, multosque apud populos aeternum mansere. Quidam statim, aut postquam regum pertaesum, leges maluere.* (Tacitus, *Annales*, III, 26)

6 [See p. 240.]

will of all, that the *more* it is the will of *all*, the *less* it is *law*: so that it would cease to be *law*, if it were, without exception, the work of *all* those who must obey it.

But as pure democracy does not exist, neither does the state of purely voluntary association. One starts only from this theoretical power to understand; and it is in this sense that one can affirm that sovereignty is born at the moment when the sovereign begins not to be *all the people*, and that it is strengthened as it is less than *all the people*.

This spirit of voluntary association is the constitutive principle of republics; it necessarily has a primitive germ: it is *divine*, and no one can produce it. Mixed to a greater or lesser degree with sovereignty, the common basis of all governments, this "greater" and "lesser" form the different *physiognomies* of non-monarchical governments.

The observer, and especially the foreign observer who lives in a republican country, distinguishes very well the effect of these two principles. Sometimes he feels sovereignty, and sometimes the spirit of community which serves to supplement it; public force acts less and above all shows itself less than in monarchies; it seems as if it defies itself. A certain family spirit, which is easier to feel than to articulate, relieves sovereignty from acting in a host of circumstances in which it would elsewhere intervene; a thousand little things go on by themselves, and—as the common phrase goes, *without knowing how*—order and arrangement show themselves on all sides; common property is respected even by the impoverished, and right down to general propriety, everything gives the observer pause for thought.

A republican people being, therefore, a people less governed than any other, we understand that the working of sovereignty must be supplemented by public spirit, so that the less wisdom a people has in perceiving what is good, and the less virtue it has in doing it of its own accord, the less it is suited to a republic.

All the advantages and disadvantages of this government can be seen at a glance; on its good days it eclipses all else, and the marvels it produces seduce even the cool observer who weighs up everything. But, in the first place, it is suited only to very small nations, for the formation and continuance of the spirit of association are difficult in proportion to the number of associates, which need not be proven.

In the second place, justice does not have that calm and impassive course which we commonly see in monarchy. In democracies, justice is sometimes weak and sometimes impassioned: it is said that, in these governments, no head can brave the sword of the law. This means that the punishment of an illustrious guilty or accused man is a true pleasure for the *plebs*, who thus console themselves for the inevitable superiority of the aristocracy, and public opinion powerfully favours these kinds of judgements; but if the guilty man is obscure, or in general if the crime does not wound the pride or the immediate interest of the majority of the people, this same opinion resists the action of justice and paralyses it.

In a monarchy, the nobility being only an extension of the royal authority, it partakes up to a certain point in the inviolability of the monarch, and this immunity (always infinitely lesser than that of the sovereign) is graduated in such a way that it belongs to fewer people the more significant it is.[7]

In a monarchy, immunity, differently graduated, is for the few; in a democracy, it is for the many.

In the first case, it scandalizes the plebs; in the second case, it makes them happy. I believe it to be good in both cases: that is to say, I believe it to be a necessary element of each government, which amounts to the same thing, for what constitutes a government is always good, at least in an absolute sense.

But when you compare government to government, it is another matter. It is then a question of weighing up the goods and ills that result for the human species from the various social forms. It is from this point of view that I believe monarchy to be superior to democracy in the administration of justice, and I speak not only of criminal justice, but of civil justice. The same weakness is seen in the latter as in the former.

The magistrate is not sufficiently superior to the citizen; he has the air of an arbitrator rather than a judge; and, forced to be circumspect even when he speaks in the name of the law, it is clear that he does not believe in his own power; he is strong only in the solidarity of his equals, because there is no sovereign, or the sovereign is not sufficiently sovereign.

One thing that follows, in particular, is that monarchy is the only government in which the foreigner is the equal of the citizen before the courts. In republics, there is no equal to the iniquity, or, if you like, the impotence

7 These infinite nuances, these admirable combinations so far above all human calculations, are designed to lead us constantly back to the contemplation of that hidden force which has set *number*, *weight*, and *measure* to everything. In the physical world, we are no doubt surrounded by marvels, but the springs driving them are blind and the laws rigid. In the moral or political world, admiration is exalted to the point of rapture when one reflects that the laws of this order, no less sure than physical laws, have at the same time a flexibility which allows them to be combined with the action of the free agents who operate in this order of things. It is a watch, all the parts of which vary continually in their forces and dimensions, and which always marks the time exactly. [cf. the analogy in *Considerations on France*, p. 53].

of the courts when it comes to deciding between a foreigner and a citizen; the more democratic the republic, the more striking this impotence. What man living near one of these states has not said a thousand times: "*It is impossible to obtain justice against these people!*" It is because the less sovereignty is separated from the people, the less it exists, if we may put it this way; it is because the associates accept that justice be done among themselves, at least as far as the interest of each individual rigorously demands it; but they refuse it with impunity to the foreigner, who cannot ask it of a sovereign who does not exist, or who does not exist entirely.

What deceives many superficial observers is that they often mistake the *police* for *justice*. One must not be fooled by a certain regulatory pedantry which the people are mad for, because it serves to annoy the rich. In a town where one is fined for leading a horse at a trot, one can kill a man with impunity, provided that the assassin was born in a shop.

> Cromwell would have been put to 'the bells' by the people of Berne, and the Duc de Beaufort on the treadmill by the Genevese.[8]

Rousseau is mistaken on two counts: if a Cromwell were born in Berne, he would be put in the irons, not by the *people*, but by *their Excellencies the Sovereign Lords of the Canton*, which is not quite synonymous.

As for Geneva, a handful of men who are not *Dukes of Beaufort*,[9] but vile scoundrels, the shame and scum of the human race, have, to the letter, just *put to the discipline* the honest people whose throats they did not slit; and the proof that the blunderers and *kings of the markets* could never be repressed as easily as Rousseau asserts, is that he, Rousseau, was never *put to the discipline*, and that he was always able, safe and sound, to be a detestable citizen in Geneva and to contaminate his country with impunity.

In general, justice is always weak in democracies when it operates alone, and always cruel or negligent when it relies on the people.

Some political scientists have claimed that one of the beautiful aspects of republican government is the wisdom of the people in entrusting the exercise of their authority only to worthy men. No one, they say, chooses better than the people: when it comes to their own interests, nothing can seduce them, merit alone governs them.

I do not know if there is not a great deal of illusion in this idea: democ-

8 *Contrat social*, 4, I.

9 [François de Vendôme, duc de Beaufort, was a prominent figure in the Fronde. Although accounts from the period describe him as a mediocre and unscrupulous character, his popularity led the Parisian mob to dub him "king of the markets".]

racy could not subsist for a moment if it were not tempered by aristocracy, and especially by hereditary aristocracy, which is perhaps more indispensable in this government than in the monarchy. The mere right to vote in a republic gives neither splendour nor power. When Rousseau tells us, in the preamble to the *Contrat Social*, that in his quality as citizen of a free state he is for his part *sovereign*, a sudden smirk breaks out in the most benevolent reader; you only count in a republic as far as birth, alliances, and great talent give you influence; a simple citizen is effectively nothing. The men of this class in Athens were worth so little that they refused to attend the Assembly; those who so refused had to be threatened with a fine; they had to be promised a salary, or, to put it better, an *alms* of three obols, to induce them to come to the square to make up the quorum prescribed by law, which must have amused endlessly the *Pentakosiomedimnoi*.[10] In the comedies of Aristophanes, one often finds jokes about these rulers at so much per session, and nothing is better known in history than the *Triobolon dicasticon*.[11]

The mass of the people therefore has very little influence on elections, as on other affairs. It is the aristocracy which chooses, and, as we know, it chooses very well. When the crowd has meddled in affairs, it was by a kind of insurrection, sometimes necessary to stop the too rapid action of the aristocracy, but always very dangerous and producing the most terrible effects. "We can, however," says Rousseau, "form an idea of the difficulties caused sometimes by the people being so numerous, from what happened in the time of the Gracchi, when some of the citizens had to cast their votes from the roofs of buildings."[12] He should have noticed that voting on the roofs accompanies cutting throats in the streets, and that at the time of the Gracchi the Roman Republic no longer existed. In calm times, the people allow themselves to be led by their leaders; it is then that they are wise, because they do little; it is then that they decide very well, because things are decided for them. When it contents itself with the power it holds from the Constitution, and without daring, so to speak, to put it to use, it relies on the enlightenment and wisdom of the aristocracy; when, on the other hand, the leaders, sufficiently restrained by the fear of being

10 "Wishing to leave all the magistracies in the hands of the well-to-do, as they were, but to give the common people a share in the rest of the government, of which they had hitherto been deprived, Solon made an appraisement of the property of the citizens. Those who enjoyed a yearly increase of *five hundred measure* (wet and dry), he placed in the first class, and called them *Pentakosiomedimnoi*." (Plutarch, *Lives*, *Solon* 18.1)

11 A payment of three obols to Athenian jurymen, instituted by Pericles.

12 *Contrat social*, 3, XV.

deprived of the exercise of power, use it with a wisdom that justifies this confidence—it is then that republics shine. But when this respect is lost on the one hand, and this fear on the other, the state marches with great strides towards its ruin.

Rousseau, in weighing the advantages of monarchical and republican governments, did not fail to grasp and exaggerate in his own way the superiority of the latter in terms of the choice of persons who occupy the places.

> An essential and inevitable defect which will always rank monarchical below republican government, is that in a republic the public voice hardly ever raises to the highest positions men who are not enlightened and capable, and such as to fill them with honour; while in monarchies those who rise to the top are most often merely petty blunderers, petty swindlers, and petty intriguers, whose petty talents cause them to get into the highest positions at Court, but, as soon as they have got there, serve only to make their ineptitude clear to the public."[13]

I have no doubt that in a republic a watchmaker's apprentice would be put in shackles who came out of his *stall* to call the first men of the state *petty blunderers*, *petty swindlers*, *petty intriguers*, etc. But in a monarchy one is less vulnerable: one can be amused by another species just as by a street performer or a monkey; one can even allow him to print his books in the capital, but this is pushing indulgence too far.[14]

Let us see, however, what may be true in this diatribe, for if the core were true, the form would be less reprehensible.

The most ancient of secular historians showed himself to be more loyal than Rousseau to a monarchy that he had every right to dislike.

> The Persians greatly esteem fine service, and among them this is the surest way to achieve the highest honours.[15]

We see that at the court of the GREAT KING, petty intriguers did not exclude men of merit; but, to generalise the thesis, I would first like it to be

13 *Contrat social*, 3, VI.

14 The French government has done itself great harm by closing its eyes too much to such excesses: it has cost the throne and the life of the unfortunate Louis XVI. "Books have done everything," said Voltaire. No doubt, because they have allowed all books.

15 Herodotus, 3.154. Elsewhere he says: "of all the men I know, none are more given to honouring those distinguished by valour than the Persians." (Herodotus., 7.238)

explained by what magic these prodigious meetings of talents which have illustrated different centuries have always exhibited their brilliance under the influence of a single man.

Alexander, Augustus, Leo X, the Medici, Francis I, Louis XIV, and Queen Anne have sought out, employed, and rewarded more great men of all kinds than all the republics of the world put together.

It is always one man who has given his name to his century; and it is only by the choice of men that he has been able to merit this honour.

What spectacle is comparable to that of the century of Louis XIV? An absolute and almost adored sovereign, doubtless no one hindered him in the distribution of favours; and what man chose men better?

Colbert managed his finances; the terrible talents of Louvois presided over war; Turenne, Coudé, Catinat, Luxembourg, Berwick, Créqui, Vendôme, and Villars led his land armies; Vauban secured France; Dugay-Trouin, Tourville, Jean Bart, Duquesne, Forbin d'Oppède, d'Estrées, and Renaud commanded his fleets; Talon, Lamoignon, d'Aguesseau sat in his courts; Bourdaloue and Massillon preached before him; the episcopate received from his hand this same Massillon, Fléchier, Bossuet, and that great Fénelon, the honour of France, the honour of his century, the honour of humanity. In his *royal* academies, the talents gathered under his protection shone with a unique brilliance; it was he who made France the true fatherland of talents of all kinds, the arbiter of fame, the dispenser of glory.

It may be said that since chance placed a host of great men under his hand, he did not even have the merit of choice. So what? Does one imagine that his century lacked mediocre men, thinking themselves fit for everything, and demanding everything? This species teems on all sides and at all times. But it is precisely here that I would confront the extreme admirers of republican government. This form of government, as we cannot stress enough, does not endure. It only exists, it only shines, by a rare confluence of great talents and great virtues, and this union is necessarily concentrated on a very small number of heads. What do we say, in effect, when we say that the people chooses its agents perfectly? We say that one wise man chooses another: this is the whole miracle.

Rousseau lived in Paris under the deplorable reign of Louis XV: he was witnessing, so to speak, the agony of France. Regarding some documents distributed by Madame de Pompadour, he hastened to write that, *in monarchies*, one saw only *petty blunderers*, *petty swindlers*, and *petty intriguers* attaining high offices. It is not to be wondered at: this man never saw but one point.

I do not deny, however, that monarchical government is more prone than any other to err in the choice of persons; but the eternal declamations on the errors of blind patronage are much less well-founded than we commonly imagine. First of all, if you listen to pride, kings always choose poorly, for there is no malcontent who does not prefer himself unquestioningly to the lucky chosen one; moreover, princes are too often accused when only the people should be accused. In times of universal degradation, people complain that merit does not prevail; but where, then, is this forgotten merit? One is obliged to exhibit it before accusing the government. Under the last two French reigns, we have certainly seen very mediocre men in important offices; but to which men of merit, then, were they preferred? Now that a revolution, the most complete that has ever been, has broken all the chains that could hold talent captive, where are they? You will find them, perhaps, joined to profound immorality; but as for talents of this kind, it is empires' very instinct of preservation that has kept them away from the high office. Moreover, as a sacred writer has said very aptly, "*there is a certain skill which is but for evil*."[16] It is this talent which has been enflaming France for five years.[17] Among even the most outstanding men who have appeared in this theatre bathed in blood and tears, if one examines carefully, one will find little or no real political talent. They have done evil very skilfully; that is the best we can say of them! Fortunately, the most famous of them have written, and when all passions repose in the grave, posterity will read in these indiscreetly traced pages that the most monstrous errors dominated these proud men, and that the previous government, which fended them off, which enchained them, which punished them, was unknowingly fighting for its own preservation.

It is, therefore, because France was degenerating, it is because it lacked talent, that kings seemed too willing to welcome the mediocrity presented by intrigue. There is a very gross error, into which we nevertheless fall daily without noticing it. Although we recognise the hidden hand which directs everything, yet such is the illusion which results from the action of second causes, that we quite commonly reason as if this hand did not exist. When we contemplate the games of intrigue around thrones, the words *accident*, *fortune*, *misfortune*, *chance*, etc., present themselves quite naturally, and we pronounce them a little too quickly without realising that they make no sense.

Man is free, no doubt; man can make mistakes, but not enough to disturb the general plans. We are all attached to the throne of the Eternal by a flexible chain which reconciles the *autocracy* of free agents with the divine

16 Ecclesiastes 21:15.

17 This date fixes that of this work. [1794]

supremacy.[18] Without contradiction, such and such a king may for such and such a time keep true talent from its proper place, and this unhappy faculty may be extended more or less, but in general there is a secret force which carries each *individual* to his place: otherwise the State could not subsist. We recognise in the plant an unknown power, a plastic force, essentially *one*, which produces and preserves, which invariably moves towards its goal, which appropriates what serves it, which rejects what harms it, which carries to the very last fibril of the last leaf the sap it needs, and fights with all its strength the diseases of the vegetal body. This force is even more visible and admirable in the animal kingdom! How blind we are! How can we believe that the body politic does not also have its law, its soul, its plastic force, and that everything is subject to the whim of human ignorance? If the moral mechanisms of empires were made manifest to us, we would be freed from a host of errors: we would see, for example, that such and such a man, who seems to us to be made for such and such an office, is a *disease* which the vital force pushes to the surface, while we deplore the *misfortune* which prevents him from insinuating himself into the sources of life. These words *talent* and *genius* deceive us every day; often these qualities are not where we think we see them, and often they belong to dangerous men.

As for those rare times when empires must perish, they depart visibly from the ordinary cycle of events. Then, all the ordinary rules being suspended, the faults of the government which is going to dissolve prove nothing against this form of government. They are merely symptoms of death, and nothing more: everything must perish to make room for new creations:

> And nothing, so that all may last,
> Lasts eternally.[19]

We must submit; but in the ordinary course of things, I invite the subjects of monarchies to lay hands on their consciences and ask themselves if they know of many true talents, and of pure talents, which are overlooked or restrained by the sovereign. If they should listen to the response of their conscience, they would learn to content themselves with the boons they possess, instead of envying the imaginary perfections of other governments.

To hear the agitators of democracy talk, one would think that the people deliberate like a senate of sages, whereas juridical murders, hazardous ventures, extravagant choices, and above all mad and disastrous wars are

18 See the opening of *Considerations on France*, p. 53.

19 François de Malherbe, *Ode au Roi Henri le Grand*, 1596.

eminently the prerogative of this kind of government.

But who has ever spoken more ill of democracy than Rousseau, who clearly determines that it is made only for a people comprised of gods?[20]

It remains to be seen how a government which is made only *for gods* is nevertheless proposed *to men* as the only legitimate government: for if this is not the sense of the social contract, the social contract has no sense.[21]

But that is not all.

> Besides, how many conditions that are difficult to unite does such a government presuppose! First, a very small State, where the people can readily be got together and where each citizen can with ease know all the rest; secondly, great simplicity of manners, to prevent business from multiplying and raising thorny problems; next, a large measure of equality in rank and fortune, without which equality of rights and authority cannot long subsist; lastly, little or no luxury.[22]

If democracy is only suitable for very small States, how can this form of government be proposed as the only legitimate form of government, and, if it may be so called, as a *formula* which must resolve all political questions?

Rousseau is not at all embarrassed by this difficulty. "It is useless," he says, "to bring up abuses that belong to great States against one who desires to see only small ones," that is to say:

> I, Jean-Jacques Rousseau, do solemnly declare, so that no person can be ignorant of it, that I DO NOT WANT a great empire. If there have been in the world Babylonians, Medes, Persians, Macedonians, Romans, Tartars, etc., all these nations were abuses, which took place only because I was not there. *I do not want* these peoples, who are *so difficult to assemble*. In

20 *Contrat social*, 3, IV.

21 Let it not be said that Rousseau expressly recognises other governments as legitimate: we must not be fooled by words; he himself has taken the trouble to outline his profession of faith. "Every legitimate government," he says, "is republican." (2, VI) And, to avoid any equivocation, here is the note: "I do not mean by this word 'government' only an aristocracy or a democracy, but in general any government guided by the general will, which is the law. To be legitimate, the government must not be confounded with the sovereign, but must be the minister of the sovereign. Then monarchy itself is a republic." (2, VI) Thus wherever the law is not the expression of the will of *all* the *people*, the government is not legitimate... we must remember this.

22 *Contrat social*, 3, XIII.

> vain does unity of language demonstrate the natural unity of these great families; in vain does the disposition of seacoasts, rivers, and mountains form vast basins plainly destined to contain these nations; in vain does the experience of all centuries serve to demonstrate the intention of the Creator. I am embarrassed neither by metaphysics, geography, or history. *I do not want great States*. I extend my philosophical measure line over the surface of the globe; I divide it like a chessboard, and, in the middle of each square of 2,000 measures per side, I build a charming city of Geneva which I fill with *gods* for greater surety.

Doubtless this tone is permissible when one comes up against errors that are so far beyond serious refutation. I do not know why, moreover, Rousseau was willing to admit that democratic government leads to minor abuses; he had found a very simple way of justifying it: to judge it only by its theoretical perfections, and to regard the evils it produces as small anomalies without consequences, which need not attract the attention of the observer.

> Our will is always for our own good, but we do not always see what that is: the people is never corrupted, but it is often deceived, and on such occasions only does it seem to will what is bad.[23]

Drink, Socrates, drink! and console yourself with these distinctions: the good people of Athens only *seem* to want what is wrong.

Such is the partisan spirit: it does not want to see, or it only wants to see one side. This ridiculousness is especially striking in the outrageous eulogies that Rousseau and his followers have delivered for democracy and especially for ancient democracy.

I remember reading in one of these panegyrics that "the superiority of popular government over government of one is alone decided by the superiority of the interest which the history of republics inspires compared with that of monarchies."

It is always the same illusion. Since democracy can only subsist by virtue, energy, and public spirit, if a nation has received from the Creator the aptitude for this government, it is certain that, in the time of its vigour, it must, by the very nature of things, give birth to a dazzling group of great men whose deeds give to its history an inexpressible charm and interest.

Moreover, in popular governments there is more action, more movement—and movement is the life of history.

23 *Contrat social*, 2, III.

Unfortunately, the happiness of the people is in peace, and almost always the pleasure of the reader relies upon their sufferings.

Let us repeat it, because nothing is more true: nothing equals the salad days of republics; but it is a flash. Moreover, in admiring the beautiful effects of this government, we must also consider the crimes and follies to which it has given birth, even in happy times; for the influence of the wise is not always sufficient—though nearly so—to keep in check the disordered action of the people.

Is it not better to be Miltiades than the favourite of the greatest monarch in the world? Yes, no doubt, on the day of the battle of Marathon. But a year later, the day this great man was thrown into prison to finish his days, the question becomes doubtful.

Aristides and Cimon were banished; Themistocles and Timothy died in exile; Socrates and Phocion drank the hemlock. Athens did not spare one of its great men.

I do not wish to deny that the Athenians were admirable in some respects, but I also believe, with one of the ancients, that they have been too much admired.[24] When I read the history of this "slight, suspicious, violent, hateful people, jealous of power,"[25] and almost never knowing how to help themselves, I am very much in favour of the sentiment of Voltaire, who called the Athenian democracy *the government of the rabble*.[26]

Condorcet was no less an enemy of this government and of all those that

24 *Atheniensium res gestae sicut ego existimo salis amplae magnificaeque fuere; verum aliquanto minores tamen quam fama feruntur*. ["The deeds of the Athenians were indeed glorious enough; and yet somewhat lesser than fame makes them out to be."] (Sallust, *The War with Catiline*, VIII) For example, in admiring the heroes of Plataea, Thermopylae, and Salamis, it is permissible to recall the exclamation of Caesar on the battlefield where he had just crushed the hordes of Asia by making sport of them: "Happy Pompey, what enemies you had to fight!"

25 *Populus acer, suspicax, mobilis, adversarius, invidus potentiae*. (Cornelius Nepos, *in Timoth. III*)

26 "When I supplicated you to be the restorer of the beaux-arts of Greece, my prayer did not go so far as to implore you to restore Athenian democracy: *I do not like the government of the rabble*. You would have given the government of Greece to M. de Lentulus, or to some other general who would have prevented the new Greeks from doing as much mischief as their ancestors." (Voltaire to the King of Prussia, 28 October 1773. *Oeuvres de Voltaire*, vol. 86, p. 51)

To say it in passing, I do not know why people have insisted on making this man one of the saints of the French Revolution, of which he would have liked only the irreligious side. He is responsible for it in large part, and yet he would have abhorred it. There shall never be men, not only more proud, but more conceited and more hostile to any kind of equality.

resemble it. He complained of the "pedant Mably who was always looking for examples in the despotic anarchies of Greece."[27]

And it is truly a great error to reason too much in politics by the examples left to us by antiquity. It is in vain that one would want to make of us Athenians, Lacedemonians, or Romans. Perhaps we should say "*Nos sumus argillae deterioris opus*" ["we are the work of inferior clay"]; at least if they were not better, they were different. *Man is always the same*, it is often said. It is rashly said; but the thoughtful politician does not make up his mind by these fine axioms, the insubstantiality of which is clear when we come to the examination of particular cases. Mably says somewhere "*It is Titus Livius who taught me all I know about politics.*" This is certainly a great honour for Livy, but I am sorry for Mably.

27 Condorcet, *Vie de Voltaire*, Paris, 1791, p. 299 – Mably being also one of the oracles of the day, it is good to have him judged *by his peers*.

Chapter V:
Of The Best Kind of Sovereignty

> The question 'What absolutely is the best government?' is unanswerable as well as indeterminate; or rather, there are as many good answers as there are possible combinations in the absolute and relative situations of all nations.[1]

This observation of Rousseau's does not admit of any reply, and he has devoted half of his book to refuting the other half; but, in truth, he has taken too much trouble, these few lines were enough.

He saw very well that it was never necessary to ask what the best government is in general, since there is not one that suits all peoples. Each nation has its own, as it has its own language and character, and this government is the best for it.

Hence it obviously follows that the whole theory of the social contract is a juvenile fantasy.

It cannot be repeated often enough: "There are as many good governments as there are possible combinations in the absolute and relative positions of peoples."

Since none of these combinations depends on men, it follows that the consent of the people plays no part in the formation of governments.

> But if it is asked by what sign we may know that a given people is well or ill governed, that is another matter, and the question, being one of fact, admits of an answer.[2]

It could not be better said: the question is never to know which government is the best, but which people is best governed according to the principles of its government.

It is precisely this question, the only reasonable one, that Rousseau has

1 *Contrat social*, 3, IX.
2 *Contrat social*, 3, IX.

treated with his usual flippancy.

"What," he asks, "is the end of political association? The preservation and prosperity of its members."

So far, so good.

"And what," he continues, "is the surest mark that they"—the members of the body politic—"preserve and prosper? Their numbers and population. Seek then nowhere else this mark that is in dispute. The rest being equal, the government under which, without external aids, without naturalisation or colonies, the citizens increase and multiply most, is beyond question the best. The government under which a people wanes and diminishes is the worst. Calculators, it is left for you to count, to measure, to compare."[3]

There is nothing so superficial, nothing so dubious, nothing so poorly reasoned as this whole piece.

Rousseau has just said that one cannot ask "What is the best government", that the question is *unanswerable as well as indeterminate*. And now, in the same chapter, he tells us that the *best government* is the one that *populates* the most, and that the *worst* is the one under which a people *diminishes* and *declines*; there is, therefore, an absolute *good* and *bad* government. Let us agree, if it even be possible, with Rousseau himself.

Will it be said that, in the second part of the chapter, he does not compare one nation with another nation, but a nation with itself, considering it at different times?

In this supposition, Rousseau wants to say that when a people multiplies, it is a sign that it is *well* governed, and that if this people declines, it is a sign that it is *badly* governed: that is to say, in the first case one *follows*, and in the second one *violates*, the principles of government which is best for this given people. Very good! But in this case, it must be admitted that the statement of such a trivial truth is an absurdity most rare, and this absurdity becomes truly transcendent when one considers that this beautiful discovery is preceded by a haughty reproach addressed to all the publicists who have not wished to agree to this infallible rule for judging governments.[4]

In a word, if Rousseau wants to say that there are essentially *bad* governments that kill men, and others that are essentially *good* that multiply

3 *Contrat social*, 3, IX.

4 "For my part, I am continually astonished that a mark so simple is not recognised, or that men are of so bad faith as not to admit it. What is the end of political association? The preservation and prosperity of its members. And what is the surest mark of their preservation and prosperity? Their numbers and population. Seek then nowhere else this mark that is in dispute." (*Contrat social*, 3, IX)

them, he is talking nonsense, and he is obviously contradicting himself. If he means that a given people is badly governed when it declines or languishes at the lowest ebb of population, and that it is well governed, on the contrary, when its population increases or sustains itself at the highest level, he is talking nonsense: the choice is yours. One may conclude, moreover, from what Rousseau says about population, that he was as profound in political economy as in metaphysics, history, and morality.

Population is not the unique thermometer of the prosperity of states; it must be combined with the well-being and richness of the people; the population must be *rich* and *available*. A people whose population is raised to the highest possible degree, and whose every individual consequently possesses only the bare necessities, would be a weak and unhappy people; the least political upheaval would overwhelm it with calamities. A nation of fifteen million men can be not only happier, which is obvious, but more powerful than another nation of twenty million: this is what economists have perfectly proved, and Mr. Young has just confirmed it by new observations in a work which is equally valuable for the truths it establishes and for the errors it retracts.[5]

5 *Voyage agronomique de France* (Arthur Young, *Travels in France during the Years 1787, 1788 and 1789*).

Chapter VI: Continuation of the Same Subject

The best government for each nation is that which, in the space of land occupied by that nation, is capable of providing the greatest possible sum of happiness and strength, to the greatest possible number of men, for the longest possible time. I dare to believe that the validity of this definition cannot be denied, and it is in following this definition that it becomes possible to compare nations in terms of their governments. In effect, although we cannot ask absolutely: *which is the best government*, there is nothing to prevent us from asking: *which people is relatively the most numerous, the strongest, the happiest, for the longest period of time, through the influence of the government that suits it?*

How odd it is that in the study of politics we do not wish to use the same kind of reasoning and the same general analogies that guide us in the study of the other sciences.

In physical research, whenever it is a question of estimating a variable force, we reduce it to an average quantity. In astronomy especially we always speak of *average distance* and *average time*.

To judge the merits of a government, the same procedure must be followed.

Any government is a variable force, which produces effects no less variable than itself, within certain limits; to judge it, we must not consider it at a single moment; we must comprehend it in its entirety. Thus, to judge the French monarchy soundly, one must add up the virtues and vices of all the kings of France and divide by 66: the result is an *average king*; and the same must be said of all other monarchies.

Democracy has one brilliant moment, but it is one moment, and it must come at a high cost. The salad days of Athens may, I agree, inspire desires in the subject of a monarchy, languishing at such and such a time under the sceptre of an inept or wicked king; nevertheless, we would be prodigiously mistaken if in comparing moment to moment we pretend to establish the superiority of democracy over monarchy, because in this judgement we neglect, among other things, the consideration of duration, which is a necessary element in these kinds of estimations.

In general, all democratic governments are only passing meteors whose brilliance excludes duration.

Aristocratic republics have more consistency because they are closer to monarchy, and the mass of the people plays no role in them. Sparta was an admirable phenomenon of this kind. However, with unique institutions, within reach only of an extraordinary people, with a certain kingship, with a strong and imposing aristocracy, within a very narrow territory, with the harshest slavery admitted as an element of government, that of Sparta lasted only roughly half the time as the kingdom of France has lasted up to our days.

Let us examine again, before leaving the ancients, the most famous government in the world, that of Rome.

Let us count, in round numbers, 700 years from the foundation of Rome to the battle of Actium: the seven kings first occupy 244 years of this period; 456 years remain for the republic. But its old age was dreadful: what man would have the nerve to call "free" the government which saw the Gracchi, the triumvirs, and the proscriptions? Ferguson,[1] in his Roman History, rightly observes that the century of the Gracchi alone produced more horrors than the history of any other nation in the world presents in such a space of time. — (He had not seen the French Revolution!)

The sedition of the Gracchi was in the 621st year from the foundation of Rome, so that 377 years remain for the government that could be called a *Republic*: this is an instant, and nevertheless it was far from being a democracy. The first merit of a political constitution consists in the extent of its possible duration; it is therefore poor reasoning to judge it by its effects at a given time. When a simple and even crude mechanism produces four inches of water for the irrigation of a meadow or for any other interesting purpose, and the most skilful mechanic comes to propose another machine which will furnish double, this man must not be listened to right away: for if the new machine is fragile, if its maintenance is expensive, if it costs ten times as much and if it should last ten times less than the other, the father of the family must reject it.

On this principle, which it is impossible to contest, if one were asked, for example, what one thought of the constitution of England, which is, however, seemingly the most perfect that can be imagined, at least for a great people, the true political scientist will not know what to answer. This

1 Adam Ferguson, *The History of the Progress and Termination of the Roman Empire*, 1783.

constitution, as it has existed since it took its last form, dates only from the year 1688: it has therefore lasted only a century, that is to say a moment; but who can answer for the future? Not only do we have no moral certitude in this respect, but there are strong reasons for fearing that this fine work will not last. "Every government," says Tacitus, "is democratic, aristocratic or monarchical: a constitution made up of these three powers mixed and tempered by each other is easier to admire than to find; or, if such a thing ever existed, IT COULD NOT LAST."[2]

Here is the English constitution condemned in advance in express terms, and by an excellent judge.

If we were to consult even the enlightened English, how many alarming replies would we not receive! A writer of this nation, deeply instructed in the finances of his country, and who has written the history of it; a writer who is in no way suspicious since he shows himself everywhere attached to the government and who wrote expressly to calm minds and to strengthen them against the system of an inevitable bankruptcy; this man, I say, nevertheless decides unequivocally that "Frugality, integrity, and propriety are not therefore to be expected in the expenditure of public money, till a political revolution shall take place in the administration of this country."[3]

Recently, in a trial famous in more than one respect, one of the first magistrates of the Crown, the Solicitor General, was heard in England to say to the nation and to Europe that "he would not disguise but that there were abuses in our government; nay, he would suppose, abominable abuses; and if the season were proper, he would himself bring forward some such propositions intended to correct them."[4]

Finally, to confine us to the present time, could the Prime Minister of this great and illustrious nation refrain from complaining, in the open House, about the members of the opposition who were tiring the administration with "the difficulty and embarrassment of a particular crisis… a moment

2 *Cunctas nationes et urbes populus aut primores aut singuli regunt delecta: ex his et consociata reipublicae forma laudari facilius quam evenire; vel si evenit, haud diuturna esse potest.* (Tacitus, *Annals*, IV, 33)

3 Sir John Sinclair, *The History of public revenue of the British Empire*, Part. III, 1790.

4 Discourse of the Solicitor General in the trial of Thomas Hardy and others, accused of high treason, 4 November 1794. *London Chronicle*, No. 5973, p. 447. One may give whatever force one likes to the hypothetical expression *he would suppose*; for the rest, to say it in passing, this great trial has made disinterested jurisconsults fear that England has proved, on this occasion, that she lacks *laws* or *justice*; but it is better to suspend judgement and believe that one would think otherwise if one saw things close up.

of embarrassment, irritation and disquietude"?[5]

The perfect formation, the completion, the consolidation of the English constitution as it now exists, has cost the English people torrents of blood: they will not have paid too much if it endures; but if ever (and *omen quidem dii prohibeant*! ["may the gods indeed prevent this omen"]) this beautiful constitution should dissolve; if this dissolution were only a century or two hence, and if the destruction of this superb machine should subject the empire to all the upheavals which preceded the expulsion of the Stuarts, it would be proved that this constitution, so much vaunted, and so worthy of being vaunted in its best days, was nevertheless bad, because it was not durable.

Fortunately, it is permissible to suppose the contrary, because liberty is not new to the English, as I have observed above: so that the state in which they now find themselves is not a forced state, and also because the balance of the three powers seems to promise this government, at least for a long time, the strength to raise itself back up again; but we are far from having any certainty in this respect. The only indisputable point is that the English constitution cannot be judged definitively, because it has not passed the test of time, and if a Frenchman, agreeing on the superiority of that constitution considered absolutely, should nevertheless argue that the government of his country was a better government on average than that of England, the legitimate judges of that assertion have not yet been born.

The consideration of the duration of governments naturally leads us to that of the greatest happiness of peoples: in effect, as all political revolutions necessarily entail great evils, the greatest interest of peoples is the stability of governments. But it is not enough to examine these particular cases; we must also weigh the goods and evils that result, for the greatest number of men, from the different forms of sovereignty, throughout their duration.

In reasoning about the various kinds of government, we do not place enough emphasis on the consideration of general happiness, which should, however, be our only standard. We must have the courage to admit to ourselves an incontestable truth which would cool enthusiasm for free constitutions a little: in any republic of a certain size, what is called *liberty* is only the absolute sacrifice of a great number of men to the independence and pride of a few. This is what it is especially important never to lose sight of when judging ancient republics, with which a great number of writers, namely Rousseau and Mably, have shown themselves to be infinitely too

5 Discourse of Mr. Pitt in reply to that of Mr. Fox, in the House of Commons, sitting of March 24, 1795. *Morning Chronicle*, No. 7939.

infatuated.

Strictly speaking, all governments are monarchies which differ only in that the monarch is for life or for a term, hereditary or elective, individual or corporative; or, if you like, for it is the same idea in different words, all government is aristocratic, composed of greater or fewer ruling heads, from democracy, where this aristocracy is composed of as many heads as the nature of things permits, to monarchy, where the aristocracy, inevitable in all government, is dominated by a single head which caps the pyramid, and undoubtedly forms the government most natural to man.

But of all monarchs, the harshest, most despotic, most intolerable is the monarch *people*. Again, history testifies in favour of this great truth, that the liberty of the few is founded only on the slavery of the multitude, and that republics have never been anything but multi-headed sovereigns, whose despotism, always less forgiving and more capricious than that of monarchs, increased in intensity as the number of subjects multiplied.

Rome, above all, to reign over her vast domains, exercised this despotism in all its fullness, and no power was ever more absolute. All the power of government, concentrated in the Capitol, presented to the trembling world only a sole head, one single power before which everything had to bow. While in modern times no capital of a vast state has been able to give it its name, Rome on the contrary, *immensi caput orbis* ["the capital of the boundless world"],[6] impressed its name on all that depended on it and did not even allow language to alter the exclusive idea of this power: thus, the empire was not *Italian*, it was *Roman*. The army was *Roman*. There was no counterweight in the provinces, no force of resistance: Rome directed everything, set off everything, struck everywhere. The name of Rome was King, and the prostrate imagination of the peoples saw only this astonishing city.

> *Quanta nec est nec erit nec visa prioribus annis.*[7]
>
> ["Than which none greater is or shall be, or has been in past ages."]

But who can help groaning about the fate of the human race when one thinks that this enormous power was the patrimony of a handful of men, and that Rome with its 1,200,000 inhabitants[8] had barely 2,000 proprietors

6 [Ovid, *Metamorphoses*, 15.435]

7 [Ovid, *Metamorphoses*, 15.44]

8 Some exaggerators have set the population of ancient Rome at 4, 8, and finally at 14 million. Brottier rightly calls these calculations *enormous and absurd calculations* (*de urbis Romae Pomoerio et magnitudine, incolarumque* numero; No-

within its walls?[9]

It was to this small number of men that the known world was sacrificed. Some readers will perhaps see with pleasure how French liberty has appreciated ancient liberty.[10] It is to satisfy them that I will quote this passage from a report made to the National Convention in the name of the three Government Committees:

> In the ancient republics, the exercise of the political rights of citizens was circumscribed within a very narrow territory, or within the walls of a single city. Outside the precinct of governments, people lived in intolerable subjection; and within their precinct, the harshest slavery was established alongside tumultuous liberty. The dignity of a few men has been raised upon the degradation of the many. In those countries whose liberty has been so highly praised, because the people have been mistaken for a small number of privileged inhabitants, the name of *liberty* could not be pronounced without exciting a shudder from a crowd of slaves; the name of *equality* could not be pronounced without hearing the sound of their chains; and *fraternity* has never been known in countries where a few free men

tae et Emend. in Tac. II, p. 375). This skilful commentator puts the population at 1,200,000. Gibbon arrived at the same result by another route. (*History of the decline and fall, etc.*, vol. I) Mr. Byres, by a calculation drawn from the size of the great circus, claimed that the population of the city and its suburbs could not be less than 3,000,000. Moor claims that if the wall of Belisarius really served as a boundary for the ancient city, it could not have contained, at any time, more than 500,000 to 600,000 souls, unless the masters of the world were very poorly housed; but he admits that if the suburbs are included in the calculation, the number of inhabitants can be raised as high as one deems appropriate. Amid these uncertainties, I can only hold to the moderate and reasoned calculation of Brottier and Gibbon.

9 This is what the tribune Philippus, haranguing the people in the year 649 from the Founding of Rome [105 BCE], said to them in order to enflame them and induce them to decide for the agrarian law: *Non esse in tanta civitate duo millia hominum qui rem habeant* ["there were in the city not two thousand men who held property"] and Cicero, who reports this fact (*de Officiis*, II, 21) in blaming the intention of the tribune, does not dispute the truth of the fact. One can judge, to say it in passing, how the multitude was influenced and how the gold of the aristocrats mocked the law *Julia de Ambitu* [the *lex Julia* penalized bribery when acquiring political offices].

10 *Ut comparatione deterrima sibi gloriam quaereret.* ["Had sought to heighten his own glory by the vilest of contrasts"] (Tacitus, Annals, I, 10) But his effrontery turns against itself, for every comparison defames it.

> have constantly held under their domination a crowd of men condemned to servitude.[11]

They have not always spoken so justly at the tribune of the National Convention; instead of extolling Roman liberty, we should think a little longer about what it cost the world, we should remember how much the proconsular haughtiness and arrogance debased the provinces. A Roman magistrate amid the subjects of the Republic was really a kind of deity, good or evil according to the play of chance. It is impossible to describe all that the provinces had to suffer from these terrible magistrates when it pleased them to do evil; there was no way of obtaining justice against them[12] and even when their conduct was irreproachable, they still made their superiority felt in the harshest manner. When they were exercising of their functions, they were not allowed to speak any other language than that of Rome: it had to be spoken on the Euphrates as well as on the Guadalquivir; they did not deign to suppose that there was any other language. There was not even an exception for proud Greece. The compatriots of Demosthenes and Sophocles came stammering before the tribunal of a proconsul and were astonished to receive orders in Latin in the middle of the Prytaneum. The most distinguished man of his country, even if he were a king, if he were not a Roman citizen, did not dare to claim the honour of embracing a provincial governor, and history shows us a king of the Parthians asking for his brother, king of Armenia, who was going to Rome, the privilege of embracing these superb magistrates.[13]

11 Session of 12 January. (*Moniteur*, No. 117, p. 482, 1795)

12 Verres, a simple praetor with an obscure name, committed all manner of crimes with impunity in Sicily; on his return to Rome, the eloquence of Cicero, thundering against him for five days in a row in the name of an entire nation, barely succeeded in getting him exiled. If one calls this *justice*, one is not difficult to please.

13 Tacitus, *Annals*, XV, 31 — Brottier reports an interesting anecdote on this place in Tacitus. It is a very interesting anecdote. "Severus, who later obtained the empire, went to Africa, whose government he had obtained. One day, walking ahead of his lictors, he met an inhabitant of Leptines, his fellow citizen, whose guest he had been for a long time. The latter, unaware or not remembering the law which forbade any provincial, and even any plebeian, from embracing a provincial governor, saw in Severus only an old friend and embraced him without reflection. Severus had him beaten immediately and during the operation, a town crier addressed these consoling words to the patient: 'Remember, plebeian, not to embrace inconsiderately an envoy of the Roman people: LEGATUM POPULI ROMANI HOMO PLEBEIUS, TEMERE AMPLECTI NOLI!' And, to avoid similar inconveniences, it was decided that the provincial governors would no longer

The most vigorous brush of antiquity having transmitted to us a faithful painting of Roman legislation under the republican regime, one will be grateful that it be placed it here. It is, in truth, a Roman history, made by the man who abridged all because he saw all.

> After Tarquin's expulsion, the people, to check cabals among the Senators, devised many safeguards for freedom and for the establishment of unity. Decemvirs were appointed;[14] everything specially admirable elsewhere was adopted, and the Twelve Tables drawn up, the last specimen of equitable legislation. For subsequent enactments, though occasionally directed against evildoers for some crime, were oftener carried by violence amid class dissensions, with a view to obtain honours not as yet conceded, or to banish distinguished citizens, or for other base ends. Hence the Gracchi and Saturnini, those popular agitators, and Drusus too, as flagrant a corrupter in the Senate's name; hence, the bribing of our allies by alluring promises and the cheating them by tribunes vetoes. Even the Italian and then the Civil war did not pass without the enactment of many conflicting laws, till Lucius Sulla, the Dictator, by the repeal or alteration of past legislation and by many additions, gave us a brief lull in this process, to be instantly followed by the seditious proposals of Lepidus, and soon afterwards by the tribunes recovering their license to excite the people just as they chose. And now bills were passed, not only for national objects but for individual cases, and laws were most numerous when the commonwealth was most corrupt.[15]
>
> […]
>
> Cneius Pompeius was then for the third time elected consul to reform public morals, but in applying remedies more terrible than the evils and repealing the legislation of which he had himself been the author, he lost by arms what by arms he had been maintaining. Then followed twenty years of continuous strife; custom or law there was none; the vilest deeds went un-

go out on foot." (Spart., *in Severus*, II) This anecdote and that of the king of the Parthians are from under the Empire, but the custom is from the Republic and could not even have begun under a monarchy.

14 We may be surprised that Tacitus did not say, in passing, what the laws of the Twelve Tables cost the Romans.

15 [Translation in the next three paragraphs excerpted from Tacitus, *Annals*, tr. Alfred John Church, William Jackson Brodribb, 1888]

> punished, while many noble acts brought ruin.[16]

This picture is neither suspicious nor attractive; but if the abuses described by this great master were so terrible within the walls of Rome, what evils they must have produced in the provinces! It is easy to form an idea of them. And so, when after the battle of Actium the government finally fell into the hands of one man, it was a fine day for the Roman Empire; and Tacitus, though very fond of the Republic, as we see in a thousand places in his works, is forced to admit that the provinces applauded a revolution which relieved them immensely.

> Nor did the provinces dislike that condition of affairs, for they distrusted the government of the Senate and the people, because of the rivalries between the leading men and the rapacity of the officials, while the protection of the laws was unavailing, as they were continually deranged by violence, intrigue, and finally by corruption.[17]

The same historian has painted in a striking manner, and probably without thinking about it, the sufferings of foreign nations under the empire of the Roman people. It is known that when Augustus took the helm, nothing changed externally, and that titles especially were always the same.[18] The title of prince with which he contented himself, far from rousing the idea of a king, was, for the Romans, below that of dictator:[19] so that Ovid, who certainly had no desire to shock the ears of Augustus, was able to say without scruple at the end of his inimitable narrative of the death of Lucretius and the expulsion of the Tarquins:

> Tarquin fled with his brood, the consul for a year took hold of

16 Tacitus, *Annals*, III, 27–28.

17 *Neque provinciae illum rerum statum abnuebant, suspecto Senatus Populique imperio ob certamina potentium, et avaritiam magistratuum; invalido legum auxilio, quae vi, ambitu, postremo pecunia turbabantur*. (Tacitus, *Annals*, I, 2)

18 *Domi res tranquillae eadem magistratuum vocabula*. ["At home things were calm, (with) the same titles of magistrates."] (Tacitus, *Annals*, I, 3) Not everyone has a clear idea of this change. The Abbé de la Bletterie painted it perfectly well in his dissertation entitled *L'Empereur au milieu dù Sénat*; it can be found in the Mémoires de l'Académie des inscriptions. [Jean-Philippe-René de La Bléterie, who wrote a biography life of the emperor Julian in 1735, subsequently cited by Gibbon.]

19 *Non regno tamen, neque dictatura, sed Principis nomine constitutam Rempublicam*. ["Yet he did not constitute the republic by kingship, nor by dictatorship, but by the name of *princeps*."] (Tacitus, *Annals*, I, 9)

the law: that was the final day for kings.[20]

A singular consequence of this order of things was that the government of the provinces did not pass abruptly and entirely into the hands of the emperor. Only Augustus, during his seventh consulship, divided the provinces, by a sort of transaction, between the people and himself. The governors for the people were called *proconsuls* and were appointed by lot, according to republican forms; those for the emperor were called legates or praetors and held their office by his choice. Now, although the despot of Rome sent into the provinces, as we may well imagine, only *petty swindlers* and *petty intriguers*, there was nevertheless in a very short time such a difference in the state of the provinces subjected to the two regimes, and the subjects of the *people* found themselves so wretched compared to the subjects of the *prince*, that when, under Tiberius, Achaia and Macedonia asked to be relieved of the taxes afflicting them, nothing better was thought of, in order to lessen their lot, without harming the public treasury, than to deliver them for the moment from the proconsular regime and to give them to the emperor.[21]

The great misfortune of the Romans and of the greater part of the known world which was subject to them, was that on the accession of Augustus the revolution was not sufficiently completed. What tears and crimes an hereditary monarchy would have spared the world! But all the ancient forms were preserved: there was a senate, consuls, tribunes, assemblies, and provincial governors *for the Roman people*. The prerogative of the emperors was rather a *de facto* than a *de jure* power: the Claudian family which reigned over opinion died out after having produced some monsters; there was no legal succession. Soon the legions revealed the *secret of the empire*, and emperors were made outside Rome. All these circumstances combined to produce a military and elective despotism, in other words, a permanent plague.

But the government of the emperors, like all the others, degraded only by degrees. Often the empire was possessed by great men, or by men of great merit. I do not believe that the Roman name was ever greater, and that the world in general enjoyed a greater sum of happiness, than under the reign of Trajan and the Antonines.

20 *Tarquinius cum prole fugit: capit annua consul*
Jura; dies regnis illa suprema fuit. (Ovid, *Fasti*, II)

21 *Achaiam ac Macedoniam, onera deprecantes, levari in praesens proconsulari imperio, tradique Caesari placuit*. ["It was satisfactory that the burden be eased for the moment by transferring Achaia and Macedonia to the proconsular imperium of Caesar."] (Tacitus, *Annals*, I, 76)

Let us put together the reigns of Augustus, Vespasian, Titus, Nerva, the Antonines, Trajan, the Severi, etc. During this period, 150 million men, who would have groaned under the rod of republican proconsuls, enjoyed a happy existence, and in Rome itself, instead of the tumultuous enjoyments of liberty, there was peace. I know all that the writers of this century have written in Paris, *with the approbation and privilege of the king*, to establish that liberty, with its daggers, wars, internal divisions, seditions, and sublime intoxication, was preferable to the shameful respite of servitude; I admire this poetry very much, but I shall always maintain that Newton was right in prose when he called respite *rem prorsus substantialem* ["an utterly essential matter"].

So? Why look at only one point? Is the whole human race to be found in the capitals? We always speak of the people, yet we count them for nothing: most political questions should be put to the vote in cottages; but by always speaking of *humanity*, *philanthropy*, and *general happiness*, it is always pride that speaks for itself and regards only itself. Leafing through Livy in his ivory tower, the young writer, tired of his obscurity, invests himself in his imagination with the role of a Roman citizen; he is the consul Popilius; he holds the famous rod and traces around the monarch the dreaded circle; nations tremble; kings bow before him; soon, his enthusiasm knowing no bounds, his imagination debauched by vanity leads him to the Capitol on the triumphal chariot; kings in chains follow him, the legions applaud, envy breathes its last: he is a god. Then he cries out: "O divine liberty; holy equality!" Do we think he is bothered about the *people* and all that *Roman* greatness cost the subject nations? These small considerations do not stop him, and with his eye stupidly fixed on the Capitol, he does not know how to see what Verres is doing in Sicily.

Not only were good emperors better than the Republic for the mass of men, but I am persuaded that, under vicious and even detestable emperors, the subjects were happier than under the Republic.

The most vicious prince is not always the most dangerous for the people. Louis XV, with his kindness, does them far more harm than Louis XI. In general, subjects have only the gangrenous vices produced by weakness to fear in their sovereigns. Those vices with a dark and cruel character dishonour the sovereign much more, but hardly weigh at all on the capitals, even on the upper classes of the capitals.

The historian Dio Cassius has made one of those sentences about the execrable Tiberius that one never forgets. "He had," he says, "a great number of good and bad qualities; and he used them alternately as if he had possessed only one kind."[22]

But what is important to observe is that the people hardly felt the former qualities. Tiberius maintained strict economy in the administration of the public revenues, he did not permit provincial governors to trample on the subjects, and, like all tyrants of his kind, he arrogated to himself the exclusive privilege of crimes. Under his reign the empire was peaceful, and the Roman armies were nowhere humiliated. Varus was avenged. Tiberius had the honour of giving a king to the Parthians and Armenians;[23] that of the Thracians was led in chains to Rome;[24] the Gauls were chastised and returned to duty.[25] The distinctive character of his administration was a distaste for novelties, and his first maxim was to leave everything in its place, lest it be spoiled. He abhorred anything that might disturb the public peace.[26] Gold had no power over him,[27] and he never obtained it by crime; he was seen to repudiate rich inheritances in order to leave them to those whom nature called to the succession,[28] and he was never willing to accept any bequests other than those of friendship;[29] he permitted army generals to apply to public monuments the wealth they had taken from the enemies of the state.[30] Without pity for that shameful poverty which is the daughter of immoral prodigality, he often came to the aid of indigent virtue[31] and harshly rejected the prayers of a ruined nobleman who asked

22 Livy, book 53. This is Tiberius, and Tiberius in full. This line is worthy of the greatest master; it belongs to Tacitus, who let it slip out by distraction.

23 Tacitus, *Annals*, II, 56; VI, 32.

24 Tacitus, *Annals*, II, 66.

25 Tacitus, *Annals*, III, 40.

26 *Nihil aeque Tiberium anxium habebat, quam ne composita turbarentur.* ["Nothing gave Tiberius such anxiety than that composed settlements not be disturbed."] (Tacitus, *Annals*, II, 65)

27 *Satis firmus, ut saepe memoravi, adversum pecuniam.* ["I recall that he was frequently steadfast enough against money."] (Tacitus, *Annals*, V, 18)

28 Tacitus, *Annals*, II, 48.

29 *Neque haereditatem cujusquam adiit, nisi cum amicitia meruisset; ignotos et aliis infensos eoque Principem nuncupantes, procul arcebat.* ["He entered into no bequest but that he merited it by friendship; he held at arms' length strangers and antagonistic men who named the prince as heir."] (Tacitus, *Annals*, II, 48)

30 Tacitus, *Annals*, III, 72.

31 *Ut honestam innocentium paupertatem levavit; ita prodigos et ob flagitia egentes… movit senatu, aut sponte cedere passus est.* ["As he relieved honest and innocent paupers, so he undertook to remove or willingly accept the resignation of the following senators… prodigal and destitute on account of their disgraces."] (Tacitus, *Annals*, II, 48)

for the means to support his great name;[32] but when an earthquake overturned twelve cities of Asia Minor in one night, Tiberius forgot nothing to console the unfortunate inhabitants, both with magnificent gifts and with tax exemptions.[33] A frightful fire having consumed the whole of Mount Celius at Rome, he opened his treasures and distributed his benefits with such impartiality, he was so good at unearthing the isolated, the timid, and the unfortunate to call him to share in his gifts, that the great and the small accorded him their admiration and their recognition equally.[34]

If the provinces brought demands to Rome, he himself brought them to the Senate; and, without letting power slip from his grasp, he enjoyed enlightening himself by discussion.[35] A thing most singular! An ever-prostrate baseness seemed to irritate this atrocious character more than austere virtue and intrepid frankness. Everyone knows his exclamation on leaving the Senate, "*O men born for slavery!*" True merit could disarm him.

Piso, clothed in the highest offices, was an honest man with impunity until he was eighty years old, and died in his bed without having been degraded once by a servile opinion.[36] Terentius was happier still, and not only did his noble and incredible boldness cost him neither life nor liberty, but Tiberius allowed the Senate to punish at his leisure the vile accusers of this brave Roman knight with exile and death.[37]

If ancient history were not, for the most part, the history of five or six capitals, we would reason better about true politics; but it is easy to imagine that the peoples submissive to Tiberius throughout his empire found themselves very happy; that the ploughman, tranquilly driving his plough, in the midst of the deepest peace, recounted with horror to his children the proconsuls and triumvirs of the Republic, and troubled himself very little with the heads of senators who fell in Rome.

32 Tacitus, *Annals*, II, 38.

33 Tacitus, *Annals*, II, 47.

34 *Actaeque ei grates, apud senatum ab inlustribus, famaque apud populum, quia sine ambitione, aut proximorum precibus, ignotos etiam, et ultro accitos, munificentia juverat.* ["He was given thanks, in the senate by the nobles, with fame among the people, for without ambition, nor by the entreaties of relatives, he had generously helped even strangers and those he had freely summoned."] (Tacitus, *Annals*, IV, 64)

35 *Postulata provinciarium ad disquisitionem patrum mittendo.* ["(Tiberius… allowed the Senate) some shadow of its old constitution by referring to its investigation certain demands of the provinces."] (Tacitus, *Annals*, III, 60)

36 Tacitus, *Annals*, VI, 10.

37 Tacitus, *Annals*, VI, 8.

Chapter VII:

Summary of Rousseau's Judgments on the Different Kinds of Governments — Other Judgments of the Same Nature — Reflections on this Subject

In hereditary monarchy, everything works towards the same goal, but this goal is not that of public felicity, and the very force of the administration is constantly to the detriment of the state.[1] *Kings want to be absolute... The power that comes from the love of the people... is not enough for them... The best kings want to be wicked if they please... Their personal interest is first that the people should be weak and miserable... Those who reach the highest offices in monarchies are, most often, only petty blunderers, petty swindlers, and petty intriguers, whose petty talents which lead to high positions in the courts only serve to exhibit their ineptitude to the public. Even when the sovereign has talents, he forgets the interests of the people and makes them no less unhappy by the abuse of the talents he has... than a ruler limited by the lack of talents he has not.*

> [In elective monarchy] He to whom the State has sold itself can hardly help selling it in his turn and repaying himself, at the expense of the weak, the money the powerful have wrung from him. Under such an administration, venality sooner or later spreads through every part, and peace so enjoyed under a king is worse than the disorders of an interregnum ... [In hereditary monarchy] apparent tranquillity has been preferred to wise administration, and men have chosen rather to risk

1 This is another of those obscure concepts that swarm in Rousseau's philosophical works: does he mean that the principle of government is contrary to that of this government? This proposition is worthy of a *madhouse*. Does he mean only that monarchy, like all human institutions, carries within itself principles of destruction? It is one of those truths that one reads on the blackboard.

> having children, monstrosities, or imbeciles as rulers to having disputes over the choice of good kings. It has not been taken into account that, in so exposing ourselves to the risks this possibility entails, we are setting almost all the chances against us ... Everything conspires to take away from a man who is set in authority over others the sense of justice and reason ... One result of this lack of coherence is the inconstancy of royal government, which, regulated now on one scheme and now on another, according to the character of the reigning prince or those who reign for him, cannot for long have a fixed object or a consistent policy—and this variability, not found in the other forms of government, where the prince is always the same, causes the State to be always shifting from principle to principle and from project to project ... But if, according to Plato, the 'king by nature' is such a rarity, how often will nature and fortune conspire to give him a crown? And, if royal education necessarily corrupts those who receive it, what is to be hoped from a series of men brought up to reign? It is, then, wanton self-deception to confuse royal government with government by a good king. To see such government as it is in itself, we must consider it as it is under princes who are incompetent or wicked: for either they will come to the throne wicked or incompetent, or the throne will make them so.[2]

Hereditary aristocracy is hastily judged. "[It is] the worst of all legitimate forms of administration."[3]

Democracy supposes too many things difficult to combine... there is no government so prone to civil wars and internal agitations... because there is none that tends so strongly and so continuously to change its form, nor that requires more vigilance and courage to be maintained in its own image... if there were a people of gods, they would govern themselves democratically. Such a perfect government[4] *is not suitable for men.*

2 *Contrat Social*, 3, VI. Let us not forget that the man who wrote these things almost always lived by choice in monarchical states, and that he used the moments he spent in his homeland to fan the flames that are still burning it at this moment.
3 *Contrat Social*, 3, V. I say nothing about the elective aristocracy that Rousseau courageously calls *aristocracy proper*. He forgets to explain what he means by this government, and I confess that if this is not democracy, I do not know what it is.
4 This *emphasized* epithet is no doubt inapplicable to democracy as we see it or have seen it on earth, for Rousseau has said all bad things possible about it. Does it apply at least to theoretical democracy? No, for in theory all governments are perfect, and it costs the imagination even less to create an excellent king than an

What results from these learned invectives is that each of the three governments is the worst of the three: this is a tremendous discovery.

Let us hope this ridiculousness should not be lost to universal morality, nor to politics which is a branch of it. It gives rise to the most useful reflections; it makes known the principal illness of this century and the character of the dangerous men who have done us so much harm.

Here is Rousseau who does not want any government, and who insults all forms of it. Monarchy is detestable; aristocracy is detestable; democracy is no better: he cannot bear any form of government; England does not have the least notion of liberty. "The people of England regards itself as free; but it is grossly mistaken; it is free only during the election of members of parliament. As soon as they are elected, slavery overtakes it, and it is nothing. The use it makes of the short moments of liberty it enjoys shows indeed that it deserves to lose them."[5]

The very duration of the Republic of Venice proves that it is worthless. "There is no better proof of this rule than the long life of the Republic of Venice, of which the shadow still exists, solely because its laws are suitable only for men who are wicked."[6]

Mably dislikes Batavian liberty. "The government of this Republic has deformed itself since it changed into an ordinary magistracy a dictatorship that was to be reserved for short and difficult times. The stadholder is still only a lion cub held on a chain; but he need only break it to become a lion; let us speak plainly: all invites this prince to ruin his fatherland."

Voltaire does not want antique liberty: he calls it *the government of the rabble*. But he likes monarchy even less, and he cries out for the civil and religious instruction of peoples:

> O wisdom of Heaven! I believe you very profound;
> But to what dull tyrants have you delivered the world![7]

An orator of the National Convention again cursed, just last year, the ashes of the Girondins for having wanted to bring the French nation down to the level of the Greeks and Romans, "They, too, wanted liberty," they said,

excellent people. What does this mean then: *such a perfect government*? Nothing. In all the pages of the Rousseau's philosophical writings one meets expressions which make no sense, whether for him or for us; often, he does not finish his thought. His equivocal concepts take on an apparent existence from the magic of style, but if the analyst arrives with his scalpel, he finds nothing.

5 *Contrat Social*, 3, XV.

6 *Contrat social*, 4, IV.

7 [Letter 51, to Madame le Marquise du Chaielet, *Oeuvres complètes*, vol. 10, p. 304]

"but as in Lacedaemon and Rome"—the monsters!—"that is to say, liberty subordinated to the aristocracy of talent, wealth, and pride."[8]

Condorcet does not think more highly of the ancients, "These men whom we had the good-heartedness to admire have never established anything but *despotic anarchies*; and those who seek lessons from them are pedants."

Yet he wants liberty: will he perhaps go seek it in the wise and peaceful Helvetia?[9] Even less so.

> The governments of this country preserve only the appearance and the language of republican constitutions; and, while carefully guarding all the forms of equality, the distinctions are no less real than those which separate the first slaves of a despot from the last of his subjects.[10]

A Swiss philosopher, no doubt a disciple of these great men, judges his country even more severely. "In the democratic states of Switzerland," he says, "if we except the intriguers, the strivers, the vile, vain, and wicked men, the drunkards and the idlers, there is not in the Republic a single happy and contented man."[11]

But had this Condorcet, who wanted liberty absolutely and who wanted to establish it on the ruins of all thrones, seen it at least somewhere on earth? No, "he had never seen a truly republican constitution", and such as he desired.[12]

What did he want, good Lord! And what do all the philosophers want, since nothing that exists or has existed can have the good fortune to please them? They do not want any government, because there is none that pretends not to demand obedience; it is not *this* authority that they hate, it is *authority itself* they cannot bear. But if you press them, they will tell you that they, like Turgot, want *a great democracy*;[13] even Condorcet had already drawn with his learned hand this *great* square circle; but, as we know, this plan did not come to fruition.

It would be useless to multiply these foolish citations; it is enough to return to the excellent phrase of Rousseau who is always justified when he speaks against himself: "If I consult the philosophers, each one has only his

8 *Garnier de Saintes*, session of September 21, 1794. (Moniteur, No. 5, p. 22)

9 [Switzerland. Maistre uses the ancient name.]

10 Condorcet, Éloge d'Euler. [*Eloge de M. Euler, introduction á l'analyse des infiniment petits*, 1786].

11 "*Moyen de faire de la République française un tout à jamais indivisible.*" (Brochure by a Swiss, *Courier républicain*, 1795, No. 558, p. 128)

12 *Vie de Turgot*, p.106.

13 *Vie de Turgot*, p.106.

voice." Mortal enemies of any kind of association, possessed of a repulsive and solitary pride, they agree only on one point: the fury to destroy; and each one wishing to substitute what displeases him with his own designs approved by himself alone, the result is that all their power is negative, and all their efforts to build impotent and ridiculous. O misguided men, learn for once at last to recognize these dangerous jugglers; let them admire themselves all alone, and rally to the national reason which never deceives. Remember that each nation has, in its laws and in its ancient customs, all that it needs to be as happy as it can be, and that in taking these venerable laws as the basis of all your regenerative works, you can unfold all your perfectibility without indulging in harmful innovations.

Raise yourselves again to higher thoughts. Eternal reason has spoken, and its infallible oracles have shown us that "pride is the beginning of all crimes"; this terrible principle has been unleashed on Europe since these same philosophers rid you of the faith of your fathers. Hatred of authority is the scourge of our days: there is no remedy for this evil but in the sacred maxims which you have been made to forget. Archimedes knew well that to raise the world he needed a fulcrum outside the world.

The enemies of all order have found this fulcrum to overturn the moral world. Atheism and immorality provoke revolt and insurrection. See what is happening before your eyes: at the first sign of revolutions, virtue hides itself, and the only action seen is that of crime. What then is this liberty whose founders, originators, and apostles are scoundrels? Ah! You have a sure way of accomplishing great and salutary revolutions. Instead of listening to the preachers of revolt, work on yourselves: for it is you who make governments, and they cannot be bad if you are good.[14]

Marchamont Nedham, a feeble precursor of Rousseau, who reasoned no better than the citizen of Geneva, but who was, moreover, dull and verbose, says that "*in a popular government* the door of dignity stands open to all that ascend the steps of worth and virtue: the consideration whereof hath this noble effect in free states, that it edges men's spirits with an active emulation, and raiseth them to a lofty pitch of design and action."[15]

14 An English preacher in 1793, on a solemn feast day, gave a sermon under this title: "Sins of government, sins of the nation," (*London Chronicle*, 1793, No. 5747, p. 58) I do not know if the title was fulfilled as it could be, but this title alone is a great truth and is worth a book.

15 *De la souveraineté du peuple et de l'excellence d'un état libre*, vol. I, p. 57, tr. Théophile Mandar, 1790. [Marchamont Nedham was a pamphleteer and propagandist during the English Civil War. His 1656 *Excellencie of a Free-State* exercised an influence in Cromwell's Protectorate, arguing for the principle of popular sovereignty.]

His French translator adds, following Shaftesbury: "A free government is for the arts what the bounty of the soil is for vigorous plants. This is what brings free nations, in a short time, to such a high point of perfection; whereas the most vast and powerful empires, when they are under the yoke of despotism, after centuries of leisure, produce only shapeless and barbarous essays."[16]

And according to Ceruti, a somewhat less respectable author: "Similar to those plants which require the most fertile soil and the most favorable climate to grow, it is only under the fortunate climate of glory, on the beneficent soil of honours, that one can hope to see eloquence sprout and fructify."[17]

Hume was of a very different opinion when he said, "I am ashamed to confess that Patru pleading for the restitution of a horse is more eloquent than our orators agitating the greatest interests in the assemblies of Parliament."[18]

Indeed, the French nation is the most eloquent of all, not only because its orators properly speaking are above all others, but because it has carried eloquence into all genres of composition, and no nation has spoken better on everything. The influence she has on Europe is due in the first place to this talent, unfortunately too well demonstrated at the time I am writing.[19]

It must therefore be admitted that the French nation was free under its kings, or that liberty is not necessary for eloquence. I leave the choice to these great philosophers. What I say of eloquence must be said of all the arts and all the sciences; it is so false that they need liberty that in free states they never shine except in the decline of liberty.

The most beautiful monuments of Athens belong to the century of Pericles. In Rome, which writers were the products of the Republic? Plautus and Terence alone. Lucretius, Sallust, and Cicero saw the Republic die.

16 *De la souveraineté du peuple*, preface, p. v.

17 *De la souveraineté du peuple*, p. 57. [Joseph-Antoine Cerutti was a writer who held a chair of humanities at a Jesuit college in Lyon at a prodigiously young age. He is noted for his *Mémoire pour le peuple française* (1789), which expressed a moderate liberalism.]

18 *Essais*. [Volume not noted by Maistre.]

19 But this talent, like Achilles' spear, can cure the wounds it has inflicted. Nations, as well as individuals, have a mission in this world; it is probable that the mission of the French nation is not completed, and as France, to fulfil the views for which it is destined, needed to preserve its integrity, it has preserved it against all human probabilities. *Populi meditati sunt inania* ["the peoples plot in vain"]. Reduced by our weak nature to attaching ourselves to probabilities, let us at least consider that there are fruitful probabilities just as there are sterile truths.

Then came the century of Augustus, when the nation was all it could be in terms of talent. The arts, in general, need a king: they shine only under the influence of sceptres. Even in Greece, the only country where they flourished during a republic, Lysippos and Apelles worked for Alexander.[20] Aristotle received from Alexander's generosity the means to compose his history of animals; and, after the death of this monarch, poets, scholars, and artists sought protection and rewards in the courts of his successors.[21]

What does Nedham mean when he argues that popular governments alone produce that noble emulation which makes for conception of the most beautiful designs?

What does Shaftesbury mean when he maintains that "free nations have carried the arts to the highest point of perfection in a short time, and that the largest and most powerful empires, when they are under the yoke of despotism, after centuries of leisure, produce only unformed or barbarous essays"?

One would be tempted to think that this is a joke. Free Sparta and free Rome neither produced a poem nor carved a column.[22] And it was not under the regime of freedom that Horace cried out:

> No, never were mortals more happy!
> We sing, we comb our hair better than those famous Greeks.

20 [Lysippos, 4th century BCE sculptor, considered one of the greatest of the classical era; Apelles, 4th century BCE painter, the foremost of his century.]

21 *Nec sacra fert quisquam sese ad certamina Bacchi,*
Suaviloquo doctus modulari gutture carmen,
Quin pretium referat dignum arte. Hinc tollere coelo
Musarum interpres vatum chorus omnis eumdem
Adproperat; neque enim diti praeclarior ulla
Res homini, quam tuta insigni gloria cantu.

["And to the sacred contests at the feasts of Dionysus
Comes no man having skill to lift his voice in tuneful song,
Whom he rewards not with some gift worthy of the minstrel's art.
In gratitude for such benefits the prophets of the Muses
Sing Ptolemy's praise. And what more glorious destiny can there be
For him who is prosperous, than to earn a fair fame among men?"]

Theocritus, Idyll XVII. *Encomium Ptolemoei*. I use the elegant translation of Mr. Zamagna. [Maistre cites a 1768 Latin translation of the Greek by Bernardo Zamagna. The English translation here is that of R. C. Trevelyan, 1925: Albert & Charles Boni, New York.]

22 *Nos etiam qui rerum istarum rudes sumus.* ["We, too, who are uncultivated in these matters."] (Cicero, *in Verrem*)

The *Aeneid* was written for Augustus; the frontispiece of the *Pharsalia* is decorated with a beautiful eulogy of Nero. Ariosto and Tasso flattered lesser princes, it is true; but they were princes nonetheless. Voltaire, born in Paris, dedicated the *Henriade* to a queen of England. Finally, excepting Milton, who shone in a moment of general frenzy and who seems to have written, says Voltaire, *only for angels, for devils, and for madmen*, all the epic poets sang of kings, to amuse kings.

A look from Louis XIV paid the author of *Cinna*:[23] it was for Louis that Racine *gave birth to his miracles*; Tartuffe[24] and Armide[25] distracted him from business; and *Télémaque*,[26] which he did not study enough, was nevertheless a production of his reign.

In our own day we have seen Metastasio, abandoning his own country too fractious for his genius, come to Vienna to seek the comfort and protection he needed.

As for great movements and great undertakings, they belong only to monarchies, for the simple reason that republics being always small and poor, whatever they do is as small as themselves.

The most famous of all was Athens; but what could a republic do when it had only 20,000 citizens, whose revenues hardly exceeded three millions of our money;[27] when it gave its ambassadors two drachmas per day, that is to say, 40 sous of that same currency;[28] to whom Demosthenes said in the moment of greatest danger: "So I propose that the whole force should consist of two thousand men, but of these five hundred must be Athenians, chosen from any suitable age and serving in relays for a specified period—not a long one, but just so long as seems advisable; the rest should

23 [*Cinna ou la Clémence d'Auguste*, by Pierre Corneille, a play apologetic to absolutism.]

24 [*Tartuffe, ou l'Imposteur*, by Molière, a satire on religious hypocrisy that was well received by Louis XIV but so scandalized the Roman Catholic Church that it was banned for five years after publication.]

25 [*Armide*, a lyric tragedy by Jean-Philippe Quinault which later served as the libretto for Jean-Baptiste Lully's opera of the same name.]

26 [*Les aventures de Télémaque, fils d'Ulysse*, a didactic novel by Fénelon, Archbishop of Cambrai. Presented to Louis XIV's grandson, it was a polemic against the Sun King's reign and so angered the king that he issued restrictions of movement on the already exiled Fénelon.]

27 Xenophon on the revenues of Athens, where, if I am not mistaken, he speaks of the mines.

28 "Athens, in the time of its greatest splendour, only paid its ambassadors two drachmas per day." (Note by M. Larcher on Herodotus, III, 131) — In place of the originals, which I lack, I can quote a modern, learned, and exact edition.

be mercenaries. Attached to them will be two hundred cavalry, fifty at least of them being Athenians, serving on the same terms as the infantry."[29]

What can such powers do in terms of enterprises and monuments? Fortify a mediocre city and decorate it.

But the pyramids, the temples, the canals, the reservoirs of Egypt, the gardens, the palaces and walls of Babylon, etc., belong only to immense countries, that is to say, to monarchies.

Was it a republican hand that weighed the air? that traced the meridian lines of Oranienburg, Bologna and Paris? that carried the pendulum to Cayenne? that measured the degrees of the meridian in Quito, Torneo, Paris, Rome, Turin, Vienna? Was it in the bosom of a republic that the four giants Copernicus, Kepler, Galileo, and Descartes were born, who overthrew the edifice of prejudice and made way for Newton?

Did not these intrepid navigators from Christopher Columbus to Cook, who discovered new lands, brought all men together, and so greatly improved astronomy, geography, and all branches of natural history, all wear a crown in their flag?

As for the arts, Greece has shone in this genre, not because freedom was necessary for it, which is a great error, but because the Greeks were destined for republican government, and no nation displays all its talents except under the government that suits it.

But if the buildings of Palmyra and ancient Rome,[30] if the mosque of Cordoba and the palace of the Alhambra, if the church of St. Peter, the fountains, the palaces, the museums, the libraries of Christian Rome, if the colonnade of the Louvre, the gardens of Versailles, the arsenals of Brest, Toulon and Turin; if the paintings of Michelangelo, Raphael, Correggio, Poussin and Lesueur; if the statues of Girardon, of Puget; if the music of Pergolesi, of Jomelli, of Gluck and of Cimarosa—if all these things, I say, which are nevertheless productions of human genius bent *under the yoke of despotism*, appear to Shaftesbury and to those who think like him, only *unformed and barbarous essays*, it must be admitted that philosophers are indeed difficult to satisfy.

The curious thing is that, while these critics of *despotism* accuse it of *stupefying* men and making them unfit for great productions of genius, others accuse it, on the contrary, of corrupting and enchaining men by turn-

29 Demosthenes *First Philippics* 21. [translation by J. H. Vince, London, William Heinemann Ltd. 1930]

30 The ancient monuments that one goes to Rome to admire almost all postdate the Republic, which was not at all tasteful. *Tu regere imperio*, etc. ["*tu regere imperio populos, Romane, memento*." ("Remember thou, O Roman, to rule the nations with thy sway.") *Aeneid* VI, 845]

ing them too much towards pleasures of this kind. "We have admired too much," says Rousseau, "those centuries wherein we have seen letters and the arts flourish, without penetrating the secret object of their cultivation, without considering their fatal effect, *idque apud imperitos humanitas vocabatur quum pars servitutis esset*."[31] ["fools called 'humanity' what was a part of slavery"] Poor monarchy! It is accused both of blunting the minds of the people and of giving them too much spirit.

Let us consider again governments with respect to population. "The best," Rousseau says again, "is that which peoples the most." He did not understand himself, as we have seen above, when he advanced this maxim; it would have to be said that "a people is well governed when, under the influence of its particular government, its population holds at the highest possible point relative to the extent of its territory, or gradually approaches this point."

But this highest possible point depends in no way on any particular form of government. An ancient poet said in a eulogy of the first of the Ptolemies: "No land else [than Egypt] hath so many towns where skilful craftsmen dwell. Therein of cities builded there stand three centuries. And thousands three, and yet again three tens of thousands more. Then twice three cities, and beside all these yet three times nine [=33,339] … Many too are the horsemen, many the targeteers that gather round his standard harnessed in gleaming bronze. In treasure he outweighs all other kings; such mighty wealth to his rich palace day by day pours in from every side; while in security his people go about their labours. For here no foeman, marching o'er the monster-teeming Nile, has raised the cry of battle among townships not his own, etc."[32]

31 *Contrat social*, 3, IX, note.

32 *Sunt scilicet omnes*
Ter centum, ter denae olli, terque ordine ternae
Triginta supra tria millia, quas regit unus.
Tot populis sceptrisque potens Ptolemaeus.
Quid me morem turmasque equitum, protectaque sentis
Agmina quae densa fremunt, atque aere corusea
Solis inardescunt radiis? Longe anteit omnes
Divitiis reges ingentibus: undique rerum
Quotidie aggeritur vis tanta in tecta, nec ullum
Interea populis sollerti in pace beatis
Cessat opps, Nemo piscosum invadere Nilum
Scilicet, ac trepidis acies inferre pedestres
Agricolis audet.

Let us suppose, if we wish, some exaggeration in the number of cities, even though it is expressed in such a precise manner. Let us suppose that the poet has abused the word *city* to a certain extent, we will always be left with the idea of truly extraordinary wealth and relative population.

Herodotus assures us that "Egypt was never happier nor more flourishing than under Amasis.[33] *This country* then contained 20,000 cities, all well peopled."[34]

"Egypt," says another historian, "was once the most populous country in the world, and even today I believe it to be inferior to no other. In ancient times it possessed more than 18,000 cities or considerable towns, as the sacred records attest; and in the reign of Ptolemy, son of Lagus, there were more than 30,000."[35]

"Calculators, it is left for you to count, to measure, to compare."[36] See how in Egypt, not only under the reign of the Ptolemies, but also under the theocratic despotism of its ancient kings, "without external aids, without naturalisation or colonies, the citizens increase and multiply most."[37]

In the session of the National Convention on 25 December 1794 it was said, in the name of the Commerce Committee, that "Spain, before the expulsion of the Moors, had eighty cities of the first rank and fifty million inhabitants."[38]

The reporter, who was apparently copying the *Précis Historique sur les Maures*, should have said that these eighty first rank cities were to be found in the states of the Caliph of Córdoba alone,[39] which also contained three

Theocritus, *Encomium Ptolemoei*. Idyll XVII, v. 94, 99, Latin translation by M. Zamagna. [English translation by Trevelyan, 1925.] One may reproach this translation, which is otherwise so exact, and whose first verses especially are a tour de force, for leaving doubt as to whether the 33,339 cities were to be found in Egypt alone, or in all the countries which obeyed Ptolemy. The text does not permit the slightest doubt on this point.

33 [Amasis II of the XXVI dynasty, reigned 570–526, the last great ruler of Egypt before the Persian conquest.]

34 Herodotus, II, 77. See the note by M. Larcher.

35 Diodorus Siculus, *Library*, I, 31. M. Larcher does not want to read here, with some manuscripts, thirty thousand (τρισμυριων). This reading seems to him to strain credibility. It agrees, however, with the testimony of Theocritus and the other ancients much better than the three thousand (τρισχιλιων) which he adopts, and which appears absolutely inadmissible if one but observes the context of ideas in Diodorus' text.

36 *Contrat social*, 3, IX.

37 *Contrat social*, 3, IX.

38 *Moniteur*, No. 96, p. 367, December 1794.

39 These states comprised only Portugal, Andalusia, the kingdoms of Granada,

hundred second rank cities and an infinite number of towns. The ambassadors of the Greek emperor came to this immense city to prostrate themselves before the caliph to obtain help against the caliphs of Baghdad who were pressing the empire of Constantinople.

The Moorish kings of Granada, in a state eighty leagues long and thirty wide, possessed fourteen large cities, more than a hundred small towns, and a prodigious number of villages. They had one hundred thousand regular troops, and this army in a time of need could easily be doubled. The city of Granada alone provided fifty thousand warriors.[40]

And these Moors, so formidable when armed, were also the best farmers, the most excellent artists, the most active merchants, and the foremost men in the world in all branches of science. Today the whole of Spain, united under the sceptre of the same sovereign, has only ten and a half million inhabitants.[41]

However, there has never been a more severe despotism than that of the caliphs, and Rousseau, who had read so many novels, no doubt remembered from the *Thousand and One Nights* this passage where the vizier says to his daughter Dinazarde: "You realize, my daughter, *that if the sultan should order me to kill you, I would be obliged to obey*."

The civil and religious despotism of the caliphs is thus "infallibly the best government,"[42] or, at least, it is worth more than tempered monarchy, since, under the same sky, on the same territory, and in the midst of the most merciless and cruel wars known to history, the general and partial population rose to a point which seems incredible, compared with what we see these days.

And what is so essential to observe is that peoples never achieve this level of population without a great moral energy which all nations have possessed, more or less, at a certain period of their political life. All the modern experts in revolt, from the cedar to the hyssop, repeat over and over again that despotism debases souls; this is another error; despotism is only bad when introduced into a country made for another government, or when it is corrupted in a country to which it is native. But while this government is in its vigour, the people are great and energetic in their own way, as much and perhaps more so than in republics.

Murcia, Valencia, and most of New Castile.

40 Florian, *Précis historique sur les Maures*, 1791, pp. 51, 57, 113.

41 According to the census made by Count Florida Blanca with all possible accuracy, and published in Madrid by order of the King, 1787. N.B. The population has increased by a million in the last eighteen years.

42 Rousseau, in the chapter just cited.

Were they, then, vile and effeminate men, those astonishing Arabs,[43] who travelled halfway round the globe, with the Koran in one hand and the sword in the other, crying: "*Victory and paradise*"? Let us transport ourselves to the century of Omar: "Asia trembles before him, and the terrible Muslims, modest in their victories, reporting their successes to God alone, preserve amid the most beautiful, richest, and most delicate countries on earth, among the most corrupt peoples, their austere, frugal morals, their severe discipline, and their respect for poverty. We see the lowest ranking soldiers suddenly stop in the sack of a city on the first order of their chief, faithfully bring back to him the gold and silver which they have taken, to deposit it in the public treasury. We see these captains, so brave, so superb with kings, leaving and resuming command according to a note from the Caliph, become in turn generals, simple soldiers, ambassadors, at his every wish. We see Omar himself, the most powerful sovereign, the richest, the greatest of the kings of Asia, drive to Jerusalem mounted on a russet camel, laden with a sack of barley and rice, a wineskin full of water and a wooden vase. So equipped, he rides through defeated peoples who crowd around him, asking him to bless them and to judge their disputes. He reached his army, preached simplicity, valour, and modesty to it; he entered Jerusalem, pardoned the Christians, preserved the churches, and mounted on his camel, the Caliph returned to Medina to offer prayers for his people."[44]

The Turks,[45] under Suleiman II, displayed all that they could be and all that they had to be; Europe and Asia trembled before them. The famous Busbecq observed them at that time, and we have the report of his embassy. There are few monuments so curious as this one. This man had a keen eye, and his public character put him in a position to see and examine everything. It is interesting to see how he judged this government. One of the things that astonished him most was the military discipline: he saw a camp; the description he left us still conveys to our hearts the feelings and emotion experienced by his own. Amid these innumerable legions of turbans, he heard not the slightest noise. Everywhere was the terrible

43 <If the Arabs had not had great natural qualities, they would not have accomplished the great things they did, and God would not have taken them to punish the degenerate Christians.>

44 Florian, *Précis historique sur les Maures*, 1792, p. 21 — Those who know the history of the Arabs will not accuse this writer of having painted from imagination.

45 What we have said of the Arabs applies no less to the Turks, whose task was not so formidable. (Editor's note).

silence of discipline;[46] nowhere was there the slightest disorder, the least agitation. Each kept to his place with the greatest ease, the general officers seated, and all the rest standing.[47] But nothing attracted his attention like the imposing aspect of the several thousand Janissaries that could be seen in the distance. Busbecq, warned that etiquette demanded a salute on his part, greeted the janissaries, who all together returned the salute in silence. *Until then*, he said, *I might have doubted whether I was seeing men or statues.*[48] The arms and equipment were magnificent, but amid this military luxury, a taste for simplicity and economy shone through.[49]

How he despises the flabbiness of our armies when he compares it to the sobriety, moderation, and invincible patience of the Turkish soldier![50]

From his pen beams the national enthusiasm of the Turks and that moral vigour which makes great things possible. He makes us see, he makes us hear this soldier dying on the battlefield, who says to those around him: *Go and tell my country that I died for its glory and for the advancement of*

46 *Nunc ades et mecum maximum multitudinem turbinatorum capitum specta… Imprimis vero in tanta multitudine silentium et modestia… nullae ibi voces; nullum murmur.* ["For the nonce, take your stand by my side, and look at the sea of turbaned heads… I was greatly struck with the silence and order that prevailed in the crowd. There were no cries, no hum of voices."] (Ogier Ghiselin de Busbecq, *Legatio turcica*, letter 4) [English translation by Forster and F. H. G, Daniell, *The Life and Letters of Ogier Ghiselin de Busbecq*, 1881.]

47 *Nulla concursatio; summa quiete quisque sui ordinis locum tuebatur. Sedebant summa capita quae ipsi Aga vocant… Vulgus stabat.* ["Neither was there any jostling; without the slightest disturbance each man took his proper place according to rank. The Agas, as they call their chiefs, were seated. … Men of a lower position stood."] (Busbecq, *Legatio turcica*)

48 *Digna erant praecipue quai spectarentur aliquot Gionizarorum millia, qui longo ordine sejuncti a reliquis, tam immoti stabant ut me diu judicii incertum redderent, hominesne essent an statuae.* ["The most interesting sight in this assembly was a body of several thousand Janissaries, who were drawn up in a long line apart from the rest; their array was so steady and motionless that, being at some distance, it was some time before I could make up my mind as to whether they were human beings or statues."] (Busbecq, *Legatio turcica*, Letter I)

49 *In tanto tamen luxu magna simplicitas et parcimonia.* ["In all this luxury great simplicity and economy are combined."] (Busbecq, *Legatio turcica*, Letter I)

50 *Turcae cum extremis difficultalibus patientia, sobrietate victus et parcimonia pugnant et se rebus molioribus servant, longe aliter quam milites nostri.* ["From this you will see that it is the patience, self-denial, and thrift of the Turkish soldier that enable him to face the most trying circumstances, and come safely out of the dangers that surround him. What a contrast to our men!"] (Busbecq, *Legatio turcica*, Letter I)

my religion;[51] he renders for us the cry of his exalted companions who exclaim: *O happiest of men!* who could not envy your fate?[52]

But when this same observer passes from the examination of the military regime to that of the civil constitution of the Turks, it is clear that he found us, in this general point of view, as inferior as we were under the particular aspect of arms. What he says about the nobility especially deserves attention. He is shocked by the exclusive privileges of this order in Christian states, and the Turks seem to him much wiser. Here, he says, "great deeds obtain honours and power; among us, it is something else: birth obtains everything and merit nothing."[53]

Elsewhere he expands further. "It is the prince," he says, "who distributes offices, and his choice is not determined by wealth, by the whim of birth, by the protection of an individual, or by the judgment of the multitude. Alone are virtues, conduct, character, and talents, taken into consideration; and each is rewarded in proportion to his merit."[54]

Finally, Busbecq, in comparing us with the Turks, could not help seeing on the one hand *all the virtues that make empires shine, and on the other all*

51 This beautiful gesture recalls the well-known epitaph of the 300 Spartans killed at Thermopylae:

Dic, hospes, patriae, nos te hic vidisse jacentes
Dum sanctis patrae legibus obsequimur.

["Go tell the Spartans passerby
That here in obedience to their law we lie."]

[Maistre cites a Latin translation of the Greek by Simonides of Ceos.]
But here it is the dying hero who gives the commission; instead of at Thermopylae, where it is the marble which speaks for the dead.

52 *O te ter felicem! etc.* ["O men thrice happy and thrice blessed!"] (Busbecq, *Legatio turcica*, Letter III)

53 *Illi rebus gestis flurent, dominantur... Apud nos aliis vivitur moribus: virtuti nihil est relictum loci; omnia natalibus deferuntur.* [Among the Turks, therefore, honours, high posts, and judgeships are the rewards of great ability and good service. (...) with us there is no opening left for merit; birth is the standard of everything."] (Busbecq, *Legatio turcica*, Letter II)

54 *Munera et officia princeps ipse distribuit in quo non divitias, non fumum nobilitatis pendit; non gratiam cujusquam, aut multitudinis judicium moratur, sed merita considerat, sed mores ingeniumque atque indolem intuetur. Ex sua virtute unusquisque ornatur.* ["In making his appointments the Sultan pays no regard to any pretentions on the score of wealth or rank, nor does he take into considerations recommendations or popularity; he considers each case on its own merits, and examines carefully into the character, ability, and disposition of the man whose promotion is in question."] (Busbecq, *Legatio turcica*, Letter II)

the vices that lead to their ruin.[55] Courage deserted him, and he was on the point of despairing of the salvation of Christianity.[56]

Mably, in Busbecq's place, would not have manifested these concerns; he knew that for the "subjects of despotic princes, and especially for the Turks, there is no other virtue than patience, and some useful qualities of slaves compatible with indolence and fear."

These schoolboy inanities would be good (for everything that amuses is good) if they did not have the disadvantage of acting on mean heads, and of making them ever falser and more dangerous.

The Turks are weak right now, and other peoples are crushing them because these disciples of the Koran have wit and schools of science, because they know French, because they exercise in the European manner: in a word, because they are no longer Turks. When we speak of their ignorance and barbarism, we may be right, but if it is with a view to blaming their government, we do not know what we are saying.

In general, we grasp almost nothing about the grand scheme of things,

55 <It is not surprising that at the moment of their advance, the Turks, in spite of their false religion, possessed civil virtues, and that, at the same time, decadent Christian nations had, in spite of the true religion, vices which brought about their ruin. Besides, *corruptio optimi pessima*. ["corruption of the best becomes the worst."]>

56 *Quae cogitantem horror corripit quid postremo futurum sit cum hanc nostram rationem cum eorum comparo; superare alteros, alteros interire necesse est; ambo certe incolumes esse non possunt. Ab illa parte stant immensae imperii opes, vires integrae, armorum usus et exercitatio, miles veteranus, victoriarum assiduitas, laborum patientia, concordia, ordo, disciplina, frugalitas, vigilantia: ab hac nostra, publica egestas, privatus luxus, deminutae vires, intracti animi, laborum et armorum insolentia, contumaces milites, duces avari, disciplina contemptus, licentia, temeritas, ebrietas, crapula; quodque est pessimum, illis vincere, nobis vinci solitum.* ["It makes me shudder to think of what the result of a struggle between such different systems must be; one of us must prevail and the other must be destroyed, at any rate we cannot both exist in safety. On their side is the vast wealth of their empire, unimpaired resources, experience and practice in arms, a veteran soldiery, an uninterrupted series of victories, readiness to endure hardships, union, order, discipline, thrift, and watchfulness. On ours are found an empty exchequer, luxurious habits, exhausted resources, broken spirits, a raw and insubordinate soldiery, and greedy generals; there is no regard for discipline, license runs riot, the men indulge in drunkenness and debauchery, and, worst of all, the enemy are accustomed to victory, we, to defeat."] (Busbecq, *Legatio turcica*, Letter III)
Quid nostra arma cum his collata valeant utinam nobis ignorare liceat! ["I hope that we do not have to know what our arms are capable of when compared to these."] (Busbecq, *Art of War Against the Turks*)

and in this we are too excusable, but we are not excused for being ignorant that this grand scheme exists. Descartes' imaginary world represents the reality of the political world quite well: each nation is a particular vortex, both acting and acted upon; the *whole* is only the assembly of these vortexes, and the nations are between themselves like the individuals who compose them. Each member of these great families called *nations* has been given a particular character, faculties, and mission. Some are destined to glide silently along the path of life unnoticed; others make noise in passing, and almost always have fame instead of happiness. Individual faculties are infinitely diversified with a divine magnificence, and the most brilliant are not the most useful; but everything serves, each is in its place; all take part in the general organisation, all invariably move towards the goal of the association.

Among this crowd of individuals there are some who seem to be born under a hidden anathema. There are madmen, imbeciles, physically and morally degraded beings; all we know of them is that they are there. What is the use of this Alpine *idiot*? — Ask the one who organised Newton's brain.

It is with nations as with individuals. All have a character and a mission which they carry out without knowing what they are doing. Some are scholars, others conquerors; and general characteristics are, again, infinitely diversified. Among conquering peoples, some are purely destructive, and others seem to destroy only to make way for creations of a new kind. The Orientals have always been contemplative; intuition seems to be more natural to them than reasoning. As they dwell so much within themselves and work less than we do on external objects, their souls are more open to spiritual impressions; hence all religions come from Asia.

Among scholarly nations, there are some who show little or no talent for this or that branch of knowledge; others seem to cultivate them all with almost equal success; others, finally, are strikingly inclined towards a certain kind of science, and then they almost always abuse it.

Thus, the Arabs, who had a prodigious talent for medicine and chemistry, have devoted themselves to magic and all theurgic operations; and the Chaldeans, who were great astronomers, gave themselves over to astrology, so much so that the name *Chaldean* became synonymous with that of astrologer. Paracelsus and even Kepler were two types of these nations.

The French invent nothing, and they teach everything. They have very little talent for medicine; and, if we except Sénac's book on the heart,[57]

57 [Jean-Baptiste Sénac, *Traité de la structure du coeur, de son action et de ses maladies*, 1749.]

which even belongs more to physiology than to medicine proper, I doubt that France has produced a single original work on this science.

The English, on the other hand, have been infinitely distinguished in this field, and while in other countries the study of medicine has led an infinite number of men, even clever men, to materialism, the English physicians, on the contrary, present a *constellation* of names as distinguished by their moral and religious character as by their profound knowledge.[58]

I would be straying from my subject if I were to push these observations further: it is enough to underscore how ridiculous we are when we accuse this or that government of debasing peoples. No nation owes to its government its character any more than its language; on the contrary, it owes its government to its character, which, in truth, is always strengthened and perfected by political institutions. If you see a nation languishing, it is not because its government is bad; it is because this government, which is the best for it, withers like all things human, or rather it is because its national character is worn out. Then nations undergo political palingenesis, or else they die. There is nothing less well-founded than our eternal discourses on the ignorance of the Orientals: these men know what they must know, they march towards a general goal; they obey the universal law as well as we who write pamphlets. — Ignorance, moreover, has nothing to do with climate, religion, or government; the character of nations has deeper roots. It is repeated daily that Mohammedanism favours ignorance; not at all. The government represses science in Constantinople; it called for it in Baghdad and Cordoba when Islamism was in its highest degree of exaltation. Some holy figures of the Christian Church, who once made roughly the same argument against science as Omar, have not prevented us from being what we are. And since we are speaking of science, I would observe that we are too accustomed, in Europe, to believe that men are created only to make books. Voltaire held to this farce to the highest degree; he believed that a nation which did not have a theatre and an observatory was not worthy of breathing. These little humanities turned his head, so much so that in an ode he composed upon the return of some academics who had gone to the pole to measure a degree of the meridian, he addressed this laughable apostrophe to the angels:

> Speak! Were you not jealous of the great Newton?

Pope was far wiser, deeper, and more spiritual when he said, also speaking of the angels:

58 This is the remark of an anonymous person in the European Magazine, 179… no. … (This note has escaped me.)

Newton was for them what an ape is for us.[59]

There are no sciences before Him who made the nations; it is not even given to the sage to be proud of what he knows, when he thinks of what he does not know. Reflecting, moreover, on the drawbacks of the sciences, without going as far as Rousseau, one could say of them what Tacitus says of precious metals, speaking of a simple people that did not know them: "It is a question of knowing whether the divinity refuses them in his goodness or in his anger."[60]

The sciences are good if they make us better and happier. In any case, let us be as knowledgeable as we can be on this sclerotic planet, and since this is our lot, let us make the best of it, but let us not always be so disposed to prefer ourselves to others. Each people fulfills its mission; we despise the Orientals, and they despise us; who can judge between us? See these pashas, these disgraced viziers! The sea offers them an assured escape; immense movable wealth promises them ease in all lands; they know our hospitality, and this zealous curiosity which makes us hastily welcome all novelties. We offer them our arts, our liberty, our courtesy; they want neither our arts, nor our liberty, nor our courtesy. They stay at home; they wait for the cord, and their descendants proudly say: "In my country one does not die in bed".[61]

The height of folly would be to maintain that the character of peoples is their own work; but when we say that they have made their government, it is the same folly in other terms.

Let us consult history: we shall see that each nation fusses and gropes, so to speak, until a certain combination of circumstances places it precisely in the situation that suits it: then it suddenly deploys all its faculties at once, it shines with all kinds of brilliance, it is all that it can be, and never has a nation been seen to return to this state after having fallen from it.[62]

59 *Essay on Man*, Epistle V.

60 *Argentum et aurum propitii, an irati dii negaverint dubito*. ["I am not sure whether benevolent or angry gods have denied them silver and gold."] (Tacitus, *Germania*, V)

61 A Turkish lady made this reply to Lady Wortley-Montagu. She had the tone of a Frenchwoman who could count among her ancestors five or six marshals of France killed on the battlefield. (See the letters of this witty lady.) [Lady Wortley-Montagu, wife to the British ambassador to Turkey. Her *Turkish Embassy Letters* described her travels to the Ottoman Empire, and her writings reflect a moderate progressivism by the standards of her time.]

62 Bolingbroke said that nations could regenerate themselves: it would have been well had he proved it. Here is what seems to me more true: it is that nations, in traversing their period of deterioration, can have, from time to time, certain

This radiant point was, for France, the century of Louis XIV. No sovereign in the world was more a king than this prince: obedience, under his reign, was a veritable cult, and never were the French greater or more submissive. Then one saw the type of the French character par excellence, in all the perfection of which it is susceptible: it was a mixture of religion, chivalry, genius, amiability, and gallantry; finally, it was a whole so daz-

bursts of strength and greatness which are themselves decreasing in a progression, as in ordinary times. Thus, the Roman Empire, in its decline, was great under Trajan, but however less so than under Augustus; it shone under Theodosius, but less than under Constantine; finally, it had beautiful moments until under the pedant Julian and under Heraclius, but the decreasing progression followed its train and did not change the law. The highest point for a nation is where its intellectual strength reaches its *maximum* at the same time as its physical strength; and this point, determined by the state of the language, has occurred only once for each nation. It is true that the state of which I am speaking is not an indivisible point, and that it is susceptible of greater and lesser degrees. Thus, not to get lost in subtleties, if we represent the growth and decadence of the Roman people by a parabola, Augustus is at the summit, and his reign occupies a certain portion of the top of the curve; we descend on the one side to Terence or Plautus, on the other to Tacitus; on the one side genius ends; on the other barbarism begins; strength continues along the two branches, but always diminishing; it was born in Romulus.

Let us consider now the phases of the French nation: it shone especially during the reigns of Clovis I, Charlemagne, Philip-Augustus, Charles the Wise, Francis I, Henry IV, Louis XIII and Louis XIV; until this last epoch it has not ceased to rise, and all that it has suffered under unfortunate reigns must be put in the rank of those painful shocks which do not regenerate nations (for no one has proved that they can be regenerated), but which perfect them when they are in their progressive period, and push them towards the highest point of their greatness.

Today there are fine questions to be asked about France: for example, can this highest point, of which we speak, be determined by contemporaries or by their immediate posterity? Can another century present yet the same phenomenon as the seventeenth: that is to say, all talents gathered to the highest degree, in France, by Frenchmen, and at the same time? Can the language of this nation be perfected? Are there, can there be proofs that the nation has begun its period of deterioration? Could the arguments one would make to establish the affirmative have been made at the time of the Jacquerie and the League? All the nations we have seen pass away similarly, that is to say, by new nations that came to replace the others on their own soil by conquest, if this does not happen, and if the most corrupt nation that one could imagine remains peaceful within its borders, can it form itself into a new nation, truly *other*, on the same soil, although it speaks the same language? The examination of these questions, on which history seems to be silent, would lead me too far afield and would moreover exceed my strength; I therefore limit myself to raising them, as the *Journal de Paris* once said.

zling that Europe bowed before this unique character, proclaimed it as the model of charming greatness, and set it up as its glory to imitate.

The general conclusion to be drawn from all these observations is that it is impossible for a nation not to be made for the government under which it displays all its moral faculties at once: now, as all nations have reached this high point of greatness under different governments, it follows that all governments are good, and, by a consequence no less certain, that there is no social contract, no convention, no deliberation on the acceptance of sovereignty in general, nor of this or that sovereignty in particular: for it is not man who has made himself sociable, and no man in particular has made himself suitable for this or that government. Nations, like individuals, are therefore, according to the expression of Thales, *only the instruments of God*, who forms them and makes use of them, according to hidden designs, of which one can but have an inkling. When nations begin to know themselves and to reflect on themselves, their government has been in place for centuries. No one can exhibit their beginnings, because they always predate all written laws, which are never more than declarations of previous rights engraved solely in the universal conscience. Great legislators, the legislators par excellence, prove nothing against this general thesis, and even confirm it. In the first place, because of their small number, they are phenomena, miracles, which attest more particularly and make palpable, literally, an action superior to human action. In the second place, as two things are needed to fashion a machine, firstly an artist capable of executing it, and secondly a material that responds to the artist's designs, so the legislator would produce nothing if he did not have at hand a *material*, that is to say, a people made to obey his action, and this people was not made as such. The great man who fashions it is already a prodigy.

Sovereignty is, therefore, foreign to the people in two ways, since they have deliberated neither on sovereignty in general nor on the particular sovereignty that governs them. In an elevated sense, the Roman people on the Janiculum are as passive as the pasha who receives the cord and kisses it. The soldier who mounts the assault certainly displays very great activity; however, he only obeys his general who sends him to victory or to death; similarly, the people that show the greatest energy for their freedom, deploy the qualities which they have received, and which make them capable of such government. Everything, therefore, leads us back to the author of all things. Power comes from him, obedience comes from him, everything comes from him, except evil...

This work goes no further; and it is only a sketch which has not even been re-read. (Author's Note)

Bibliography

BACKGROUND

Paul H. Beik. **"The French Revolution Seen from the Right: Social Theories in Motion, 1789-1799."** In Transactions of the American Philosophical Society Vol. 46, No. 1 (Philadelphia: American Philosophical Society, 1956).

Jacques Léon Godechot. **The Counter-Revolution: Doctrine and Action, 1789-1804** (New York: Howard Fertig, 1971).

Charles-Augustin Sainte-Beuve. **Les grands écrivains français: XIXe siècle; philosophes et essayistes** (Paris: Garnier 1930).

Alain de Benoist. **Bibliographie générale des droites françaises, Vol. 4** (Paris: Editions Dualpha, 2005).

Larry Alan Siedentop. **The Limits of the Enlightenment: A Study of Conservative Political Thought in Early Nineteenth-century France with Special Reference to Maine de Biran and Joseph de Maistre.** PhD thesis, Oxford University, 1966.

POLITICAL AND RELIGIOUS THOUGHT

Richard Lebrun. **Throne and Altar: The Political and Religious Thought of Joseph de Maistre** (University of Ottawa Press, 1965).

Richard Lebrun. **"Joseph de Maistre: How Catholic a Reaction?"** In Study Sessions, 1967, of the Canadian Catholic Historical Association (Ottawa: Canadian Catholic Historical Association, 1967).

John Courtney Murray. **"Political Thought of Joseph de Maistre."** In Review of Politics Vol. 11, No. 2 (Cambridge University Press, 1949).

Emile M. Cioran. **"Essai sur la pensée réactionnaire. A propos de Joseph de Maistre."** English translation in Anathemas and Admirations (New

York: Arcade Publishing, 1991).

Owen Powell Bradley. **"A Modern Maistre. The Social and Political Thought of Joseph de Maistre."** In European Horizons (University of Nebraska Press, 1999).

Peter Davies. **The Extreme Right in France, 1789 to the Present: From De Maistre to Le Pen** (Milton Park: Routledge, 2002).

INFLUENCE

Isaiah Berlin. **"Joseph de Maistre and the Origins of Fascism."** In The Crooked Timber of Humanity: Chapters in the History of Ideas (Princeton University Press, 1959).

Mother Mary Alphonse. **The Influence of Joseph de Maistre on Baudelaire.** PhD thesis, Bryn Mawr College, 1943.

Richard Lebrun, ed. **Joseph de Maistre's Life, Thought, and Influence: Selected Studies** (McGill-Queen's University Press, 2001).

SECONDARY SOURCES

E. D. Watt. **"The English Image of Joseph de Maistre: Some Unfinished Business."** In European Studies Review, Vol. 4, Issue 3 (California, European History Quarterly, 1974).

Index

www.ingramcontent.com/pod-product-compliance
Lightning Source LLC
Chambersburg PA
CBHW022348180125
20596CB00006B/32

* 9 7 8 1 9 2 2 6 0 2 2 2 0 *